STRATEGIC LEADERSHIP

STRATEGIC LEADERSHIP

A Multiorganizational-Level Perspective

Edited by
Robert L. Phillips
and
James G. Hunt

Afterword by Robert J. House

QUORUM BOOKS
Westport, Connecticut • London

Library of Congress Cataloging-in-Publication Data

Strategic leadership : a multiorganizational-level perspective /
  edited by Robert L. Phillips and James G. Hunt ; afterword by Robert J.
  House.
    p. cm.
  Includes bibliographical references and indexes.
  ISBN 0-89930-756-6 (alk. paper)
  1. Leadership—Congresses. I. Phillips, Robert L. (Robert
Leslie), 1937-   II. Hunt, James G., 1932-
HD57.7.S78   1992
658.4'012—dc20   92-8383

British Library Cataloguing in Publication Data is available.

Library of Congress Catalog Card Number: 92-8383
ISBN: 0-89930-756-6

First published in 1992

Quorum Books, 88 Post Road West, Westport, CT 06881
An imprint of Greenwood Publishing Group, Inc.

Printed in the United States of America

The paper used in this book complies with the
Permanent Paper Standard issued by the National
Information Standards Organization (Z39.48-1984).

10 9 8 7 6 5 4 3 2 1

To Ralph M. Stogdill, a mentor to Bob Phillips and role model to both of us.

Contents

Tables and Figures

Preface

This book is based on contributions prepared for a conference supported by the U.S. Army Institute for the Behavioral and Social Sciences and by the U.S. Army War College. The conference was held at Carlisle Barracks, Pennsylvania, February 11-14, 1991. In it, civilian and military experts came together to explore a number of cutting-edge aspects of strategic leadership, using Elliott Jaques's "Stratified Systems Theory" (SST) as a point of departure.

Prior to the conference, a number of individuals who were engaged in work related to strategic or top-level leadership research were contacted. They were sent a packet of materials, including SST background papers, and were asked to prepare papers of their own, showing ways in which their work and SST could be mutually beneficial. They then attended the conference and used the insights obtained there, together with reviewer comments, to revise their work. Those revisions were then further reviewed and revised (some, several times), ultimately resulting in the chapters comprising this book.

The chapter authors have a mix of backgrounds; although primarily from leadership, strategic management, and organizational behavior/organization theory, they also cover areas such as military sociology. As indicated, support for the conference and this book came from military sources. Nevertheless the contents are largely "context-free" (phenomena free of the specific organizational context in which they are found). Thus, while there are some military examples, there is also an emphasis on other kinds of organizations.

In terms of acknowledgments for help with this book, we would like first to recognize the Army Research Institute and Army War College for their support. We also wish to recognize our Texas Tech faculty colleagues, John Blair, Kimberly Boal, and Carlton Whitehead, who authored book chapters and helped in other ways, and Mark Peterson, whose help included manuscript reviewing.

We also owe a debt of gratitude to William Gardner, Michael Hitt, and Robert Hooijberg, who assisted with manuscript reviews. Those involved with manuscript preparation in various ways, were Catherine Duran, Shelly Jenkins, Chrene Johnson, Ralna Merriott, Francis Pinkerton, and Joan Rivera.

Finally, in addition to the above, acknowledgments are in order for individuals who provided additional comments or other help for the authors of some of the chapters. For Chapter 5, these are Ellen Austin and Robert Hooijberg. Chapter 6 draws heavily on earlier joint research efforts on stakeholder management with Myron Fottler, Timothy Nix, Grant Savage and Carlton Whitehead and the various joint publications cited in the chapter. For Chapter 7, Robert Hoojberg and Mark Peterson were helpful in terms of comments, as were William Gardner III, Robert Hooijberg, and Kirsi Myllys for Chapter 11.

To all the organizations and individuals just mentioned we give our heartiest thank you. Without their help, this project could not have been completed. Of course, as always, we as editors bear the responsibility for any errors.

I

Setting the Stage

1

Strategic Leadership:
An Introduction
Robert L. Phillips and James G. Hunt

What do the steel industry, Xerox, the auto industry, Kodak, the U.S. Army, and many other industries and organizations have in common? The answer is that all are in the process of restructuring, doing more with less, and developing the flexibility to deal with environments changing at an increasing rate as well as ever-greater international competition. Kanter (1989b) considers such organizations as elephants or giants "learning to dance."

These types of issues are so far-reaching that many would see traditional leadership approaches, based on face-to-face interactions at lower organizational levels, as being of little use or even irrelevant. How important can a first-level supervisor's consideration or initiating structure be when Xerox has restructured to the point where direct labor accounts for barely 10 percent of total cost (Jacobson and Hillkirk, 1987)? How important can such leadership be when productivity increases have come from drastic cuts in the size of steel-making crews to deal with worldwide competition (Hoerr, 1988)? These kinds of questions, especially when combined with the earlier views of those who have argued that leadership doesn't matter (at least when compared with other variables; see Gupta, 1988; Romanelli and Tushman, 1988, for a review), might suggest the demise of leadership as a serious topic of study.

However, though scholarly interest in leadership as an area of study waxes and wanes (Campbell, 1977; Fleishman, 1973), the topic will not die. Indeed, when all else fails, leadership is emphasized, by practitioners and scholars alike, as a romantic notion to explain the inexplicable (cf. Meindl, Ehrlich, and Dukerich, 1985). Leadership is especially prized in North America (cf. Hunt, Sekaran, and Schriesheim, 1982).

Rather than dying, the study of leadership reappears in new forms. A crucial new form, consistent with societal demands of the 1980s and 1990s is "strategic leadership" (Hambrick, 1989). The emphasis on strategic leadership as a systematic field of study (as opposed to earlier less systematic treatment) is so recent that

Hambrick (1989) tells us its domain is "relatively diffuse and uncharted" (p. 6). He adds that "we don't even have a well agreed-upon name for the topic" (p. 6). He proposes both a name and a definition that serve as the starting point for the contents of the present book: "The study of *strategic leadership* focuses on the people who have overall responsibility for an organization—their characteristics, what they do, and how they do it. The people who are the subjects of strategic leadership research can be individual executives (e.g., CEO's or division general managers), more broadly defined 'top management teams,' or other governance bodies (e.g., boards of directors)" (p.6).

The key aspect that sets off the study of strategic leadership from the traditional leadership approaches mentioned earlier is its emphasis on those individuals or teams with the overall responsibility for the organization. The traditional leadership approaches, emphasizing lower-level, face-to-face influence, comprise more than 90 percent of the leadership literature (Hunt, 1991).

As we pointed out earlier, this lower-level, face-to-face focus does not go far enough in terms of dealing with the major issues facing organizations today. Development of participative, high-productivity systems in the steel industry (Hoerr, 1988), restructuring of Xerox to "out Japanese the Japanese" (Jacobson and Hillkirk, 1987), and both restructuring of the army to deal with the battlefield of the future (Hunt and Blair, 1985) and substantial downsizing of the army to deal with new world realities and provide a peace dividend—all call for leadership to be conceptualized in its strategic context in addition to its more traditional, lower-level focus.

Models such as those proposed by Hambrick (1989), Hambrick and Brandon (1988), and Jackofsky and Slocum (1988) and one discussed by Hunt and Blair (1985), based on earlier work by Hunt, Osborn, and Martin (1981) and Hunt and Osborn (1982), are consistent with this strategic leadership emphasis. Hambrick's model illustrates the essence of these approaches. It considers important strategic elements (settings, organizational form and conduct, and organizational effectiveness) and representative connections among them (e.g., settings influencing strategic leadership, strategic leadership affecting organizational form and conduct).

FOCUS OF BOOK

The previous discussion serves as a backdrop for the contents of this cutting-edge collection, and the top-level strategic emphasis serves as an important start. However, the title *Strategic Leadership: A Multiorganizational-Level Perspective* suggests something more. The "something more" is an important extension that ties both strategic and lower-level leadership together through a multiple-level perspective. Interest in leadership at different organizational levels has had intuitive appeal for at least fifty years (cf. Holden, Fisk and Smith, 1941). And there has been some empirical work (for reviews see Bass, 1990; Hunt, 1991; Yukl,

1989a). Although most of this literature has lacked much of a conceptual foundation, Parsons (1960), Katz and Kahn (1966, 1978), and a few others (e.g. R. Katz, 1970; Mintzberg, 1973; Osborn, Hunt, Jauch, 1980; Simon, 1977; Tosi, 1982) have made starts in this direction.

An approach developed by Elliott Jaques and discussed in several recent publications (e.g., Jacobs and Jaques, 1987, 1990; Jaques and Clement, 1991) has combined some of Jaques's earlier work with directions suggested by those such as Katz and Kahn into Stratified Systems Theory (SST). The notions underlying SST are deceptively simple; however, their conceptualization, measurement, and application are not.

Essentially, SST argues, first, that there are critical tasks that must be performed by leaders if an organization is to function effectively. Because of an increasingly complex setting as one moves higher in the organization, these critical tasks become increasingly complex and qualitatively different. One way of measuring their complexity is in terms of time span (the maximum allowed completion time of the longest tasks, assignments, projects, or programs for which an individual in question is held accountable). These time spans range from up to three months for workers at the very bottom of the organization to twenty years or more at the top (e.g., some decisions by Roger Smith, ex-General Motors board chair). The critical tasks can be divided into organizational levels, the number of which are argued to vary as a function of the organization's size, time span, and the requirement that each level add value to both its higher and its lower level. By and large, it is assumed that, even for the very largest organizations, the number of levels will not exceed seven from the worker to the very top (Jacobs and Jaques, 1990).

Accompanying this increasing organizational critical task complexity by level is a related argument—there must be an increasing level of leader cognitive complexity or capacity. In other words, consistent with requisite variety notions (Ashby, 1952), there needs to be a rough match between individual leader complexity and organizational critical task complexity at each organizational level. (More details are provided by Jacobs and Lewis in this book.)

This book uses the earlier general strategic approach suggested by Hambrick, along with SST, as points of departure and a rough organizing framework in its multiple-level view of strategic leadership. However, the cutting-edge contributions go far beyond these. Essentially, then, the book is concerned not only with strategic leadership at the top of the organization but with a wide range of "indirect effects" as these cascade down the organizational hierarchy (e.g., impact of a given set of top-level policies on those deep within the organization). As we show later, the chapters in this collection address a number of issues important in considering contemporary industry and organizational restructuring of the kind mentioned earlier—downsizing, long-range strategic vision, long-term developmental implications for strategic and lower-level leaders, dealing with multiple stakeholders, and the like.

These chapters have been prepared by authors with an interest in strategic management and leadership. These individuals have been asked to relate their own cutting-edge work to some key strategic leadership and SST notions and to show (1) how their work could extend these and (2) how these could extend their work. The extensions range from modest ones to far-ranging critiques of SST, together with some suggested alternative formulations. The intent throughout is to enhance the understanding of strategic leadership as systematically reflected at the top, middle, and bottom reaches of the organization. We hope to sensitize readers to an expanded, multiple-level view of strategic leadership, such as reflected in this collection, in the hope that they will begin to incorporate this increasing sensitivity in their own work.

CONTENTS OF BOOK

In addition to a Preface, the book consists of 16 chapters divided into five parts, each with a major strategic leadership thrust. Each part contains from two to five chapters:

•Part I: Setting the Stage (two chapters)
•Part II: Environment, Strategy, and Structure (five chapters)
•Part III: Leadership Capabilities and Development (three chapters)
•Part IV: Temporality and Dynamic Change Processes (two chapters)
                                    and
•Part V: Application and Concluding Commentary (three chapters and Robert J. House's Afterword)

The parts emphasize basic themes for grouping the chapters, and we elaborate briefly on these themes, below. In addition, not surprisingly, there are a number of topics that cut across parts and chapters and occur several times throughout the book. We summarize these in Table 1.1, after we present the brief discussion of each part and the chapters it contains. Finally, at a more specific level, we present short editors' summaries at the beginning of most chapters to run through some high points.

Part I, through its two chapters, sets the stage for the book beyond that provided in the Preface. Chapter 1, by Phillips and Hunt, summarizes the justification for the book, lays out the organizing framework, and provides the background for the parts and chapters to follow.

Chapter 2 (Jacobs and Lewis) presents conceptual and empirical highlights of stratified systems theory and its implications, as these authors see them, for the organization and leadership area. The empirical thrust summarizes earlier and recent work, especially work done with the military. Essentially, this chapter is a scenario serving as a backdrop for the wide range of strategic leadership approaches covered in the ensuing parts and chapters.

Part II is broad in nature and groups together five chapters, covering environment, strategy, structure, or some combination of these. Chapter 3 (Segal) leads off with a detailed description of environmental events taking place in the United

States and the world since World War II, with a special focus on their military implications. He covers the strategic environment, manning environment, demographic environment, and fiscal environment during this post-World War II period. Though oriented toward the military, his detailed environmental analysis and description provide a feel for what would be involved in the time spans of twenty years or more of very top-level "systems" leaders. The changes since World War II are so great that the mind boggles at the complexity of what leaders with long time spans would have to deal with. Indeed, Segal raises a question of the feasibility of such long time spans, given the extensive environmental changes taking place.

While Segal primarily focuses on the military, our contention is that many non-military organizations probably have had to face environmental changes of similar magnitude. Be that as it may, careful reading of his chapter serves to convey the environmental complexity faced by organizations and strategic leaders across time.

In Chapter 4, Hitt and Keats's combine Segal's environmental theme with organizational strategy and structure implications of organizational downsizing. As mentioned previously, downsizing or restructuring has assumed increasing importance during the 1980s and 1990s as organizations have tried to become "lean machines." One key contribution to understanding such downsizing, in terms of strategic leadership, is Hitt and Keats's reciprocal model. That model looks at both the impact of strategic leadership on downsizing throughout the organization and the impact that such downsizing has on strategic leadership. As a part of these reciprocal implications, at various organization levels, this chapter reinforces Segal's contribution by again conveying the flavor of some of the effects of a changing environment—this time leading to downsizing and restructuring.

Chapter 5 (Cowan, Fiol, and Walsh) continues the underlying multilevel and environment, strategy, and structure themes by developing a midrange, cognitive, strategic leadership approach. The approach focuses on a combination of strategic choice processes, first as action and then as thought, at various organizational levels. Thus, it extends SST's cognitive emphasis by including behavior. As we shall show, a key aspect of a number of contributions in this volume is an emphasis on a combined thrust such as this.

Chapter 6 (Blair and Rivera) and Chapter 7 (Gardner and Schermerhorn) are in a number of respects both similar and different. They are different in that Blair and Rivera stress strategic leadership via strategic management of stakeholders at multiple levels, while Gardner and Schermerhorn emphasize a mix of strategic and operational leadership throughout the organization. They are similar in that they argue for the accompaniment of systems-level strategic leadership with that of stakeholder management (in the case of Blair/Rivera) and operational leadership (in the case of Gardner/Schermerhorn). Each also argues for both of these at all levels, although their specific mix and details differ by level. Finally, both approaches convey a heavy strategic thrust throughout their discussions.

Part III moves from Part II's primary emphasis on environment, strategy, and structure into leadership capabilities and development and consists of three chapters. The focus of this part is particularly important for it brings altogether separate arguments for the primacy of leader cognitive complexity or what Lewis and Jacobs in Chapter 8 call "conceptual capacity," over that of a group of individual psychological variables ranging from skills to traits, argued for by Sashkin in Chapter 9. More specifically, Sashkin emphasizes a combination of such behavioral competencies as visionary leadership and culture building and the personal capabilities of self-efficacy and socially oriented power, in addition to the cognitive complexity of SST. He then interprets his visionary leadership theory within this context. Lewis and Jacobs, in contrast, have little use for any concept but conceptual capacity. The chapters, in combination, provide a healthy emphasis on several different strategic leadership aspects, and in this they go beyond most current leadership literature. Both chapters also discuss training and development, and Lewis and Jacobs present very interesting early results comparing two different, long-term developmental approaches.

Chapter 10 (Hooijberg and Quinn) continues the developmental thrust by first tying together cognitive complexity with what they term "behavioral complexity," based on Robert Quinn's (1988) competing values framework. The chapter then discusses a recent program designed to aid in developing behavioral complexity.

Once capabilities and development are treated in Part III, Part IV examines temporality and dynamic change processes. These are covered in two chapters and are a particularly important aspect of strategic leadership in general and stratified systems theory in particular. In Chapter 11, Hunt and Ropo show the symbiotic effects of interpreting the results of a dynamic case study of high-level Finnish bank leaders in terms of SST and argue for the contributions of this dynamic case-study approach to understanding SST. They make the point that while SST explicitly emphasizes temporal aspects, current work involving SST is not always temporal or processual in nature. Such processual empirical results are the key contribution of their work.

Chapter 12 (Phillips and Duran) adds to the dynamic emphasis of Part IV by examining a number of processual organization change models (e.g., logical incrementalism, J. Quinn, 1981; intraorganizational ecology, Burgleman, 1991) within a strategic leadership context. The chapter considers both adaptive and nonadaptive change implications in terms of planning and implementation, and sketches emerging organizational structures that facilitate change.

Part V is an epilogue with an applications chapter and concluding commentary. It consists of three chapters, plus the Afterword by House. Chapter 13 (Malone) emphasizes applications aspects and describes in detail what happened in a U.S. Army Corps when a new systems-level, three-star general took over. This new commander's strategic leadership was seen as providing direct and indirect empowerment effects up and down his command. Malone's vivid

Table 1.1
Major Focus and Cross-Cutting Themes in the Book's Content

Part/Chapter	Major Focus	Cross-Cutting Themes							
		Organizations as hierarchies	Critical tasks, managerial work	Capacity, skills, competencies, behaviors, etc.	Transformational, charismatic, visionary leadership	Organizational culture, climate	Leader succession: selection, development, training	External environmental changes	Temporal aspects
I/2 Jacobs & Lewis	SST highlights and latest developments	X	X	X		X	X	X	X
II/3 Segal	Military strategic leadership challenges of long-term external environment changes	X	X	X			X	X	X
II/4 Hitt & Keats	Reciprocal consequences of strategic leadership and organizational restructuring		X	X	X	X	X	X	X
II/5 Cowan, Fiol, & Walsh	Strategic leadership midrange theory of choice-as-thought and influence on organizational effectiveness	X		X	X				X
II/6 Blair & Rivera	Implications of managing stakeholders strategically at various levels on strategic leadership and organizational effectiveness		X	X					X
II/7 Gardner & Schermerhorn	Appropriate mix of directional responsibility (strategic vision) and operational responsibility (internal organizational capacity) at various levels	X	X	X	X				

Table 1.1 (continued)

Part/Chapter	Major Focus	Organizations as hierarchies	Critical tasks, managerial work	Capacity, skills, competencies, behaviors, etc.	Transformational, charismatic, visionary leadership	Organizational culture, climate	Leader succession: selection, development, training	External environmental changes	Temporal aspects
					Cross-Cutting Themes				
III/8 Lewis & Jacobs	Strategic leadership capacity, why important and how developed		X	X			X		X
III/9 Sashkin	Strategic leadership capabilities and how developed		X	X	X	X	X		
III/10 Hooijberg & Quinn	Competing values, SST, and strategic leadership developmental theories		X	X			X		X
IV/11 Hunt & Ropo	Dynamic case study approach, SST, and process study of strategic leadership	X	X	X	X		X	X	X
IV/12 Phillips & Duran	Current strategic leadership processual models used to develop new model examining adaptive/nonadaptive change implications	X	X	X	X	X		X	X
V/13 Malone	Strategic leader's developing and sustaining lower-level empowerment climate/culture in Army corps		X	X.	X	X	X		X

Table 1.1 (continued)

Part/Chapter	Major Focus	Cross-Cutting Themes							
		Organizations as hierarchies	Critical tasks, managerial work	Capacity, skills, competencies, behaviors, etc.	Transformational, charismatic, visionary leadership	Organizational culture, climate	Leader succession: selection, development, training	External environmental changes	Temporal aspects
V/14 Boal & Whitehead	Key limitations and extensions of stratified systems strategic leadership theory	X	X	X	X		X	X	X
V/15 Hunt & Phillips	Synthesis and implications of book's content for multiple-level strategic leadership perspectives	X	X	X	X	X	X	X	X

description seems to confirm these effects and to show how culture and climate were reshaped to the point where the sergeants "act like they're running the damn army."

Chapter 14 (Boal and Whitehead) critiques and extends a number of aspects of stratified systems theory. These aspects cover environmental, organizational, temporal, and personal considerations and add considerable insight to the study of strategic leadership. The Boal/Whitehead contribution is joined by Chapter 15 (Hunt and Phillips), which contains our concluding thoughts. It elaborates in some detail on the themes shown in Table 1.1 and helps put the book's contents into overall perspective.

Chapter 16 (House's Afterword, not covered in Table 1.1) discusses the book from the perspective of one of the world's foremost leadership scholars. That discussion tends to be very different indeed, from the rest of the book's content. Thus it enriches the reader's understanding as one would expect from a good Afterword.

HIERARCHY AND THE THIRD EUROPEAN FORCE

The previous discussion emphasizes organizations as hierarchies. Until recently this emphasis would not have been questioned. Now, however, accompanying the kinds of restructuring mentioned earlier, there has been a question of the continuing viability of bureaucracy as an organizational form. The argument essentially is that increasingly turbulent environments and economic conditions, the success of Japanese organizations, and increasing pressures for humanization, flexibility, and workplace democracy all lead inexorably away from hierarchy and that bureaucracy is dead (cf. Bennis, 1966; Drucker, 1988a; Kanter, 1989b; Peters, 1988).

Proponents of this view continue to be vociferous and eloquent. However, the fact remains that hierarchy is still far and away the preponderant organizational form (Robbins, 1990), and, as we show in more detail in our concluding chapter, there are strong forces supporting the continuance of such hierarchies even in the presence of the kinds of pressures mentioned by their denigrators (cf. Miewald, 1970; Robbins, 1990).

An important counterpoint to the antihierarchy arguments is provided by Lessem (1991). He contends that, in addition to individualistic Anglo-American (great leader) organizational approaches and Japanese-style, group-oriented approaches (personified by those arguing for the demise of hierarchy), there is a "third European force" approach. Here, hierarchy is not dead but rather is reflected in a Continental or Central European perspective that emphasizes using hierarchies but making them responsive to human and social needs. For Lessem, such structures form the basis for the well-known German "economic miracle." This "third force" view is consistent with the thrust of this book.

SUMMARY OBJECTIVES OF THE BOOK

We can recap the book's focus, content, and audience in the form of the following summary objectives.

- showcase cutting-edge, conceptual, and empirical contributions focusing on a wide range of strategic leadership areas
- show how these contributions and general strategic leadership and stratified systems approaches can mutually extend and reinforce one another in a multiple-level perspective
- sensitize a broad range of readers to the usefulness of such a wide-ranging, multilevel strategic leadership approach in their own research and applications and in recognizing the relevance of this leadership perspective to important organizational issues

While the origins are military in nature, the proposed book is designed to be "context-free" (Blair and Hunt, 1986). That is, while it contains a militarily oriented applications chapter and should be particularly relevant to current military interests, the authors and editors attempted to make their contributions general enough to apply to nonmilitary settings as well.

2

Leadership Requirements in Stratified Systems

T. Owen Jacobs and Philip Lewis

This chapter provides a summary of key aspects of stratified systems theory (SST) sufficient to provide a base for the remaining work in this volume. Included here are arguments for why a theory such as SST is needed; its key underlying assumptions; areas where it is argued to apply and not apply; and summaries of work exploring some of the many questions that it suggests. The authors also summarize some suggestive key issues as they see them. All of this discussion lays the groundwork for the succeeding chapters, each of which shows the interplay between its own perspective and that of SST, with the intention of extending SST and the chapter's perspective and enhancing overall strategic leadership knowledge.

INTRODUCTION

At first glance, the term *stratified systems* appears to be an oxymoron. However, virtually all natural systems are differentiated (Miller, 1978), with various specialized functions accorded to the differentiated parts. It might be argued that increasing differentiation of specialized functions does two things. First, it increasingly formalizes the specific specialized functions, thereby limiting discretion within those functions. But, second, it establishes a basis whereby the limiting complexity of system responses to external complexity itself may be increased, thereby increasing discretion at the level of the integrated system. As just described, this type of differentiation would be predominantly horizontal.

Though the emphasis in general systems theory seems to have been more on the horizontal than the vertical, it is not difficult to argue that most natural systems are vertically differentiated. Perhaps most important, it might be argued that the complexity principle applies to hierarchical as well as horizontal differentiation within a natural system, that is, assuming the requisite information processing capacity, the degree of differentiation governs the degree of environmental complexity with which it can deal.

The principle that system complexity must match environmental complexity is the law of requisite variety. As such, it has been applied in various contexts, for example, in cognitive science in relation to the construct of "cognitive maps" (Jacobs and Jaques, 1987) and in organization theory (Thompson, 1967). The theory is that as the external complexity increases, the internal complexity must also increase if it is to "pattern" the externality in a veridical manner. The naive assumption is that both may increase with only very broad limits.

However, as the theory applies to formal organizations, there are many perplexing questions. They include the issue of just how complex complex can be, how complexity—particularly the complexity of work—can be measured in an absolute sense, how considerations of requisite variety might apply to vertical differentiation in formal organizations, and the implications these considerations might have for leader/manager succession planning and development.

That vertical differentiation does have substantial implications for managerial performance can hardly be in doubt. Organizational theory has long recognized differentiated performance requirements for managers at successively higher organizational levels (Barnard, 1938; Katz and Kahn, 1966; Simon, 1977, to mention only a few of many). However, in the approaches of these authors and others, the precision necessary for a science of organizational design as it relates to managerial and organizational performance is still lacking. It is toward this objective that the present volume is aimed.

Based on observation and experience in a variety of large-scale organizations, Jaques (1976, 1989) formulated a precise theory that specifies parameters for the vertical differentiation of a class of hierarchical organizations he terms "bureaucracies." (These are defined as accountability hierarchies—organizations chartered and governed by higher bodies, e.g., boards of directors, and accountable to external constituencies, e.g., shareholders, to perform specific functions. They are different from "associations," such as universities and churches, within which accountability is handled in very different ways.) With Gibson and Isaac (Jaques, Gibson, and Isaac, 1978), Jaques began the task of describing the complexity of work at each of the differentiated levels of a requisitely structured organization and relating that complexity to human capability.

Using these specifications, Jacobs and Jaques (1987) began the task of laying out the leadership performance requirements of managers at these differentiated levels, with the ultimate objective of understanding and influencing the process whereby progressively more complex "cognitive maps" are developed. (For all successful large-scale organizations, the development of executive talent is an extraordinarily high priority. One specific application of better understanding of developmental processes would be to increase the pool of available talent in formal organizations, hopefully thereby enhancing organizational performance.)

In the remainder of this chapter, key Stratified Systems Theory (SST) concepts will be summarized briefly (as they currently appear in SST); it is beyond the scope of the chapter to provide the extensive detail that can be found elsewhere

(Jaques, 1989; Jaques and Clement, 1991). Where possible, these concepts will be briefly supported from the empirical literature. However, there are many unknowns, and it is likely that the current formulation of SST is deficient in some respects. The objective is to stimulate inquiry and test, to illuminate areas where evidence is lacking, and to identify those aspects of the theory that can be made more veridical.

STRUCTURE

Implicity in Stratified Systems Theory are many of the assumptions underlying open systems theory, for example, that the organization exists in a world environment in which other organizations of like type compete for resources and that the effectiveness and efficiency with which resources can be used to create outputs of value will determine its competitiveness. SST is thus primarily a theory of organizational structure in relation to the competitiveness required for survival in a world environment. Second, it is a theory of managerial performance requirements derived from that structure and of managerial capability necessary to deal with the performance requirements.

Levels (Strata)

SST specifies that requisitely structured organizations have no more than six levels of effective management discretion and no more than seven levels of vertical differentiation of function. In each of these seven levels, there is an explicit complexity of work, which may be defined not only by the scope and scale of the work (Bentz, 1990) but also by the required cognitive processes of incumbents. As Figure 2.1 shows, the seven levels are divided into three broad domains: production, organizational, and strategic systems. The functions of these domains and levels within domains have been described at length by Jaques (1976, 1989), Jaques and Clement (1991), and Jacobs and Jaques (1987).

Both domains and levels are differentiated by the functions required, the time spans of discretion imposed, and the cognitive skills employed. The domains in a large-scale organization are, respectively, concerned with direct production of goods and services, organizational management, and strategic integration of organizations within a larger corporate entity. Jaques (1989) postulates that the operations required at successively higher levels (strata) differ qualitatively from one another, as shown in Table 2.1. For example, he specifies that the distinguishing operation at Stratum III is "alternative paths," that is, creating and following linear, sequential pathways toward goals, one at a time. The qualitative difference between Stratum III and Stratum IV is that at IV the incumbent is expected to create and use multiple pathways schemes toward goals, doing trade-offs between the

Figure 2.1
Stratified Systems Theory Domains and Strata

Stratum	Time Span	Domain	Domain Function
VII	Beyond 20 Years	STRATEGIC SYSTEMS	Incumbents operate in the world political, economic, sociocultural, and technological environments; conceptualize feasible futures, build consensus on them, and develop necessary resource base. Create subordinate strategic business units. Create corporate culture and values consistent with corporate aims and sociocultural context.
VI	Beyond 10 Years		
	_____ 10 Yrs. _____		
V	Beyond 5 Years	ORGANIZA-TIONAL	Incumbents operate bounded open systems (Strategic Business Units) which may be part of larger corporate structures. Develop business strategies, operating procedures, product lines. Maintain organizational climate. Responsible for Profit-and-Loss bottom line.
IV	Beyond 2 Years		
	_____ 2 Yrs. _____		
III	Beyond 1 Year	PRODUCTION	Operates mutual recognition or mutual knowledge subsystem or groups engaged in specific differentiated functions. Stratum III manages interdependency with other similar units. Stratum II interfaces within a formalized structure—context and boundaries set by the larger system. Stratum I is the shop floor.
II	Beyond 3 Months		
I	Up to 3 Months		

Source: Reprinted by permission of Greenwood Publishing Group, Inc., Westport, CT, from *Human Productivity Enhancement*, Vol. 2, edited by J. Zeidner. Copyright 1987 by Praeger Publishers and published in 1987 by Praeger Publishers, 521 Fifth Avenue, New York, NY 10175, a division of Greenwood Press, Inc.

various pathways as the need arises. The particular trade-off that distinguishes this stratum is between tangibles and intangibles, for example, time for money in a complex task that has been charted using the Program Evaluation and Review Technique (PERT) to show the various pathways. This formulation clearly has implications for the cognitive skill requirements of incumbents at the various levels.

Whether one is persuaded or not by the thesis of qualitative differences across strata, there appears little difference of opinion with regard to domains. Jacobs and Jaques (1987) postulate that there are very large qualitative differences in performance requirements from one domain to the next and that these are reflected in very substantial capability differences among incumbents. The various typological performance requirements are shown in Table 2.1 and discussed below following the section on time spans.

Table 2.1
Operations Required by Level in SST

Stratum	Operation	Action
I	Direct Judgment	Overcome obstacles in linear pathway.
II	Diagnostic Judgment	Overcome obstacles in linear pathway while at the same time reflecting on experience and things learned so as to diagnose emerging problems and initiate actions to prevent or overcome the problems identified.
III	Alternative Paths	Find a path that stands a chance of coping with short-term requirements while at the same time providing the initial stages of a realistic path toward long-term goals of a year or more. Change to alternative paths if the initial choice is unsatisfactory. (Direct judgment plus diagnostic accumulation, but also to encompass the whole process within a plan that has a pathway to goal completion with pre-planned alternatives if the path does not work.)
IV	Parallel Process	Run several interacting projects, pacing them in relation to one another in resourcing and in time. Make trade-offs between tasks in order to maintain progress along the composite route to the goal. (This is a number of Stratum III paths that are interconnected.)
V	Unified Whole System	Cope by means of judgment with constantly shifting kaleidoscope of events and consequences with too many variables to map on a PERT chart—sense interconnections between the variables in the organization and the environment, constantly adjusting them in relation to each other, sensing second- and third-order effects.
VI	Worldwide Diagnostic Accumulation	Develop networks so as to accumulate diagnostic information and create a friendly environment throughout the world, making it possible to judge corporate investment priorities, to enhance the value of corporate assets as reflected in the balance sheet and to contribute to corporate long-term success and survival.
VII	Put Business Units Into Society	Develop and pursue alternative worldwide strategic plans, producing Stratum V units by development, acquisition, merger, or joint ventures, drawing upon internationally supported financial resourcing.

Source: Based on Jaques and Clement (1991).

Time Span and Discretion

According to the theory, there is an orderly progression of complexity from one level to the next higher level. This progression is marked by increasing time span and by increased complexity of the cognitive processes required of the incumbent. Jaques (1964) defined time span as "the longest period which can elapse in a role before the manager can be sure that his subordinate has not been exercising marginally sub-standard discretion continuously in balancing the pace and the quality of his work'' (p. 17). The concept of discretion is essential to the construct. In essence, Jaques, as do others (e.g., Hunt, Osborn, and Martin, 1981; Osborn, Hunt, and Jauch, 1980), differentiates between the formalized and proceduralized part of the job and the part that is not. It is largely through the unproceduralized part of the job that a leader or manager adds value. Value is added by the extent to which the incumbent produces self-initiated, independent outputs as required by the organizational level this person occupies.

The emphasis is on self-initiated and independent outputs because the primary contribution of the leader/manager at higher organizational levels is the result of thinking—information processing. Being told what to do in detail implies that someone else has done much or all of the difficult thinking. Given that the formal organizations with which SST deals are defined as accountability hierarchies, it follows that objectives generally are defined at the topmost levels and that performances required to achieve the objectives are given successively more concrete definition by successively lower leaders and managers (Jacobs and Jaques, 1987; Thompson, 1967) until the level of direct output is reached.

The capacity to function proactively—exercise discretion—within this chain of successive translations is essential for value to be added. Lacking it, as when the required cognitive skills are absent or when the organization is overlayered, the incumbent cannot add value to the required extent, and the organization then suffers either from inefficiency (operations cost more than they should) or from ineffectiveness (the organization is not sufficiently responsive to changing contingencies because information-processing failures or costs, e.g., time, are excessive).

The relevance of time span thus is clear. It is an index of the incumbent's scope of vision of action over time. As such, it permits the incumbent to encompass the scope of action of subordinates—with their shorter time spans—within a broader pattern of whole tasks with which they must be synergistic. By visualizing the broader pattern, the leader thus is able not only to provide ''do this'' instructions but also to know that the ''do this'' is meaningful. Perhaps more important, this broader pattern permits the leader to show the subordinate how his or her work fits into the larger whole and thus to give it meaningful purpose. (It is well established in the leadership literature that explication of meaningful purpose has excellent motivational value (Lange and Jacobs, 1960.) Time span thus is also a measure of the leader's ability to provide a meaning context for subordinates, thereby increasing the motivational value of the work itself.

Time span may also be correlated with the effectiveness of managerial decision making. Streufert, Pogash and Piasecki (1988) use a simulation to assess the extent to which a player integrates current actions with contingent future actions. It can be argued that time span is an index of the length of path of integrated actions an individual can visualize. If so, it is attractive to hypothesize that Streufert's unidimensional-multidimensional, differentiation-multidimensional integration progression is related to successively longer time spans. The value in either case is that with longer forward view, current actions are less likely to be in the wrong direction and thus to waste resources in "making up lost ground."

Domain Cognitive Complexity

Streufert's early conceptualization of cognitive complexity is an attractive model to use in conjunction with Table 2.1 and Figure 2.1. The tasks in the production domain, within most large-scale organizations, are procedurally specified operations dealing with tangible "things." The operations thus can involve linear pathways and may require little in the way of abstraction. It would be logical to hypothesize that a "concrete, linear" (unidimensional—cognitively simple) thinker could succeed as a leader/manager within this domain. It is not logical to hypothesize that this will be the best leader/manager; nor would it be logical to suppose this unidimensional thinker would have a great deal of upward mobility from the production domain. The hypothesis simply is that unidimensional cognitive resources would be sufficient for the performances required.

However, the situation clearly changes with movement into the organizational domain. The scope and scale of the performance requirements at this level appear qualitatively different, and the complexity is simply much greater. First, time frames are quite a lot longer. Second, because of the existence of multiple functions and subsystems the requirement for parallel processing is nonnegotiable. Finally, managers at this level must deal with intangibles in their trade-off assessments. If the law of requisite variety holds, successful performance within this domain requires a substantially more complex "cognitive map" with which to pattern events, assign plausible causality, and develop strategies to influence outcomes. (Even at this level, it is assumed that "problem situations" appear that have some degree of prior development and that must be dealt with through "interventions." This kind of problem situation is probably more prevalent at the systems level, however.)

If these suppositions are allowed, it seems reasonable to postulate that incumbents can no longer be unidimensional and concrete. They must be multidimensional, in Streufert's terms, because they must deal with broader systems characterized by equifinality; they must also have some capacity to deal with abstractions, since many of the influential variables in the organizational domain are intangible, for example, organizational climate. This logic suggests that multidimensional differentiation skills—a greater level of cognitive complexity—are necessary for the abstract analytic performances required in this domain.

The complexity is considerably greater still in the strategic domain. The extended time frames required for the execution of long-term acquisitions and developments preclude successful performance through the exercise of abstract analytic skills alone. In doing the work of creating and disestablishing strategic business units—indeed, whole industries in some cases—incumbents at this level must be concerned with broad political, economic, sociocultural, and technological developments. In general, extrapolation of current trends to permit anticipation of future contingencies is too risky. Showstoppers simply do occur, and corporate executives cannot "bet the farm" on courses of action that are subject to showstoppers. Some kinds of trends at this level, for example, demographics, are stable enough to be trusted. However, analytic methodologies do not appear to be sufficient.

What does appear to work in this domain is synthesis. This would correspond to Streufert's multidimensional integration. A number of studies of executive skills (Harris and Lucas, 1991; Isenberg, 1985; Jaques, Clement, Rigby and Jacobs, 1986; Klauss et al., 1981; Kotter, 1982; Markessini, 1991) have appeared in recent years. Predominant among these various descriptions of executive modes of action is the sense that executives do not exercise influence in the same manner as do managers in the organizational domain. In the latter case, decision analysis techniques frequently can either strongly support or drive decision processes. However, at the top such techniques are supportive at best. Because of the gross uncertainties at the strategic level, as discussed previously, executive influence is more likely to be in the form of creating options that are assessed through a consensus-building process. Jacobs and Jaques (1987) provide a considerably more detailed analysis of these differences.

INDIVIDUAL COMPLEXITY

It would appear without question that the complexity of leadership performance requirements is higher at successively higher levels of accountability hierarchies. However, the nature of the skills required to deal with the complexity and how to develop them is not nearly so clear-cut. At least three lines of work currently are addressing the complexity issue.

Streufert (Streufert, 1986; Streufert et al., 1988), for example, describes simulation-based training that produces significant increases in simulation-measured skills that in theory ought to be positively correlated with managerial performance. However, Streufert's subjects are primarily middle management or below. While he has demonstrated that his simulation-based training increases performance in the skill areas measured, for example, diversity of action, use of strategy (forward integrations), he has not demonstrated that increases in these skills are precursors to improved managerial performance, especially at the more senior levels.

Stratified Systems Theory makes assertions about both the nature of performance demands and the nature of the conceptual skills required to deal with them (Jaques, 1989; Jaques and Clement, 1991). There is very good evidence that these assertions have merit. Stamp (1988) developed an assessment interview, Career Path Appreciation (CPA), which is based on the progression of cognitive skills hypothesized in SST. The methodology essentially locates the subject at a given point of development as defined by where she or he would fit, in terms of skills, into the requisite organization at that time. Given the subject's age in addition, the technique then permits identification of the growth (or progression) curve she or he happens to be following. That, in turn, permits predictions about the subject's probably future growth and ultimate level of achievement within that organizational structure.

By 1988, Stamp had accumulated nearly 200 inteviews, which had occurred from four to fourteen years previously. She followed up on these to determine how accurate the predictions were. The correlation between organizational level predicted and actually achieved was .71.

Two conclusions must be drawn from this work. First, the CPA clearly must measure one or more attributes that are critical for managerial progression. Second, because the CPA was built around the progressions hypothesized in SST and relies on progression curves developed by Jaques (1968), the strength of the correlation reported by Stamp is strong evidence for the theory itself.

However, as was the case with Streufert's work, perplexing questions remain. First, Jaques postulates that "conceptual power," which is what he thinks the progression curves are based on, develops at its own rate almost without regard for environment or experience. (Skill is another matter; it does require experience.) Thus, if a subject is located on a given progression curve, there is a degree of confidence that the subject will remain on that curve with a high degree of reliability. It is clear that this postulate is subject to empirical test.

In addition, there is the issue of what drives development and what constitutes potential. Markessini (1991) recently completed a systematic review of the cognitive science literature. Four "higher-order cognitive skills" with relevance to executive performance were identified: mapping ability, problem management/solution, long-term planning (envisioning), and creative thinking. She also asserted the importance of meta-cognition.

Markessini (1991) then did a reanalysis of a general officer interview database developed by Jaques, Clement, Rigby, and Jacobs (1986), looking for evidence of these cognitive skills. She found frequent mention, as well as evidence, of awareness of mention (meta-cognition). Further, four-star general officers more frequently mentioned these cognitive skills than did three-star general officers. Preliminary evidence is that one- and two-star general officers show even lower frequencies of mention.

The evidence thus is that these cognitive skills are seen by incumbents themselves to be important. Of course, the same theoretical issue resides here, as was the case with complexity. Does the cognitive skill lead to selection for the position, or does it develop as a result of exposure to the complexity of the position? While some combination of both could be the final answer, there is an even more important observation: awareness (meta-cognition) is more in evidence at higher levels. This observation suggests the possibility that for those with high potential, the formative mechanisms may be operative at relatively early stages of development, and the individual's level of development at any given time is the result of its operation to that time. If this statement is the case, early identification of high potential amounts to identifying the presence of the formative mechanism. This line of logic is much like that which Jaques would endorse.

However, there is a third area of relevant work. Stewart and Angle (1992) report evaluation of a creativity course that has been taught at Southern Illinois University at Carbondale for over fifteen years. It is experiential, with the objective of making students more self-aware, particularly with regard to their assumptions and filters, and less bound by stereotypic approaches. The course produces increments in "creativity," as thus defined. Perhaps more important, Stewart and Angle found mental rotation and intuition (the raw N score from the Meyers-Briggs Type Indicator) to correlate with the degree of improvement that occurred. It might be argued that both of these are relatively enduring attributes, as opposed to learned skills.

The research evidence is simply not sufficient to permit reliable conclusions at this time, beyond noting the very great importance of those cognitive skills required to deal proactively with complexity.

ISSUES

The discussion to this point clearly leaves a number of issues unresolved. The following are just a few examples:

- What are the useful gradations of complexity within a vertically differentiated system? SST postulates seven levels and three domains. Are they right? Are there conditions other than those specified in SST when they are not right?
- What drives time span? SST postulates fairly specific time span limits for the various strata. Are these absolute? Why are they what they are? Are there conditions under which these time spans do not hold, other than the "time compression" conditions that SST already recognizes? For example, in noncapital, intensive, technology-based enterprises, such as software development, do these same time spans mean the same thing with regard to complexity?
- Can complexity of work be measured in an absolute sense? (Otherwise, it would appear that design becomes circular.)
- What is the nature of "cognitive power," and what dynamics drive its development? Does increasing complexity reflect the coming on-line of higher-order processes or the continually more complex results of application of developmental processes that are active over a very long span of years?
- Can the fundamental operations SST postulates by stratum be taught, and, if so, can they be taught independently of the specific work that requires those processes? If taught, do they generalize to other content domains?

Clearly, many other issues could be raised, and many are raised by other authors in the present volume. Hopefully, raising these issues will lead to further testing of SST or, indeed, to the generation of a successor to SST. Whichever outcome occurs, the broad need remains for a theoretical basis for the early identification and systematic development of executive potential, within the context of this nation's egalitarian culture. The broad outlines of such a theory must incorporate understanding of (1) the dynamic operation of the variables that determine requisite structure for a given organization, (2) the general nature of the leader/manager performance requirements generation process (as a function of stratum and functional area), and (3) processes that will reliably develop executive potential in a sequential and progressive manner.

Hopefully, SST is a start in that direction. Even more hopefully, this volume will push the field forward toward those ends.

II

Environment, Strategy, and Structure

3

Environmental Challenges
for Strategic Managers
David R. Segal

A key assumption of SST is that time span of feedback increases as one moves higher in the organization. At the very top strategic level, spans are hypothesized to be twenty years or even longer. In other words, definitive feedback on current decisions will not be available for two decades or more. Segal's detailed discussion of the sweeping environmental changes that have taken place for the U.S. military helps readers to understand what is truly implied by time spans of this duration. To what extent would decisions made in the Cold War era of the 1970s be relevant for the post-glastnost and perestroika era of the 1990s? To what extent were General Motors's decisions of the 1970s appropriate for the immensely competitive era of the 1990s and beyond? To what extent could these decisions have foretold the substantial restructuring now taking place?

These are the kinds of issues Segal's chapter addresses. The implications are especially significant in complex organizations, such as the military, that rely exclusively on internal labor markets for their leaders. Implications for organizations utilizing external labor markets, while not quite as significant, are, nevertheless, still quite far-reaching.

A key aspect of Segal's discussion involves the implications of these kinds of issues for SST.

INTRODUCTION

Directing the activities of complex organizations involves a hierarchical division of labor, usually pyramidal in structure and differentiated by the cognitive complexity of the tasks involved. At its base is oversight of day-to-day production. Its broad middle range involves integration of organizational components. Its apex involves tasks relating the organization to its current and future social environment (e.g., Jacobs and Jacques, 1987, pp. 20-25).

Historically, leadership studies have focused at the base of this pyramid, where first-line supervisors oversee the efforts of workers directly involved in production.

Activites closer to the apex of this structure, which cannot be achieved simply by directing human labor but rather involve the manipulation of nonhuman resources such as time and capital as well as abstract reasoning and planning, have been regarded as management (Segal, 1981).

Organization theories that seek to incorporate this range of activities have sought to identify the dimensions that differentiate functions across levels of the hierarchy. For example, Jaques as cited by Jacobs has proposed that "the level of work of any position in a hierarchical organization can be objectively measured by its time span" (Jacobs, 1991a, p. 1). The major function performed at the apex of the organization (Jaques's Stratum VII) is long-term strategic planning, requiring a time frame of twenty or more years.

Jaques's research on flag-rank officers in the Office of the Joint Chiefs of Staff, where one would expect to find this strategic planning function performed in the defense establishment, did not find evidence of this time span. In his interviews with army generals, he found that while half of the eight four-star generals he interviewed stated work time spans of more than twenty years, the other half noted work time spans of ten years or less (Jacobs, 1990).

Given the rate of sociopolitical, economic, and technological change in the world, it may, in fact, not be possible to operate with a twenty-year planning horizon in many arenas. Time span may be a poor surrogate for the cognitive complexity of management tasks. While it is essential to anticipate alternative futures, major new research, development, and procurement programs based upon assumptions regarding the future—one of the major functions of the top stratum of strategic management—may turn out to be counterproductive as organizational environments change. This counterproductivity may be particularly true for organizations that operate as internal labor markets and select their top strategic managers from among people who have had long, successful careers—and intense organizational socialization—rather than recruiting strategic managers laterally from the pool of people who have proven themselves at this task in other settings.

The officer corps of the American armed forces are internal labor markets. The purpose of this chapter is to use the case of the U.S. Army to highlight areas in which a twenty-year time frame for strategic planning might or might not be realistic. While I am not willing to concede that the same time frames are necessarily appropriate for military and civilian organizations, I would argue that neither is the military necessarily unique. Particularly in sectors of the economy subject to major market shifts or unpredictable technological change, attenuated time frames may be unrealistic.

THE ARMY'S STRATEGIC MANAGERS

The senior generation of strategic managers in the U.S. Army today grew up in the World War II and subsequent Cold War era, when national security concerns justified large defense budgets and military service was regarded as a duty of citizenship. They were commissioned into a conscription-based, virtually all-male, and, for the oldest among them, only recently racially integrated army. They spent their careers living under the shadow of a perceived communist threat backed by nuclear technology. Their primary mission was deterring Warsaw Pact aggression in Central Europe. In the event that deterrence failed, they were to execute successfully the third major twentieth-century land war in Europe. The Korean War took place in their youth, and in virtually all cases they saw action in Vietnam.

The ascending generation of tomorrow's strategic managers was born after World War II and in many cases after the Korean War, but the Cold War provided the context in which they grew up, and, in most cases, they were company-grade officers in Vietnam and commanded battalions in an era in which American foreign policy was oriented toward containment of a perceived communist threat to nations with market economies. The major mission of the army was the deterrence of Warsaw Pact aggression, and a secondary mission was to be prepared to address the spread of communism and political instability in less developed nations in our own hemisphere, reflected, for example, in the Cuban missile crisis, in American intervention in the Dominican Republic in the mid-1960s, in Grenada in 1983, and in Panama in 1989.

During the 1950s and 1960s, while there was widespread fear of the Soviet Union in America, the People's Republic of China became the most dramatic manifestation of the communist threat, as we waged unanticipated and ultimately unsuccessful wars in Korea and Vietnam. After the Soviet invasion of Afghanistan in 1973, both public opinion and military concern with the communist threat focused once again on the Soviet Union. Although both the Korean and the Vietnam wars did not have the level of public support that World War II elicited, public support for the military institution remained high since World War II—a factor not fully appreciated by military professionals who felt embattled on the home front, particularly during and after the Vietnam War (Segal and Blair, 1976).

The world has changed during the careers of these officers, producing an army and a future very different from that for which their early professional socialization prepared them. The army was racially integrated during the Korean War. Conscription ended in 1973. Significant strides have been made toward gender integration since the advent of the all-volunteer force, although army policy still excludes women from participation in offensive line-of-sight combat insofar as possible. The issue of manpower accession regardless of sexual preference looms on the horizon.

In the international arena, social movements toward democratic government in many of the nations allied with the Soviet Union in the post-world War II era reached a zenith of drama on November 9, 1989, when the Berlin Wall was opened for East Germans to transit into West Berlin, signaling the ultimate deconstruction of the Warsaw Pact. East Germany, the major military power of the pact outside the Soviet Union, formally withdrew from the pact in September 1990, in anticipation of a reunified Germany participating in the North Atlantic Treaty Organization (NATO).

In the face of a huge federal deficit and a quest for a "peace dividend," the army is likely to be reduced in size during the decade going into the twenty-first century, by 25 to 50 percent. However, the world has not necessarily become a safer place with the reduction in NATO-Warsaw Pact tensions; if anything, it has become less stable. There are still over 300,000 Soviet troops in eastern Germany, and the Soviet Union is experiencing its own instabilities. If one departs from a Eurocentric view of the world, in other regions of the world whose instability has been constant but less present in our national consciousness, like the Middle East, the challenges become dramatically apparent.

The challenge for the army's strategic managers is to adapt the force to new missions oriented toward regional and internal wars and peacekeeping, with fewer resources in terms of people, dollars, and weapons systems, in a society that is likely to perceive a decreased need for military force. This challenge will require those managers to overcome a great deal of organizational socialization and experience, factors that in the past have led the army to be more prepared for the last war than for the next one. Some of the factors operating now could have been anticipated by strategic managers twenty years ago; most could not.

THE STRATEGIC ENVIRONMENT

For almost half a century, the army has been poised for its least likely but most threatening combat scenario: a major confrontation in the polarized, post-World War II European theater, possibly accompanied by a strategic exchange between the United States and the Soviet Union. The European war did not occur, perhaps because it was a polarized conflict situation in which the major actors were constrained to act responsibly, perhaps because the logic of deterrence was correct.

The democratic revolution in Eastern Europe has removed the Warsaw Pact threat as conventionally conceived. However, it has not necessarily pacified Europe. As Eastern European nations break away from the Warsaw Pact, as republics within the USSR seek their own greater autonomy, and as these states seek to make the transition from imposed socialist economies to modern market economies, the democratic revolution will be conflated by a revolution of rising expectations that will, in the short run, most certainly be unmet. The result will be major political instability in Eastern Europe, with a multitude of actors, rather than just one.

The Soviet Union itself has been destablized by the same two factors. The democratic revolution has produced demands for greater autonomy and, indeed, for independence among its constituent republics, some of which we formally regard as subordinate to Soviet sovereignty and others of which we have regarded as occupied territories. As the role of the Soviet military as defender of an empire decreases, its role in the maintenance of internal social control is likely to increase, but no union is likely to be maintained for long by military power alone. The prospect of a Soviet nuclear threat controlled by Moscow was worrisome. The prospect of Baltic or Muslim republics' breaking away and potentially gaining control of nuclear weapons is horrifying, not because they would pose a direct threat to the United States but because of the implications for world order.

Much of the future stability of the Soviet Union rests on the success of Gorbachev's economic and social reforms. As is the case in the smaller Eastern European nations, the possibility exists for the failure of a smooth transition to a market economy to kindle a revolution of rising expectations that will seek to reject or reverse the reform process. The army's contemporary strategic managers cannot discount a major American military role in Europe in 2010. Neither can they assume it.

Increased potential for instability exists in Western Europe as well. Many observers—myself included—were surprised by the speed with which West Germans accepted the economic burden of modernizing the East and with which Germany's neighbors both to the west and to the east accepted the principle of reunification. The fact that Poland—the wellspring of the democratic revolution in the East— requested the continued presence of Soviet troops on her soil reflects at least residual unease regarding German reunification and reclamation of sovereignty from the Four Powers. West Germans are now belatedly beginning to chafe at the cost of modernizing the East, and as the implications of those costs that they will bear become apparent to the other nations of the European Economic Community, the potential for politico-military instability in the West increases. At a minimum, to the extent that economic development in the eastern regions of Germany is delayed, it would not be surprising for Germany to have to use military force for controlling more disadvantaged segments of its own population, while if development moves apace, force might have to be used increasingly in border regions to deal with the discontent and relative deprivation of neighboring, less affluent populations.

The increased instability of Europe, east and west, notwithstanding, the decreased tension level among superpowers allows the United States to adopt a less Eurocentric view and more consciously to acknowledge the existence of other bases of cleavage that might lead to military conflict in other areas of the world. In the best case, if industrialization of a market-economy Europe is successful, the resentments of the 80 percent of the world's population that live in less developed areas and that are not likely to share in this largess are likely to increase. Ironically, reduced tensions between the United States and the Soviet Union may well reduce demand for strategic minerals, directly injuring less developed, extractive economies.

Military conflicts in the developing nations—including so-called wars of national liberation—have heretofore been associated largely with the process of decolonization. There are still residues of that process ongoing, reflected, for example, in the recent use of French and Belgian troops to sustain the regime in Rwanda in the face of intertribal conflict. However, conflict based on decolonization is being replaced by conflict based on other cleavages.

Economic differences produce increased hostility between haves and have-nots.

Racial antagonisms persist in the world. Nationalistic appeals cause abrasions among neighbors at disputed borders, and religion, which has been the basis for the plurality of humanity's wars, continues to strain the fabric of the world order. In a world in which American soldiers sent to Saudi Arabia, accompanied by allies from other Western nations in the wake of the Iraqi invasion of Kuwait, are portrayed in parts of the Arab world as modern-day crusaders threatening the holy places of Islam, a major confrontation pitting Moslem nations and peoples against the Judeo-Christian world is not unthinkable. The army's strategic managers today clearly have to regard the Middle East as a potential market for military operations in 2010.

Despite constant demonstrations of the persistence of politico-military cleavages throughout the world, from the post-World War II years through the 1970s, as noted above, the combat doctrine of the U.S. Army was oriented toward a high-intensity conflict, possibly of long duration, in Central Europe. Combat units were configured and trained and equipment was prepositioned for that armor-heavy war. Relatively little attention was paid, in terms of training, doctrine, or organization, to other forms of military conflict.

The revelation in September 1979 that the Soviet Union had more than 2,000 heavily armed combat troops in Cuba; the seizure of the U.S. embassy in Teheran, Iran, two months later; subsequent failure of at least one attempt by American military units to rescue the embassy hostages; and the invation of Afghanistan by 85,000 conventionally armed Soviet troops—the first time that Soviet troops had been used outside Eastern Europe since World War II—all demonstrated the salience and unpredictability of what came to be called low-intensity combat (LIC) scenarios in parts of the globe other than Europe and the inability of the United States to respond to them. The global dispersion of potential battlefields has increased. However, the designation of the battles to be fought on them as "low intensity" is questionable. If the first American paratroopers to arrive in Third World Saudi Arabia had to battle advancing, Soviet-built Iraqi armor supported by French-built, high-performance aircraft, they would not have felt that they were in low-intensity combat.

America's strategic military managers did not plan for large-scale military operations against Iraq twenty years ago. President Jimmy Carter had recognized the geographical shortcoming in American military capability. Presidential Review Memorandum 10 (PRM-10), issued in the early months of his administration, had noted the potential for conflict in the Persian Gulf region, and the Special Coordinating Committee of the National Security Council had subsequently recommended the establishment of a rapid deployment force (RDF)—a recommendation approved by President Carter in Presidential Directive 18 (PD-18), issued in August 1977.

However, neither the State Department nor any of the military services had been enthusiastic about the RDF concept, and the administration, despite its recognition of other conflict scenarios, had been preoccupied with the European theater: the SALT II negotiations and negotiations with NATO allies. It took the discovery of Soviet troops in Cuba, the capture of embassy personnel in Iran, and the Soviet invasion of Afghanistan to turn the administration's attention away from Europe and toward the implementation of PD-18.

Largely as a result of increasing recognition of national security interests in the Persian Gulf, the Rapid Deployment Joint Task Force was established in 1979—slightly more than a decade ago—as a subordinate command to Readiness Command. The Reagan administration upgraded Carter's rapid deployment force to a separate headquarters under the Joint Chiefs of Staff in 1981 and elevated it to the level of a unified command headquarters, U.S. Central Command (CENTCOM), in 1983. CENTCOM, with responsibility for Southwest Asia, the Araban Peninsula, the Horn of Africa, and the Red Sea and Persian Gulf regions, was established with neither basing facilities nor airlift and sealift capabilities appropriate to its mission. The cutting edge of CENTCOM land-power resources is airborne and light infantry army divisions and marine amphibious forces: smaller and less encumbered by armored and motorized vehicles than are heavier mechanized infantry or armored divisions and therefore more rapidly deployable, but not configured to confront heavy forces without forms of support that are not as rapidly deployable.

Thus, the major evolution of the configuration, coordination, and management of the forces to be used in the projection of American power in some of the most strategically important parts of the world outside Europe is only slightly more than a decade old. Indeed, despite the recognition that rapid deployment required a great deal of interservice cooperation, it was not until January 1984, after much public discussion of problems of interservice coordination during the October 1983 invasion of Grenada, that the Joint Special Operations Agency was established. "Jointness" was to become a military goal for the late 1980s. As Jacobs (1991a, p. 5) notes, this interservice collaboration, requiring long time spans, was sought, but not found, by Jaques in his interviews with flag-rank officers in the Office of the Joint Chiefs of Staff.

That interservice coordination became a problem is not surprising. The army and navy evolved as autonomous, cabinet-level agencies with different missions, technologies, and strategic theories. It was not until 1949—slightly more than forty years ago—that these services, together with the new air force—with its own definition of mission, technology, and strategic theory—were made subordinate to the new Department of Defense (Allard, 1990). Even within this structure, neither the navy nor the air force saw the delivery of ground combat troops to combat theaters as its primary mission. Nor did the air force emphasize close support of ground combat troops. Both the maritime and air services focused on their roles in a strategic exchange with the Warsaw Pact.

The requirement for increased interservice coordination for conflicts outside Europe contributed a new dimension to the army's strategic environment. The recent change in the posture of the Soviet Union with regard to international security produced an even greater complexity in this environment. For most of the history of the United Nations (UN), conflicting goals between the United States and the USSR in the Security Council had prevented the UN from achieving its goal of peace through strength—a doctrine that had been developed following the failure of the League of Nations doctrine of peace through democracy—and had limited UN military operations, in most instances calling for constabulary forces. This standoff in the UN had left the United States relatively free, in emerging peacekeeping situations, to act unilaterally, with allies, or under the auspices of other international organizations. While such actions have sometimes involved U.S. troops in multinational military operations in conjunction with nations with whose military forces we rarely operate, it has given us some leverage in influencing the establishment of systems of command and control. For example, the Multinational Force and Observers (MFO) in the Sinai, set up as an autonomous organization under the Camp David Accords, has three maneuver battalions: one each from the United States, Colombia, and Fiji. It has support elements from eight other nations, and it has a clear chain of command (Tabory, 1986). By contrast, the multinational force sent into Lebanon in the early 1980s, although consisting of U.S. and European forces accustomed to operating with each other, had no unified chain of command and was far less successful than the MFO (Mackinlay, 1989).

With the Soviet Union cooperating in the United Nations and seeking to expand the role of that organization in pursuit of collective security, coordination, as we see in Saudi Arabia, will increasingly extend beyond interservice cooperation to international cooperation, sometimes again involving nations with which we have not undertaken joint military operations in the past and probably, as in the Saudi case, under conditions of ambiguity regarding command and control. Strategic managers twenty years ago were not planning for these contingencies.

THE MANNING ENVIRONMENT

An additional set of complexities is introduced by changes in the way the U.S. Army fields a force (Segal, 1989). For most of our military history, with the major mission of our land forces being continental defense, we drew upon militia or, more recently, National Guard organization. In the world wars and Korea, these were supplemented—increasingly heavily—by national military conscription. In Vietnam, we virtually ignored the National Guard and other reserve components and raised our army through enlistment and an increasingly unpopular military draft. Ironically, service in the army reserve and National Guard became means of avoiding going to war in Vietnam while at the same time fulfilling the citizenship obligation of military service.

The distribution of participation in combat became sociodemographically inequitable under this system, and military conscription became one of the major institutional casualties of the Vietnam War. In 1973, we gave up the principle of military service as an obligation of citizenship in favor of the all-volunteer force market principle that wars should be fought by those who need the work.

That same year, faced with the massive cost of maintaining a large peacetime force without conscription at market wages and with the recognition that such a force would still not be sufficient to sustain a major war, we increased our military dependency on the reserve components. We moved from a system that had made the reserves a refuge from combat to a system in which the army could not go into combat without the reserves. The Total Force policy, suggested by the secretary of defense in 1970 and promulgated by the army in 1973, made the reserve components, on paper, full partners with the active forces. From the perspective of strategic planning, this mix of active and reserve forces, designed in the early 1970s, would comprise the army we would deploy if we went to war in the 1990s and represents an interesting test of the time horizon in Jaques's theory.

This partnership between active and reserve forces assumed, probably unrealistically, that the reserve components would achieve equal degrees of readiness with the active forces. Not only would a significant number of the army's divisions be in the reserves, but active divisions would require "round-out" brigades from the reserve components to be brought to full strength. A significant amount of the army's strength was put in the reserves.

Today, almost as much of our combat force is in the army National Guard as in the active army (44 percent versus 49 percent, with the remaining 7 percent in the army reserve). The plurality of our combat support structure is in the active army (48 percent, as compared to 33 percent in the reserves and 19 percent in the guard). However, more than 90 percent of our combat service support is in the reserve components (78 percent in the reserves, 13 percent in the guard, and only 9 percent in the active army). Thus, the manning level, equipping, quality, and training of both the active and reserve components are critical factors in our national security posture.

Through the last decade we have demonstrated in every combat or potential combat operation involving our ground forces, regardless of the size of the operation—Grenada, Panama, Saudi Arabia—that our active forces cannot go to war without the reserves. A fundamental principle of the Total Force concept has been demonstrated; however, the actual mechanisms of the concept appear to be flawed. A widespread mobilization of reserve units for Operation Desert Shield and Desert Storm has seen transportation units, medical units, and military police units called up, but the reserve combat units that round out active divisions deployed to the Arabian Peninsula were not sent with their divisions. The 24th Infantry Division (Mechanized), trained for desert warfare and needed for its weight in confronting an armor-heavy Iraqi force, was deployed from Fort Stewart, Georgia, without its round-out brigade, the 48th Infantry Brigade from the Georgia National Guard. Instead, it was rounded out with troops from the 197th Mechanized Infantry Brigade at Fort Benning. After an extensive period of training and evaluation of the 24th Infantry Brigade, the brigade commander was relieved.

The army also deployed the 1st Cavalry Division from Fort Hood, Texas, without activating its reserve round-out brigade. Instead, it was brought to full strength by adding a brigade from the 2nd Armored Division, which was being dismantled as part of the army's force reduction in the face of political change in Eastern Europe and budgetary pressure.

In terms of combat readiness and given the luxury of not immediately being in a ground war on the Arabian Peninsula, the deployment of active, rather than reserve, round-outs made sense. The army has found it difficult to train the reserves to the same level as the active forces (Segal and Segal, 1991). Reservists are frequently trained on equipment other than what they will be expected to use in combat. Many reservists are not trained to perform critical parts of their jobs, frequently due to lack of equipment. Reserve unit training tends not to be as realistic as required by army policy and regulations, and although the army has begun to train reserve units at the National Training Center at Fort Irwin, California, and at the more recently established Joint Readiness Training Center at Fort Chaffee, Arkansas, many reservists do not learn battlefield survival skills.

Reservists have less total time to train than do active duty soldiers, and administrative requirements cut deeply into the time available. Moreover, not all reservists who are supposed to train with units do so. In 1989, about 18,000 soldiers serving in army reserve units were classifed as "unsatisfactory participants" for missing nine or more drills. They were transferred from their units to the Individual Ready Reserve, from which they might be drawn as individual replacements to fill out active units. These soldiers accounted for about 7 percent of the strength of army reserve units.

The General Accounting Office found that in fiscal years 1987 and 1988, at most 60 percent of reserve component soldiers took the army's Skill Qualification Test (SQT), despite the fact that reservists are required to take the SQT every two years. Moreover, of the 156,000 reservists who did take the test in 1987, only about 65 percent passed, compared with 92 percent of active duty soldiers during the same period. Similarly, although reservists are required to be tested every two years on performance of soldier tasks common to all military specialties, in fiscal years 1986 and 1987, only 37 percent of army reservists and 50 percent of National Guard soldiers were tested. While most reserve component soldiers who took the test successfully completed most tasks, the percentage of tasks failed by reservists was twice as high as the percentage of tasks failed by the average active duty soldier. In 1987, the army reserve achieved a readiness rating of 55 percent.

The pattern of reserve call-ups in support of Desert Shield and Desert Storm reflects the army's belief that readiness is frequently higher in reserve support units than in reserve combat units, even if the combat units are round-out units for active divisions that must be rapidly deployed. Many reservists in support functions practice their military skills in their civilian job, while reservists in armored units are unlikely to have civilian occupations that resemble driving tanks or loading and firing tank guns. Thus, combat skills are seen as "more perishable" than are support skills in reserve units.

The reserve components—the army's citizen-soldiers—are an important facet of the task environment of the army's ascending generation of strategic leaders. They are inheriting a force structure based upon a set of assumptions about reserve readiness made two decades ago that have not yet been met and may be unreasonable. They are faced with the task of imposing reality on this structure. Should they not do so and should there be a war of sufficient scale to require the use of reserve combat units, they will be faced with the task of fighting the war within the constraints of this structure.

THE DEMOGRAPHIC ENVIRONMENT

Military manpower is one domain in which current knowledge reduces future uncertainty for strategic planners. Recent birthrates indicate how many native-born Americans will be in the military age-eligible population twenty to thirty years from now. One can probably make more reasonable assumptions about immigration and about the gender composition of the labor force at that time than about the geographical "markets" for military operations or about major changes in military technology.

The army's ability to recruit sufficient numbers of high-quality young Americans for both the active and the reserve forces will be influenced by demographic processes. At the high end of the age distribution, these same processes will increase the apparent costs of national security. This consideration is not trivial in a budget-conscious era.

The American population is growing; it will reach about 283 million people in the year 2010. However, the fertility rate has been below the replacement rate for more than a decade, contributing to an increase in the average age of the population and a decline in the military age-eligible population. The number of eighteen to twenty-four year-olds was about 30.5 million in 1981. It will decline to about 23.5 million in 2010. Thus, the size of the army's recruiting pool will decline into the middle of the 1990s and may not regain its 1981 level for a century. Increased longevity also contributes to the aging of the population and results not only in an older labor force but also in an increased number of retirees, including military retirees. Not only is the recruitment pool for new military personnel declining, but, in addition, career personnel will increasingly draw retired pay for more years than they drew active duty pay.

With fertility lower than the replacement rate, the growth in the population is explained largely by immigration, both legal and illegal. In 1980, about one-third of the nation's population growth was attributable to immigration, and we can estimate that the figure will not drop below one-fifth in the near future. The nation is confronted with interesting policy decisions regarding the degree to which the citizenship obligation of defending the state should be borne by noncitizens and the degree to which such activity can earn citizenship.

Population growth is not equal among all racial and ethnic groups. The population within the army recruits will have declining percentages of non-Hispanic,

Euro-Americans and increasing percentages of immigrants, Hispanics, Asian Americans, and African Americans: another manifestation of a world that is increasingly less Eurocentric.

The non-Hispanic, Euro-American population, which comprised 78 percent of the total population in 1985, will decline between 5 and 10 percent by 2010. By contrast, Asian Americans, the fastest-growing minority group, will roughly double between 1985 and 2010, and Hispanics—the several ethnic groups of Spanish or Latin American descent—will increase from about 7 percent in 1985 to more than 10 percent in 2010. Given higher fertility rates among Hispanics, their percentage growth will be even higher among the young, constituting up to 13 percent of military-age cohorts.

The army has had the largest percentage of African American personnel among nonprior service accessions of the four Defense Department services since the advent of the all-volunteer force: 26 percent in fiscal year (FY) 1989 compared with 22 percent in the navy, 18 percent in the Marine Corps, and 12 percent in the air force. The army has also led the navy and Marine Corps, although it has lagged behind the air force, in the accession of nonprior servicewomen, with FY 1989 figures of 14 percent, 12 percent, 6 percent, and 21 percent, respectively. About 40 percent of all enlisted personnel are members of racial or ethnic minority groups, and among enlisted women, the figure is greater than 54 percent.

Regarding the labor force, the most dramatic change beyond a population that is older and increasingly composed of racial and ethnic minorities is the employment of women. In 1971, about 31 percent of mothers with young children were working. By 1985 this figure had increased to almost 50 percent. More than 70 percent of women aged eighteen to forty-four were in the labor force. In 1990, almost two-thirds of all new job applicants were women. For a traditionally masculine military force that has moved markedly toward gender integration but maintains gender-linked combat exclusion policies, such a profound change in labor market composition is consequential (Segal, 1990).

The reentry of women into the labor force in part reflects changing family patterns in America that are also consequential for the army, although there are interesting divergences between the military and civilian populations in this arena. Americans generally have been getting married later, and couples have been having their first children later, spacing their children more widely, and having fewer children. However, in contrast to their civilian counterparts, soldiers have been marrying and having their first chidren earlier and have been having more children. As of June 1989, 72 percent of American officers and 53 percent of enlisted personnel were married. Thus, with regard to both male and female personnel, the strategic leaders of the army must be increasingly sensitive to the competing demands made on the serviceperson by military and family duties if they are to maximize readiness and effectiveness (M.W. Segal, 1989). The Persian Gulf deployment has demonstrated strains for military personnel at the interface between the work organization and the family that were not anticipated twenty years ago.

In addition, while marriages have been delayed on average in America, divorce has increased markedly, and we have seen a rapid increase in the number of single-parent families—about 20 percent of all families in the mid-1980s—and this increase is likely to continue. Moreover, single-parent families are more common among racial and ethnic minorities. Thus the military age-eligible recruiting pool consists of young Americans many of whom have family responsibilities and more than one-fifth of whom do not have a spouse with whom to share child-rearing duties.

Army recruiting in this environment is a challenge. After a generally successful decade through most of the 1980s, the army fell 2 percent short of its quarterly recruiting goal in the fall of 1988, and accessions from the top half of the mental aptitude distribution dropped 14 percent. With the recruitment pool declining, entry-level civilian wages at their highest point in recent history, and unemployment at a decade-and-a-half low, the army had to reenlist larger numbers of first-term soldiers in FY 1989 to offset a shrinking market of first-term recruits.

The subsequent beginning of a drawdown of the army in 1990 might have reduced recruiting pressure for a smaller force, and recruit quality did improve. In FY 1990, the army had to recruit fewer than 90,000 soldiers, compared with more than 120,000 in FY 1989. Ninety-five percent of the FY 1990 recruits were high school graduates, exceeding the previous record figure of 93 percent in 1988, and two-thirds of the FY 1990 recruits were in the top half of the mental aptitude distribution. Equally important, if we are to take the Total Force concept seriously, 95 percent of FY 1990 enlistees in the army reserve were high school graduates, compared with 86 percent in 1989.

However, events in Saudi Arabia required the army to increase its recruiting goals in the autumn of 1990, and the combination of reduced cohort size, the inertia of the drawdown, and the threat of war in the Middle East made enlistment less attractive to young men and women who might have been motivated to join the army for educational opportunities, job training, or peacetime employment but who really do not want to be warriors. At the same time, the virtual certainty of an eventual drawdown might deter some career-oriented potential recruits who see career opportunities in the army diminishing. The future recruiting environment is by no means clear.

THE FISCAL ENVIRONMENT

Anticipating the availability of financial resources for defense with a twenty-year lead time is not an enviable task. The defense budget has changed markedly during the past decade, first under pressure to reduce a federal deficit approaching $3 trillion in the mid-1980s and more recently in the quest for a "peace dividend" in the wake of the collapse of the Warsaw Pact (Zakheim, 1990). The world has not become a demonstrably safer place, but these pressures remain as environmental constraints within which the army's strategic leaders must work.

After a period of minimal growth during the Carter administration, the defense share of the federal budget was increased markedly under President Ronald Reagan, supported by a public worried about the Soviet invasion of Afghanistan and the revolution in Iran. The increase affected the services differentially, largely as a function of the balance of capital and labor in their war-fighting doctrines. The army, having begun to emphasize low-intensity conflict, was probably disadvantaged by this process.

Reagan's FY 1986 budget of $313.7 billion represented a 40 percent increase (in constant 1986 dollars) over Carter's FY 1981 budget of $224.2 billion. Most of the gain during the Reagan years supported capital-intensive rather than labor-intensive views of the military. The procurement budget grew by 75 percent. The research, development, test, and evaluation budget grew by 86 percent. By contrast, the military personnel account increased by only 17 percent. Interestingly, this growth supported increases in the size of the navy, air force, and Marine Corps, but not the army.

While the transition from Carter to Reagan saw an increase in the budget share allocated to defense by the administration, the mid-1980s saw the potential for a taxpayer's revolt, fueled by the deficit, focused on perceived abuses in the capital defense accounts that had been favored by Reagan, particularly in the procurement process, reflected in public opinion opposing growth in defense spending, and manifested in the passage by the Congress, in late 1985, of the Gramm-Rudman-Hollings Balanced Budget Act. Sequestration under this act led to a FY 1986 defense budget reduction of $5.1 billion in outlay and $11 billion in spending authority.

The Reagan administration continued to budget the Defense Department on the basis of an assumption of future budgetary growth, continued to budget capital programs with low initial outlays but extensive out-year commitments, and canceled no major weapon systems. President George Bush, early in his administration, announced his intention to reduce FY 1990 defense funds to the level necessary to keep pace with inflation, but he projected growth above inflation from 1991 to 1994, continuing a pattern of disregarding fiscal reality and avoiding hard choices. In late 1989, Secretary of Defense Richard Cheney announced plans to cut the defense budget by $180 billion during the FY 1991-1994 period. However, his base was a FY 1990 Bush administration budget submission that had no chance of passage, and that represented a reduction in budget authority less than three-quarters as large as the reductions in the defense budgets during the previous four fiscal years had been.

As this is written, Operation Desert Storm represents a temporary budgetary reprieve, as the deployment of more than 500,000 American military personnel to the Saudi Peninsula/Persian Gulf region distracted attention from the long-term budgetary pressures. The $288 billion 1991 defense budget—about $18 billion less than the Defense Department had requested in January 1990—will reduce force size for an army that stood at 744,170 soldiers in October 1990 but is projected to be cut by 42,000 soldiers, to 702,170 by October 1991, and to be cut by an additional 224,170 soldiers, to an end strength of 520,000 soldiers, by October 1995. The 1991 defense budget allows Secretary Cheney to keep up to 20,000 additional military personnel on active duty across all services if they are necessary for Operation Desert Storm, and reserve call-ups of up to 1 million people have been authorized, but the long-term drawdown will go on.

Budgetary pressures will lead to continued reductions in army Reserve Officers' Training Corps (ROTC) units—the major source of officer accessions in the army—since fewer officers will be required in a downsized force. There will also be a reduction in the size of the U.S. corps of cadets at West Point, although this will not produce significant budget savings. Changes in officer accession in any given year will have implications for the management of the officer corps for an additional two decades.

Budgetary pressures will certainly lead to additional base closings, a process that got bogged down last year in political battles. The 1991 defense appropriation calls for the appointment of a new base-closing commission that will operate under rules similar to those of the 1988 base-closing commission. Once bases are identified under the complex rules of the new commission, it is likely that they will be closed. The only domestic bases closed in recent years had been identified by the 1988 commission.

Moreover, if fiscal responsibility is imposed on the services by the Defense Department—an occurrence presaged by Secretary Cheney's cancellation of the navy's multibillion-dollar A-12 aircraft development program—the army may have to forego material acquisitions that are currently high on its wish list. These are fiscal pressures to which the army's strategic managers will have to adapt, going into the twenty-first century.

DISCUSSION

All of these changes pose challenges for the army's strategic managers. Western ideologues have long predicted the greater longevity of market economies than of planned socialist economies, and most Western military analysts have assigned very low probabilities to an actual shooting war between NATO and the Warsaw Pact. Nonetheless, it was the focus of the army's strategic planning through the Cold War period. It is unlikely that twenty years ago, as the Vietnam War and the system of military conscription that supported it were winding down, the senior strategic managers of the army were anticipating that in 1991 the Warsaw Pact would have collapsed, that we would be withdrawing troops from Europe, that we would be downsizing the army and closing domestic bases under budgetary pressures, and that at the same time we would be deploying a large volunteer force, with a significant representation of female personnel, to the Middle East, with Egypt, Saudi Arabia, and Syria among our major allies. Given the assumptions of Stratified Systems Theory, today's four-star generals must be able to conceptualize this magnitude of change as they steer the army toward the year 2010. These generals learned the profession of arms as small-unit leaders during a Eurocentered Cold War period. Except in the manpower domain, the parameters with which they have had to work have been both uncertain and volatile.

Lieutenant generals today are faced with a slightly less ominous task: they need merely the cognitive flexibility and vision to be able to see over the cusp into the twenty-first century. The mission of today's major generals, by contrast, involves time scales still within the current century. Understanding of concrete trends that are already unfolding is probably more important to their task performance than is the vision necessary to anticipate and deal with intangibles. Brigadier generals are responsible for managing the operational problems of today.

There is a very imperfect fit between the number of stars a flag-rank officer wears and the time scale that he or she must deal with, but the fundamental assumption that time horizon must increase with hierarchical level probably holds in all large organizations. The success of chief executive officers (CEOs) in large corporations may well be determined by their ability to make correct decisions about long-term resource allocations in the face of the uncertainty of the future. However, military organizations probably deal with more environmental uncertainty and, indeed, a more complex environment, with considerably greater downside risk, than do other organizations.

The potential loss of tens of thousands of human lives as the cost of being wrong has far greater social and political consequence than the loss incurred when a new automobile model or a new fighter aircraft is developed for which there is no market. This loss of life aspect makes military management unique. At the same time, military management operates in an internal labor market. Unlike in other corporate organizations, senior strategic managers cannot be recruited from among the ranks of CEOs of the Fortune 500 corporations, laterally to bring in senior executives who have demonstrated their ability in other arenas to operate with broad temporal horizons. The army's senior strategic managers must be homegrown.

If the time horizons specified by this approach are correct, then the army—and any other organization whose most senior management is promoted from among candidates with long careers within the organization—faces two major personnel tasks. First, the organization must be able to select, educate, and train executives who, for the first decade of their employment will be able to fulfill the detailed, everyday requirements of immediate productive functions (in the case of the army, company-level leadership and battalion staff responsibilities) but some number of whom, two decades after that, will have the vision to plan two additional decades into the future. Second, in such organizations, career progression must be managed to maximize the likelihood that the people best suited for strategic management roles rise to that level.

4

Strategic Leadership and Restructuring: A Reciprocal Interdependence

Michael A. Hitt and Barbara W. Keats

Major corporations and government units, in response to poor performance and/or competitive pressures, are undergoing restructuring—a phenomenon of the 1980s and 1990s. The focus of this chapter is strategic leadership's impact on this restructuring and, in turn, restructuring's impact on strategic leadership.

The exercise of strategic leadership during restructuring requires the mentoring of strategic thinking and the nurture and maintenance of organizational core competences (organizational skills around which competitive advantage can be built). The authors show how these competences must be buffered during restructuring. Management and professional development, appropriate organizational culture creation and maintenance, long-term commitment to the organization, and development and maintenance of long-term strategic control systems are all critical to sustaining core competences.

Hitt and Keats embed all the previously mentioned considerations within SST to show how the interplay can enhance our knowledge of both SST and restructuring.

Work force reductions have become an integral part of the modern organizational environment. A survey of 1,000 top human resource managers revealed substantial work force reductions in 39 percent of their organizations in 1988 and 1989 alone (Greenberg, 1989). Examples include Bank of New England (approximately one-third of work force), Digital Equipment (5,000 jobs out of 124,000), Bank of Boston (1,500 out of 18,500), Saks Fifth Avenue (700 out of 12,000), Pan Am Corporation (2,500 out of 29,000), Chase Manhattan Corporation (5,000 out of 41,000), and the combined armed forces of the United States, facing a 25 percent planned reduction in total personnel over the period 1990-1995, including 4,600 positions in the air force alone (Bureau of National Affairs, 1990; Ginovsky, 1990; Kalish, 1990). In fact, U.S. firms cut twice as many jobs in the first nine months of 1990 as in all of 1989 (Kantrowitz et al., 1990). These reductions in force may be implemented for a number of reasons, but in recent years they have been couched principally in terms of "downsizing" or "restructuring."

The decade of the 1980s exhibited an unprecedented wave of organizational restructuring, as reflected in mergers and acquisitions, downscoping (reducing the number of business or product service offerings in which the organization participated), and downsizing (reducing operational slack, subtracting administrative layers, and so on). Work force reductions generally reflect organizations' responses to signals indicating poor performance, as might be generated by an inability to compete effectively in increasingly global markets. As a result, they may be implemented hastily or in a reactive posture and guided almost solely by economic considerations, such as an immediate felt need to reduce costs. While layoffs generally are expected in response to economic downturns, historically they have been confined to blue-collar and/or unskilled labor. However, work force reductions of the 1980s and 1990s reflect a pervasive trend toward inclusion of the white-collar and executive ranks. This trend is reflected in figures that suggest as many as 70 percent of the newly jobless in 1990 were white-collar workers. On Wall Street alone, staffing dropped from a peak of about 265,000 in 1987 to about 215,000 in late 1990 (Kantrowitz et al., 1990.)

Therefore, downsizing and downscoping actions are far-reaching and sometimes caused by abrupt environmental changes. As a result, even executives who have strategic long-term vision may not perfectly anticipate the need for restructuring. This notion is congruent with Hunt and Ropo's (this book) suggestion of the development of general long-term visions (which may lack specificity in some areas, particularly as the focus is further into the future). However, maintaining an alternative of exercising strategic leadership during downsizing and/or downscoping actions may allow appropriate flexibility to respond properly to environmental requirements for restructuring. In other words, strategic leaders need to develop alternative scenarios because of the inability to predict the future with 100 percent accuracy. Restructuring actions would be one of those alternative scenarios.

Our focus in this chapter is on strategic leadership as it affects and is affected by reductions in force associated with downscoping. Thus, we examine restructuring processes in terms of the relationship between strategic skills and long-term organizational health. We approach this relationship from two reciprocal perspectives: (1) the role of strategic leadership in restructuring efforts and their outcomes and (2) the impact of restructuring efforts on development and maintenance of strategic leadership. A model depicting the reciprocal relationship between strategic leadership and restructuring is shown in Figure 4.1. We then develop an integrative position regarding the critical issues that emerge from the analysis and offer some recommendations for effective strategic leadership after organizational restructuring. The general framework for our analysis is provided by current theory and research on the nature of strategic leadership skills (e.g., Hambrick, 1989; Hitt and Hoskisson, 1991; Prahalad and Hamel, 1990; Westley and Mitzberg, 1989)

Figure 4.1
Reciprocal Interdependence Between Strategic Leadership and Restructuring

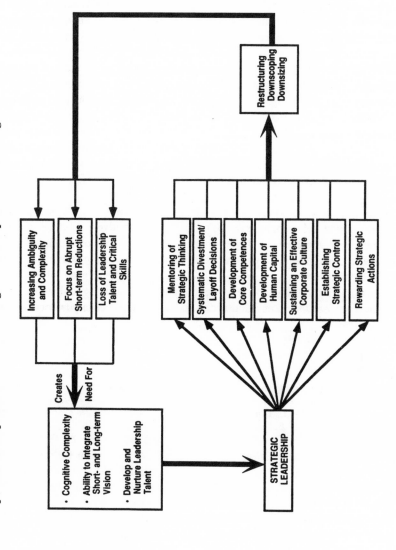

the concept of Stratified Systems Theory (Jaques, 1976, 1986; Jaques and Clement, 1991), the multilevel leadership model (Hunt, 1991), and the developmental theory of expert judgment advanced by Dreyfus (1982) and extended in Dreyfus and Dreyfus (1986).

According to Hambrick (1989), strategic leadership is involved with external and internal spheres of the organization, is embedded in ambiguity, complexity, and extensive information processing, is multifunctional, and largely involves managing through others. Therefore, the exercise of strategic leadership is integrative in nature and highly complex. Under normal conditions it is difficult, but under conditions associated with restructuring, strategic leadership is extremely complex and challenging. As a result, there may be multiple intended and unintended (similar to indirect effects proposed by Hunt and Ropo, this book) consequences from restructuring efforts.

POTENTIAL OUTCOMES FROM RESTRUCTURING

There are many possible outcomes from restructuring efforts, both positive and negative, intended and unintended. For example, a positive, intended outcome might be increased efficiency. However, unintended negative outcomes might be reflected in low employee morale, low commitment and loyalty, and higher levels of turnover (Wheeler et al., 1990). As noted by Brockner, Davy, and Carter (1988), survivors of layoff activity often experience severe guilt, insecurity, and distress. Table 4.1 denotes some of the potential intended and unintended consequences of restructuring actions.

Table 4.1
Potential Intended and Unintended Consequences of Restructuring

Intended Consequences	Unintended Consequences
Strategic Refocusing	Increased Turnover
Organizational Regeneration	Lower Employee Commitment
Increased Efficiency	and Loyalty to Organization
Decreased Costs	Survivor Guilt, Insecurity, and
Improved Productivity	Distress
Improved Quality Output	Penalties for Bad Decisions
Enhanced Competitive Advantage	Emphasized
Institute Major Organizational Changes	Managerial Risk Aversion
Inculcate New Basic Values (Culture)	Resistance to Change
Build New Sources of Synergy in the	Reduced Innovations
Organization	Short-term Emphasis

Beyond effects on individual employees (which, of course, affect organizational functioning), restructuring undertaken in response to performance downturns or environmental shocks is likely to produce a pervasive, crisis-oriented atmosphere (Cameron, Kim, and Whetten, 1988). In such circumstances, rewards for good decisions may be overshadowed by the penalties for bad decisions (Whetten, 1988). If, as a result, managers then become more risk-averse, they may sacrifice strategic, long-term thinking to focus on the current crisis. Such orientations often lead managers to limit their data-gathering and decision-making activities to protection and survival of their "turf." Over time, the organization may experience a lack of long-term planning and innovation, scapegoating, resistance to change, fragmented pluralism, and debilitating conflict (Cameron, Kim, and Whetten, 1988).

Thus, although the intent of restructuring efforts is generally directed toward organizational regeneration and enhanced competitive advantage, the actual outcomes may be degenerative and dysfunctional. These potentially negative outcomes may be averted or, at least, anticipated through development of proactive planning efforts. It is incumbent upon the strategic leadership of the organization, then, to recognize potential problems associated with restructuring efforts and develop effective structural and behavioral safeguards. Given that the exercise of strategic leadership is complex and difficult under stable conditions and/or "normal" growth goals, the additional challenges presented by restructuring efforts will tax even the most creative and smoothly functioning top management team.

Behn (1988) suggested that during downsizing, management should focus on maintaining morale, attracting and retaining high-quality personnel, developing support from key constituencies, and creating opportunities for innovation. While this suggestion presents management with a noble agenda, it also suggests the paradoxical nature of the task (Cameron, Freeman, and Mishra, 1990). In general, Cameron, Freeman, and Mishra (1990) imply that managers often must design and implement restructuring actions for immediate impact. However, they also must preserve the long-term goals to enhance competitive position and organizational growth and survival (Thompson, 1967). In response to these concerns we consider the potential impact of restructuring efforts on the development and nurturance of currrent and future strategic leadership in the organization.

THE IMPACT OF RESTRUCTURING ON STRATEGIC LEADERSHIP

As noted earlier, the human resource targets of restructuring actions increasingly include members of the midlevel and upper echelons. Thus, there are important strategic implciations for the future of many organizations. Three approaches to handling human resources generally taken in a downsizing or downscoping mode are (1) reducing the ranks of highly paid, upper-echelon members, often accomplished through virtually random election by such personnel to accept early retirement inducements, (2) eliminating middle management layers in order to resemble a "lean machine" and (3) implementing across-the-board layoffs, often with little evaluation of the relative importance or contribution of functional specialties or particular units to the organization's strategic mission and objectives. While such efforts may provide some short-term relief or sense of action in the face of crisis, the manner in which they are conceived and implemented may have serious and pervasive consequences for the long-term growth and survival of the organization.

Consider some recently articulated sources of organizational malaise: mid-level managers at General Motors express concern over the absence of a perceived career path; managers at both General Motors and Georgia Pacific sense a crisis of leadership due to the dual process of early retirement incentives and replacement of older, experienced management with perhaps talented, but undeveloped, people (Byrne, 1988). Such experiences are being coupled with the emerging pressure on organizations to shift away from traditional pyramid structures toward hourglass organizations (Byrne, 1988; Fisher, 1988). The emergence of these areas of concern is a direct outgrowth of the process that has come to be known generally as "restructuring."

The strategic management literature suggests that strategic leadership requires an ability to accommodate and integrate both external and internal context. As noted earlier, it involves managing ambiguity and complex information processing. It is multifunctional and largely involves managing through others (Hambrick, 1989). Furthermore, it requires anticipation, vision, flexibility, and ability to empower others to create strategic change (Byrd, 1987). However, only recently has theoretical and empirical work emerged to suggest the substantive nature of the strategic leadership process and factors underlying its development (Hunt, 1991; Jaques, 1986).

According to Jaques (1986), leadership is not simply an idiosyncratic characteristic of some individuals. It is a systemic property derived from the interaction of the requirements of critical organizational tasks, the critical functions those tasks serve, and the problem-solving characteristics of the actors in "leader" roles. The nature of the critical functions and tasks is related to organizational level. Hunt (1991) expanded those concepts and incorporated them into a multilevel model of leadership. His model provides an integrative perspective on the type of leadership required, critical tasks, individual capabilities needed, and the importance of organizational culture/subcultures at each organization level.

For example, Hunt argued that leaders at the systems level, which relates most closely to Hambrick's (1989) notion of strategic leadership, must have a ten-to twenty-year vision, given the critical tasks (e.g., goals/mission development, development strategy, design of the organization, design of subsystems—planning, information, control, and so on) at this level. According to Hunt (1991), effective leadership at each organizational level requires development of a frame of reference—a "cognitive map"—that reflects the level of complexity produced by the combination of the foregoing situational elements. Furthermore, each level requires specific leadership skills and individual predispositions. Such suggestions are consistent with the developmental model advanced by Dreyfus (1982).

Dreyfus (1982) postulates that information processing and decision making commensurate with what we are calling "strategic" depend on the successive transformation of four mental capacities through five distinct stages. The four capacities, each with a primitive and sophisticated form, are component recognition, salience recognition, whole situation recognition, and decision. The five stages proposed by Dreyfus (1982) and extended by Dreyfus and Dreyfus (1986) and Hunt (1991) are novice, advanced beginner, competency, proficiency, and expert. At each stage, development reflects movement toward a more holistic and intuitive approach to information processing and decision making. Dreyfus (1982) clearly indicates that development of this holistic and intuitive capability can be obtained only through "vast experience with concrete, real world situations" (p. 146). Clearly, Hunt's (1991) notion of the differences in leadership by organizational level and the requisite tasks and demands provides this critical context for development of strategic "expertise." One would expect strategic leaders to be at the expert stage and thus to function as what Quinn (1988) calls master managers. For example, we might expect master managers to be able to anticipate and prepare for critical environmental jolts that necessitate downsizing/downscoping.

In general, then, development and validation of an appropriate "map" are one of the most important growth objectives for executives. Such development depends on both individual cognitive capacity and experiential opportunity. The primary factors underlying this experiential opportunity are interaction with the critical tasks of multiple organization levels and a process of "guided discovery," or mentoring. Such development is congruent with the perspectives proposed in the chapters in this book by Sashkin and by Lewis and Jacobs. Thus, the organization's task is to recognize the long-term nature of these developmental processes, the long-term value associated with providing for them, and the danger of short-term solutions to current economic problems that fail to account for them. We address these concerns in the following paragraphs.

Restructuring and Developmental Tasks

Jaques's (1986) model of cognitive development, when placed in the context of separate organizational levels, suggests that a person's inherent cognitive "equipment" is a necessary, but not sufficient, condition underlying acquisition of higher-order management skills. Beyond that condition, one is constrained at any particular moment by the limits of one's experience to that moment. The critical attribute of this constraint is one's maximum temporal horizon, which sets the boundaries of the "world of purpose and intention within which one lives, constructs patterns, and organizes one's life and aspirations" (p. 374). Expansion of that temporal horizon is dependent upon both direct experience and "guided discovery," the process of monitoring.

Restructuring that is singularly focused on cost reduction and implemented through early retirement incentives to highly paid executives risks losing the very individuals needed to serve in such mentoring roles. For example, Jaques (1976, 1986) and Hunt (1991) suggest that the relevant time frame for the strategic level of decision making, and thus for strategic leaders, extends to twenty years and beyond. An organization that makes cutbacks among upper-echelon members is left with individuals whose time span horizons extend no further than about ten years. As a result, there is no one in the organization with the appropriate cognitive map to engage in true "strategic" thinking or to mentor those at lower levels to develop strategic expertise. In the context of Dreyfus's (1982) and Hunt's (1991) work, the organization has effectively eliminated the individuals most likely to have developed holistic, "expert" strategic problem-solving capabilities.

If, on the other hand, the target of work force reduction actions is middle management, the organization stands to lose those individuals who are just beginning to form cognitive maps of the requisite complexity to cope with higher-order organizational strata. Such issues are likely to surface, for example, in the response to the increasingly pervasive cutbacks among students in the Reserve Officers' Training Corps (ROTC) at more than 1,000 college campuses in the United States (Pasztor, 1990). With the noncommissioned officers (NCOs) forming the ranks of first-level managers in the military, ROTC programs, as important sources of entry-level commissioned officers, provide primary development of lower middle managers for the armed services. Although one of the easiest means to "slim down" may be to reduce "intake," unless great care is taken to preserve an appropriate threshold level of critical organizational skills and abilities, such reductions may severely limit the availability of a pool of potential future strategic leaders by short-circuiting the requisite developmental processes inherent in the models proposed by Dreyfus (1982), Jaques (1986), and Hunt (1991). As noted by Tichy (1987), organizations are increasingly challenged to focus on a commitment to nurturing leadership.

The third common means of making reductions in force, across-the-board layoffs, may offer the simplest decision path but can be quite harmful to the organization. Separate functional areas often make differential contributions to organizational performance that are ignored in across-the-board reductions. As a result, the organization may lose many individuals who perform critical tasks. Their loss may diminish the organization's capacity to achieve long-term success. Therefore, executive decisions to restructure should involve careful analysis of the relative contribution of the various functions and skills to organizational performance and achievement of long-term goals. The functions and skills should be prioritized, and greater reductions should come from less critical areas. While difficult, this exercise of strategic leadership will help to ensure the preservation of skills required for the continued exercise of strategic leadership in the future.

Such considerations appear to have guided Richard Miller's actions at Wang after he was hired as CEO in 1989. He and a special team of managers identified assets that could be sold to raise about $600 million in cash. In so doing, $500 million worth of loans were paid off. However, in choosing assets to be divested, they protected assets that could be developed and contribute to the firm's long-term success. For example, some managers recommended selling a small subsidiary that provided voice mail services to other larger firms. Miller rejected that idea because he believed that business fitted into Wang's long-term strategy of offering customers information in all forms, text data, image, or voice (Dumaine, 1990). As a result, Miller preserved functions and skills he felt were important to Wang's long-term strategy. That is, he retained the skills necessary to continue to develop and offer customers systems for voice mail services.

Summary

Effective restructuring does not mean across-the-board work force reductions. The implementation of such approaches often neglects the critical, if time-consuming and potentially conflict-laden, process of evaluating future as well as present strategic skills needed by the organization. It also affects both the selection of the best candidates to be mentored and the provision of that mentoring. If restructuring is to be of long-term value to the organization, appropriate evaluative processes will require assessment of critical organizational functions and organizational core competences in light of long-term goals and assessment of individual skills and developmental potential in the context of those requisite skills and goals. Furthermore, it will require establishment of incentives, policies, and procedures designed to attract and/or retain those targeted individuals (rather than leaving such attraction/retention to some relatively random process of self-selection, as often occurs).

We will offer some observations regarding the reciprocal relationships proposed and some suggestions for the proactive and integrative exercise of strategic leadership in the process of organizational restructuring.

THE EXERCISE OF STRATEGIC LEADERSHIP IN RESTRUCTURING

Our second major consideration is the exercise of strategic leadership in the process of restructuring. While difficult, exercise of strategic leadership is critical to the success of the process and involves thoughtful and creative attention to a number of critical variables. For example, investment in new technology, often a victim of short-term thinking, should not be neglected. As suggested by the work of Clark (1987) and Young (1988), strategic investment in new technology and in the continuous upgrading of employee skills it requires reflects some of the most critical areas of strategic decision making for regeneration and renewal. Effective strategic leadership also depends on recognition of the increasing degree to which all organizations are part of a global market. Adoption and maintenance of this perspective, even in the context of domestic competition, emphasize the important role of future, long-term growth goals. Also, there is a focus on continued environmental mastery, so critical to capitalize on selected advantages associated with various international markets, exploits differential core competences and shared resources across businesses in development of new forms of organizational synergy (Barney, 1986; Lei, Hitt, and Bettis, 1990; Porter, 1990).

In general, the focus of strategic leadership in the context of restructuring should be on balancing short-term needs with long-term growth and survival, continued development of, and investment in, core competences, continued development of human capital, and fostering a strong organizational culture. Each of these areas is addressed in more detail in the following sections.

Core Competences

The work of Hambrick (1989), Hitt and Hoskisson (1991), Prahalad and Hamel (1990), and Westley and Mintzberg (1989), among others, suggests explicit inclusion of strategic leadership focus on the nurture and maintenance of "core competences" as a potential basis for competitive advantage and long-term survival. Core competences, discussed in more detail later, are similar to what others termed distinctive competences (e.g., Hitt and Ireland, 1985, 1986; Snow and Hrebiniak, 1980). Core competences are organizational skills around which a firm builds a competitive advantage. Examples include research and development at Merck, marketing and promotion at Phillip Morris, and development and transfer of innovation to the market at 3M.

Prahalad and Hamel (1990) define core competences as "the collective learning in the organization, especially to coordinate diverse production skills and integrate multiple streams of technologies" (p. 82). The competences represent the core skills, capabilities, and knowledge on which organizational learning is focused (Lei, Hitt, and Bettis, 1990). Core competences often relate to functional skills, (for example, manufacturing, marketing, research and development (R&D).

When these core skills are developed and applied through the organization, they create the opportunity for gaining competitive advantage. The ability to develop and utilize a core skill across separate businesses, markets, and locations may be distinctive and highly difficult to imitate by competitors, thereby creating a sustained competitive advantage (Barnery, 1988).

Lei, Hitt, and Bettis (1990) argued that the development, nurture, and application of core competences on a firmwide basis can greatly facilitate managing important interrelationships within global firms. Although the sharing of resources has been shown to be an important source of competitive advantage in diversified firms (Gupta and Govindarajan, 1984, 1986; Porter, 1985), globalization greatly complicates resource sharing across country borders. Domestic markets, informal rules of competition, cultural differences, government regulations, and other trade barriers make resource sharing difficult.

While the sharing of tangible resources may be complicated in global firms, sharing of intangible resources represents an opportunity. Intangible resources refer to knowledge or skills. Strategic leaders can thus promote the sharing of intangible resources across business units. In particular, if they identify and nurture core competences, they can build linkages among diverse units throughout the organizations. To do so, they must (1) emphasize continuous learning focused on core competences, (2) take a systemic approach to application of core competences to add value, and (3) take advantage of the unique capabilities to create a sustainable competitive advantage (Lei, Hitt, and Bettis, 1990).

The development and application of core competences help facilitate information processing by executives. In fact, because of the cognitive complexity required to undertake an SST approach to leadership, particularly during restructuring efforts, application of core competences can lessen information-processing demands on top executives (thereby lowering often unrealistic requirements for cognitive complexity). With core competences, executives and middle managers may have similar critical technical skills. Therefore, executives may delegate certain decisions to middle managers that otherwise could not be delegated. Additionally, emphasis on core competences may place more realistic boundaries on the strategic vision required (narrows focus of vision). As a result, development and application of core competences complement and extend the SST framework for strategic leadership.

A classic application of a core competence for competitive advantage can be seen in the Phillip Morris acquisition of Miller Brewing Company. Phillip Morris had a core competence in advertising, promotion, and marketing of consumer goods. It transferred this competence to Miller Brewing Company and revised a stagnant, if not declining, firm. With frequent creative advertising and the development and promotion of new products, such as ''lite'' beer, Miller moved from an ''also ran'' to number two in the beer industry behind Anheuser-Busch.

A systemic approach to nurturing and applying core competences helps the firm achieve economies of both scale and scope. Core competences often allow firms to gain first-mover advantages. Furthermore, a systemic approach facilitates more efficient skill transfers. For example, learning and skills accumulated from experience in one set of businesses can potentially be transferred to new business opportunities, thereby reinforcing existing competitive advantage (Hamel and Prahalad, 1989).

Additionally, while idiosyncratic skills may not be easily imitable, systemic applications of core competences also may be difficult to imitate, to create competitive advantages. 3M, Nestle, Procter and Gamble, and Heinz exemplify firms that apply core competences on a global basis. All four firms participate in, and dominate across a spectrum of, different end product markets, but they have built leading positions in global markets by focusing and continuously refining their core competences.

Therefore, in restructuring, executives must be careful not to harm core competences that exist in the organization. These core skills should be buffered from major disruption during downsizing and downscoping actions. For example, individuals who have the critical skills (e.g., have important leadership skills as noted by Sashkin, 1992, i.e., work in a function considered a core competence) should be protected from layoffs. Furthermore, units and businesses where core skills can be applied to greatest advantage should be maintained. The resulting streamlined organization should have an even stronger emphasis on application of core competences after restructuring efforts are completed. Therefore, strategic leaders should understand and appreciate the importance of the firm's core competence(s). Additionally, they must ensure that these skills are integrated and emphasized throughout the newly refocused organization.

Human Capital Development

Hitt and Hoskisson (1991) argued that the development of human capital is critical for strategic competitiveness. Nussbaum (1988) argued that U.S. firms have invested billions of dollars in capital equipment only to learn later that there was a shortage of skilled labor to operate that equipment. He concluded that human capital has been neglected for years and that this neglect has now reached crisis proportions.

The importance of human capital is further shown by the fact that one-third of the growth in the U.S. gross national product from 1948 to 1982 has been attributed to increases in the education level of the work force. Fifty percent of the growth resulted from technological innovation and knowledge that depend heavily on education. Only 15 percent of the growth was attributed to more investment in capital equipment (Nussbaum, 1988). Duffey (1988) argued that human capital is U.S. firms' greatest competitive advantage.

Doz and Prahalad (1981) suggested that change from a domestic to a global strategy requires shifts in the cognitive and strategic orientation of strategic business unit (SBU) managers. Thus, these managers' critical tasks change, thereby requiring a change in their cognitive map as described by Hunt (1991) and denoted earlier herein. These shifts may be achieved, at least partially, through effective management development programs. Management development programs can help socialize (SBU managers on the importance of a global and overall firm view. Thus, management development may help inculcate core values and systemic focus. However, effective management development also includes objectives of skill acquisition and new motives (Kerr and Jackofsky, 1989) and the development of appropriate reward systems to reinforce such acquisition.

Reward and incentive systems should be designed to maintain a balance between decision-making activities focused on the current situation and long-term data gathering and decision making with a reasonable amount of risk assumption (Hoskisson, Hitt, and Hill, 1992; Hoskisson et al., 1989). In response to shifting resource allocations and perhaps declining resource bases, training and skill building in conflict management methods should be emphasized.

Development programs facilitate communication among employees by providing a common language, building professional networks, and constructing a common vision of the organization. They promote cohesion primarily as a socialization agent and help inculcate a common set of core values. Development programs also influence flexibility by helping to improve critical skills necessary to respond effectively to competitive challenges (Kerr and Jackofsky, 1989).

Change affects the effectiveness of employee skills. For example, employees must become increasingly sophisticated to manage new technology. The required skills necessary to manage new and sophisticated technology are exemplified in the military. Furthermore, because of the need to have cost-efficient operations (particularly after restructuring), workers will have less supervision and be required to become more self-managing (Miles, 1989). Overall, such change suggests the need for higher-skilled employees.

While development of human capital is critical, buffering such programs during restructuring efforts will require strong and committed strategic leadership with a long-term focus and appreciation of the value of human resources. Often during cutbacks or reductions in force, the training and development function is drastically curtailed. For example, after T. Boone Pickens attempted a raid on Phillips Petroleum Company, the firm was forced to make major reductions to pay the costs of newly acquired debt. One of the moves included the elimination of its corporate training and development function, in which it had recently made major investments.

Some reductions in development program investment may necessarily follow general reductions in budget outlays in restructuring efforts. However, injudicious and drastic cuts could exacerbate human resource problems mentioned earlier. To show sensitivity to remaining employees and to develop core competences, continuing investment in development of human capital is critical. Thus, strategic leadership would entail not only maintaining appropriate investments in development programs but also designing new, innovative programs to build and take advantage of surviving employees' skills. Hunt (1991) specifically refers to the importance of integrating education, training, and experience in the development of human capital.

Development of human capital does not always require formal classroom training. In fact, Richard Miller, CEO of Wang, believes that to develop star employees, a leader provides the vision but delegates much responsibility and authority. In doing so, he argues that bright people with creative ideas will surface. However, in delegating responsibility, leaders will find it necessary, at times, to ''manage'' the decision process in order to develop less experienced, but highly talented employees. This approach exemplifies the mentoring described earlier, which is necessary to develop strategic thinking and is congruent with the development notions advanced by Lewis and Jacobs (1992).

In addition, strategic leadership requires effective conflict management skills, particularly during the implementation of restructuring. Leaders must minimize, to the extent possible, inevitable conflict between units that receive differential resource reductions. All survivors of the reduction in force must be made to feel important.

As noted earlier, survivors often feel pressure and experience guilt and distress. Thus, continued development of human resources across units can help overcome negative feelings and provide visible support for the importance of human capital in the organization (see Sashkin, this book, for further development of these ideas).

Organizational Culture

Organizational culture provides a system of shared meanings and values that serve as an interpretational system for organizational members. Hunt (1991) explained that managing culture ranges from sustaining the current culture to actively attempting to change it. Sustaining the current culture could be a significant challenge and may be the most desirable path. On the other hand, restructuring presents a dramatic crisis (Hunt, 1991) that may provide an opportunity for needed cultural change. Work by Tichy and others (Tichy, 1987; Tichy and DeVanna, 1986a; Tichy and Ulrich, 1984) suggests the importance of sensitivity to cultural factors in organizational restructuring efforts. The underlying theme of their work is the anticipation, recognition, and management of both organizational and individual dynamics associated with any change process.

Their model assumes, first, that organizations initiate change in response to some trigger, ranging from an impending cash flow crisis to vague projections of diminishing future competitiveness. The trigger(s) elicits mixed feelings among organizational members, often including highly defensive postures. If the organization has already engaged in some layoffs, the survivors are likely to develop serious morale problems (Brockner, Davy, and Carter, 1988). As a result, they may devote substantial energy to nonproductive activities (such as thought and efforts to seek a new job outside of the organization) and counterproductive psychological responses (such as disengagement, hostility, and so on).

At the organizational level, Tichy's work suggests the danger in responding to resistance with defensive, quick-fix transactional leadership behaviors or cookbook solutions. Rather, the appropriate course of action ("transformational leadership") involves three programs. First is the creation of a vision. To create vision, the leader must be capable of integrating analytic, creative, intuitive, and deductive thinking (see Sashkin, this book). If this job is done well, the culture of the organization becomes infused with this vision, creating the basis for the second and third stages.

The second stage involves mobilization of commitment. This may be initiated in some intense fashion, for example, at a retreat, but requires a willingness on the part of the leadership to engage in repeated and continuing dialogue and exchange with organization members. The heart of the process, however, is the third stage—institutionalization of change. This stage involves literally shaping and reinforcing a new culture. Various mechanisms are available to serve as tools in this process. These include communication, decision-making and problem-solving systems, and selection, appraisal, and reward systems. The effectiveness of transformational leadership in initiating change is supported by the work of Seltzer and Bass (1990). They found that the exercise of transformational leadership provided intellectual stimulation and affected individual behavior even more than it did group behavior. Change must begin and be institutionalized with individuals if it is to be effective.

Creative leaders will anticipate organizational members' responses to impending or experienced change. For example, they will assist in the recognition of, and coping with, endings—colleagues' relationships, old behavior patterns, and so on. They will expedite passage through the transition phases and create an environment in which members may learn from the past, but not dwell on it, and learn new "scripts" for behavior rather than reenacting old, inappropriate ones. Again, this process requires exceptional creativity and perseverance on the part of the strategic leadership of the organization. It requires a commitment to the creation of new systems of behavior and decision making and the willingness to implement reward and incentive systems to support them.

The work of Martin et al. (1983) and Trice and Beyer (1984) suggests the value of managing the outward manifestations of culture. Thus, in the process of restructuring the organization, effective strategic leaders will consciously reinforce the vision created by managing the use of symbols, rites, and stories. These important aspects of culture communicate values to organizational members, reward behavior consistent with the new vision, and help to reinforce the commitment among organizational members. Lee Iacocca was successful in creating a strategic vision and thereby implementing change at Chrysler in the 1980s. He did so by organizing a team that developed the vision. Thus, his management team helped develop and implement the strategic vision. This process helped to inculcate and reinforce new values at Chrysler (Westley and Mintzberg, 1989).

Restructuring actions often disrupt an organization's culture. Basically, downsizing and downscoping actions can produce uncertainty and job insecurity. As a result, surviving employees become risk-averse and short term-oriented. Culture provides a means of controlling the premises for employee behaviors and attitudes. A reward system consistent with the new cultural norms provides a powerful means of achieving control (Kerr and Slocum, 1987). After restructuring, the culture should be managed so that it promotes the pursuit of opportunity with rewards and minimizes the penalty for failure. Rewards should be consistent and based on individual achievement and innovation.

It is critical, then, that the culture promote diversity and individuality instead of conformity. It should promote risk taking rather than risk-averse behavior. To do so, rewards must be based on long-term as opposed to short-term performance (Hoskisson et al., 1989). Furthermore, the culture should foster an entrepreneurial spirit. To the extent possible, authority should be decentralized and employees involved in important operating decisions. Importantly, new product and idea champions should be identified and rewarded (Ahrandt and A. Blair, 1986).

Strategic Control Systems

All organizational control systems should be reviewed for potential conflict with long-term needs. For example, based on their study of large, diversified firms, Hitt and Hoskisson (1991) concluded that a focus on acquisition strategies and a resulting emphasis on financial control systems produced an overemphasis on short-term goals. Therefore, it is critical for firms undergoing restructuring to ensure the use of strategic controls. Strategic control focuses on the content of strategic actions rather than their outcomes. Focusing on outcomes alone, as is the case with financial controls, often produces short-term, risk-averse decisions. Alternatively, strategic control encourages managers to make decisions that incorporate moderate and acceptable risk and that focus on long-term returns.

Jack Welch restructured General Electric (GE) to regain strategic control. By selling off some units and reorganizing others, he was able to restructure approximately forty separate businesses into fourteen strategic business units. In so doing, his span of control was reduced by some twenty-six general managers. As a result, he was better able to exercise strategic control over the fourteen SBUs (as opposed to the forty businesses).

To seize the opportunities of a newly restructured organization, strategic leadership will be required to change or avoid the use of short-term financial controls. While it is natural to assume more centralized control in newly restructured firms, this tendency should be fought. The newly downsized firm, with fewer and more similar operating units, represents an opportunity to reinstitute strategic controls. In other words, top executives can control the strategic actions/behaviors of the various units instead of focusing on outcome controls. Use of strategic controls often promotes a longer-term focus and more innovation (Hitt, Hoskisson, and Ireland, 1990; Hoskisson and Hitt, 1988).

The use of strategic controls should be coupled with reasonable operating autonomy for the various units. This coupling is necessary to achieve competitive advantage in the various markets. Strategic controls can ensure appropriate strategic behavior along with the promotion of resource (tangible and intangible) sharing among interdependent units. At the same time, operating autonomy allows the flexibility and innovation necessary to take advantage of specific market opportunities (or avoid competitive threats). Therefore, strategic leadership should promote the simultaneous achievement of autonomy and strategic controls.

CONCLUSION

Downsizing and downscoping are increasingly common in our economic environment. As a result, effective strategic leadership during restructuring efforts must balance short-term needs with long-term growth and survival. In so doing, effective strategic leadership must cope with a number of challenges (refer to Figure

4.1). Therefore, it requires visionary and creative managers.

Work force reductions during restructuring have increasingly included middle- and upper-level executives. If care is not taken in selecting and implementing reductions, strategic leadership as described by Hambrick (1989), Jaques (1986), and Hunt (1991) may be seriously disrupted. By eliminating many middle managers, restructuring efforts may have laid off employees who had the greatest capability to develop holistic, expert, strategic problem-solving skills (Dreyfus, 1982).

If executives are able to exhibit strategic leadership that achieves a long-term focus, promotes development and application of core competences, emphasizes the development of human capital, develops an effective culture, and achieves strategic control simultaneously with the allowance of autonomy, restructuring efforts are more like to be successful. Effective exercise of these tasks depends on the development of appropriate cognitive models (Barr and Stimpert, 1990). The model of strategic leadership described herein complements and extends the SST framework for leadership. While preservation of organizational systems responsible for such development may tax the available resources, the potential outcomes of such investments (and the consequences for failure to do so) are critical to long-term survival and effectiveness.

5

A Midrange Theory of
Strategic Choice Processes

*David A. Cowan, C. Marlene Fiol, and
James P. Walsh*

This chapter explores some intriguing interrelationships between individuals and
organizations. By doing so, it provides a focus on some of the dynamics underlying the strategic choice process. The contribution of the chapter arises from the
authors' attempt to merge aspects of the environmentally deterministic view of
organizational performance with the strategic choice perspective. Historically, these
two views have stood in contrast—one claiming that understanding follows organizational actions and the other claiming that understanding precedes organizational
actions, linked to them by strategic choices. The authors propose that the
paradigmatic debate arising from this contrast between choice-as-action and choice-
as-thought is unfortunate because it has diverted attention away from integrative
efforts.

With the purpose of adding enrichment to SST, this chapter helps inform some
of the ways in which leadership cognitions may weave their way through organizational processes to appear later as organizational actions. Further, it provides some
insight to help explain why it often seems that leaders have no influence on organizational performance. To accomplish this purpose, the authors review theories of
choice-as-thought and choice-as-action and then develop an integrative, midrange
theory of strategic choice. This midrange stance proposes that efficacy expectations of leaders interact with the goal-oriented alignment within an organization,
in order to frame interpretations of strategic issues in terms of opportunities and
threats. These interpretations, in turn, cue various, but different, choice processes.
The product of integrating these ideas is a preliminary theoretical framework that
begins to answer the question, How do strategic executives make a difference to
firm performance?

The strategic choice perspective has long stood in contrast to a deterministic view
of organizational adaptation. It argues that the destiny of organizations depends
at least partially on the choices that they make (Child, 1972). This perspective is
consistent with the assumptions of Stratified Systems Theory (Jacobs and Jaques,

1987; Jaques, 1976), which assert that leaders must mature in their ability to handle tasks with more distant time horizons if they are to succeed in making strategic choices. Researchers who work within the framework of strategic choice have attempted to differentiate their approach from deterministic perspectives, which hold that a firm's destiny lies in forces outside of its control. They have been less concerned with integrating the various and disparate theories that have emerged in support of the general paradigm.

Several competing streams of research have emerged within the strategic choice perspective. First, coarse-grained approaches to the study of choice in organizations treat the whole organization as a decision-making unit (Miles and Snow, 1978; Smith, Guthrie, and Chen, 1989; Snow and Hrebiniak, 1980). Broad and encompassing typologies suggest different choice processes as characteristic of entire firms. In contrast, finer-grained approaches treat top management teams or dominant coalitions within organizations as the authors of choice (Hambrick, 1989). Leader typologies suggest choice processes as reflections of individual traits and characteristics.

Different assumptions underlie each of these approaches. Typically implicit, they vary in the extent to which they portray choice as primarily action-driven or thought-driven. The differing emphases revolve around beliefs about the primacy and roles of understanding, intention, and action in choice processes. Choice-as-action perspectives argue that the selection from among decision alternatives occurs as a result of actions taken. Cognitive elements of understanding and intention represent little more than subsequent justifications for such actions. Choice-as-thought perspectives, in contrast, argue that the selection from among decision alternatives is essentially a cognitive process, based on decision-maker understanding and intentions. The former assigns minimal importance to the potential for individuals to shape and change the processes by which choices are made in organizations. The latter assigns minimal importance to the organizational context that may constrain and shape the discretionary impact of a leader (cf. Jacobs and Jaques, 1987).

This chapter argues that neither approach alone adequately describes strategic choice processes in organizations. Choice processes may sometimes reflect characteristics of a leader, other times, they may be embedded in organizational routines that lie beyond a leader's reach. They may sometimes result from cognitive deliberations and other times result from unreflective actions. In all cases, these choice processes result from reciprocal interactions between individuals and their organizational contexts (e.g., Bandura, 1977b). By explicitly considering the elements of choice—understanding, intention, and action—at the intersection of individuals and their organizational context, the framework we develop integrates these different characterizations of strategic choice. The framework explores the individual-organization interactions that give rise to various types of choice processes and therefore enables a richer understanding of the organizational contexts in which theories like Jaques's (1976) stratified systems focus.

DIRECT LINKS TO STRATIFIED SYSTEMS THEORY

Stratified systems theory (SST) provides important insights about the nature of strategic leadership and organizational change (e.g., Jacobs and Jaques, 1987). Its major contribution lies in the articulation of how the time horizons of tasks facing leaders and the corresponding cognitive capabilities required by them differ by level in an organization's hierarchy (Jaques, 1976). Leaders at the apex of an organization consider issues that take ten to twenty years or more to resolve, in contrast to lower-level employees, who deal with tasks that provide daily performance feedback. Just the same, the leaders of a firm are thought to exercise control over their organization's destiny. As Jacobs and Jaques (1987) noted, "Leadership is a *discretionary* function, that is, it is outside the application of established process structure, though establishing process structure generally is a leadership function" (pp. 26-27). As such, SST falls within the choice-as-thought paradigm.

SST holds practical implications for the selection and development of strategic leaders. Jaques (1986) pointed out that leaders must develop the cognitive power to mold a facility with shaping, reflective articulation, linear extrapolation, and transforming systems. While his major contribution to our understanding of the executive's role in choice processes focuses on these cognitive issues, he does note that successful strategic leaders will need to develop "other necessary 'equipment'" as well (Jacobs and Jaques, 1987, p. 51). Another purpose of this chapter, then, is to consider what some of this "equipment" might be.

TRADITIONAL APPROACHES TO THE STUDY OF STRATEGIC CHOICE

Studies of strategic choice have tended to focus either on choice-as-thought or on choice-as-action. Few authors have attempted to address a synthesis of these perspectives; Weick's (1983) "managerial thought in the context of action" indirectly represents one attempt. Choice-as-action models assume that actions drive choice processes, which culminate in retrospective cognitive justifications. Choice-as-thought models, in contrast, assume that cognition drives choice processes and that these culminate in action. Figure 5.1 depicts links between cognition and action-based models of strategic choice. Action models depict a counterclockwise movement beginning at the top of the figure; cognitive models depict a clockwise movement beginning at the bottom of the figure. We briefly describe each model.

Choice as Action

Models of strategic choice-as-action build on the underlying assumption that choice results from unintended actions (Starbuck, 1983). Starbuck (1983) stated

Figure 5.1
Competing Models of Strategic Choice Processes

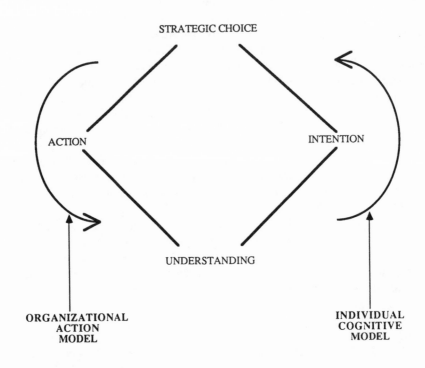

that "most of the time organizations generate actions unreflectively. To justify their actions, organizations create problems, successes, threats, and opportunities" (p. 91). Behavior progams shape organizational realities. Cognition becomes important only as a retrospective justification for those realities.

An important characteristic of this perspective is the primacy of the organization as the relevant unit of analysis. Organizations act. Organizations then ascribe intentions to those actions, and these intentions enable them to understand themselves in relation to the decision context. Individuals hold no place except as pawns of a larger, embedded organizational ideology (Starbuck, 1983).

Such a view of organizations as a gestalt, or a system of crystalized ideology, is not Starbuck's creation. Miles and Snow (1978) and later Miller and Friesen (1984), among others, similarly characterized an organization as a complete system. Strategic choices and choice processes are believed to follow a predictable and identifiable pattern that derives from historically embedded "crystals" (e.g., Starbuck, 1983). None of these gestalt views of organizational choice processes allows much room for variance in established patterns. None allows for intentional changes as discretionary influences brought about by any given individual. Though perhaps not environmentally determined, strategic choice in this view follows historical patterns of action.

A number of empirical studies cast doubt on the validity of typing an organization as a single and enduring gestalt (Hambrick, 1983; Smith, Guthrie, and Chen, 1989; Snow and Hrebiniak, 1980; Zajac and Shortell, 1989). These studies sought empirically to confirm the clusters that define Miles and Snow's (1978) different strategic types. All of them came up with partial, rather than full, confirmation. For example, Smith, Guthrie, and Chen (1989) found, contrary to predictions, that their "Defenders" defined markets more broadly and had more different products and broader skills than their "Prospectors." The other studies similarly were unable to type organizations fully according to Miles and Snow's (1978) stable typology. Moreover, Zajac and Shortell (1989) reported that more than half of the firms in their study shifted from one to another of Miles and Snow's (1978) strategy types in response to environmental changes, suggesting again the dangers of assuming a stable and ingrained action pattern as the sole determinant of strategic choices.

In a recent review and critique of the Miles and Snow (1978) typology, Dunbar and Nachman (1989) argued that "the details Miles and Snow provide to describe the different types . . . are probably more obfuscating than enlightening" (p. 26). They suggested the need for a more contextually sensitive approach to categorize organizational forms of adaptation. One important question raised by the attempts to validate Miles and Snow's (1978) typology is the extent to which a leader or dominant coalition with a new vision can redirect a firm's historical patterns of action. We turn next to a largely separate body of research that has examined this question.

Choice as Thought

Models of choice-as-thought build on the underlying assumption that intentions drive choice processes. For our purposes, thought represents the linked processes of understanding and intention. According to this view, free will and choice imply that decision makers have reasons for doing what they do and that they use information accordingly (e.g., O'Reilly, 1983). The strategic management paradigm, as set forth by Schendel and Hofer in 1978, is built on the notion that strategic decision making results from intentional actions in the name of individual or collective purpose. The paradigm accords central importance to the cognitive elements of understanding and intention as basic drivers of strategic choice. Managerial thought is critical to processes of strategy formulation, for example, which require managers to envision and prioritize future states that are appropriate and proper (Andrews, 1980). Similarly, managerial thought is critical to environmental analysis, which requires managers to forecast and make predictions (Pant and Starbuck,

1990). These tasks all depend on individual cognitive capabilities (e.g., Lewis and Jacobs, this book; Sashkin, this book) and on cognitive processes such as attention, perception, reflection, and understanding (e.g., Hunt, 1991; Stubbart, 1989).

How do such individual cognitive variables relate to choice and actions at the level of the organization? Few management researchers accept the economists' simplifying assumptions that managers "all reason in the same logical way, all notice the same threats and opportunities, and all pursue the same goals" (Stubbart, 1989, p. 326). Thus, the focus of choice-as-thought models has been on the ways that reasoning differs among individuals and the impact of such differences at the level of the organization. The research interest in cognitive mapping techniques has resulted in a focus on individuals as the critical unit of analysis. Although methodologies for mapping the "organization mind" now exist (Huff, 1990), most research on strategic choice-as-thought has examined the cognitive processes of key people in organizations (Walsh, 1990). It is not surprising, then, that renewed interest in cognition has been accompanied by renewed interest in strategic leadership (e.g., Blair and Rivera, this book; Hambrick, 1989).

Research on strategic leadership tends to assume that the values and cognitions of leaders affect choices in organizations. It places leadership activities alongside organization and industry characteristics such as size (Miller, Kets de Vries, and Toulouse, 1984), industry concentration (Salancik and Pfeffer, 1977a) and industry structure (Finkelstein, 1988). It tends to ignore how leaders' understanding and intentions relate to organizational outcomes. Those outcomes, the focus of the choice-as-action stream of research, have remained largely unexplored in the choice-as-thought stream. To us, this seems an unfortunate oversight.

ELEMENTS OF CHOICE PROCESSES IN ORGANIZATIONS

Understanding, intentionality, and action are important elements of any model of choice in organizations. Though different views of strategic choice assign different sequences and different casual links between these elements, they represent building blocks of any choice model. Theories vary in how they treat the organizational context in which they occur. Models of choice that view the organization as a gestalt portray ingrained patterns of action as driving strategic choice processes. Cognitive elements of decision-maker intention and understanding, then, are embedded within an organization's routines (Argyris, 1985; Argyris and Schön, 1978). Models of choice that view individuals at the helm of an organization portray intention and reflection as driving strategic choice processes (Child, 1972). The organization represents the arena for decision activity within this paradigm, rather than as a consequential component of any decision process.

Differences between the two general approaches to strategic choice processes become irrelevant during periods of organizational stability. The constructs represented in Figure 5.1 emerge as a consequence of reciprocal influence (cf. Wood and Bandura, 1989) and become intertwined over time. Thus, important research questions have to do with the possibility and source of unlearning during times of needed organizational change. That is, we need to understand how decision makers intentionally intervene in this cycle of reciprocal influence. An organization-based action mode of strategic choice predicts that crises can break the cycle and produce unlearning. When organizations discover that their behavior programs are producing undesirable results, some "organizations replace their leaders, reorient, and survive . . . more [of them] unlearn and then die" (Starbuck, 1983, pp. 100-101). The key to reorientation and survival, however, is not just to replace the organization's leaders. The culture, transformations, structures, and ecology that supported past strategic directions need to be refocused to support the newly intended direction. Attempts to change an organization will fail unless the inertial forces embodied in organizational memory are redirected (Walsh and Ungson, 1991).

An individual-based cognitive model of strategic choice also predicts that crises can break the cycle and produce unlearning. This view, however, suggests that the success of unlearning and relearning depends on the focused vision of those at the organization's helm (e.g., Hambrick, 1989). Rather than assigning the task of renewal to "organizations," this view regards it as a critical task of the individuals responsible for an organization's survival and growth—its leaders. Executives' second-order learning (Argyris and Schön, 1978) may become the key to survival in these times, as might their capacity for independence of thought and their ability to anticipate second- and third-order effects of their decisions (Lewis and Jacobs, this book).

Both bodies of theory provide useful insights toward understanding strategic decision processes. Choice-as-action models help explain why some organizations fail to adapt to environmental changes despite the fact that their top management team recognizes and understands the need for strategic change. Choice-as-thought models help explain why some organizations, steeped in historical action routines, successfully break the cycle, unlearn, relearn, and perhaps survive. Whereas the choice-as-thought models highlight the role that executive attention and vision can play in strategic adaptation and renewal, the choice-as-action models suggest that executives have only limited influence. Thus, each body of theory provides partial insight into strategic choice processes. However, there remains a need for a midrange theory to bring together important strands of each approach.

Mintzberg and Waters (1984) traced the beginnings of such a midrange theory. Following Mintzberg (1978), they distinguished deliberate from emergent characteristics across different types of strategies. Thus, planned strategy results from the precise intentions of central leadership, and entrepreneurial strategy results from the personal unarticulated vision of a single leader. Further, ideological strategy results from intentions that represent the collective vision of all actors, and disconnected strategy results from action patterns in the absence of central or common intentions. The authors concluded that strategy-making processes in organizations exhibit both deliberate and emergent aspects—deliberate to provide direction and emergent to accommodate learning and to respond to unexpected patterns in an organization's actions.

Mintzberg and Waters's (1984) typology of strategy making is an important first step toward establishing a midrange theory of strategic choice. However, their typology does not describe the particular characteristics of organizational contexts and leaders that might lead to different choice processes. In the remainder of this chapter, we develop a midrange theory of strategic choice that builds on such leader-organization interactions. This blends theories of individual psychology with a multilevel decision-making perspective to delineate when and how individual choice makes a difference in organizational contexts. Our discussion is grounded in the cognition literature that posits a relationship between cognition and organizational performance but never explicitly addresses this linkage. This effort also benefits from those who focus attention on cognitive capabilities and cognitive potentialities at higher levels within an organization's hierarchy (e.g., Boal and Whitehead, this book; Jacobs and Jaques, 1987; Lewis and Jacobs, this book; Sashkin, this book).

STRATEGIC CHOICE IN ORGANIZATIONAL CONTEXTS

In this section, we identify several factors that influence strategic choice processes. Our purpose is to integrate existing characterizations of strategic choice by illuminating the psychodynamics of those involved. The selected factors represent an insider's understanding of strategic issues, which involves the concepts of self-efficacy (Bandura, 1986b, 1989) and effective synergy (Cattell, 1948, 1951). In a broad sense, these concepts parallel locus of control (Rotter, 1966) and organizational culture (Schein, 1985), respectively, but we choose to focus on self-efficacy and effective synergy to enable a more precise orientation. Together, they provide enabling conditions that influence the interpretation of strategic issues as threats or opportunities (cf. Jackson and Dutton, 1988).

Interpreting Strategic Issues

Since organizations exist in complex, ambiguous environments (Ackoff, 1970; Daft and Weick, 1984; Mason and Mitroff, 1981), strategic issues usually do not emerge as self-evident, objective entities (Dutton and Jackson, 1987). Thus, strategic issue diagnosis requires that individuals interpret equivocal stimuli (Dutton, Fahey, and Narayanan, 1983) and that those involved work toward shared understanding of events, expectations, and the like. Since such diagnosis necessitates social and often political processes (Lyles and Mitroff, 1980; Mintzberg, Raisinghani, and Theoret, 1976), leaders must possess not only cognitive capacities for interpretive activities but additional capacities for effectively handling multifaceted social situations (e.g., Sashkin, this book).

Throughout the strategic formulation process, labeling situations as categories is a crucial step because it enables differentiations among ongoing, interconnected events (Smith and Medin, 1981). In this way, categories serve as fundamental ingredients for understanding. They focus subsequent attention (Taylor and Crocker, 1981), enable communication (Donnellon, 1986), and serve both to mobilize effort and to guide action (Dutton and Duncan, 1987; Meyer, 1982). Understanding the role that categories play in strategic choice helps link individual cognition to organizational outcomes. Without these linkages, a midrange theory of strategic choice processes is impossible to formulate.

Certain categories appear to play a more significant role in strategic choice processes (e.g., Mintzberg, Raisinghani, and Theoret, 1976). The categories of opportunity and threat appear most closely associated with strategic choice and are widely employed for understanding environmental stimuli (Christensen et al., 1982; Dutton and Jackson, 1987). Empirical evidence suggests that three attributes accompany the concept of an opportunity: (1) controllable, (2) potential gain, and (3) positive; similarly, three attributes accompany the concept of a threat: (1) uncontrollable, (2) potential loss, and (3) negative (Jackson and Dutton, 1988).

The interpretation of strategic issues as opportunities or threats underlies the type of choice process in which the organization will engage. In the face of issues perceived as threatening, organizational action responses will focus on internal administrative solutions (Jackson and Dutton, 1988). By contrast, in the face of issues perceived as opportunistic, organizational action responses will focus on achieving externally oriented change.

In the following section, we build on the work of Bandura (1977b) and Cattell (1948, 1951) to delineate factors that lead to the interpretation of strategic issues as opportunities or as threats. This delineation helps explain in greater detail the cognitive capabilities (cf. Sashkin, this book) that executives employ when interpreting strategic issues. Further, it enriches the SST perspective (Jacobs and Jaques, 1987) by expanding on the relevance and significance of cognitive maps. By doing so, it begins to explore the context in which these interpretations occur, as other authors in this book are doing in alternative ways (e.g., Blair and Rivera; Boal and Whitehead; Hitt and Keats).

Self-Efficacy and Effective Synergy Underlying Understanding. Patterns of stimuli labeled as strategic issues are complex and relatively ambiguous. This complexity and ambuguity often creates a high degree of uncertainty and disagreement among those who seek to understand them, usually attributed to insufficiency, equivocality, or ambiguity of available information (Jacobs and Jaques, 1987). In addressing the categorization of such issues as threats or opportunities, we explore selected factors that help link individual interpretation with organizational action.

For the CEO or the few influential top figures in an organization (cf. Hambrick and Mason, 1984; Prahalad and Bettis, 1986), Bandura's (1977a, 1986a) concept of self-efficacy seems particularly informative. "Perceived self-efficacy concerns people's beliefs in their capabilities to mobilize the motivation, cognitive resources, and courses of action needed to exercise control over events in their lives'' (Wood and Bandura, 1989, p. 364). Though related to the broader concept of internal locus of control (Rotter, 1966), self-efficacy is more relevant in the context of strategic issue interpretation since it relates more particularly to specific information contexts rather than to one's general state of mind. Self-efficacy helps us to understand the potential influence of single organizational members on organizational choice processes (Wood, Bandura, and Bailey, 1990), since it induces effort (e.g., Gardner and Schermerhorn, this book) by enhancing ''one's belief in one's self as an effective 'agent' in (and on) one's environment'' (Sashkin, this book).

Self-efficacy affects not only the level of effort that one will exert but also the duration of perseverance that one will endure, the level of stress that one will sustain in threatening situations, and the relative degree to which one's thought patterns will enable or detract from intentions (Wood and Bandura, 1989). Each of these helps inform different aspects of the complex, dynamic, and social contexts of strategy formulation. Combined, these aspects of self-efficacy help establish vital linkages between individual characteristics and organizational performance. As Locke and Latham (1990) noted: ''Self-efficacy is significantly and positively related to future performance, even more so in some cases than to past performance. Furthermore, extensive research strongly supports this claim'' (p. 68).

In an attempt to link individual strategic issue interpretation to the organizational process involved, we also employ Cattell's (1948, 1951) concept of effective synergy. It offers an important distinction to the commonly employed term, group synergy (Hackman, 1987), and helps establish a relationship to strategic leadership approaches, which attempt to account for group-level concerns, like multiple stakeholder perspectives (e.g., Blair and Rivera, this book). The term *group synergy* represents one of a class of variables that ''can potentially lead to improvements in a group's level of effort, its application of member knowledge and skill, and the appropriateness of its task performance strategies'' (Hackman, 1987, p. 324). Group synergy contributes to effort, common understanding, and task performance by ''creating shared commitment to the team and its work'' (p. 326). In this sense, Hackman argued that even in the face of adversity, a team may interpret stimuli as challenging because of the presence of this ''can do'' attitude. Individuals are more likely to accept a group-supplied understanding of reality.

Drawing on Hackman's (1976, 1977) insights about group synergy, we add a distinction enabled by Cattell (1948), who proposed that a group's energy can be directed either toward maintaining the existence and harmony of a group or toward achievment of a group's purpose. He designated the first direction maintenance synergy and the second direction effective synergy. Effective synergy is the ''energy expressed in gaining the outside goals for which the group has come together'' (Cattell, 1948, p. 55). It pertains to particular decision makers or stakeholder groups rather than to entire organizations, as is the case with broader concepts like culture. The concept of effective synergy identifies the portion of a group's energy that enhances its "can do" attitude, providing an endowment of sorts to help make sense of equivocal stimuli related to common goals.

Together, the concepts of self-efficacy and effective synergy offer helpful means for understanding some of the dynamics involved in strategic choice. The interactions of these factors are depicted in Figure 5.2 and suggest that certain conditions lead to relatively clear categorizations of issues as opportunities or as threats. The "can do" energy state provided by the presence of higher levels of self-efficacy and effective synergy is more likely to promote understanding of issues as opportunities (Jackson and Dutton, 1988).

Interactions between these two factors also result in conditions that lead to an incongruence between the CEO's and the relevant others' interpretive orientations.

Figure 5.2
Interpretation of Strategic Issues

In these instances, low CEO self-efficacy may exist in concert with relatively high effective synergy, or high CEO self-efficacy may exist with low effective synergy. For example, a strong leader may be placed in a poorly performing, disintegrating company. A situation of this sort will likely affect the degree to which a leader can effectively use leverage to enhance effective synergy among others (cf. Gardner and Schermerhorn, 1991). Incongruities result in interpretive tensions whereby a CEO understands an issue as a threat yet others understand it as an opportunity, or when the CEO understands an issue as an opportunity and others understand it as a threat. Though we acknowledge that situations exist with highly varied interpretations, we believe it is helpful to begin with an understanding of these more extreme instances. We specify some proposed effects of these scenarios on strategic choice processes in the following section.

Effects of Issue Interpretation on Strategic Choice Processes

We propose that the four situations depicted in Figure 5.2 will affect the strategic decision process in ways that we illustrate in Figure 5.3. Before describing the specifics involved, we identify several significant patterns. First, if we look back at Figure 5.2, it is important to remember the pattern involving congruency of interpretations around opportunities and threats. Second, it is useful to note the pattern of controllability that accompanies these interpretations. Conditions of higher self-efficacy and effective synergy more likely support perceptions of controllability, which in turn undergirds interpretations of opportunity.

When we map these patterns onto Figure 5.3, particular relations become salient. The congruency condition between self-efficacy and effective synergy promotes a bias toward action, when both are high or toward understanding when both are low. In the upper right quadrant, the bias toward action enables opportunity interpretations because of the presence of perceived control; thus, understanding precedes choice. In the lower left quadrant, the bias toward understanding suggests the presence of threat interpretations due the absence of perceived control. Figures 5.2 and 5.3 thus trace the linked effects of efficacy expectations on managerial interpretations and on strategic choice processes. The proposed links are consistent with Jackson and Dutton's (1988) view that the interpretation of issues as threats will lead to an organizational focus on internal adaptive adjustments and that the interpretation of issues as opportunities will lead to an external focus on proactive strategic change. Our model extends their view by adding the proposed effects of efficacy expectations on both managerial interpretations and choice processes. This orientation posits efficacy as a learning phenomenon.

Highly efficacious individuals within a synergistic decision unit (upper right quadrant of Figure 5.3), will ''see'' equivocal stimuli as opportunities to exert their mastery over the world. This ''seeing'' is consistent with the concept of primary control (Rothbaum, Weisz, and Snyder, 1982). Strategic choices in these instances

Figure 5.3
Effects of Issue Interpretation on Strategic Choice Processes

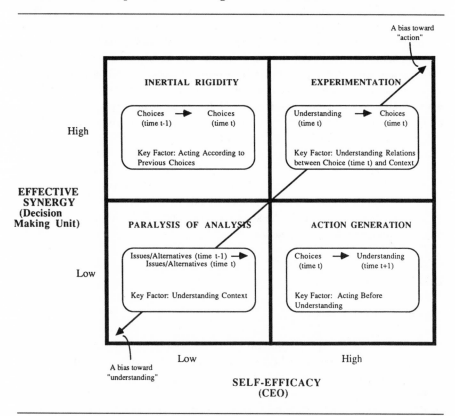

embody proactive attempts to control an organization's destiny. However, when controllability is low (as depicted in the lower left quadrant of Figure 5.3), issues are likely interpreted as threats, and an understanding bias emerges. In these instances, the overriding activity is geared toward understanding the nature of the perceived threat (Mintzberg, Raisinghani, and Theoret, 1976; Nutt, 1984). Consistent with the notion of secondary control (Rothbaum, Weisz, and Snyder, 1982), inefficacious individuals attempt to understand the uncontrollable events that seem to befall them. This understanding rarely leads to proactive action responses.

In situations with patterns of incongruence, strategic choice processes reflect a tension within the decision-making unit. It is likely that these decision situations will occur mostly at the systems level of the organization (Jacobs and Jaques, 1987), where discretionary alternatives are most prominent (Hambrick and Finkelstein, 1987). When low self-efficacy of a CEO combines with high effective synergy on the part of others in the decision-making unit, inertial rigidity is likely to occur.

By this we mean that actions will likely take place as they have before, since cohesive forces will help sustain previous actions (Festinger, Schachter, and Black, 1950; Hackman, 1976; March and Simon, 1958). A CEO in such instances will provide little direction for change and few inducements to redirect current efforts (Gardner and Schermerhorn, this book). Rather, he or she will devote most energy toward understanding the equivocal decision stimuli seen as threatening.

In the alternative case of high CEO self-efficacy and low effective synergy of the decision-making unit, it is more likely that certain actions will be encouraged, with attempts to understand deferred until later. In these instances, the CEO interprets stimuli as an opportunity, even though the rest of the decision unit does not. Since timing is crucial in taking advantage of opportunities, action generators (Starbuck, 1983) likely will have a stronger presence in this case to ensure that something gets accomplished. Accordingly, there likely will be a push for action from the CEO, with activity geared toward understanding delayed. Such instances of CEO action in the face of recalcitrance by others are often cited as the essence of leadership situations within the strategic choice paradigm—those that generate the need for discretionary behavior.

DISCUSSION

Implications for Research

Our theory of strategic choice processes provides some insight on the "Do managers make a difference?" debate that has persisted without resolution in the organizational sciences for many years. Typically, researchers in this area have monitored a firm's clear success or failure and, once established, have linked the outcome to managerial behavior (or misbehavior). Such monitoring often has entailed examining managers' compensation packages (Jense and Murphy, 1990) or employment status (Friedman and Singh, 1989) following various kinds of organizational performance. The results of such outcome-oriented studies are often weak or equivocal.

More process-oriented research suggests that poor organizational performance may follow from cognitive pathology in the executive suite (Starbuck and Hedberg, 1977). Such results might lead one to conclude that managers "make a difference" for poor firm performance, if not for good performance (Lieberson and O'Connor, 1972; Thomas, 1988). The attributions of poor performance, however, are not always seen as evidence of managerial potency but rather as evidence of managerial scapegoating (Gamson and Scotch, 1964). Thus, after three decades of inquiry, the research community still does not really know to what extent managers make a difference to organizational performance and how such differences occur.

The research community's general inability to establish robust accounts of managerial influence stands in marked contrast to the conclusions of the business press, that routinely attribute organizational success to the leadership abilities of those in the executive suite (Meindl, Ehrlich and Dukerich, 1985). Further, this research community perspective stands in marked contrast to a substantial and growing body of theoretical support for SST (e.g., Jacobs and Lewis, this book; Jacobs and Jaques, 1987; Jaques, 1986; Lewis and Jacobs, this book). Given what we know of self-serving attribution biases (Nisbett and Ross, 1980), we can only surmise that executives themselves agree with the conclusions of the business press and with the inherent logic of SST.

This confusing and often acrimonious debate sustains an interest because it often pits one academic paradigm against another (Astley and Van de Ven, 1983). Moreover, when managers are found to have less influence on firm performance, the voices criticizing what happens in schools of business around the world can only be expected to grow louder and more strident (Oviatt and Miller, 1989). Since all human life is inexorably tied to the success or failure of organizations, the interest in this debate extends far beyond the university's walls. Anyone touched by an organization's performance could benefit from knowing how this performance can be directed, controlled, and enhanced. Our view is that we can begin to resolve the debate only if we can specify how managers make a difference.

Managers, indeed, make choices frequently, and strategic managers frequently make strategic choices. Whether their choices involve studying a situation or acting to alter a situation, making choices is the essence of managerial and leadership work. Before we can determine how much variance such choices explain in organizational performance, however, we need to understand various choice processes better. As we have seen, there is little agreement in the academic communitiy about how these choices are made. The choice-as-action and choice-as-thought paradigms have been unable to find sufficient common theoretical ground, even though they address the same outcomes of a given circumstance. Our theory helps provide some common ground by illuminating the important role that efficacy expectations play when interpreting strategic issues. We showed how various decision processes emerge from the multilevel (i.e., both the CEO and the decision-making group) interpretation of equivocal decision stimuli. In so doing, we employed the assumption that these supposedly competing choice paradigms essentially are not competitive. Rather, they describe different choice processes that accompany different interpretive conditions.

A key research implication of this theory is that organizational scientists need to examine choice processes even when choices are not obvious to an observer. In many important respects, this point is consistent with the SST framework (Jacobs and Jaques, 1987; Jaques, 1976), since longer-range decisions are inevitably less visible in current manifestations. Strategic choices occur even in environments that external observers may consider uncontrollable.

Another implication from this work is that organizational actions emerge as efficacy and effective synergy vary within an organization's context, not just as environmental constraints permit. This emergence supports the relevance of what Gardner and Schermerhorn (this book) call strategic operational leadership for creating supportive work environments. One can infer from this perspective that the cause of an organization's paralysis lies not only in the environment but also in the efficacy expectations and effective synergy of its membership. Efficacy expectations, through their effects on managerial interpretations of environmental stimuli, contribute to the definition of an organization's environment. Thus, we cannot entirely divorce ''internal'' choice processes and ''external'' environmental conditions as determinants of organizational performance. Our proposed model stresses efficacy expectations (at both individual and group levels) as a critical link between the two sets of influences.

While our goal is to develop a midrange theory of strategic choice processes, we cannot help but speculate about which kind of process is most likely related to superior firm performance. Given our attention to ''analysis paralysis'' and its connotation (cf. Boal and Whitehad, this book), the reader may rightly conclude that we favor a particular hypothesis about which kind of decision process will most likely enhance firm performance. Our perspective is consistent with Bandura (1986b), who proposed that human behavior (and by extension, firm behavior) is multi-determined. Choices made within organizations at least compete with environmental factors in shaping firm performance, if not enabling a firm to prevail over such factors (cf. Amburgey, Kelly and Barnett, 1990). Therefore, purposive organizational actions are a contributing factor in determining performance. In response to this line of reasoning, a relevant question involves the kind of managerial actions most likely to have systematic and robust effects on performance. In this light, actions stemming from efficacious experimentation in the face of strategic opportunities are likely to compete with, if not occasionally outweigh, environmental determinants of performance. A practical challenge is to discover how to engender an appropriate sense and level of efficacy among an organization's leaders in order to promote experimentation; in some respects, this is the challenge addressed by Gardner and Schermerhorn (this book) and indirectly by Sashkin (this book). In all cases, this general issue helps inform the kind of conceptual and social skills embodied in strategic choice processes, which serve to enrich our understanding of the SST framework (Jaques, 1976).

Implications for Management Practice

As a practical matter, our theory suggests that managers in organizations need to ensure that they and their subordinates hold high efficacy expectations with respect to the completion of all tasks. While the notion of a general efficacy expectation has some appeal, which moves toward the notion of internal locus of control (Rotter, 1966), efficacy seems the more critical concept in strategic choice situations since it connotes a more domain-specific focus (Bandura, 1986a). For example, though an accountant's sense of efficacy about completing a client's audit may be high, it may far outweigh his or her sense of efficacy regarding the firm's strategic reorientation. Since efficacy involves domain-specific forethought, or the ability to envision a completed task (Bandura, 1989) within a particular content area, Jaques's (1976) distinctions between time frames associated with different tasks in an organizational hierarchy become particularly relevant.

Jaques (1986) more recently discussed intellectual capabilities needed to meet particular task demands. He spoke in terms of "cognitive power," which is "the ability of individuals to form and pattern the world in which they live in a manner that allows them to construct goals and organize their approaches to achieving them" (p. 382). The demands for cognitive power increase as one rises in a corporate hierarchy. Our theory suggests the need for more attention to the development of efficacy expectations and skills that enable decision-making units to develop effective synergy in social contexts. These considerations addressed some of the requisite "equipment" that Jacobs and Jaques (1987) left unidentified and suggest the need to account for the effect of purposeful contexts on the deliverance of such capabilities. It is likely that some individuals will possess efficacy expectations only with respect to tasks of relatively short time horizons. Knowledge of this sort may better inform the leadership processes involved in building and managing efficacy expectations among subordinates as they pertain to strategic issues within different contexts.

CONCLUSION

In conclusion, our midrange theory supports the notion that efficacy expectations and effective synergy help establish the necessary infrastucture to make and implement strategic choices in organizations. Thus, not only must a strategic leader hold a sense of efficacy about decisions that may take five or even fifty years to unfold, she or he must foster synergy among those in the organization who implement decisions (e.g., Covey, 1989) and must attend carefully to contextual factors that support or hinder these efforts. In these ways, our chapter offers a perspective to help inform some of the linkages among the strategic, organizational, and production domains comprising the SST framework. Our theory suggests that leaders who more successfully create an experimenting organization within proactive contexts may be more likely than those who do not to "make a difference" in firm performance.

6

A Stakeholder Management
Perspective on Strategic Leadership

John D. Blair and Joan B. Rivera

In addition to strategic leader macro activities involving the whole organization, strategic leaders are involved with key micro activities involved in managing important stakeholders. The authors link these two concepts at the "mesolevel" and show the crucial interplay among the leaders at all levels of the organization. Blair and Rivera also use this interplay to emphasize the role of stakeholder management in extending SST.

Overall environmental and organizational conditions seem far removed from the daily interaction situations facing leaders, who may find it difficult to integrate meaningfully the overall organizational issues with the day-to-day activities generated by their in-boxes, meetings, and phone calls. The results experienced by leaders from interaction with others may have little apparent direct impact on how well the organization does (as opposed to how well leaders are evaluated by the organization). For example, does a "successful" phone call have any real impact on return on investment? The feedback from a negotiation episode may be quite immediate, while the results from organizational strategy are often not evident— even over an extended period—and are certainly not clear in the short run.

The separation of management research into microlevel and macrolevel has divided organizational theorists and behaviorists. This distinction carries over into the strategic management field and conceptually underpins, in part, the distinction between strategy content (cf. Fahey and Christensen, 1986) and strategy process (cf. Huff and Reger, 1987).

At the macrolevel, strategy is concerned with the type of business to be in as well as the scope and competitive advantage of the strategy content. Strategy at the microlevel is concerned with approaching behavioral processes with clear strategies in mind, such as negotiating strategically. (These definitions of macrolevel and microlevel strategy apply throughout this chapter and will be expanded upon in later sections.) These microlevel strategies (and their effective implementation) may well, in turn, impact the effective implementation of corporate or competitive strategy (at the macrolevel).

For example, an executive may formulate an overall strategy to negotiate a particular contract with a key supplier of products or services. This strategy may be designed to achieve certain goals during the course of negotiations (Lax and Sebenius, 1986). If the executive succeeds in negotiating according to that strategy, that is, successfully implements that microlevel strategy, that microlevel behavior may have considerable impact on the successful implementation of a macrolevel strategy that requires the organization to ''differentiate'' its services (Porter, 1980, 1985). If that supplier's cooperation in providing scarce products or services is essential to making that competitive strategy work, microlevel negotiation strategy leading to a mutually acceptable contract is clearly linked to successful implementation of the macrolevel competitive strategy of differentiation. The chapter by Gardner and Schermerhorn in this volume on directional and operational responsibilities of strategic leaders parallels our micro-macro notions.

In this chapter we are dealing with three mutually exclusive concepts: middle-range theory, ''mesolevel'' of analysis, and the middle levels in a hierarchy. Middle-range theory as originally conceptualized by Merton (1957) is designed to be a level of abstraction that is less ambiguous than grand theory, yet encompasses more than making sense out of empirical observations. It provides an intermediate level of theories—theories applicable to limited ranges of data—that more effectively link broad theoretical issues to practical problems. Middle-range theories ''consolidate otherwise segregated hypotheses and empirical uniformities'' (Merton, 1957).

The mesolevel of analysis described by Hage (1980) is distinguished from middle-range theory. We use the mesolevel of analysis to develop middle-range theories. Our focus is on a level of analysis that is midway between and links the macrolevel and microlevel of reality. Furthermore, we concentrate on strategic leadership and not on middle hierarchical levels of an organization. Stakeholder management is a middle-range theory focusing on the mesolevel of analysis, which is applicable to all hierarchical levels. There is considerable difficulty in fully conceptualizing the meso phenomenon. Additional insights on this issue have been provided by our colleagues[1].

A building-block approach is used to develop this chapter. First we review the strategic management paradigm as the theoretical basis of our approach to strategic leadership. As part of this macro overview we examine Stratified Systems Theory (SST), along with strategic leadership. Next we consider the microside of strategy, followed by the stakeholder approach and how it integrates strategy at the macrolevel and microlevel. We then integrate stakeholder management with the earlier topics of strategic leadership and SST.

STRATEGY AT THE MACROLEVEL

The fundamental strategic management research paradigm based on Fahey and Christensen (1986) encompasses three basic components: conditions, strategies, and results. This basic paradigm indicates that strategy is developed after the environmental conditions have been assessed. At this level, leaders responsible for strategic planning in the organization attempt to create overall corporate and competitive strategies that will most closely align the organization with the environment. The tighter the fit between the organization and the environment, the more successful the organization will be in achieving the desired results. This paradigm of planned strategies is based on the economist's view of rational decision making (Murray, 1978). Such a view assumes that decision makers possess comprehensive knowledge of the environment and are acting to attain some agreed-upon goal such as profit maximization. The choice model by Cowan, Fiol, and Walsh in this book is a variation of this view.

At the macrolevel, many environmental and organizational conditions affect the formulation of specific competitive strategies. These conditions also have considerable impact on the results of these planned strategies, given their appropriateness in terms of the organization's strengths and weaknesses and the threats and opportunities in the environment. A pure model of planned strategic management would indicate that strategy is developed at the apex of the organizational hierarchy, that is, by "strategic leaders." Members of the organization would have knowledge of this strategy, and the strategy would drive their actions. In addition, the planned strategy would also be the actual or realized strategy that would impact on (if not completely determine) overall organizational results (Mintzberg and McHugh, 1985).

SST Model of Organizations

Jacobs and Lewis present a recent summary of SST in this book. Three primary advantages of SST are its broad focus, unique critical tasks, and open systems perspective. SST offers a unique perspective on leadership at different levels; it transcends face-to-face interaction with subordinates. SST recognizes the importance of matching the cognitive complexity of leaders to the degree of task complexity inherent at the various levels. That is, higher-level leaders require greater cognitive power—greater ability to differentiate and integrate more elements (Streufert and Swezey, 1986)—than do lower-level leaders. The nature of their tasks calls for a variety of skills: the capacity to deal with uncertainty and abstraction (Jacobs and Jaques, 1987), effective negotiating, political skills, shaping public opinion about the organization, and understanding national society and culture (Jacobs, 1991a; Mintzberg, 1973). A proactive philosophy permits the systems domain to work toward creating a future context that will allow the desired future state to become reality (Jacobs and Jaques, 1987).

SST links leader function to specific organizational function by level (Jacobs and Jaques, 1987). We believe the elements of Fahey and Christensen's (1986) strategic management paradigm apply to SST and to the strategic leadership component implied by SST. Strategic leaders assess the environmental setting and formulate strategy, both of which actions impact on performance or results.

SST uses open systems notions and recognizes that systems domain leaders operate within an unbounded environment. It conceptualizes increasingly complex leadership requirements as one ascends the organizational hierarchy (Hunt, 1991). For example, systems domain leaders engage in national and international networking, negotiations, and interaction with representatives from outside the leaders' organizational realms of operation.

Its benefits notwithstanding, SST places undue emphasis on top leaders' unilaterally conditioning the external environment. Not only is the external environment influential, stakeholders internal to an organization also exert influence. SST does not explicitly address the fulfillment of stakeholder needs. Its primary concern appears to be fulfillment of an organization's own needs. Here we have considered the macro strategic paradigm and elements of SST. We have used SST to introduce the topic of leadership, which we will continue discussing in the next subsection.

Strategic Leadership

In the literature ''there are almost as many definitions of leadership as there are persons who have attempted to define the concept'' (Stogdill, 1974, p. 259). Most definitions of leadership involve influence (Yukl, 1989b) at the bottom of an organization (Hunt, 1991). Yukl (1989b) adopts a rather broad definition, which includes influencing objectives and strategies, among other things. Hunt (1991) notes the growing interest in studying leadership at several levels, including CEO level. His multilevel approach extends the leadership paradigm and acknowledges the importance of environmental and organizational factors. Top levels are involved with defining the mission, setting strategy, and organizational design. They also define an organization's values and ''create a social structure which embodies them'' (Selznick, 1957, p. 60).

Westley and Mintzberg (1989) see strategic vision as a marriage between leadership and strategic management. As the needs and expectations of stakeholders change, so, too, must those of the visionary leader, if he or she is to remain in that role. According to Hosmer (1982), strategic leaders create an overall sense of purpose that guides an organization's strategy. Leaders' micro behaviors coalign organizations with the environment. Open systems theory is particularly relevant because of the strong influence of the environment (Katz and Kahn, 1966, 1978).

Leaders' tasks at the strategic apex transcend the traditional face-to-face interaction with subordinates (Hunt, 1991). Leaders survey the complex economic, technical, political, and social environment and subsequently engage in planning, organizing, and other functions needed to reduce uncertainty for lower levels (Jacobs and Jaques, 1989). The strategic apex may include more than the CEO of an organization (Mintzberg, 1979); it is charged with ensuring that an organization serve its mission as well as the needs of its stakeholders. Strategic leaders engage in both micro and macro behaviors: direct supervision, strategy formulation, and managing the organization's relations with its environment. They use microlevel strategies to build and maintain relationships, to manage conflict, or to achieve key substantive outcomes. (Savage, Blair, and Sorenson, 1989, provide detailed coverage of what is involved in negotiating strategically.)

Strategic Leadership and Strategic Management. Strategic management as used in this chapter refers to leadership at the top of an organization. Because of executive-level involvement in determining organizational policy and consistency with earlier arguments, we will use the terms *strategic leadership* and *strategic management* interchangeably. Hambrick (1989) defines strategic leaders as those who have overall responsibility for an organization (not just a small portion), who are concerned with internal as well as external spheres of influence, and who are surrounded by ambiguity and complexity. As Figure 6.1 illustrates, strategic

Figure 6.1
The Strategic Leadership Model

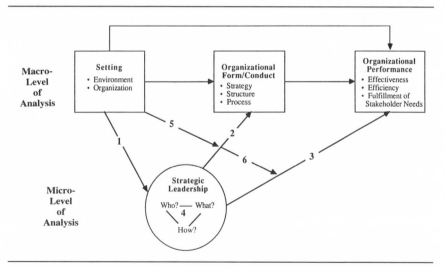

Source: adapted from Hambrick (1989). From Guest Editor's Introduction, *Strategic Management Journal,* copyright 1989 by John Wiley & Sons, Ltd. Reprinted by permission of John Wiley & Sons, Ltd.

leadership is affected by setting, both environmental and organizational. It influences organization form and conduct, which includes strategy, structure, and process. Strategic leaders influence organizational performance as well (Hambrick and Mason, 1984). Fulfillment of stakeholders' needs is an important aspect of performance already recognized to some extent in the strategic leadership literature (Hambrick, 1989; Hambrick and Mason, 1984).

Hambrick's theoretical connections between leadership and strategy, which have been described in the introductory chapter, identify six broad research areas of strategic leadership. SST notions may also be applied to these six issues. As we outline Hambrick's connections and cited research examples, we will incorporate some SST notions.

1. Settings affect strategic leadership. Mintzberg (1973) reported the effects of firm size on the chief executive's role behavior. SST notes the need for increasing cognitive complexity of leaders to match the increasing environmental complexity (i.e., setting) inherent in one's critical tasks as one ascends the hierarchy.
2. Strategic leadership affects organization form and conduct. The chief executive's personality affects organizational structure (Miller and Droge, 1986). In terms of SST, senior levels interpret the environment and structure organizations accordingly (Jacobs and Jaques, 1987).
3. Strategic leadership affects organizational performance. The scope of a leader's influence affects the likelihood of organizational failure when the leader departs (Carroll, 1984). As previously mentioned, SST's requisite structure is designed to enhance organizational performance and long-term success; it is the senior leaders who design organizations.
4. Certain aspects of leadership affect other aspects of leadership. The degree of demographic dissimilarity within a top management team affects the rate of member turnover (Wagner, Pfeffer, and O'Reilly, 1984). The cognitive complexity requirements outlined by SST determine one's potential for strategic leadership; not all leaders are capable of assuming positions in the systems domain.
5. The association between strategic leadership and form/conduct depends on the setting. Certain settings may enhance or restrict the amount of executive discretion (Hambrick and Finkelstein, 1987). SST applies primarily to bureaucratic organizations. Elsewhere in this volume, however, Whitehead and Boal argue that SST leadership theory is most relevant in bureaucratic organizations operating in relatively stable environments. They do not accept the presumed generalizability of SST.
6. The association between leadership and organizational performance depends on the setting. The association between top management team heterogeneity and organizational performance depends on the dynamism of the environment (Hambrick and Brandon, 1988; Hambrick and Mason, 1984). In line with SST, the complexity of the environment necessitates design of a requisite structure to enhance organizational success.

Strategic Leaders and Stakeholders. Several themes echo throughout this survey of some recent descriptions of strategic leadership. Hambrick (1989) calls it an "expansive domain" that can benefit from multidisciplinary research and studies relating it to other elements of the strategy paradigm. Today's strategic leaders function within a dynamic environment characterized by increasing complexity. Implicit in the environment is the continual presence of stakeholders. Stakeholder management is becoming an important approach to conceptualizing and performing the management role in all organizations (Carroll, 1989; Freeman, 1984; Mason and Mitroff, 1981). Stakeholders have a vested interest in the organization. More specifically, they are the individuals, groups, and organizations that (1) have a stake in the decisions and actions of the organization and (2) may attempt to influence those decisions and actions.

Contributing to the complexity of today's environment is a more pronounced series of stakeholder relationships than existed in the past. This blossoming of activist stakeholders is due in part to changing social values and the subsequent rights movements. Although stakeholders have existed since the inception of organizations, only during the past few decades have they become forces to be reckoned with (Blair and Fottler, 1990; Freeman, 1984; Mason and Mitroff, 1981).

For example, prior to the civil rights movement and passage of the Civil Rights Act in 1964, managerial actions concerning employees were more arbitrary than they are now. Today employee stakeholders have legal protections that they use to influence managerial behavior. Similarly, the role of consumer stakeholders has changed to have more of an impact on business. Besides current legal restrictions, there are consumer advocates attempting to shape organizations' future activities. These are but a few of the many groups vying for attention. Leaders are concerned with managing stakeholders so that strategic decisions are compatible with stakeholders' vested interests in an organization. The stakeholder management approach shares some common perspectives with Smith and Peterson's (1988) event management approach; it is beyond the scope of this chapter to address these linkages systematically.

Just as SST adds a perspective to the strategic management paradigm, so, too, do the strategic leadership notions in Figure 6.1 enhance our understanding of SST. However, strategic leadership as it relates to SST does not explicitly address stakeholder management. Strategic leadership and stakeholder management are two dynamic research directions, neither of which is mutually exclusive to the other. Stakeholder notions can be used to augment further our knowledge of strategic leadership. In the next section we introduce the micro aspects of strategy, followed by an elaboration on the stakeholder management perspective. Stakeholder management concepts will be used to show how micro behaviors occurring at the strategic apex are manifested in leader's actions that attempt to influence macrolevel phenomena.

STRATEGY AT THE MICROLEVEL

People involved in strategy formulation and implementation activities do not operate in a vacuum, nor are all planned strategies ever realized. Leaders do not directly deal with dimensions of the environment such as complexity or munificence. What they deal with every day is other people. Most of stakeholder management deals with the immediate or task enviromment, which is particularly relevant to achieving effectiveness. Organizations must interact with specific stakeholder groups in order to grow and survive. In addition, lobbying government stakeholders, advertising to the public, and other forms of influence activities occur that are directed at the general environment. Thus, much of macro environmental reality actually appears to the leader doing his or her daily tasks as people (1) who represent either themselves or other individuals, groups, and organizations that hold a stake in the decisions and actions of the leader's organization and (2) with whom the leader will likely interact through telephone calls, meetings, or memos.

Strategic management research at the microlevel refers to individual or group interactions. These interactions need not be restricted to face-to-face discussions but may also be mediated by documents. A report of recommendations from a committee to a top management team is one such example (Peterson, 1991). In the next section the mesolevel phenomenon is introduced as a linkage between micro and macro strategies.

At the microlevel, the basic research paradigm of conditions, strategies, and results also applies. Here, interaction situations serve as the conditions that affect the microlevel strategies (such as collaboration, subordination, or competition) to be used by executives to negotiate, to manage conflict, or otherwise to interact with others inside or outside the organization. Such interactions involve management attempts to balance stakeholder inducements and contributions. The realized strategies lead to the results of the interactions. Results of specific negotiation, for example, depend on both the appropriateness of the strategy in terms of the executive's desired outcomes and its appropriateness given the other party's desired outcomes to the negotiation (Savage, Blair, and Sorenson, 1989).

Microlevel interaction is inherently episodic. In the interaction episode, the actual communication takes place between the leader and other people. The leader in this episode may be the CEO of the company or one of the lower-level leaders. This microlevel of strategy is not meant to represent the lower levels of leadership, but rather strategic interactions between people, that is, interpersonal behaviors that are influenced by strategy-based choices on the part of one or more of the participants.

STAKEHOLDER MANAGEMENT AS A MESOLEVEL PHENOMENON

Here we introduce the concept of mesolevel of analysis as a means for furthering the development of leadership theory (Hage, 1980). The development and use of middle-range theory, focusing at the mesolevel on stakeholders as phenomena between overall organizational/environmental conditions and micro interaction situations, permit the researcher as well as the executive to go from the interesting, but broad and abstract, notion that stakeholders are important to the organization to a conceptually informed and organized way to understand and manage key stakeholders. Researchers have looked at how one can manage stakeholders "strategically" by formulating and implementing explicit strategies that will make stakeholders more supportive and/or reduce their threat to organizations. (Throughout this and the following section on stakeholder management and strategic leadership we will draw portions of our discussion from Blair et al., 1990; Blair and Fottler, 1990; Blair, Savage and Whitehead, 1989; Blair and Whitehead, 1988; Fottler et al., 1989; Freeman, 1984; Mason and Mitroff, 1981; Savage et al., 1991; Whitehead et al., 1989).

We believe that neither the practitioner nor the researcher has had available either the systematic theory or the practical guidance to tie everyday working activities to the macrolevel of strategic management. To fill that gap, we propose the stakeholder management approach. The mesolevel of stakeholder management provides a model that allows analysis of the impacts of microlevel and macrolevel on each other through examination of mesolevel phenomena as they impact the content and process of strategy.

At the mesolevel or midlevel of analysis, some sort of relationship (condition) exists between the organization and the stakeholder. This organization/stakeholder relationship impacts on stakeholder management strategies such as proposed by Freeman (1984), Blair and Whitehead (1988), and Savage et al. (1991). To manage key stakeholders, leaders must first seek those stakeholders who are likely to influence the organization's decision. Then, executives must make the two critical assessments about these stakeholders: (1) their potential to threaten the organization and (2) their potential to cooperate with it. When determining this "stakeholder bottom line," leaders should account for such factors as stakeholders' relative power and the specific context and history of the organization's relations with those stakeholders and those of other key stakeholders influencing the organization. These activities are key elements in the process of assessing the stakeholder elements in the organization's environment (conditions) prior to the formulation of stakeholder management strategy.

Again applicable is the basic strategic paradigm of conditions serving as contingencies for strategies that are presumed to impact results. At this level, existing relationships between organizations and their key stakeholders serve as the conditions that affect the content of strategies, such as collaboration, involvement, defense, or monitoring, to be used by executives to "manage" those stakeholders. The results of the attempt to manage stakeholders strategically are based on (1) the appropriateness of those strategies in terms of the stakeholders' overall potentials for threat and cooperation and (2) the extent to which the planned, deliberate strategy is realized or, alternatively, (3) the emergence of an emergent, but appropriate strategy that is then realized.

Figure 6.2
Using Stakeholder Management Concepts to Integrate Strategic Leadership at Macrolevel and Microlevel of Analysis

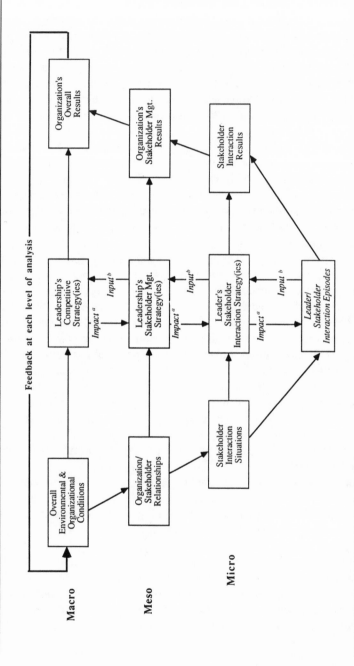

a -Deliberate/Planned Impact on Strategy Implementation   b - Emergent Patterns as Input to Strategy Formulation/Reformulation
Source: Adapted from Blair et al. (1990). Used by permission.

Using the Stakeholder Approach to Integrate Strategy at the Macrolevel and Microlevel

Figure 6.2 illustrates how we believe the mesolevel of analysis fits between the macrolevel and the microlevel. The boxes in the middle of each level represent strategy of each level. At each level, there is an assessment of conditions between conditions and strategy, and at each level there is the actual or realized strategy between (intended) strategy and results. However, the levels do not exist independently of each other. The vertical arrows in the model represent impacts and inputs that connect the levels.

Figure 6.2 illustrates a cascading effect, along the lines of SST's notion of successive strata. The lower-level conditions existing between an organization and its stakeholders are affected by the overall environmental conditions at the upper levels. In fact, environmental reality, we would argue, is concretely manifested primarily as organizational stakeholders.[2] In turn, organizational/stakeholder relations provide the context for the situation within which the interaction episode with a representative of the stakeholder will take place. The results of microlevel strategy affect overall organizational results by facilitating or hampering them. Thus, results of individual negotiations will affect overall organizational results—mediated by their impact on the organization's relationships with its stakeholders, which will, in turn, facilitate or hamper the effectiveness of the realized macro strategy to bring about desired overall organizational results.

This model shows how consideration of stakeholders affects the different levels of strategy. Although we briefly discussed interaction episodes earlier in the chapter, the introduction of stakeholders into the integrated model produces the means to reconceptualize the practice of leadership by explicitly including episodic, but strategic, interactions with key stakeholder representatives.

Now that we have looked at the various levels of strategy, we continue to develop the meso phenomenon of stakeholder management as we return to topics presented earlier—strategic leadership and SST.

A STAKEHOLDER MANAGEMENT PERSPECTIVE ON STRATEGIC LEADERSHIP

In this chapter we can indicate only some of the conceptual connections between the stakeholder management perspective and the set of issues considered to be in the domain of study of strategic leadership. In Figure 6.3 we return to Hambrick's (1989) strategic leadership framework and examine some of its theoretical connections to stakeholder management. Earlier we examined the strategic leadership connections to SST. In Figure 6.3 we integrate our multiple levels of analysis perspective (described in Figure 6.2) with Hambrick's strategic leadership model. The six specific research propositions raised by this synthesis are:

Figure 6.3
Stakeholder Management Perspectives on Strategic Leadership

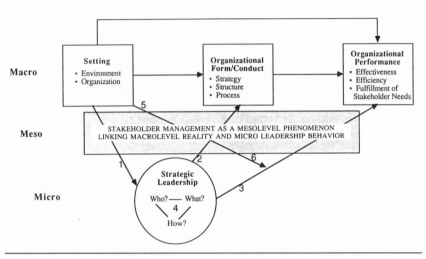

Source: based on Hambrick (1989).

1. Setting (the complexity of both the external environment and internal organization) affects strategic leaders who represent stakeholders in both arenas. Not only
   does setting affect what they do (i.e., manage stakeholders), but it also affects
   how they do so (i.e., via stakeholder management techniques).
2. Strategic leadership affects organizational form/conduct. Strategy formulation and
   implementation are stakeholder management issues. Structure may be designed
   to manage key stakeholders, for example, a personnel department for employee
   stakeholders and marketing and public relations departments for external groups.
3. Strategic leadership affects organizational performance. Proactively managing
   stakeholders should contribute to enhanced performance. Proactive management
   includes willingness to reconsider analysis when new information becomes
   available and reevaluate one's original assessment. One may need retroactively
   to manage stakeholders that were misdiagnosed or for which the situation has
   changed. A passive approach, on the other hand, is an impediment.
4. Certain stakeholder management aspects of leadership affect other aspects of leadership. Stakeholder management systematically integrates strategic management,
   leadership, organizational politics and social responsibility (Fottler et al., 1989).
5. The association between the stakeholder management aspects of strategic leadership and organizational form/conduct depends on the setting. Depending upon
   the number of stakeholders that are key to a particular organization, different
   organizational structures will apply. Additionally, different strategies will be
   applied to the various groups.

6. The association between stakeholder management aspects of leadership and organizational performance depends on the setting. Organizational stakeholders increase in number, diversity, and power, but their level of supportiveness may well decrease (Whitehead et al., 1989). As a result, there is increasing pressure on executives to deal with them (Fottler et al., 1989). The CEO's role is to maintain the health of an organization—to serve stakeholders and guard the direction and values of the organization.

Continuing with this last notion, the CEO's maintenance role is fulfilled internally as well as externally. The CEO not only is involved in strategy formulation but shares that strategy with the rest of the organization. Equally important are conducting effective stakeholder reviews and interacting with stakeholder representatives.

Freeman (1984) tells us that externally, CEOs spend the bulk of their time dealing with a range of stakeholder matters, ranging from meetings in Washington to discussions with union officials. Along with other senior leaders, they serve as spokespersons in negotiations with key stakeholders, are politically and socially active, and build coalitions. For example, in 1984, Charlie Brown of AT&T participated in negotiations and testimony with the U.S. Justice Department that played a role in getting an antitrust suit dropped. Lee Iacocca participated in advertisements targeted at the public during Chrysler's turnaround (Freeman, 1984). Blair, Savage, and Whitehead (1989) provide a diagnostic and action-oriented framework to guide leaders in conducting stakeholder negotiations strategically.

No single person manages all stakeholders (Fottler et al., 1989); however, the ultimate responsibility for balancing conflicting demands rests with top leadership. Due, in part, to stakeholders, most policy-planning and strategy problems are "wicked"—"an ensnarled web of tentacles" surrounded by uncertainty, ambiguity, and conflict (Rittel, 1972). By virtue of the definition of stakeholders and their potential to exert influence, executives seek to maximize what Mitroff (1983) calls "supporting" stakeholder relationships and minimize the "resisting" ones (Whitehead et al., 1989). Blair and Fottler (1990) refer to top management as minimally satisfying the needs of marginal stakeholders while maximally satisfying key groups.

The strategic leader-stakeholder relationship as discussed here is of an autopoeitic (self-creating) nature (Smith, 1984). Leaders in the microcosm or task environment adapt to their general environment—the macrocosm—and condition it to their advantage by managing relationships with stakeholders. By minimizing the adversity of potentially threatening stakeholders and taking advantage of supporting stakeholders, leaders are, in essence, creating the type of environment needed for survival. The organization is linked to a network of relations that constantly re-creates the conditions necessary to sustain it. Systems domain leaders are concerned with new relationships and issues resulting from changes in strategy and how best to respond to them.

Stakeholder management will be effective if it is integrated into broader strategic management, which, as we have shown in Figure 6.3, is linked to strategic leadership.

Strategy formulation and implementation are the result of interaction with both internal and external stakeholders. Interaction may range from obscure to purposeful. An idea may be conceived with no conscious awareness of stakeholders, yet as it is acted upon, their role becomes evident.

The stakeholder management approach is not without its critics, who point to the complexity and time-consuming nature of identifying, assessing, and responding to stakeholders. However, the stakeholder perspective is the most consistent with today's business environment (Carroll, 1989) and needs to be explicitly addressed by SST. The final section of this chapter addresses this stakeholder management-SST linkage.

A STAKEHOLDER MANAGEMENT PERSPECTIVE ON SST

Microlevel versus macrolevel distinctions represent conceptually clear, but artificial, designations in management, and they have proven useful for theorists because they are conducive to parsimonious study and organization of the research literature. However, leaders and other members of the top executive team may find that macro and micro theories of strategy fail to address certain key aspects of everyday management situations. Indeed, part of the management literature has indicated that the strategy process cannot simply be described with either macro or micro theory that emphasizes planned, rational processes. Strategy process may be better characterized by terms such as "muddling through" (Lindblom, 1959) or seen somewhat more systematically as "logical incrementalism" (J. Quinn, 1980, 1985).

In terms of SST, macrolevel and microlevel do not correspond to systems and organizational domains. SST explicitly considers organizational hierarchy, where stakeholder management does not. Both macro and micro strategies can be formulated and implemented by the same persons, such as an organization's chief executive officer. In fact, implicit or explicit micro strategies are formulated by all leaders who interact with significant parties affected by the organization's macro strategy, although most may only be asked or directed to help implement that macro strategy. Gardner and Schermerhorn in this book discuss similar notions.

SST clearly acknowledges the importance of the environment to strategic leaders and may benefit from the incorporation of stakeholder management notions. An organization's internal environment is no less important than the external environment. Each of the strata may be considered stakeholders, as each one has a key stake in the behavior of the others. Across strata in the organizational and systems domains, parallel relationships become stakeholder relationships. As one ascends the hierarchy, moving from a bounded to an unbounded environment, the primary stakeholder focus changes. As will be discussed later, within the bounded environment internal stakeholder concerns dominate; within the unbounded environment, external stakeholders increase both in number and in importance. The primary thrust of SST appears to be with influencing the unbounded external environment. In that sense, executive levels deal with an unlimited number of external stakeholder groups. External stakeholders are a natural concern in the formulation of strategic vision. Not to be ignored are the equally important internal stakeholders who are key to strategy implementation. Each successive level of leadership "adds value" by reducing uncertainty for lower levels. Top levels plan strategy, provide clarity, and even define tasks for the next stratum (Jacobs and Jaques, 1987). Internal stakeholders at lower levels implement strategy.

Ultimately, strategic leaders (those in the systems domain) are concerned with survival. Survival is dependent upon ensuring the flow of needed resources from the immediate environment. Stakeholders are the source of resources (employees, customers, suppliers, regulators, the media, and so forth). Unless strategy formulators take stakeholders into account, so that an organization is properly aligned with its environment, there may be no implementation of strategy. Internal stakeholders play a particularly critical role in this regard. Implementers of strategy possess power that can influence further strategy (Provan, 1989). Top levels formulate strategy, but that does not ensure implementation.

As Rowe et al. (1989) argue, without implementation there is no strategy. Overall strategy evolves from a cohesive pattern of decisions that account for behavioral and organizational factors. Thus, internal groups that are expected to implement an intended strategy must first accept it. Their acceptance or resistance directly impacts whether or not strategic vision becomes reality, so that the formulation process ought to be sensitive to those involved in implementation (Reid, 1989).

Stakeholder concepts are grounded in systems theory (Katz and Kahn, 1966, 1978). They have wide applicability in the systems domain of SST, where strategic leaders face a relatively unbounded environment. Involvement with stakeholders occurs at lower strata as well. Table 6.1 is a hypothetical matrix illustrating three examples of the stakeholder management-SST relationship across domains. Stakeholder priorities are likely to vary by organization, depending upon the specific time period, the focal stakeholder group, and the stakeholder group level, if any (as in the case of multiple levels of government). As indicated in Table 6.1, all organizational levels interface with stakeholders of one form or another, to differing degrees. Primary stakeholder concerns within the systems domain differ from those of the organizational and production domains; the systems and organizational domains are concerned with longer time horizons for their key stakeholders.

The examples in Table 6.1 indicate the changing stakeholder relationships as one ascends the organizational hierarchy. Because they operate in a more limited, less complex environment, lower strata are directly involved with fewer, primarily internal stakeholders over more immediate time horizons. Their stakeholder maps would be less encompassing than those of CEOs in the systems domain who interface with an unlimited range of predominantly external stakeholders, over longer time spans.

The government stakeholders in the table exist at multiple levels—local, state,

Table 6.1
Nature of Stakeholder Involvement by Organizational Domain

		Selected Stakeholder Group		
		Employees	*Government*	*Public Interest Groups*
	Systems Domain	No direct employee involvement; primarily concerned with broad strategic human resource management issues[a]	Anticipating and influencing the future state of regulations via lobbying and testifying before legislative bodies[b]	Considering the influence of these groups over the long term and their impact upon the organization's future desired state[c]
SST Leadership Domains	*Organizational Domain*	Setting detailed human resource management policies; planning for requirements for the near future[b]	Interpreting regulations, adjusting policies, and preventing lawsuits resulting from noncompliance; structuring activities at lower levels to correspond with regulatory requirements[c]	Identifying key groups; public relations responsibilities and face-to-face interaction/ negotiations with key groups[b]
	Production Domain	Day-to-day human resource management responsibilities[c]	Addressing day-to-day problems associated with regulations; following regulations applicable to specific functional areas[a]	Little, if any, concerns[a]

[a] least direct involvement
[b] moderate direct involvement
[c] most direct involvement with stakeholder concerns

national, and international (Freeman, 1984). One would expect interaction between leaders and government at commensurate levels. Heads of large, multinational corporations and three- and four-star military generals, for example, have dealings with different societal cultures and high-level political officials (*Executive Leadership,* 1988). Senior leaders need political skills to engage in fishbowl management of diverse groups. They deal with considerable abstraction insofar as values and social issues surrounding stakeholders are concerned (Freeman, 1984). Dealing with such a "messy environment" (Mason and Mitroff, 1981; Mitroff, 1983) naturally requires a higher degree of cognitive complexity and holistic thinking, because leaders face dissimilar problems with various, sometimes interdependent groups.

As others have indicated (Lewis and Jacobs, this book; Sashkin, this book; Thurman, 1991), strategic leadership tasks entail greater uncertainty, larger numbers of variables, a greater rate of change, and a higher degree of interdependence than does leadership at lower levels. This difference is due in part to the multitude of stakeholders, internal as well as external, with which strategic leaders interact. The strategic leader envisions the future—sets macro strategies—and then engages in micro strategies for getting there. An important part of these micro behaviors is the strategic leader's communication competencies, which include public speaking, persuasiveness, listening (Thurman, 1991), and other behavioral competencies emphasized by Sashkin. These are all critical skills as far as stakeholder management responsibilities are concerned.

Cognitive complexity may be operationalized as the number of stakeholders, the level of change occurring in stakeholders, their relative importance, and their interconnectedness. For example, a functional manager (such as a marketing manager) has fewer stakeholders to deal with than does a CEO, who deals with a wider range of issues and decisions. Along these lines, greater demands are placed on the CEO to differentiate—acknowledge the existence of—numerous stakeholder groups and integrate their potential influences on the organization. Lewis and Jacobs in this book elaborate on cognitive complexity via their notion of "conceptual capacity."

We are indebted to a colleague's insights on how stakeholder management follows a different tack than SST along two dimensions. First, stakeholder management replaces SST's concern with time by using an incident analysis approach to understanding social process. (Also check the Lewis and Jacobs chapter in this book, which proposes a way to transcend time.) Second, stakeholder management argues that cognitive complexity as a leadership skill could theoretically be expanded to include a whole range of cognitive and social skills to understand and engage in internal and external negotiations with representatives of key stakeholders (Peterson, 1991). These social skills would include negotiation, communication, and resolution of conflict. Stakeholder management is a critical task of leaders that requires skills beyond cognitive complexity.

DISCUSSION AND IMPLICATIONS

This chapter has looked at several separate, but related, concepts: strategic management, strategic leadership, SST, and stakeholder management. Leaders at all strata need to be concerned with stakeholders in one way or another. As shown here, more than one stratum may be involved with the same stakeholder group, though in differing degrees. Different strata are likely to have primary responsibility for particular groups, depending upon the critical issue faced and the skills required to manage various stakeholders.

Stratified Systems Theory can influence and be influenced by strategic management, strategic leadership, and stakeholder management concepts. SST highlights the various organizational strata and how stakeholder management differs across these strata. SST clarifies the unique strategic management responsibilities of top leaders and how activities at the different strata prepare leaders for strategic-level roles. Proactive stakeholder management ideas may make SST leaders and, subsequently, their organizations more effective. The stakeholder management concept of mesolevel of analysis has been used to demonstrate how leaders connect what they do on a daily basis with what is strategically important for the organization.

Threats to the organization resulting from the actions or inactions of key stakeholders create problems for strategic leaders, so minimizing them is as important as seeking opportunities. According to SST, systems domain leaders have critical tasks spanning ten to twenty years and more. Therefore, it is within the systems domain of an organization, where the strategic leaders are situated, that stakeholder management is of the utmost importance for the long-term success of an organization. There the visions of the organization are conceptualized. If these visions are to become reality, leaders need proactively to manage their stakeholder-filled environments.

Strategic leaders will be concerned with managing different stakeholders over considerably longer periods than will those at lower levels. The nature of stakeholders is such that they may facilitate or inhibit an organization's realization of its strategies. Without systems domain leaders acknowledging the importance of fulfilling stakeholder needs, the ultimate result of strategic management, organizational performance, may fall short of the results promised by SST. Future research could benefit from incorporating critical stakeholder tasks into SST, particularly the systems domain. Work is needed to make explicit the nature of these relationships, and it is hoped this will be a future direction taken by scholars.

NOTES

1. Level of analysis notions derive from the idea that organizations exist as formal structures. Analyzing characteristics of, and interactions among, individuals is microlevel research. Analyzing characteristics of organizations and interactions among organizations is macrolevel research. Interactions between individuals and organizations may better be described as a mesolevel process intervening between the microlevel and macrolevel of analysis. Alternatively, meso may be viewed as a kind of temporary structure that consists of a negotiating group comprised of representatives from the interacting organizations, for example, an individual (free agent) intracting with an organization. Another alternative is to eliminate the concept of level of analysis and instead focus on processes that do not map on to individuals, organizations, or any other particular formal social structure (Peterson, 1991). Hunt (1991) discusses configurations and archetypes along similar lines.

2. This conceptualization of the environment is consistent with enacted environment concepts of Weick (1979) and Smircich and Stubbart (1985).

7

Strategic Operational Leadership and the Management of Supportive Work Environments

William L. Gardner III and
John R. Schermerhorn, Jr.

The major theme of this chapter is that while top-level leaders are responsible for strategic or what Gardner and Schermerhorn term "directional leadership" (focus on vision, purpose, mission), both these leaders and those at lower organizational levels are also responsible for operational leadership (focus on day-to-day performance outcomes). This theme leads into discussion of such currently popular notions as leadership versus management, transformational versus transactional leadership, and the like. More importantly, it leads to the development of Gardner and Schermerhorn's operational leadership framework, which shows how leaders at all levels can go about providing the supportive environment needed to enhance organizational goal accomplishment.

As a part of this discussion, Gardner and Schermerhorn link their approach to SST and point out ways in which their approach helps broaden some of SST's underlying organizational assumptions.

When a human resources vice-president telephoned to ask for Peter Drucker's assistance as a leadership consultant, she was surprised by his reaction. "We'd like you to run a seminar for us on how one acquires *charisma*," she said (Drucker, 1988b, emphasis added). He responded that there is more to leadership than the popular interest in "personal dash" or "charisma" would lead one to believe. "Leadership," said Drucker, "is *work*" (emphasis added). After listening, the vice-president replied, "But that's no different at all from what we have known for years are the requirements for being an effective manager." "Precisely," said Drucker.

This incident introduces three points developed in this chapter. First, the chapter provides an inventory of some of the competing perspectives on leadership and its relationship to management. Second, the chapter raises implications for the Stratified Systems Theory (SST) perspective, serving as the conceptual framework for this book. Third, the chapter brings specific attention to day-to-day "operational" leadership concerns—ones, as Drucker suggests, that may be easily overlooked in today's clamor for charisma.

The present chapter focuses on leadership in organizations where the leaders are managers, that is, persons held directly accountable by a higher level of authority for the performance accomplishments of people working under their supervision. We advance the premise that a necessary condition for effective leadership in such situations rests with the leader's ability to create high performance outcomes on the part of all followers and their work units on a daily basis. Indeed, effective leadership—at any level of authority—may be defined as that which results in the greatest number of people achieving high performance results every day in tasks that are critical to the attainment of organizational goals. We call this approach "strategic operational leadership."

PERSPECTIVES OF LEADERSHIP AND MANAGEMENT

Recent writings on leadership and management include the three viewpoints shown in Table 7.1. They are highlighted here as background for our discussion.

Table 7.1
Three Basic Perspectives of Leadership and Management

Perspective	Description	Representative Authors
Leadership = Management	Leadership involves selecting talented subordinates, providing them with goals and direction, and establishing followers' trust by backing up one's words with actions; the management functions of planning, organizing, and controlling represent critical components of the leader's job.	Drucker (1988b)
Leadership and management are separate, but complementary processes	The primary function of leadership is to produce constructive or adaptive change; in contrast, the primary function of management is to ensure that an organization achieves its goals on time and on budget. Both processes are needed for an organization to prosper.	Kotter (1990); Bass (1985); Jaques (1989); R. Quinn (1988)
Leadership ≠ Management	Leaders and managers have fundamentally different temperaments. Managers perceive work as an enabling process; management is an orderly and stabilizing process. Leaders risk disorder and instability as they seek out opportunities for change; leadership is a creative force.	Zaleznik (1977, 1989a, 1990); Burns (1978)

Leadership Is Synonymous with Management

At one extreme is Drucker's (1988b) view that effective leadership is synonomous with effective management. Rather than viewing charisma as the key to great leadership, he sees it as the undoing of many leaders (e.g., Stalin, Hitler, and Mao) who become self-centered, inflexible, overconfident, and unwilling or unable to change. Indeed, Drucker contends that good leadership is "mundane, unromantic, and boring." He considers good leaders to be managers who successfully accomplish these primary tasks: (1) select and develop quality personnel, (2) set goals, priorities, and standards, and (3) establish trust through consistent actions.

Similar concerns and ideas have been voiced by others. In this volume, for example, Sashkin states, "Charisma is in the beholder, not the leader, and is the affective consequence, not the cause, of the leader's behavior." Like Drucker, he argues that charisma-producing behaviors are neither sufficient nor necessary to achieve success in leadership. This being the case, there is no reason to expect the "charismatic leader" automatically to be either effective or socially responsible. For this reason some leaders who succeed in eliciting charismatic affect among their followers may fail to achieve their vision (e.g., John DeLoreon) or pursue sinister and self-serving goals (e.g., Saddam Hussein, Jim Jones).

Tosi (1982, 1985) also views effective management as the basis for effective leadership. He seems in agreement with Drucker that leadership is much more mundane than popular charismatic imagery suggests. Tosi (1985) observes:

> With few exceptions, behind the popular charismatic image, the leader acted as a manager. A good deal of time was spent acquiring resources, making decisions, assigning responsibilities, and so forth. These managerial practices may account for as much of the individual's success as do the personal qualities, which are the base of charisma. If this is so, then any theoretical construction of leadership influence which does not include such managerial elements is likely to be far too inadequate (p. 225).

Leadership and Management Are Radically Different

At the opposite extreme is Zaleznik's (1977, 1989a, b, 1990) view that leadership and management are fundamentally different. Zaleznik sees management as an orderly and stabilizing process, while leadership is a creative and often radical force for change. In fact, he attributes productivity problems of U.S. industry to a preoccupation with management and a dearth of leadership. Interestingly, though, both Drucker and Zaleznik agree that leadership is real work.

Zaleznik's distinction between leaders and managers is similar to one Burns (1978) makes between transactional and transformational leaders. Burns's transactional leader offers subordinates rewards in exchange for desired work efforts or services.

This transactional leader resembles Zaleznik's "manager." His transformational leader inspires followers to pursue higher-order needs and make extraordinary work contributions and is consistent with Zaleznik's "leader."

Leadership and Management Are Complementary Processes

In between these extremes is an intermediate position exemplified by Kotter's (1990) work. He suggests that while management and leadership are different phenomena, each is required for organizational success. The primary function of management is to achieve the organization's goals on time and on budget; the primary function of leadership is to produce constructive or adaptive change.

Many leadership theories are consistent with this intermediate position. For example, Bass's (1985) theory of transformational leadership assumes that (1) most leaders exhibit both transactional and transformational leadership, although in differing amounts, and (2) organizations need both forms of leadership to be effective. Bass's research also suggests that transactional leadership is based on two fundamental management practices—management by exception and contingent rewards. Such leadership seems consistent with traditional views of management. Similarly, Quinn's (1988) competing values model supports the notion that "master managers" perform both management and leadership responsibilities by playing eight key roles—producer, facilitator, coordinator, director, monitor, mentor, innovator, and broker. Importantly, he believes the need to fulfill both responsibilities actually increases as one moves up the hierarchy and the issues facing managers become more complex.

LEADERSHIP AND MANAGEMENT FROM A STRATIFIED SYSTEMS THEORY PERSPECTIVE

Stratified Systems Theory (SST), as reviewed in this book by Jacobs and Lewis, is consistent with the intermediate perspective just advanced. It is derived from work by Jaques (1989), who specifically states that a manager is "a person who is held accountable for the output of others and for sustaining a team capable of producing those outputs" (p. 13). Management, in turn, is defined as "the act of managing subordinates" to fulfill this accountability. Leadership, on the other hand, is seen as a discretionary process that energizes members to perform the critical tasks required for the adaptation, effectiveness, maintenance, and efficiency of the system (Jacobs and Jaques, 1987). This view echoes Katz and Kahn's (1978) notion of "incremental influence" and the construct of "discretionary leadership" advanced by Hunt and Osborn (1982). It is also consistent with Kotter's view of leadership as creating adaptive change. In sum, SST contends that management is rooted in accountability and the hierarchy of authority, while leadership operates more "at the margin" and in tandem with the leader's ability to elevate followers to high levels of commitment and performance. Both leadership and management thus seem critical and complementary processes in SST.

DIMENSIONS OF STRATEGIC LEADERSHIP AND MANAGEMENT

Strategic leadership in organizations may usefully be considered as having two dimensions of action responsibility. First is the leader's directional responsibility. It involves creating and communicating a unifying and inspirational "vision" and sense of "purpose" for the organization or group as a whole. Discussion, advice, and observations relevant to this responsibility now abound in the scholarly literature (e.g., Kotter, 1990; Sashkin, 1988) and in popular business or trade books such as those by Bennis and Nanus (1985) and Kouzes and Posner (1987). The notion of directional leadership is often implicitly associated with charisma (Conger and Kanungo, 1987; Nadler and Tushman, 1990). But, as Sashkin notes in this book, visionary leaders need not be charismatic. Rather, they must possess and apply the personal capabilities of cognitive complexity, self-efficacy, and a strong power motive. Specifically, they apply these capabilities to (1) define a value-based vision, (2) develop policies and programs for attaining that vision, and (3) engage in personal practices and behaviors that model the values that underlie the vision. This behavior is clearly directional leadership.

A second, perhaps less visible but no less important, dimension of strategic leadership involves operational responsibility. This creates the internal capacity in an organization or group actually to pursue desired direction through sustained, day-to-day performance. It has much in common with what Kotter (1990) refers to as management, Bass (1985) as transactional leadership, and Nadler and Tushman (1990) as instrumental leadership. While less "best-seller" appeal than the visionary and charismatic elements in directional leadership, operational leadership responsibility is nonetheless essential and necessary to true success in any setting. Organizations and groups depend on it, and someone has to do it.

Figure 7.1 depicts the interrelationship between these two leadership dimensions using the analogy of an arrow. The arrow's bold outline represents the leader's "directional responsibility," and the shaded interior represents the "operational responsibility." Both the bold outline and shaded interior are as integral to leadership as they are to the figure. While the outline establishes the overall sense of direction, the interior shading fills in the substance needed to hold the shape over time. One without the other is incomplete. So it is, too, with directive and operational leadership.

Figure 7.1
Two Dimensions of Strategic Leadership

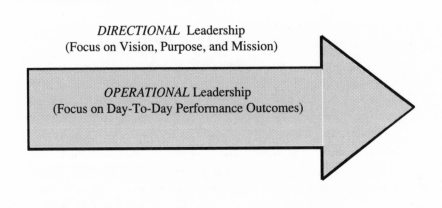

DIRECTIONAL Leadership
(Focus on Vision, Purpose, and Mission)

OPERATIONAL Leadership
(Focus on Day-To-Day Performance Outcomes)

LEADER RESPONSIBILITIES ACROSS LEVELS, FUNCTIONS, AND STRUCTURES

Both leadership responsibilities apply within the SST arena. They are essential at all organizational levels. It is just as important for a department head to maintain a sense of direction and integrate that department with others, as it is for a CEO to give direction to the enterprise as a whole. By the same token, it is as critical for senior executives to make sure their direct reports can and do accomplish daily tasks, as it is for the production manager. This argument is consistent also with Hooijberg and Quinn in this book who indicate that "masters of management" are effective in fulfilling a variety of roles that vary somewhat by organizational level. Of course, there may be differences in the emphasis leaders place on these responsibilities across levels, functions, and structures.

Jacobs (1991a) notes the time span for Stratum VII positions (e.g., CEOs of multinational conglomerates or four-star generals in the military) may exceed twenty years. Here, the leader's directional responsibilities focus on providing long-term direction while operational responsibilities focus on ensuring day-to-day progress toward these objectives. Operational leadership thus supports the primary responsibility of directional leadership. As one moves down the hierarchy, overall direction comes from higher-stratum leaders. Lower levels thus devote progressively more attention to operational aspects of implementation and work with comparatively short (three months to one year) time frames. Nevertheless, these leaders must still provide followers with the direction required to achieve work unit goals.

SST implies that these distributions of leadership responsibilites may be rather precise in the traditional pyramid sense of an organization. But of Mintzberg's (1983, 1989) five structural configurations, for example, only two—the machine bureacracy and the divisionalized form—resemble the requisite organization assumed by SST and described by Jaques (1989). Thus, a leader's directional and operational responsibilities may be less hierarchically determined in a broader mix of organizations. In other settings, the extent to which leaders emphasize directional versus operational responsibilities may have as much or more to do with the functions they perform than level.

Consider the highly flexible and responsive adhocracy as described by Mintzberg. Here, directional and operational responsibilities are more likely dispersed across both levels and functions. This structure may be adopted when an organization places a heavy emphasis on innovation and strategic opportunism. All internal stakeholders, in a sense, can have a say in shaping the organization's strategies. Moreover, some directional responsibility may even be externalized to regulators (e.g., elected political leaders, in the case of the military, or the Joint Commission on the Accreditation of Health Care Organizations, in the case of hospitals).

Even in the divisionalized organizational form, strategic leadership may be more broad-based than SST implies. Because division managers are held accountable for the performance of their units, they place a heavy emphasis on both responsibilities. Because leaders in top corporate management positions provide division managers with substantial autonomy, they are less concerned with its strategic activities than they are with its operating performance. Of course, if a division's performance is deficient, its activities will be closely scrutinized.

STRATEGIC LEADERSHIP AND INDIVIDUAL PERFORMANCE

The fulfillment of directional and operational responsibilities appears essential for all leaders, although the relative emphasis on them may vary by level, function, and structural configuration. Thus, there is much to be gained by ensuring that operational responsibility is not neglected—in practice or in theory—even as attention is given to expanding our understanding of, and success with, the directional aspects. The remainder of this chapter is devoted to specific elements of strategic "operational" leadership.

An Operational Leadership Framework

High-performing individuals are foundations for effective work groups; high-performing groups are foundations for effective organizations. To be effective, therefore, operational leaders must have high-performing followers. One way to expand operational leadership effectiveness is through improved awareness of the factors that influence individual performance. A useful framework is offered in this individual performance equation:

Performance = Ability × Support × Effort

The equation identifies three ''high performance factors'' that must be present for any individual to achieve high performance in a work situation—ability, support, and effort. It is consistent with research on individual work performance summarized by Campbell and Campbell (1988). The three performance factors are defined by Martin, Schermerhorn, and Larson (1989, p. 182) as:

- Ability—the capacity to perform created by the aptitudes and skills through which a person's performance potential is developed.
- Support—the opportunity to perform made possible by providing individuals with what they need for best use of their capabilities in a job.
- Effort—the willingness to perform represented by the individual's decision actually to work hard at the job.

For present purposes, the important initial point is that the absence of any one or more of the three performance factors severely limits the performance level a person can attain. Thus the equation shows multiplicative relationships among the performance factors. A lack of ability, for example, clearly compromises the performance of even the most willing and best-supported worker. A lack of support can compromise the performance of the most capable and hardworking individual. Finally, an unwillingness to work hard can compromise the performance of a capable and well-supported individual.

On the positive side, by contrast, high performance outcomes can be maximized when an organization's leaders successfully address the ability, support, and effort variables for each and every person under their immediate supervision (Schermerhorn, Gardner, and Martin, 1990). This premise applies regardless of level, function, or structure. As Campbell and Campbell (1988) note, the factors can and should become important ''points of influence'' for leaders interested in improving the performance of others in a work situation (p. 89).

A framework for ''high performance'' operational leadership, that is, leadership focused on positively influencing the individual performance factors, is diagrammed in Figure 7.2. The model implied by this figure is generally consistent with the expectancy theory of motivation (Vroom, 1964) and has ties to the associated path-goal theory of leadership (House and Mitchell, 1974). As described, the framework has important and tangible leadership implications.

Leadership and the Ability Factor

The first insight of this framework is that each of the leader's immediate subordinates must have the ability to perform at a high level. If an individual does not have the requisite ability to master the tasks at hand, absolute limits to the level

Figure 7.2
A Framework for "High Performance" Operational Leadership

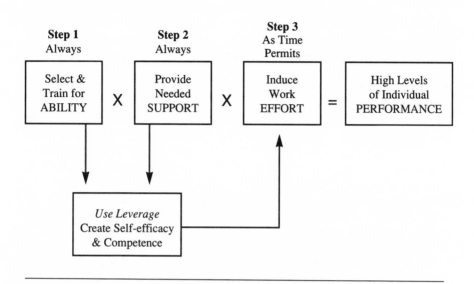

of attainable performance are set. This performance ceiling may be difficult to raise even if the individual is well-supported and hardworking.

Our use of the term *ability* here is similar to the concept of working capacity, which Jaques (1989) defines as "the highest level of work of *a given type* that an individual can carry out." SST also includes the concept of potential working capacity, which is equivalent to our notion of a performance ceiling. Potential working capacity is a function of one's cognitive power, that is, the maximum scale and complexity of the world that a person is able to construe.

Both the individual performance equation and SST imply that an effective leader must recognize the critical role of ability. Success in operational leadership, accordingly, is earned, in part, by those leaders who take any and all actions necessary to select capable people for the work to be done and then regularly train and develop these people to maintain their job capabilities over time. As suggested earlier by Drucker, the work of a good leader involves selecting talented people and then developing them into highly capable followers.

Given the importance of ability, it is always the performance factor that gets the effective operational leader's first attention. That is, such leaders believe that there is no substitute for ability among followers. By always addressing the ability factor for each individual performer, the effective operational leader maximizes the height of the performance ceiling that governs the group or organization in question. Moreover, because ability is a substitute for task-oriented leadership

(Howell, et al., 1990; Kerr and Jermier, 1978), attention to this factor in the short run can save the leader enormous amounts of time and energy in the long run.

Leadership and the Support Factor

Second, this framework points out that each individual under the leader's immediate supervision must have the support needed to perform at a high level, that is, each person is given every chance to apply his or her talents to maximum advantage at work. Jaques (1989), recognizes this responsibility within SST when he asserts that "managers must be able to *add value* to the work of their subordinates, in particular by *setting an effective context* for their work" (p. 61). "Support" in this sense is a multifaceted high performance factor. It ranges from making sure that the performance goals are understood and the individual has the necessary technology and resources to accomplish those goals, to the elimination of job constraints that inhibit one's work accomplishments.

An effective leader knows that support is critical to sustaining high levels of work performance. Success in operational leadership, accordingly, is earned, in part, by those leaders who take any actions necessary to support properly the daily work efforts of their subordinates. As again suggested by Drucker, good leaders maintain support through such activities as setting goals, priorities, and standards and keeping them clearly visible, as well as by being consistent and making sure that actions always back up their words.

Once every effort has been made by the leader to ensure followers' abilities, the effective operational leader always finds the time to fulfill the support factor. This leader does everything possible every day to ensure that followers have the support needed to take full advantage of their talents and capabilities. This fact is as true at the upper levels of the organization as it is at the lowest. Indeed, the importance of support may actually increase as one moves up the hierarchy since the critical tasks become more complex and far-reaching in scope. This is not to say that executives spend a great deal of time monitoring their direct reports' work on a daily basis—they do not. The major reason they don't is that there are many subordinate (e.g., need for independence, a professional orientation), task (e.g., intrinsically satisfying duties), and organizational (e.g., cohesive work groups, organizational rewards outside the leader's control) substitutes for leadership support at this level (Howell et al., 1990; Kerr and Jermier, 1978). Nevertheless, effective executives—like their lower-level counterparts—do take actions to ensure continually that their direct reports have all of the support they need to perform their jobs.

Leadership, the Effort Factor, and Performance Leverage

Third, this framework points out that each individual under the leader's immediate supervision must work hard enough to perform at a high level. This is largely an issue of individual motivation (Ilgen and Klein, 1988). An unmotivated person will not exert much effort; a highly motivated person will. It is part of every leader's job to ensure that every person comes to work and experiences sufficient motivation to excel at the job.

An effective leader understands that a willingness to work hard is essential to high performance. Success in operational leadership, accordingly, is earned, in part, by those leaders who create motivational work environments for their subordinates. But there is an aspect to this latter responsibility that differentiates it from those described for the other two performance factors.

To begin, the effective operational leader understands that the strongest motivation comes from within. Rather than expending scarce energy, time, and other resources trying externally to manipulate individual motivation to work, the effective operational leader first pursues an alternative strategy. Almost acting contrary to common sense, this leader refrains from devoting attention to the effort factor until he or she is well satisfied that the ability and support factors are properly addressed. That is, this leader is directly concerned about individual efforts only as time otherwise permits.

The reason that the effective operational leader can and should do what we have just mentioned is leverage. Performance leverage is achieved when the leader is able to do things, even small things, whose ultimate performance impact is both continuing and magnified. In this sense, leverage is similar to the SST notion of the "positive value added" by effective leaders to the work of persons at lower levels (Jacobs and Jaques, 1987). The leader who takes advantage of leverage invests scarce resources in activities whose ultimate impacts on performance are far-reaching. This is an important means of expanding the leader's influence, given the fact that time and other resources are often scarce. Simply put, an effective leader always does first those things offering the most leverage for performance.

The framework depicted in Figure 7.2 identifies how the effective operational leader gains performance leverage on the effort factor through understanding the motivational importance of self-efficacy (Bandura, 1977a, 1978; Cowan, Fiol, and Walsh, this volume; Gist, 1987; Sashkin, 1988, this volume) and feelings of personal competence (White, 1959). Self-efficacy involves confidence that one can produce the required behavior. Note that this construct is conceptually similar but distinct from the expectancy theory constructs of expectancy (Effort⟶ Performance Expectations) and instrumentality (Performance⟶ Outcome Expectations) (Gist, 1987). However, because self-efficacy judgments depend on more than effort considerations (e.g., ability to cope with stress, internal motivation), they encompass variables that are not reflected by the expectancy construct (Bandura, 1978; Gist, 1987). With regard to instrumentality, Bandura (1978) distinguishes it from self-efficacy as follows: "An efficacy expectation is a judgment of one's ability to execute a certain behavior pattern, whereas an outcome expectation is a judgment of the likely consequences such behavior will produce" (p. 240).

The key implication of self-efficacy for strategic operational leadership is that people can be expected to work harder when they experience a sense of felt competence in their jobs. Therefore, to the extent that a leader can create such feelings among followers, the power of motivation "from within" can be leveraged to influence the effort factor. As shown in our framework, one way to develop self-efficacy is to make sure that people have the abilities and support needed to do their jobs well. If a leader is successful with the ability and support factors, the leverage achieved can extend the benefits of these investments to the third factor—effort.

Leadership and Attribution Errors

Unfortunately, attribution theory and research (Mitchell, 1984) suggest that many leaders are prone to systematic errors that deny them full advantage of the leverage opportunities just described. This situation is particularly true with respect to the implicit value of the support factor as an important point of leadership influence. Research by Schermerhorn (1986) with a group of health care supervisors showed, for example, that they were prone to attribute the causes of poor subordinate performance to a lack of either ability or effort. In other words, the performance problems were due to deficiencies that were the subordinates' responsibilities. When asked about their own performance problems, however, these supervisors overwhelmingly identified a lack of support as the critical factor. That is, they felt their own performance problems were due to deficiencies beyond their individual control. Importantly, evidence of this "self-serving bias" has been repeatedly obtained in a wide variety of contexts by both social psychologists (for reviews see Bradley, 1978; Miller and Ross, 1975; Zuckerman, 1979) and management researchers (Mitchell, Green, and Wood, 1981).

The critical leadership question in this example was posed by Schermerhorn to the supervisors. "Why," he asked, "if you only need more support to do your jobs better, can't the same be said about your subordinates?" With this question he redirects their attention and ours toward the support factor as a potentially neglected leadership variable. We believe SST and other leadership perspectives can be enhanced by spelling out in more detail the ways in which strategic operational leadership can be greatly enhanced by leaders who actively support the work efforts of their followers.

SUPPORTIVE OPERATIONAL LEADERSHIP

A supportive operational leader is someone who leads by making sure that capable people have the support they need to do their jobs well. This kind of leadership involves creating a day-to-day work environment that makes people confident and competent and thereby enables and empowers them to excel at tasks that are critical to the organization's mission or overall direction. Although the support concept is clearly within the domain of leadership theory, with roots as diverse as Likert's (1967) "System 4" theory and House's path-goal theory (House and Mitchell, 1974), it gains a unique identity when considered from the operational perspective of enhancing individual performance, as just described.

Supportive operational leadership also reflects a commitment to action that can be shared by leaders across the organizational levels with which SST is concerned. Indeed, one of the major reasons it is so powerful is that it can serve as a downward or upward influence across strata. Because subordinates, at any level, add value to the work of their superiors when they become capable of higher performance, such leadership can ultimately serve to facilitate upward influence. Moreover, as a review of Blair and Rivera's chapter in this book suggests, capable leaders and professionals at the middle and lower levels can even provide the organization with its strategic direction. Thus we can speak of stratified operational leadership, without limiting ourselves to the top-down perspective of SST.

Stratified Operational Leadership

While supportive operational leadership facilitates upward influence, one should recognize that it is, by definition, a means of downward influence since support is provided by a superior to a subordinate. This form of downward influence is always required regardless of the organizational level. For example, even at the highest levels, the leaders must ensure that their immediate subordinates have the support they need to perform their jobs effectively. In essence, upper- and middle-level managers fulfill multiple leadership roles, which include being the leader of their work unit as a whole and the supervisor of their immediate staff (Neal and Fiedler, 1968). With regard to the former role, these leaders seek to create a supportive culture for their work unit by serving as role models and fostering the internalization of desired values (Sashkin, 1988, this volume; Trice and Beyer, 1984). With respect to the latter, they attempt to provide support through daily interactions with subordinates.

Positive value added. It follows that the supportive aspects of strategic operational leadership will cascade down the hierarchy into the depths of the organization, as long as leaders at each level succeed in adding "positive value" by performing their critical tasks (Jacobs and Jaques, 1987). When top management effectively supports middle management, when middle management effectively supports first-level management, when first-level management effectively supports operational workers, and when all these things are accomplished with a clear sense of total direction, the full human resource potential of an organization can be realized. As Jaques (1989) notes, however, "negative value" can just as easily be added if critical tasks at a particular stratum are performed poorly, if the organization is not properly structured, or if a subordinate subverts the efforts of a superior.

Importantly, this observation is consistent with our argument that if either ability, support, or effort is deficient, an individual's performance will suffer. If, instead, leaders at each level are able to unlock the potential "magnifying effect" of supportive operational leadership, positive value can be added throughout the organization—from top to bottom—and back up again.

Fixed and variable operational support. A model of the specific ways in which managers at different organizational levels can and should exercise supportive operational leadership is depicted in Figure 7.3

Whereas all levels may share responsibility for certain "fixed" support needed by followers at any level of operations, they may also have "varied" responsibilities in response to the distinctive support needs of their immediate followers. For example, the right side of Figure 7.3 recognizes three different needs for variable support:

- Total system support—provided by the top to middle levels in the form of external environmental understandings and the communication of organizational strategies.
- Integrated subsystem support—provided by the middle to lower levels in the form of internal system understandings and subsystems integration.
- Internal subsystem support—provided by the lower levels to non-managerial personnel in the form of subsystem understandings and intra-subsystem activities.

Figure 7.3
A Cascade Model of Supportive Operational Leadership in a Stratified Organizational System

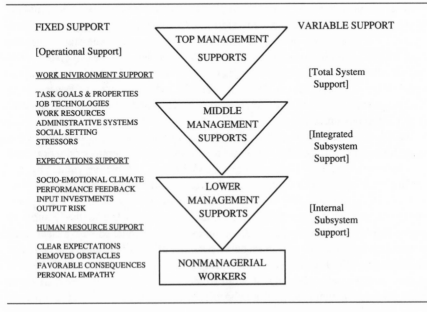

In addition to these broadly defined variable aspects of leadership support, however, each of the dimensions of work environment, expectations, and human resource support listed in the left column of Figure 7.3 can and should be applied at all levels of leadership responsibility in organizations. We examine these forms of support in detail below by discussing three distinct, but complementary, points of view regarding supportive leadership.

Work Environment Support

Earlier, Martin et al. (1989) have examined the motivational aspects of supportive work environments. They include the following as critical support elements in any work situation: task goals and properties, job technologies, work resources, social setting, administrative systems, and stressors. Briefly, we can now highlight major points of leadership attention for each of these key aspects of a supportive and motivational work environment.

Task goals and properties. A key point of leadership attention relates to the tasks people are assigned and the performance goals expected of them. The significance of task goals and properties is well covered in organizational research (Locke, et al., 1981). Here, it can simply be noted that any leader's operational responsibilities involve making sure that each and every direct report has clear and understandable goals, achievable but moderately challenging task goals, and a job whose requirements match individual abilities.

Job technologies. Proper tools, equipment, and other resources are required for high performance. They create an opportunity for persons to use their abilities to maximum advantage in a task assignment. The effective operational leader is alert to the importance of making sure that each and every subordinate has the latest in appropriate job technologies, that is, the technology is only as sophisticated as necessary for the task at hand and the capabilities of the person assigned to the work. For lower-level positions, this appropriateness may simply involve supplying the individual with proper tools and equipment. At the highest levels, however, such a match may involve scanning the environment to anticipate technological innovations and ensuring that subordinates have the capability to acquire and/or develop the technology needed to sustain long-term success.

Work resources. Having the resources needed to perform one's job is one of the most important everyday considerations faced by most workers. An effective operational leader makes sure that each work unit member has the resources needed to achieve high performance. These resources include adequate budgets for financial, material, and human resources, as well as facilities, working conditions, and other physical aspects of the job environment. Once again, the scope of the resources required is likely to vary by organizational level. At the lowest levels, these resources may be limited to supplies and materials. At the highest levels, they may include multimillion-dollar budgets, competitive information, the authority to hire high-quality personnel, and physical facilities.

Social setting. The social setting of the workplace has an important impact on the behavior and accomplishments of individual workers. An effective operational leader always strives to create a social setting that responds to the maximum extent possible to the relatedness needs of people at work. Key aspects of the social setting that merit leadership attention are interpersonal harmony, group norms and cohesiveness, informal groups, socioemotional support, and task-related mentoring and interactions.

Administrative systems. Job and situational constraints are recognized for their potential to impact individual performance adversely (Peters and O'Connor, 1980). In many cases, the individual may want and try to perform as expected but be severely hampered by the presence of unnecessary constraints. Effective operational leaders continually ferret out and eliminate such job constraints, which only serve to add "negative value" (Jaques, 1989). Elimination of such constraints means that daily attention must be given to the efficiency of administrative systems. Things to be especially on guard against include poor planning and scheduling, improper work flow requirements, cumbersome or irrelevant policies and procedures, restricted or unnecessary communication channels, and insufficient delegation.

Stressors. Stress can add positive or negative value to the performance of individuals at work. It is suggested that people need a moderate amount of stress to achieve and maintain the creative and/or high performance edge (Selye, 1976). While finding the moderate stress level for each person is a tricky task, it can be said that the effective operational leader does not allow stress to exert a destructive force at work. In particular, the leader is continuously on guard against excessive stress caused by improper role definition. For example, the leader eliminates role ambiguities caused by unclear job expectations, role conflicts caused by mutually exclusive job expectations, and role overloads or underloads caused by inappropriate job expectations. In addition, care must be taken when filling vacant positions to ensure that the individual possesses the cognitive power required to perform the critical tasks (Jacobs and Jaques, 1987; Jaques, 1989). Finally, attention should be given to buffering the work impacts of nonwork stressors such as external commitments and the pressures of family responsibilities or personal life events (Beehr, 1985; Blau, 1981; House, 1981).

Expectations Support

Eden's (1990) concept of the "pygmalion effect" has direct implications for supportive leadership. To Eden, support in the form of high and appropriate expectations is the key to producing the pygmalion effect in leadership. This means that an effective leader communicates performance expectations to create self-fulfilling prophecies for member performance. When applied to operational leadership, the dimensions of such expectations support are as follows.

Socioemotional climate. The effective operational leader provides a supportive socioemotional climate that serves as a point of encouragement for each individual and as a model of interpersonal relationships. Specifically identified are such things as looking subordinates in the eye, smiling, using warm voice intonations, and being attentive during conversations. Furthermore, at the upper levels of the hierarchy, the effective operational leader also operates to create a culture and value system that communicate respect for the individual and foster a supportive social climate (Bass, 1985; Jacobs and Jaques, 1987; Trice and Beyer, 1984). Here again, desired behaviors that are role-modeled by the executive, such as active listening, truthfulness, and shows of respect for others, tend to be copied by lower-level leaders as these behaviors permeate through the organization to foster a supportive culture (Sashkin, 1988, this book).

Performance feedback. Performance feedback promotes learning and helps reinforce successful work behaviors. Eden considers it outright neglect on the part of leaders when such feedback is withheld from deserving subordinates. Key commitments in this realm of leadership support include making sure that followers are evaluated for their performance accomplishments and always know exactly where they stand in terms of progress and expectations.

Input investments. Support occurs when the leader demonstrates a willingness to invest personally in a follower. At the lower levels of an organization, this may mean staying overtime to help subordinates with an important task, listening to their concerns, giving extra explanations, personally demonstrating how to do a task correctly, and taking advantage of all training opportunities. At the middle and upper levels, these inputs may involve serving as a mentor and making a commitment to the career development of subordinates (Jaques, 1989).

Output risk. This aspect of supportive leadership is consistent with the currently popular concept of empowerment (Sashkin, this volume). The supportive leader is willing to assume "output risk" by granting subordinates the authority and latitude to make critical decisions about their work. By empowering others, the leader makes a useful demonstration of support and commitment. Although this involves output risk, it signifies the leader's confidence and trust in the subordinate.

Human Resource Support

Another approach to supportive leadership builds on a human resource management point of view. Odiorne (1987) directly identifies a "supportive" boss as someone who, in addition to clarifying expectations and providing favorable consequences, removes any and all obstacles to the performance success of subordinates. Being supportive requires going beyond providing the right resources, technologies, and so on and into the elimination of "blocking" or contradictory signals that may interfere with their work performance. Odiorne suggests that the supportive boss asks, "Is there anything I could do or refrain from doing to help my subordinates succeed?'' Finally, he, too, recommends that proper attention be given to such things as the individual health, stress, personal problems, and work habits of subordinates. Importantly, Odiorne's position is consistent with findings from the stress and mental health literature that indicate that social support by the supervisor is negatively related to work stress (Beehr, 1985; Blau, 1981; House, 1981).

CONCLUSION

It is time to recognize the need to move beyond the insights and contributions of purely directional leadership approaches. Every leader's commitment to fixed and variable, day-to-day, operational support responsibilities must be maintained. This commitment must be evidenced even while most external attention seems to go toward more emotional and popular appeals for personal vision and charisma (see, e.g., Bennis and Nanus, 1985; Kouzes and Posner, 1987). Once again, Sashkin's chapter in this volume presents a practical view on the essential foundations of a visionary role and directional leadership. It stresses the importance of the leader's providing an enlightened sense of direction for the organization or group as a whole and then enthusing everyone through special personal qualities to work hard in pursuit of this direction. But it must still be recalled that this directional aspect of leadership is a necessary, but not sufficient, condition for effective leadership overall. Allowing one's concerns to become dominated by it alone may cause the leader to overlook important advantages to be gained by leveraging individual performance accomplishments through the support factor.

The charismatic concept of leadership responsibility, in particular, is tied to the effort factor in the individual performance equation. While charisma is fine in concept, important, lingering questions exist regarding every appointed leader's capability to deliver on the charismatic dimension. Yet there is no doubt that every leader can deliver on the supportive operational dimensions. In fact, the role of self-efficacy and felt competency as described in Figure 7.2 may be viewed as a potential leadership ''substitute'' (Howell et al., 1990; Kerr and Jermier, 1978) for otherwise direct and personal charismatic contributions of a leader. In effect, efficacy and felt competency helps unlock the people's capacities charismatically to lead themselves. This notion of internal charisma may be most significant of all. The exact significance of this proposition is a matter for future research and scholarly consideration.

The guiding framework of this book, Stratified Systems Theory (SST), offers many opportunities for advancing leadership thinking. Practically speaking, however, SST can benefit from a basic reminder implicit throughout this chapter: an effective leader makes sure every day that each individual follower has the ability, support, and motivation to perform at a high level of accomplishment. Said more specifically, the three daily checks for effective operational leadership are: (1) Is each of my followers capable of doing the job?, (2) Is each of my followers well supported in the job?, and (3) Is each of my followers highly motivated to work hard in the job?

Strategic operational leadership views individual performance as the essential building block of organization or group performance—the ultimate criterion of leadership effectiveness in any setting. It builds from the basic premise that an effective leader must, at a minimum, have high-performing followers. While not denying the importance of "top-down" and more directional leadership considerations, it suggests that vision and charisma alone are insufficient to ensure long-run success for any organization or group and therefore for its leader(s). Somehow, the everyday work of leadership must get done. We believe the concept of strategic operational leadership as advanced in this chapter can help all leaders—working at all levels and in various responsibilities in organizations of all types—who share the goal of wanting to do their jobs exceptionally well.

III

Leadership Capabilities and Development

8

Individual Differences in Strategic Leadership Capacity: A Constructive/Developmental View

Philip Lewis and T. Owen Jacobs

The central concept of this chapter is what its authors term "cognitive capacity"—a broad interpretation of SST's underlying cognitive complexity notion. They develop the cognitive capacity concept in great detail. Whereas the literature tends to ignore or consider cognitive complexity (capacity) in combination with other variables, for Lewis and Jacobs, cognitive capacity's centrality makes it so crucial that it cannot be ignored. While, for them, cognitive capacity cannot be ignored, other variables have no, or far less, importance in predicting effective leadership.

Consistent with this philosophy, the chapter describes developmental aspects of cognitive capacity in considerable detail. It also provides some preliminary empirical evidence concerning cognitive capacity development.

INTRODUCTION

The personal demands of strategic leadership are enormous. As Hitt and Keats have noted elsewhere in this book, the strategic leader operates in a highly faceted, rapidly changing, probabilistic environment where the consequences of strategic decisions will often not be known for several years. To operate effectively in such an environment requires the vision, perspective, and strength of character that are thought to come only from years of experience in the real world. Yet, as the growing literature on managerial "derailment" illustrates (McCall and Lombardo, 1983; McCauley and Lombardo, 1990), experience alone does not seem to impart strategic leadership capacity. The corporate landscape is littered with enterprises brought to ruin by "experienced" leaders who failed to anticipate the ruinous consequences of their strategic decisions. It seems unlikely that these leaders failed because they lacked specific managerial skills. Although a few may have had significant character flaws, most leaders with such defects are identified and their career progression halted before they reach the highest levels of leadership.

What, then, does distinguish effective strategic leaders from ineffective ones, if not experience and skill levels? In this chapter we seek to extend the Stratified Systems Theory (SST) position, articulated most recently by Jaques and Clement (1991), that what most often distinguishes between effective and ineffective strategic leaders is their level of conceptual capacity. Simply stated, SST includes the proposition that leaders who lack the conceptual capacity to construct an understanding that matches or exceeds the complexity of their work will be unable to carry out their most critical tasks effectively (Jaques and Clement, 1991). As is clear from a careful reading of SST, conceptual capacity is more than mere cognitive complexity. In this chapter we will argue that conceptual capacity is a broad set of "constructive" capacities that include the capacity for integration, abstraction, independent thought, and the use of broad and complex frames of reference. As such, conceptual capacity is used herein to denote a set of individual attributes that subsume and broaden what has traditionally been referred to as cognitive complexity. We will further argue, and present preliminary evidence suggestive of the notion, that high levels of conceptual capacity are most likely to be found in individuals who have achieved a high level of personal differentiation, a developmental achievement variously referred to by structural developmental theorists as personal autonomy (Loevinger, 1976) or psychological self-definition (Kuhnert and Lewis, 1987).

As we will explain shortly, our definition of personal differentiation is based on structural features of the way in which the individual creates meaning, rather than the content of the individual's values or preferred leadership style. In our opinion, it is not nearly as important to discover what a potential strategic leader believes (a values issue) or how he or she prefers to operate (a style issue) as it is to know how the leader structures an understanding of the strategic environment. With a few notable exceptions (cf. Streufert and Nogami, 1989), these constructive processes have been most neglected by leadership theorists and researchers.

In trying to encompass notions about personal differentiation and conceptual capacity within a broad constructive/developmental framework, we intend to clarify the nature of conceptual capacity in a fashion that clearly distinguishes it from other relevant, but less central, individual features of strategic leaders. We agree with Sashkin (this book) and others (House, 1988; Hunt, 1991; McClelland and Burnham, 1976; Miner, 1978) who assert that a desire to exercise power and influence and a belief that one can be effective doing so (Bandura, 1982) are essential leader qualities. Nonetheless, no amount of motivation will make up for a lack of conceptual grasp. Indeed, the vigorous pursuit of strategies born of a narrowly conceived understanding of the organization and its dynamics may prove especially disastrous.

THE OVEREMPHASIS ON LEADERSHIP STYLE

The fact that nearly everyone has had some direct experience with both disappointingly ineffective leaders and surprisingly effective ones has led to the common-sense belief that there are important personality differences between good and poor leaders. Most people reject out of hand the competing idea that effective leaders are created wholly by circumstances (e.g., being in the right place at the right time) and that the enduring personal qualities of the leader are largely irrelevant to effective leadership. It is quite disconcerting, therefore, to discover that most of the classic reviews of leadership research (Hollander and Julian, 1969; Mann, 1959; Stogdill, 1948) suggest that personality traits, independent of other variables (House, 1988), do not distinguish effective from ineffective leaders. This lack of support for the direct effect of personality traits on leader effectiveness has not, however, deterred contemporary leadership theorists from trying to identify personality style differences that they feel are relevant to leader effectiveness. Driver, Brousseau, and Hunsaker (1990) describe two dimensions of decision-making style, information use and focus, which they combine to identify five basic decision-making styles. Thus, their decisive style is characterized by the rapid use of a minimal amount of information to arrive at one clear solution. The other styles are flexible, hierarchic, integrative, and systemic.

Driver, Brousseau, and Hunsaker (1990) assert that these managerial styles have a significant impact on organizational outcomes. Similarly, Kirton, who studied the ways in which organizational innovation gets implemented, has identified two other managerial styles that he thinks are implicated in organizational effectiveness. Using a relatively brief questionnaire, Kirton seeks to identify "adaptors" and "innovators" (Kirton, 1976) and indicates that they operate in work organizations with very different problem-solving styles. Interestingly, like most theorists who claim to have identified key leadership style differences, both Kirton and Driver et al. are careful to point out that no single style is better than any other style. Rather, each is said to have its advantages and disadvantages. Driver, Brousseau, and Hunsaker (1990) recommend that managers seek to develop more than one style so that they will be able to adapt to the demands of different situations. Similarly, Kirton suggests that organizations will benefit from a mix of adaptive and innovative managers. Clearly, then, a close reading of these contemporary proponents of leadership style approaches reveals them to be unwilling to assert that they have identified personal characteristics that distinguish between effective and ineffective leaders. This is not to say that style differences are irrelevant to leader effectiveness. Rather, the flexible use of multiple styles may, as Streufert and Nogami (1989) suggest, be particularly important in the complex and fast-changing world of senior leaders.

DISTINGUISHING BETWEEN CONCEPTUAL CAPACITY AND LEADERSHIP STYLE

Before proceeding further, we need to be clear about what we mean by the term *style* and how we view it as different from what we are calling "conceptual capacity." By leadership style we are referring chiefly to preferred ways of operating in the leadership role. For example, Driver, Brousseau, and Hunsaker (1990) distinguish between people who prefer to gather only enough information to arrive at one or two "good enough" solutions to a problem (the "satisficers") and those who prefer to gather all relevant information before arriving at a decision (the so-called maximizers). Driver, Brousseau, and Hunsaker (1990) point out that while most people can shift styles as situational demands change, people typically prefer one or the other way of operating when faced with a decision. As such, the decision-making style is a preference and is a summary of how the individual is likely to behave in most, but not all, circumstances.

Consistent with a constructive/developmental metapsychology (Kegan, 1982), conceptual capacity is not viewed by us or by Stratified Systems Theory (Jaques and Clement, 1991) as a behavioral preference. Rather, conceptual capacity describes the breadth and complexity with which an individual organizes his or her experience. As such, conceptual capacity is not a disposition to act. Rather, it is the level of sophistication of an individual's organizing processes and is antecedent to action. With Jaques (1989), we subscribe to the constructivist view that people do not react to an objective real world. Rather, they react to the meaning they have attached to that world. Conceptual capacity is a description of the nature of the meaning-making process. Just as one's organizing process can be seen as giving rise to one's behavior, these processes can also be seen as giving rise to certain motivational states. Stated simply, if you can't "see" something, you can't care about it.

Another major difference between managerial styles and conceptual capacity concerns their dimensionality. As Streufert and Nogami (1989) pointed out in their review of cognitive styles, styles are usually described in terms of bipolar dimensions (e.g., adaption versus innovation; satisficing versus maximizing). Each end of the dimensions is viewed as having value under certain circumstances. In contrast, the elements of conceptual capacity (e.g., breadth of perspective, level of abstraction) are not bipolar. Rather, they range from little or none of the capacity to a great deal of it. Even more importantly, levels of conceptual capacity are thought to be hierarchical in the sense that each succeeding level encompasses the lower levels. For example, Jaques and Clement (1991), in describing the thinking processes used by leaders at successive organizational strata, point out that the individual who uses the highest thinking process, parallel processing, can and does also use declarative processing, data accumulation, and serial processing, the latter three being less complex and developmentally earlier ways of processing information. Indeed, the information that is processed in parallel (simultaneously) by the individual functioning at the highest level is sets of information that the individual has already processed serially. To summarize, styles are usually viewed as alternative bipolar dispositions or preferences (e.g., extroverted vs. introverted), each with its own advantages and disadvantages. In contrast, conceptual capacity concerns increasing levels of sophistication, where higher levels of capacity encompass lower levels rather than being alternatives to them.

A third major difference between most managerial style variables and conceptual capacity (as we are defining it here) is that the former are cast in terms of individual differences while the latter are cast in terms of developmental level. This distinction has a number of implications for leader training and development, which we will consider below. Here we merely wish to point out that conceptual capacity is thought to develop through an invariant series of hierarchically ordered stages or levels (Jaques and Clement, 1991; Kegan, 1982). Individual differences in conceptual capacity are thought to represent differences in developmental level, and it is not believed that people can be moved from lower to higher levels without their passing through each intervening level. In contrast, styles are thought to be a function of each individual's learning history and (perhaps) physiological constitution. It is theoretically possible, therefore, to train individuals to modify their managerial styles in whatever direction is believed to be most useful. Indeed Quinn (1988) describes a systematic educational program that he claims has accomplished just this goal.

The recent work of Robert Quinn (1988) is also worth mentioning for another reason, because it represents a potential bridge between the leadership style approaches that we are critiquing and ours and SST's constructive developmental approach. Quinn (1988) has provided a rough developmental model of how one progresses from being a novice manager to being a "master" manager (a status few seem to achieve). Quinn asserts that whereas novice managers tend to be purposive, linear thinkers who emphasize only one or two managerial approaches, master managers take an "integrative" view, which allows them to tolerate, consider, and employ both purposive and holistic frames of reference. It is clear that he is not merely asserting that the master manager is a sort of stylistic jack-of-all-trades who can, chameleonlike, adopt whatever style best fits the moment. Rather, he mentions a "transformational" process that permits the master manager to move to a new "metalevel" (Quinn, 1988, p. 165). What Quinn lacks, however, is an effective way of conceptualizing this transformational process. Transformation is not compatible with the behavioral metapsychology that underlies much of the recent theorizing about leadership style. Constructive developmental theory, in contrast, provides an elegant framework for encompassing transformational change (Kuhnert and Lewis, 1987).

Finally, leadership style and conceptual capacity typically differ with respect to the way in which they are assessed (Streufert and Nogami, 1989). Style is typically assessed using paper-and-pencil questionnaires where respondents are asked to indicate which of two or more descriptions or adjectives is most like them (the forced choice approach) or how much they are like a particular word or description (the rating scale approach). An exemplar of the forced choice approach is the Myers-Briggs Type Indicator (McCauley, 1981), a widely used measure of personality style based loosely on Jungian personality theory. Quinn's Competing Values Leadership Instrument (Quinn, 1988) is a good example of the rating scale approach to the assessment of managerial style differences. Consistent with our definition of style is the fact that the person being rated is described in terms of either a general behavioral preference or a preferred way of operating in the leadership or managerial role.

Because conceptual capacity concerns how an individual constructs meaning or organizes information, it is typically not effectively assessed using paper-and-pencil questionnaires (Streufert and Nogami, 1989). When assessing conceptual capacity, one is not interested in what people think. One is interested in how they think. As Streufert and Nogami (1989) have pointed out, most people are unable to tell you how they think. For these two reasons, assessment of conceptual capacity (including cognitive complexity) requires that individuals being assessed engage in a task that demands the demonstration of their conceptual capacity. This is the principal reason the current technique for assessing conceptual capacity in SST, Stamp's Career Path Appreciation (Stamp, 1986), includes a problem-solving task (Brunner's symbol-sorting task) and the individual is questioned extensively about how he or she approaches work tasks. In short, assessment of conceptual capacity typically entails demonstration of capacity while assessment of style typically entails self-description.

THE PRIMACY OF DECISION-MAKING COMPETENCE

Despite our gut-level feeling that there are important stylistic differences between effective and ineffective leaders, differences in interpersonal style, decision-making style, or other personal preferences may not be directly related to leader effectiveness. Approaches that focus on leadership style tend to ignore what is most fundamental about leadership. Leaders add value to their organizations by exercising discretion and making sound decisions that others in the organization are not in a position to make. The style with which those decisions are made is not, ultimately, very important. What is important is the quality of those decisions. Jaques and Clement (1991) have stated it very well:

> If a corporation is doing very well *over the long haul* (emphasis added), look to the competence of the CEO as the most likely overriding cause. It is not a function of market circumstances or other lucky breaks "out there," for those factors can be relied upon only in the short term. A highly competent CEO takes advantage of changing market conditions, creates opportunities out of new situations and new technologies and sustains a team of competent subordinates in a rich talent pool. Our argument is that in order to get effective leadership and excellence at the top, there is one essential condition that must be met; namely, competence at a level required by the work (pp. 36-37).

What Jaques and Clement are suggesting is that the critical individual difference variable in leader effectiveness is the conceptual competence to do the required work. Good leaders are, first and foremost, competent to undertake their leadership responsibilities. Poor leaders are not. For this reason leader personality style is given little emphasis in SST. A leader's awareness of his or her preferred style and that of others may marginally improve communication, but it will not, ultimately, get the right decisions made.

It must be acknowledged that a number of respected, contemporary leadership theorists make a strong case for including preferences and values among the individual difference variables associated with leader effectiveness (Hunt, 1991; Gardner and Schermerhorn, this book; Sashkin, this book). Sashkin (this book), for example, asserts that a broadly conceived power motive is essential for leader effectiveness. However, Sashkin also acknowledges that individuals lacking a strong need for power seldom put themselves in leadership positions. Hence, even though need for power may be an important characteristic of senior leaders, it is not likely to be an important differential predictor of leader effectiveness. The same argument might well be made with regard to the predictive utility of self-efficacy, another key leader capability identified by Sashkin (this book) and Cowan, Fiol, and Walsh (this book). Most senior leaders are likely to be high in self-efficacy; they believe they can be an effective agent of change in their work role. In line with the position quoted above by Jaques and Clement (1991), whether they actually turn out to be effective has to do with their competence in role, not their belief about their potential efficacy.

If we were to stop here, we would be at risk for creating a useless tautology. It would go something like this: Leader effectiveness is a function of leader competence. What is leader competence? That which makes leaders effective. Fortunately, Stratified Systems Theory (Jacobs and Jaques, 1987; Jaques, 1976, 1989; Jaques and Clement, 1991) provides a way out of this potential conundrum by specifying the essential nature of managerial work. Key to this specification is the idea that the nature of managerial work is qualitatively different at each of several successive organizational levels. As one moves up the organizational hierarchy, the nature of the critical tasks at each successive level undergoes qualitative changes. In Stratified Systems Theory this specification of level of work is linked directly to specification of the conceptual requirements needed to do that work. For this reason, leader competence can be specified a priori in terms of the conceptual requirements inherent in the level of work required by the leader's principal job tasks. These conceptual requirements become the basis for judging a critical component of individual differences in leader competence, conceptual capacity. The interested reader is referred to Jacobs's and Lewis's chapter in this volume for an overview of Stratified Systems Theory.

THE "CONSTRUCTIVE" NATURE OF STRATEGIC LEADERSHIP CAPACITY

Behavioral science in general and psychology in particular have been hampered by a tendency to view leader capacity in terms of the possession of requisite skills and behaviors. While useful, behavioral approaches to the assessment of leader capacity ignore a fundamental feature of human experience. Human beings do not respond directly to an objective, "real" world. Rather, humans actively "construct" a view of the world that then becomes the world within which they live and work (Kegan, 1982). As such, adults generally live in a "larger" world than do children. Similarly, executives or strategic leaders generally live in a "larger" world than do supervisors or first-line managers. The crucial point is that strategic leaders behave differently than lower level leaders not principally because they have better managerial skills but because they "see" more than others see. If we accept the central proposition of Stratified Systems Theory that managerial work becomes more complex as one moves up the organizational hierarchy, then the ability to represent that work cognitively becomes the critical feature of leadership capacity. Strategic leaders must have the capacity to represent conceptually, through considerable periods of time, the highly complex, volatile, and probabilistic environments within which they are expected to operate. Lacking the capacity to construct such a "vision," they are likely to fail.

How can leader differences in these "constructive" capacities be best understood? Two different, but related, answers to this question will be offered. The first is derived from the constructive/developmental theory of Kegan, a psychologist working at Harvard University (Kegan, 1982; Kegan and Lahey, 1984). The second is provided by Stratified Systems Theory, particularly as presented in Jaques's and Clement's (1991) recent book on executive leadership. A brief summary of the two approaches will be followed by a summary of preliminary research examining the level of conceptual development found in a sample of highly successful military officers.

THE DEVELOPMENT OF PERSPECTIVE

Kegan, writing about the process by which people construct meaning across the life span, has presented an elegant and comprehensive theory about how people develop increasingly broad perspectives of themselves in relation to the world (Kegan, 1982). He has identified five major levels or stages in the progression from a narrow, sensory-based perspective found in infancy to a broad, transcendent perspective found (only rarely) in late adulthood. Most adults function at Kegan's third stage, which is characterized by the use of shared or "coconstructed" frames of reference (Kegan, 1982), which require the capacity to consider two perspectives simultaneously. Those who manage to develop beyond this stage of consensually shared perspectives do so by personally constructing a frame of reference that they can bring to bear on the coconstructed or shared frames characteristic of the earlier stage. Achievement of this fourth stage in the development of meaning frameworks imparts a capacity for independent thought that is lacking at earlier stages. Individuals at this fourth stage can think about, rather than thinking with, consensual points of view.

It is in this metacognitive sense that Kegan's stage 4 thinking is broader than thinking at developmentally earlier stages. Being able to think reflectively about shared views also imparts psychological independence or differentiation of the self from, and objectivity about, those shared views. Stated slightly differently, individuals who have achieved Kegan's fourth stage of meaning making have the capacity to operate their own judgmental processes unconstrained by the standards, values, or points of view of others. The nature of the work at strategic levels would appear to require just such a capacity.

LEVEL OF THINKING PROCESSES

A somewhat different view of conceptual capacity is contained in the latest version of Stratified Systems Theory (Jaques and Clement, 1991). As indicated above, Stratified Systems Theory suggests that successively more complex levels of managerial work require successively more complex thinking processes. If you put someone into a leadership position for which that person lacks the requisite thinking processes, he or she will be unable to do the job. Jaques and Clement (1991) provide the first comprehensive summary of the nature of the thinking processes that they believe are required to do successive levels of managerial work. They describe four hierarchically ordered reasoning processes that, when combined with four orders of conceptual abstraction, combine to yield distinctly different, hierarchically ordered ways of processing information. Although in theory this combination yields sixteen categories or levels of cognitive processing (four ways of processing information by four levels of abstraction), only eight are relevant to the assessment of managerial capacity. These eight correspond to the eight levels of work or task complexity identified in Jaques's theory of organizational hierarchy (Jaques, 1976).

The four levels of abstraction identified by Jaques and Clement (1991) are (1) simple denotation, (2) symbolic labeling, (3) abstract conceptualization, and (4) universalization. Most managerial work at lower organizational levels can be accomplished by using symbolic labeling (the use of symbolic labels for elements that have concrete referents). However, at higher managerial levels, conceptual information processing is typically required (the use of abstract conceptual models that do not translate directly to concrete elements). So, for example, while midlevel managers can understand their work using such analytic tools as performance targets, turnover rates, and monthly sales figures, the work of upper-level managers requires use of abstract concepts such as resource depreciation, talent pool development, and community infrastructure. Unlike the former, none of these latter concepts can be directly decomposed into concrete events.

The second dimension used by Jaques and Clement to describe hierarchical differences in thinking processes concerns how information (at different levels of abstraction) is put together. The simplest process is declarative. The person merely asserts or declares the validity of a particular idea or situation, for example, "Quality is job one" or "The customer is always right." At the next level of complexity there is a process that entails the accumulation of relevant data in support of an idea or view that at the previous level was only asserted, not supported with data. In other words, the individual reaches conclusions by systematically amassing data relevant to the decision alternatives being considered. When arguing for a particular decision, the individual who uses this thought process not only asserts the validity of the preferred alternative, but also marshals evidence in support of it. For example, she or he might assert, "We've got to keep pushing product quality because if we don't, our competitors are going to use quality differences to achieve a competitive advantage."

At the third level of complexity identified by Jaques and Clement (1991), the individual thinks by using serial processing, putting information together in a sequential form where events are connected through time and lead to an envisioned conclusion. The individual using serial processing might argue for a particular decision as follows:

> We used to emphasize volume of output at the expense of quality. And we got the reputation of making an affordable but lower-quality product. That was fine until the Japanese came into the market with a comparably priced product that was of higher quality. Then we had to play catch-up with the Japanese for several years. Now we're competitive again, but if we don't emphasize quality from the start with this new product, we're going to be right where we were before, when the Japanese come in with their version of the product.

The most sophisticated thinking process identified by Jaques and Clement is what they term "parallel processing." This entails organizing information into a number of separate serial processes and then dealing with the information in each process in parallel with the other processes. Explicit linkages are made among ongoing parallel processes.

An individual using parallel processing might construct an argument somewhat as follows: "You see, there are two fundamental issues here, quality control and unit cost. You've got to have quality control because when we didn't have it from the start, we were forced to build it in later when the Japanese came into the market. And unit cost has to be kept down, too, because you can bet that there's somebody out there who will figure out how to do it cheaper. But you can handle that if you build in your start-up costs to come out of the first couple of years. Then you can begin reducing your prices after the start-up costs have been absorbed. But if you fail to build in quality from the start, then just when you need to begin reducing prices to meet competition, you have to start paying more attention to quality, and that keeps your costs too high to be able to lower prices." Here we have a speaker who not only presents serial arguments about quality and unit cost but also explicitly links the two arguments.

It should be noted that each of the four examples given above was couched in terms that fall at Jaques's and Clement's second order of abstraction, where the concepts used (competition, product quality, customer satisfaction, and unit cost) all have concrete referents. In other words, one could point to concrete data or events that reflect the abstract concept being used. As such, the four examples illustrate thought processes considered to be requisite at Jaques's Levels I, II, III, and IV (Jaques, 1976). Work at Level V, the general manager level, and higher levels is thought to require the use of abstract conceptual models that do not have direct concrete referents. The move from bottom line to balance sheet accounting illustrates this transition from symbolic to conceptual modeling.

These ideas about the progressively more sophisticated thinking processes considered by Jaques and Clement (1991) to be necessary for effective functioning at successive organizational levels are an interesting extension of SST. They have promise for providing an alternative to time span of discretion as an index of managerial capacity.

PRELIMINARY RESEARCH ON CONCEPTUAL CAPACITY

We turn now to a research project conducted by the present authors that explored the conceptual capacities of fast-track military officers and civilian managers and examined the convergence between breadth of perspective and the SST concept of conceptual work potential. The project focused upon the executive capacity of an opportunity sample of forty-eight war college students and was conducted at the U.S. Army War College and the Industrial College of the Armed Forces.

The first issue to be explored was whether these midlevel leaders could be reliably assessed for breadth of perspective. If they could be reliably assessed, were they all functioning at a level of self-definition, or were a significant number still psychologically embedded in a shared context? The assessment approach, closely related to the subject/object interview of Kegan and his colleagues at Harvard University (Lahey et al., 1988), focused upon the extent to which each war college student was able to bring an independent frame of reference to bear on his or her work experiences. Interrater reliability was established, and Lewis assessed each student, using an intensive, interactive interview.

On the basis of these interviews, it was determined that only about half of the students sampled had differentiated themselves from their work to a point where they could view their work environment objectively, that is, from outside the organizational context within which it was taking place. The other half were prone to using prevailing organizational ''wisdom'' to construct an understanding of their work context. To borrow a term from Piagetian theory, half of the study participants were unable to ''decenter'' from the shared organizational or interpersonal frames of reference prevalent in their work setting. Lacking the capacity independently to construct a frame of reference that could encompass and thereby transcend prevailing organizational views, these individuals were unable to ''see'' their work organizations in broader terms. While only descriptive (i.e., the predictive utility of the interview ratings was not examined), these findings suggested that breadth of perspective is one way that highly successful midlevel leaders differ from one another in terms of the level of sophistication of their conceptual processes. Furthermore, preliminary results suggest that there may be a surprisingly strong link between Kegan's concept of the differentiation of self or breadth of perspective and Jaques's concept of conceptual work capacity.

Using a variation of Stamp's interview measure (Stamp, 1986), Jacobs assessed the current work capacity of twenty-eight of the forty-eight war college students who participated in the breadth of perspective interviews. Stamp's measure of work capacity is based directly on SST's view of the nature and development of cognitive capacity, or what Jaques (1989) has termed "conceptual work capacity." This conceptual work capacity interview is quite different in structure from the interview used by Lewis to assess breadth of perspective. While the breadth of perspective interview consists of asking a series of "why" questions designed to elicit the interviewee's broadest frame of reference for viewing significant work incidents, the work capacity interview is much more structured. The conceptual work capacity interview consists of three parts: responses to a series of phrase cards, a problem-solving task, and a work history. The conceptual work capacity interview yields an estimate of each individual's current highest conceptual work capacity, expressed in terms of the eight SST work strata.

Twenty-four of the twenty-five military officers interviewed by Jacobs had successfully completed a battalion command or its equivalent (one naval officer had not yet commanded a ship, though he had been selected to do so), and the three civilians interviewed by Jacobs had been successful program managers. Such positions are thought to represent the highest level of direct leadership and are at the top of Jaques's third stratum of work complexity (Jacobs and Jaques, 1987). Not surprisingly, therefore, Jacobs found that the lowest level of current work capacity of his twenty-eight interviewees was at the top of Jaques's third level of work complexity (Level III). Eight of Jacobs's interviewees were determined to have a conceptual capacity at this level. A larger group of Jacobs's interviewees (N = 16) showed the conceptual capacity to handle work at Jaques's fourth level of work complexity (Stratum IV), what has been broadly defined as the lower of two levels of "organizational" work (Jacobs and Jaques, 1987). The remainder (N = 4) demonstrated the capacity to think about work, using conceptual skills equal to the complexity of high-level "organizational" work (SST's Level V).

Overall, Jacobs found that two-thirds of the highly successful direct leaders whom he interviewed already showed the conceptual capacity to function at indirect leadership levels. This finding is consistent with Jaques's notion that there are advantages to having a conceptual work capacity that somewhat exceeds one's current conceptual work requirements (Jaques, 1989). This allows incumbents to understand more fully the nature of their superior's work context and requirements. It is also quite possible that senior raters, who can generally be expected to have higher work capacities than their average subordinate, recognize and value high work capacity in their subordinates and provide stronger performance evaluations for their higher-capacity subordinates. Both mechanisms would be expected to yield high performance ratings for higher-capacity officers, performance ratings of the sort needed to gain admittance to the war colleges.

Perhaps the most intriguing finding of the executive capacity study was the strong positive correlation between the SST measure of work capacity (as assessed independently by Jacobs) and the Kegan measure of breadth of perspective (as assessed independently by Lewis). Despite the fact that there was a restricted range of scores on both measures (from Kegan's stage 3 to stage 4 on the breadth of perspective measure and from Jaques's high-Level III to mid-Level V on the current work capacity measure), the product-moment correlation between the two was .59. Given the restricted ranges and the fact that the two assessment procedures are directed toward the assessment of conceptually distinct cognitive capacities (breadth of perspective versus conceptual work capacity), the strength of the relationship is most surprising. One possible interpretation of this finding is that there may be a structural capacity that underlies both breadth of perspective and current work capacity.

Another possibility, suggested by the pattern of results obtained (see Figure 8.1), is that one must achieve a certain independence of thought before one can develop the conceptual capacity to handle highly complex managerial work. Inspection of the pattern of results shown in Figure 8.1 suggests that in general, unless one has attained a full stage 4 breadth of perspective, high levels of conceptual work capacity will not be present. This finding is somewhat puzzling, since to be scored at the

Figure 8.1
Conceptual Work Capacity as a Function of Breadth of Perspective for Twenty-eight War College Students

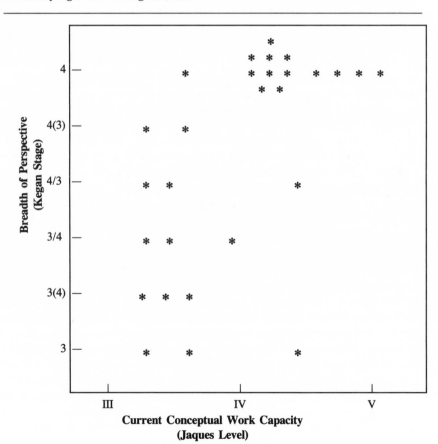

transition points shown as 3/4, 4/3, and 4(3) in Figure 8.1, subjects must demonstrate that they can exercise a stage 4 independence of thought in some circumstances. Even though they also show that they are still susceptible to reverting to narrower, stage 3 thinking, they appear to possess the structural capacity for broader, stage 4 thought. One interpretation of the pattern of results shown in Figure 8.1 is that only those subjects who are not at risk for being drawn back into narrower, shared points of view are likely to be judged as having the conceptual capacity thought to be necessary to handle the demands of indirect leadership positions. This finding is most intriguing and is being investigated further by the present authors.

The finding that virtually all the individuals who showed the conceptual capacity to operate as indirect leaders had achieved independence of thought (Kegan's stage 4) bears directly on one of the criticisms leveled at SST by Boal and Whitehead (this book). They suggest that because SST indicates that conceptual capacity develops within an organization's existing structure and process, organizational leaders are embedded in organizational frames of reference that may prove inadequate during times of rapid changes in the strategic environment. Boal and Whitehead suggest that these "embedded" leaders cannot be expected to generate "frame-breaking" organizational changes. The data presented above suggest that Boal and Whitehead's contention is not, in fact, typically true of leaders who possess organizational level (Level IV and Level V) leadership capacity. Of the sixteen war college students who were identified by Jacobs as showing a conceptual work capacity equal to work at mid-Level IV and higher, only three had failed to achieve a full stage 4 breadth of perspective. The hallmark of stage 4 functioning in the assessment process used in the Lewis and Jacobs study was the capacity to construct an independent perspective on important events at work. In other words, more than 80 percent of those individuals who could be expected to function effectively at the so-called indirect or organizational domain of leadership (Jacobs and Jaques, 1987) demonstrated a lack of embeddedness in the organizational context.

PRACTICAL IMPLICATIONS

That both theories of the nature of cognitive capacity described herein are couched in hierarchical developmental terms has a number of implications for the selection and development of strategic leaders. Foremost is the idea that the conceptual capacities required for strategic leadership are probably not a matter of individual differences in conceptual style or conceptual preference. Rather, strategic leadership competence with regard to the capacity to construct a broad and complex understanding of the strategic environment is a function of the achievement of a high level of conceptual development. Stated in terms of the two theories briefly described above, strategic leadership potential is, first and foremost, a function of the capacity for generating an independent perspective on the strategic environment (Kegan, 1982) and thinking using abstract conceptual models (Jaques and Clement, 1991).

Second, since progressively higher managerial levels require progressively more complex ways of conceptualizing the strategic environment and one's relationship to that environment, success at one's current level of work is not necessarily predictive of success at higher levels of work (Jaques and Clement, 1991). Failure to assess a promotion candidate's capacity to understand the conceptual demands of the higher position will result in a significant number of "Peter Principle" (Peter, 1969) promotions, where the newly promoted manager lacks the conceptual capacity effectively to carry out critical features of the new role. Such promotions can be very costly to the organization and to the incumbent who must struggle to accomplish work for which he or she lacks the requisite conceptual tools. The new leader's lack of conceptual grasp is not always easily detected, partly because the inadequate decisions that result from the lack of conceptual grasp may not yield negative outcomes for many months or even years and, particularly, because at the executive level the incumbent's high motivation, technical knowledge, and interpersonal skills may cause one to look elsewhere for the cause of the emerging problems. Unfortunately, most organizations lack the expertise needed to assess work level (the conceptual demands of work at each organizational level) and, particularly, the expertise needed to assess conceptual level (the conceptual capacity of managers who are expected to work at each level). As a result, poor hiring and promotion decision are made with alarming regularity. The resulting cascading effects of managerial incompetence can be disastrous.

TRAINING VERSUS DEVELOPMENT

Our constructive-developmental view of managerial conceptual capacity has implications not only for selection decisions, but also for managerial training and development programs. Most important is the implication that skill-based training programs are not likely to have a significant impact on managers' conceptual capacity. In contrast, management development programs may prove useful. Our distinction between training and development rests on an important distinction between skills and capacities (Sashkin, this book). Skills are typically defined as relatively discrete behaviors that can be taught, using standard instructional methods. Capacities (or, as Sashkin calls them, capabilities) are an individual's ways of construing experience and his or her relatively enduring motivational features. Capabilities are relatively impervious to training and change slowly over extended periods of time. Slow and progressive changes in the way a person constructs experience occur not primarily as a result of being taught better ways of making sense of the world but, instead, in response to directly experiencing the limitations of one's current way of making sense of experience (Kegan, 1982).

The reason traditional instructional methods typically fail to have an impact on conceptual capacity is that the information presented can often be assimilated to the student's current cognitive structures. When they cannot, the instructional materials are typically such a small part of the individuals' experience that persons can compartmentalize the resulting dissonance and thereby avoid changing their fundamental conceptual orientation to their larger world. Only when one experiences a failure to master one's larger world is there the possibility that one's views of the world will expand. The heart of managerial development, therefore, should be the planned assignment of high-potential leaders and managers to successively more challenging work roles where a mentor is present who can help the individual better understand the new, more complicated world in which the new manager must now operate. Here again, the organization must have the expertise needed to assess both the manager's current level of conceptual capacity and the conceptual demands of the proposed developmental position. Too often, such "developmental" job changes result in a change in the nature of one's responsibilities (e.g., a move from logistics to personnel) without any change in the level of conceptual demands in the new position. Such job transfers may require the individual to learn a new job content, but they will not require a more complex mode of thinking. Accordingly, little managerial development will result.

SUMMARY AND CONCLUSIONS

In this chapter we have argued that the fundamental individual difference variable that most often distinguishes successful strategic leaders from unsuccessful ones is the extent to which leaders' conceptual capacity meets or exceeds the conceptual demands inherent in their work. Those promoted to strategic leadership positions typically already possess the requisite interpersonal and technical skills needed to be successful. These skills and the motivation to lead will usually already have been amply demonstrated at lower managerial levels. What is often not known is whether the new strategic leader has the conceptual capacity to grasp the complexity, scope, ambiguity, and volatility of the circumstances that must be grasped if sound decisions are to be made at the strategic level. The reason organizations typically lack this information is that the nature of managerial work changes qualitatively as one moves from one organizational level to the next. This qualitative difference in the nature of work at various levels is thought to demand qualitatively different thinking skills. For this reason demonstrated competence at an individual's current level of work may reveal little about that individual's capacity to grasp the nature of the work at higher levels.

One absolutely fundamental requirement for effective promotion decisions, particularly at senior levels, is the assessment of the conceptual capacity of the candidate for promotion (or selection), in conjunction with an assessment of the conceptual demands of the new position (since the new position, while a "promotion," may not actually represent a higher level of work, as defined in Stratified Systems Theory). Furthermore, since conceptual capacity, in our view, has to do with the way in which persons construct an understanding of their experience, it cannot be assessed using passive assessment approaches, such as standard paper-and-pencil questionnaires. Assessment approaches are needed that require an active organization of complex, ambiguous stimuli of the sort encountered in managerial work. Such approaches are the sine qua non of the assessment of conceptual capacity (cf. Streufert and Nogami, 1989).

We have also asserted that conceptual capacity develops slowly in response to real world experiences that call into question the adequacy of one's current best way of making sense of the world and one's own relationship to that world. This developmental view of conceptual capacity differs from the maturational view contained in SST. But until we make systematic attempts to modify conceptual capacity (based, of course, on a clear conception of just what it is), we will not know if increases in conceptual capacity can be systematically developed or accelerated. Our hierarchical, developmental view of the growth of conceptual capacity has implications for training and development efforts. Skill-based training programs are not likely to result in appreciable changes in conceptual capacity. What should be more effective in promoting the development of the conceptual development of managers is the provision of challenging job assignments that require an upward revision of thinking and envisioning processes. Such an upward revision can be best accomplished if there is a mentor available who possesses the required conceptual skills at a level that allows the mentor to communicate them effectively to the manager being mentored.

Theories concerning the conceptual demands of progressive levels of managerial work and the requisite cognitive capacities to master those levels of work complexity are in their infancy. In this chapter we have identified two promising approaches, the Stratified Systems Theory of Jaques and his colleagues and the constructive developmental theory of Kegan. We have also presented preliminary research suggesting that the development of conceptual work capacity as defined in SST (Jaques and Clement, 1991) and differentiation of self as defined by Kegan (Lahey et al., 1988) are related and that a level of differentiation of self that imparts independence of thought may be requisite for the development of higher levels of conceptual work capacity. This research is continuing, and it is hoped that it and other efforts will yield assessment and development methodologies that will make it possible in the not too distant future to ensure that individuals occupying critical decision-making positions have the conceptual competence to make sound decisions. The world of work will be much the better for such efforts.

9

Strategic Leadership Competencies
Marshall Sashkin

Sashkin's chapter does a very nice job of discussing the importance of understanding strategic leadership by using a whole panopoly of what he terms competencies, namely, behavioral skills and the three competencies of cognitive complexity, self-efficacy, and power motive. He discusses each of these and their interaction in great detail and shows their role in his visionary leadership theory. That theory, while not inconsistent with SST, extends SST notions in very interesting and insightful ways and includes an emphasis on culture building through visionary symbolic leadership. Particularly important are Sashkin's comments concerning leader development and training within the combined context of SST and his own work.

I have become increasingly convinced of two facts relevant to the Stratified Systems Theory approach developed by Jaques (1986) and elaborated more recently in several publications by Jacobs and Jaques (1987, 1990, 1991). First, I am certain that the cognitive complexity variable (first identified as "time span of discretion" and often still labeled as such) is crucial for understanding the nature of organizational leadership (and for the practice of leadership, as well). Second, I am convinced that this factor is not the only one responsible for leadership effectiveness (or failure), but that there are other, noncognitive, individual psychological variables that are crucial for effective organizational leadership (as well as behavioral-skill and social-organizational factors).

I will use my own leadership approach, "visionary leadership theory," or VLT, as the central organizing framework for this presentation. While it would be nice to think that readers will find my own approach even more useful and sound than Stratified Systems Theory, my aim is more modest: I hope only to convince the reader that visionary leadership theory can be a useful adjunct to Stratified Systems Theory, an approach with which visionary leadership is highly compatible.

There is, in fact, a more pragmatic reason than either my personal preference or the general compatibility between SST and VLT for using VLT as an underlying framework for this chapter. That is, SST is lacking in the clarity with which it permits a description of how leaders, especially those at higher systems levels, actually go about constructing and operating organizational structures. Visionary leadership theory does not conflict with SST notions but instead adds to SST a more concrete understanding of how leaders actually carry out leadership tasks at various organizational strata. Thus, another aim of the present chapter is clarification of how leaders actually lead. I will show how certain competencies are used by leaders at higher organizational levels to construct organizational cultures (Sashkin, 1984; Schein, 1985).

In Jaques's (1979, 1986) theory the CEO of an organization is typically at the sixth level or "stratum." In the present analysis I have chosen to ignore lower-level strata (I through IV) and to concentrate on Strata V and VI. The reason is that leadership, as used here, does not really apply at lower organizational levels. At those levels, often called supervisory and middle management levels, what is going on can, for the most part, be described as supervision and management. These are certainly legitimate and important areas for study and action, but they are quite different from leadership. (See Sashkin and Fulmer, 1988, for more detail about this distinction which is there referred to as the difference between "operational" and "executive" leadership.)

A QUICK SKETCH OF STRATIFIED SYSTEMS THEORY

SST is an approach developed by Jaques (1986, 1989) and extended by Jacobs and Jaques (1987, 1990). It is based on Jaques's (1986) "general theory of bureaucracy," which postulates that organizations can be thought of as composed of six levels or "strata." At each stratum the primary tasks and activities of organization members are similar in that they require a typical time span.

The reason for using the term *strata* is that each stratum is separate and apart from its neighbors in a qualitative sense. Thus, it makes sense to speak of a range of time span for activities of increasing complexity within a particular stratum, but not across strata; discontinuities exist at strata boundaries, because the nature of task activities differs qualitatively from one stratum to the next. At Stratum III, for example, managers create and carry out plans to implement policies that have been developed at higher levels. That is, they define and implement ways to carry out fairly clear assignments. In contrast, at Stratum V, executive leaders are in charge of operating an entire, complex organization. This means defining the ways that the various task activities being carried out at lower levels fit together and are coordinated to attain a larger aim.

Individuals operating at different strata require different levels of what Jaques initially called "time span of discretion." Later, that term was reserved to describe the key characteristic of task activity at different strata. Other terms used to refer to this individual capability include conceptual complexity, conceptual skill requirements; the ability to build cognitive maps and, on the basis of those maps, make effective decisions; abstract analytic and integrative skills; and, most simply, thinking skills. All of the above terms are used by Jacobs and Jaques in the same paper to refer to the same thing, which I shall call "cognitive complexity."

Although the basic outline of SST is relatively straightforward, the apparent isomorphism between task characteristics and the individual characteristic can generate confusion. Moreover, many important details are less than perfectly clear (e.g., the exact nature of tasks within each stratum, especially at higher levels). The beauty of the theory is that it provides a new way of understanding the nature of leadership, both in the sense of a personal characteristic and in terms of organizational tasks.

In this chapter I build on SST in three ways. First, I define in concrete detail the specific behavioral skills and activities of leaders at Strata V and VI. Second, I extend the set of personal characteristics required for effective leadership. Third, I define in more specific terms the strategic tasks of leaders at Strata V and VI and show how they apply certain behavioral skills and how they make use of the personal characteristics I have defined to exercise effective executive leadership.

A SLIGHTLY JADED LOOK AT COMPETENCIES

The recent popularity of "competencies" in management is just another of the many fads to which the study and practice of management have been subject over the past few decades. As such, it is good that the fad is dying down. I say this for two specific reasons, each relating to a serious flaw in the approach to competencies that has typically been followed. First, competency approaches have typically failed to distinguish among behavioral skills, knowledge, and personal characteristics or traits. This is a critical flaw; skills and knowledge are, for the most part, learnable, often with relatively little effort, while characteristics may or may not be modifiable and traits are typically thought of as relatively fixed aspects of individuals' personality structures.

Second, there is an even more severe problem with respect to the so-called validation of competencies. What generally takes place is the identification of high and low performers as midlevel managers. This identification is often acomplished by methods that are questionable, if not obviously flawed. For example, performance ratings might be used to identify individuals in each group. Performance ratings, however, are notoriously inaccurate as measures of actual performance achievement. An alternative approach often used is to have superiors nominate exceptional performers. Again, such a process is inherently fraught with bias. What happens next is worse: superiors are interviewed and asked to identify the characteristics of the high performers that separate them from average or poor performers. This procedure, of course, simply compounds the potential for bias, bringing in the superiors' own "implicit" theories of leadership and performance, which may have little or nothing to do with real performance (e.g., see Eden and Leviatan, 1975).

The first flaw can be avoided by understanding the differences between, and by carefully separating, behavioral skill competencies and "competencies" that are actually personal characteristics, perhaps even traits. To use the competency concept in a meaningful and valid way, it is crucial to distinguish between what I will call "skills" and what I refer to as "personal capabilities." The second problem of validity can be addressed by ensuring that competencies are identified and validated on the basis of sound, quantitative research. Both of these requirements, separating behavioral skills from personal characteristics and using well-designed, quantitative research as the basis for selection and validation of competencies, are part of visionary leadership theory.

BEHAVIORAL SKILLS AS LEADERSHIP COMPETENCIES

Our understanding of behavioral skill leadership competencies comes from both empirical studies of the specific actions of leaders describing instances of exceptional leadership (e.g., Kouzes and Posner, 1987) and more theory-based examination of the nature of leadership activity (e.g., Bennis and Nanus, 1985; Sashkin and Burke, 1990). These independent sources converge on a relatively small set of behavior categories. While the specific behaviors within each category vary somewhat, depending on the SST stratum, both categories and specific behaviors are stable when we confine ourselves to Strata V and VI[1]. Later on I will necessarily turn back to the topic of behavioral skill competencies. My primary concern in this chapter is with the personal capabilities side of the competency concept, for this is of special relevance and importance to Stratified Systems Theory.

PERSONAL CAPABILITIES AS LEADERSHIP COMPETENCIES

Many people think that Stogdill's (1948) classic review of personality research and leadership concluded only that there was no evidence for any such personality characteristics. This is not so. In fact, Stogdill observed that while there was no single trait or small number of traits that clearly and strongly stood out, there was some evidence for certain trait clusters. Several of the clusters Stogdill identified are similar to one or another of the five factors that are coming to be regarded as the primary dimensions of personality (Digman, 1990). Both Stogdill's clusters and these "big five" personality factors are related to the three personal capabilities I shall discuss.

One of these three personal capabilities central to my approach is none other than the SST variable, cognitive complexity. The second, self-efficacy, comes out of social learning theory as developed for the past two decades by Bandura (1977b, 1982, 1986b, 1988) and his associates. The third is a construct developed by McClelland (1975) and his associates (McClelland and Burnham, 1976; Winter,

1973, 1987): the need for power directed in a socially productive manner. These three capabilities, all of which are malleable, at least to a degree, are prerequisite to the successful application of behavioral skill competencies (which are generally much easier to develop).

As each of these three personal capabilities is examined, bear in mind that the sense in which they are requisite or required for effective leadership is not simply a conceptual abstraction. These capabilities are requisite in the sense that only through actions based on using and applying these competencies can leaders effectively construct or change organizational cultures.

Cognitive Complexity

Cognitive complexity is the central and, until recently, the sole individual variable in Jaques's theory (Jaques, 1979; Jaques and Clement, 1991). It is not, however, adequate for a complete or a practically useful understanding of leadership or leadership effectiveness in organizations. There are at least two other very important personal capabilities, variables not recognized in SST but, nonetheless, critical competencies for organizational leadership: self-efficacy (used by others in this book) and the need for power directed in a socially productive manner.

Self-Efficacy

This term, coined by Bandura (1977b, 1982, 1986b, 1988), refers to one's belief in oneself as an effective "agent" in (and on) one's environment. Thus, some speak of this construct as "agency theory." In many respects, self-efficacy is very similar to internal control (Rotter, 1966). That is, self-efficacious individuals believe that they can control or have an impact on their world by what they do, by means of their own actions. In one sense, self-efficacy is little more than self-confidence, yet self-confidence may be based on little more than hope and narcissism. In contrast, self-efficacy is the result of life experiences that teach one that one can, in fact, take actions that will effectively have an impact on one's environment.

The concept of self-efficacy is deeply interwoven with that of the self-fulfilling prophecy (Eden, 1990; Merton, 1948; Rosenthal, 1976). Consider a child whose teacher says, "I expect that you will be in the top 10 percent of this class." The child's study of the subject matter is followed by high test scores and good grades. Thus, the child learns that he or she can control his or her academic success. This is more than simple self-confidence; it is consequence of action—study—for which belief in the possibility of success was prerequisite.

Now consider a child whose teacher exhibits low expectations of him or her. It has been repeatedly shown that in such circumstances children perform poorly;

having concluded that success is not possible, the child chooses not to study. Performance is, unsurprisingly, poor, fulfilling the teacher's prophecy.

What really was the cause in the first case? Was it the child's agency assumptions, or was it the child's study habits? What was the cause in the second case? Was it the child's conclusion that he or she could not perform as an effective agent in the school environment? Or was it simply failure to study? In both cases it was both the belief and the action. Self-efficacy is prerequisite, but if the child had not studied, self-confidence would not by itself have resulted in good grades. Had the second child studied, he or she might have achieved good grades, but the teacher's actions, communicating low expectations and thus reducing the child's sense of self-efficacy, helped to ensure that the child would not study and would not, therefore, achieve good grades.

Without the foundation provided by self-efficacy, individuals can and do assume that nothing they do will make a difference; the next logical step is to do nothing. Without a strong sense of self-efficacy, it is unlikely for a person willingly to take on a leadership role or to want to be a leader.

Power Motive

McClelland (1975; McClelland and Burnham, 1976) showed that (1) it is the need for power, not achievement, that characterizes successful managers in organizations and (2) the need for power has "two faces," one that looks to others as the independent means by which organizational success is achieved, the other that looks to people as implements to be used to further one's own self-centered desires.

It should not be assumed that leaders have no need to achieve. By direct measure, leaders' need for achievement is generally at least moderate. Leaders, however, attain their greatest achievements by means of power and influence. Possession of a high need for power, socially directed, reflects a sophisticated understanding of the nature of achievement in organizations, since the leader recognizes that it is through power and influence that things are accomplished by and in organizations. But to achieve through power requires a certain level of maturity and development.

By a low or immature level of development, McClelland means that the person's sense of self depends on seeing that he or she can have an impact on others by means of control over them. A low level of development of the need for power, in terms of McClelland's (1975) four-stage model, is characterized by a very high power need accompanied by low "activity inhibition" or "impulse contol." This simply means that the individual is not able to delay gratification of needs and acts upon impulse to obtain what he or she believes will bring immediate gratification. Combined with a very high power need, low impulse control indicates that the person is indiscriminate in his or her use of power to attain what are primarily personal, not organizational, goals.

Regardless of level of development, the need for power is characteristic of individuals who strive for positions of leadership in the organization. Absent this need, most individuals would not act to put themselves in leadership positions. Activity inhibition is independent of power need, so individuals with low activity inhibition may well become high-level executives—that is where the power is. Research conducted by McClelland (1975) and his associates (McClelland and Boyatzis, 1982; McClelland and Burnham, 1976) shows, however, that long-term success and effectiveness as a leader are typically achieved only when high activity inhibition accompanies a strong power need. McClelland and Boyatzis (1982) labeled this combination the "leadership motive syndrome."

The leadership motive syndrome permits the power need to be directed in a "prosocial" manner, toward the attainment of organizational goals that benefit many, if not all, organization members, not only the leader. Without activity inhibition, a strong power need is apt to be aimed at the immediate gratification of an individual's narcissistic (self-serving) impulses.

Interactions of the Three Personal Capabilities

I have already implicitly referred to some of the ways in which the three personal capabilities interact. All three are requisite elements for successful leadership. Deficit in any one of the three will surely limit greatly, if not doom, an individual's capacity to function effectively as a leader.

As already noted, without a strong sense of internal control or direction—self-efficacy—a person would simply not act as a leader, or at all, for that matter, regardless of the level of cognitive complexity present. It might be argued that a high level of cognitive complexity, commensurate, for example, with the requirements for Stratum IV or higher, would automatically show the individual that his or her actions could have consequences. This is not an unreasonable assertion, but it is by no means proven. Moreover, the research is quite clear in showing that self-efficacy is a learned motive pattern. Intellectual insight, no matter how powerful, may not be sufficient for effective leadership absent the sort of experiences that provide a person with evidence that he or she can (at least to a degree) control his or her world.

A leader without a strong and mature need for power will not and cannot use social influence processes in organizations to empower members to achieve organizational aims. Such a prosocial learned power motive pattern derives from a learned developmental process (McClelland, 1975). It is crucial not merely because the absence of a strong need for power, socially directed, would leave one uninterested in (unmotivated toward) the design of organizational structures and achievements, but persons not at this level of power motive development cannot understand how people are enlisted—by being empowered—in efforts to accomplish major organizational aims and thus cannot effectively implement organizational visions, no matter how sophisticated those visions may be in concept.

MOTIVE AND MEANS

It should now be obvious that the personal capabilities I have discussed are actually of two very different, but equally important, types. Jaques (1986, 1989) deals with one type, the cognitive capability. I believe that a second, motivational type of variable is also crucial for effective organizational leadership. Thus, I assert that these motivational, affective factors—self-efficacy and need for power (n Pow)/pro-social—are prerequisite for effective leadership in organizations.

Cognitive complexity is a means for constructing social systems that can attain certain organizational aims (or visions). As such, it is prerequisite for leadership success, but while necessary it is not sufficient. Unless an individual has the requisite self-efficacy, he or she will simply not bother to undertake any actions to implement his or her vision, no matter how acute that vision due to a high level of cognitive complexity. Such a person may dream grand dreams, but they will remain just that, dreams. They may not even be shared with others; after all, what would be the point? The dreamer "knows" that his or her dream cannot become reality. Perhaps some such individuals become great storytellers. Certainly great novels often describe and sometimes create complex social systems and descriptions of interactions within such social systems; consider, for example, Dostoyevsky's *Crime and Punishment,* Dickens's *A Tale of Two Cities,* or Steinbeck's *The Grapes of Wrath.*

Even if an individual of high cognitive complexity is self-efficacious, believing that he or she can, through action, make a difference, that person may still not become a leader. Unless a person also wants to lead, wants power and influence in order to empower others and thus achieve certain effects through his or her committed actions, a high level of cognitive complexity may be used as a theoretical physicist, to conceptualize the nature of the universe, as an artist, to express one's deepest feelings to others, or as an engineer, to design complex new machinery. That cognitive capability will not, however, be used to construct social organizations with certain aims that are attained through the concerted efforts and cooperative actions of their members.

ORGANIZATIONAL LEADERSHIP:
STRATEGIC APPLICATIONS OF COMPETENCIES

Our discussion here will examine the "how" of organizational leadership, how leaders form (or transform) "cultures" that facilitate effective operations while incorporating and inculcating in members values that support effective operations, internally and externally, now and in the future.

The competencies I have identified are crucial requisites for effective leadership because they are instrumental for defining and, as Schein (1985) says, "embedding" in the organization's culture and inculcating in the organization's members the shared values and beliefs that enable organizational achievement. That is, the organizational culture is the means for constructing the leader's "vision" of organizational achievement. Moreover, the competencies are crucial for carrying out three especially important actions:

- defining a value-based organizational vision or philosophy
- creating and using (and empowering others to create and use) policies and programs that express the philosophy and direct the accomplishment of the vision that the leader has defined
- engaging in certain personal practices and behaviors so as to model consistently the values that underlie the leader's vision and embed them within the organization's culture, thus further strengthening the culture and making more likely the realization of the leader's organizational vision

These are the three broad strategies for constructing organizational cultures. Within each, certain of the personal capabilities and behavioral skills discussed earlier will be applied tactically. I shall consider in more detail how each of these three action-elements of organizational leadership unfolds.

An Organizational Philosophy: Applied Vision

In one sense, defining a philosophy or vision is the most abstract aspect of organizational leadership, calling for a high degree of cognitive capability. In another sense, the development of a value-based philosophy calls not just for the use of one's cognitive capability but for effective application of behavioral competencies, too. These are needed to work effectively with top executives, developing a philosophy that these key executives can and will support in action. This value-setting activity is, then, a crucial first step in culture building.

Note that self-efficacy is prerequisite, as usual, since without it the leader would have no reason to act to begin with. It is obvious that cognitive complexity is requisite, since without the appropriate degree of cognitive complexity, the leader could "see" neither the value-building process nor its long-range aims. Less obvious, perhaps, is the role played by the need for power, but unless the leader can begin building culture by empowering executives, the process will break down at the very start.

The act of developing a philosophy is best undertaken not in isolation but as a joint activity, with senior executives (Frohman and Sashkin, 1985; Tregoe et al., 1991). This can be a difficult and conflictual process, but unless the top group will support the values contained in the leader's vision and philosophy, the leader's efforts will be crippled from the start. Moreover, the conflict that may be exposed can be used productively by the leader as another culture-building tool, rather than being hidden, only to arise later in what is likely to be a destructive eruption.

Working with a top team to define a philosophy and develop a vision may be accomplished formally or informally; the matter of import is that it be accomplished. By doing this, the leader illustrates a supportive policy and models the sort of value-based behaviors that will strengthen the culture the leader is trying to shape.

Several of the specific behavioral skill competencies I alluded to earlier are particularly relevant to, and useful in, the value-setting process. That is, a leader uses vivid metaphors to get across essential values that might otherwise remain abstract. More generally, the leader must apply sound communication skills, such as active listening, questioning, and feedback, in working through the value-setting process. The leader must convey respect for others while continuing to insist on the preeminence of certain values. The leader invites others to join in, to accept the leader's values and the organizational challenges that accompany them. Thus, at least four of five behavioral competencies first identified by Bennis (1984; Bennis and Nanus, 1985) and measured by Sashkin (1984, 1990) are important tactics for building organizational culture by defining a value-based philosophy or vision.

Policies and Programs: Empowerment in Action

All three personal capabilities are important for defining a value-based organizational philosophy, even though cognitive complexity is, perhaps, of greatest significance. Similarly, all three are needed for embedding values in the culture through policies and programs that are designed to enact those values. Still, if any of the three personal capabilities is of special relevance for this second strategy, it is the need for power used in a prosocial manner, that is, to empower and enlist others in actions designed to further the culture-building process.

There are at least three major categories of policies and programs: (1) policies aimed at selecting organization members whose values are consistent with those of the philosophy; (2) programs that create opportunities for organization members not only to engage in but to take charge of and "own" specific projects that carry into action some element of the leader's vision; and (3) policies for rewarding or punishing the actions of organization members, defined in terms of the values their actions illustrate, support, or act against.

Selection by values. One of the first acts of new leaders is typically to bring into the organization individuals who will act to strengthen and reinforce the values on which the leader's organizational vision is based. Leaders also try to identify key persons in the organization who share their values and who can then become part of the leader's cadre or inner circle, acting to support the leader's values and vision. Of course, it is equally important to remove persons who, by their actions, demonstrate values that are seriously incompatible with those being inculcated as the basis of the leader's vision and the organization's culture. The new leader will, finally, implement a general selection process that, insofar as possible, will help to ensure that new members of the organization will share these values. Value-based selection is a crucial aspect of empowerment. If key staff are known by the leader to share in the values that undergird the leader's vision, the leader can feel secure in sharing his or her power with those persons.

What might be the behavioral skill competencies that are useful here? Perhaps the most obviously important is that the leader possess the basic communication skills needed to identify just what values individuals hold. Without such listening, questioning, and feedback skills, the leader would be unable to determine what those values are and would, therefore, be at a loss to tell whether or not an individual's values were consistent with the leader's.

Programs that empower others. A three-level schema first developed by Katz and Kahn (1966) is consistent with, and in many ways a precursor to a similar three-level approach developed by Jacobs and Jaques (1987), as well as the one described by Hunt (1991). At the top level, chief executives define and create organizational structures. At midlevels these structures set the limits within which policies and procedures are defined and applied. Policies and procedures are, then, developed so as to fit within the structures (and, perhaps, the philosophies) defined by CEOs. At the lowest managerial levels, these policies and procedures are implemented and administered.

At midlevels a special sort of process is in action. Through this process the CEO's vision is translated into policies and transformed into sets of activities—programs. These programs are designed to get those at this midlevel deeply involved in constructing the organizational mechanisms that will serve to implement, to make real, the leader's vision. This is an important aspect of empowerment, the process by which individuals and groups come to feel a sense of personal control and ownership of programmatic activities.

Thus, it should be no surprise that one of the specific behavioral skill competencies I have identified as associated with visionary leadership is the ability to create new opportunities, chances for others to "buy in" to the leader's vision by taking on new challenges and becoming responsible for—owning—specific programs or sets of activities. I initially labeled this "risk taking." Leaders do not, however, see as risky the creation of programs that provide options and opportunities for others to take on, take charge of, own, and make succeed. This is partly because of the leader's self-efficacy belief, his or her certainty that goals can be accomplished. It is even more the result of the leader's ability to see clearly (as a result of the leader's level of cognitive complexity) what others see only as "through a glass, darkly."

That is, the leader can, as Jacobs and Jaques (1987) point out, see causal chains and how they interconnect. Moreover, the leader can also see where—and how—to intervene in such chains of events, so as to produce the results that are desired. Thus, there are no uncertainty and no risk; if actions a, b, and c are taken in the correct manner, in the right order, and at the right time and if they connect properly with actions x, y, and z, then the leader knows that the program will succeed. The only question is whether these actions will be done in the correct manner.

Reward and promotion policies. In most organizations managers would assert that rewards and, to a degree, promotions are made on the basis of performance. But performance is often poorly defined, determined by subjective ratings or performance appraisals that have no basis in reality. To serve as a means of empowerment and a tactical tool for constructing an organizational vision and creating or changing an organization's culture, reward and promotion policies must be focused on successful actions that further the organizational vision and philosophy.

The previous argument means rewarding those who have demonstrated that they share the values that are the basis for the organizational philosophy and the leader's vision. Value-based actions are therefore reinforced, and the values themselves are strengthened. Values that are not seen as the basis for rewards or sanctions are not likely to be operative in defining or directing behavior. They may be loudly espoused, but they will be essentially irrelevant to the organization, except that the more overt the espousal and the more divergent it is from enactment (reality), the more the leader's vision is likely to be undercut and weakened. Nothing destroys culture more quickly than hypocrisy.

Value-based promotion policies that are driven by achievements that are consistent with and that further the leader's values and vision will also make it more likely that those entering higher organizational strata will possess not only the requisite degree of cognitive competency but also the motivational and behavioral competencies required for effective leadership. This not only helps increase organizational effectiveness but results in leaders at higher levels who have been empowered and will empower others, because doing so is consistent with their previous actions.

Personal Practices: Self-Efficacy in Action

There are at least two tactics for inculcating values in organization members (and thus embedding those values in the organization's culture) that rely primarily on the leader's own interpersonal behaviors. Thus, in using these tactics, leaders must possess and use most or all of the five behavioral skill competencies I have studied (Sashkin, 1990; Sashkin and Burke, 1990).

At the core of these behavioral tactics is the personal competency of self-efficacy. Perhaps more than in any other of the strategies or tactics for culture building that have been discussed so far, personal practices depend on the leader's self-efficacy beliefs, for without such beliefs no action makes much sense. What is more, by engaging in these strategic behaviors, the leader is modeling self-efficacy, along with other values and beliefs. Modeling, in a more general sense, is one of the most effective ways of building culture. A more specific, but still quite powerful, tactic involves using conflicts to define or clarify values and get organization members overtly to commit themselves to those values. I will briefly discuss each of these value-focused tactics for shaping organizational culture.

Modeling. Perhaps the most powerful of what Schein (1990) labels "primary embedding mechanisms" is deliberate behavioral modeling by the leader. Modeling permits group members to internalize the leader's values and assumptions. By modeling, leaders exhibit their values and show that those values are not merely espoused, "nice" statements that belong on a wall plaque but are enacted in the leader's own real, day-to-day behavior.

Effective modeling is not a one-shot strategy; it must occur over time and with consistency. The behavioral skill competency I have labeled "trust" is of special importance for modeling, for trust is the result of consistent action over time. Only repeated action ensures that others will clearly see the values one models as guiding that action. Only when actions are consistent in illustrating the same or complementary values will those values be seen as an operative aspect of the organization's culture and not just espoused sentiments. Moreover, for maximum effect the leader must model crucial values in many different ways, through many different behaviors that, when woven together, form a strong fabric with a clear and visible pattern. This is not an easy task; success requires not merely behavioral skill but the vision (cognitive complexity) to see the pattern of action that one is trying to construct.

In sum, leaders model the values they wish to inculcate among organization members; their own actions are therefore a primary tool for culture building. On a superficial level this means that their actions conform to and illustrate their espoused values and beliefs. More subtle, and a far more difficult task, is the way leaders "design" their values into their actions, not just now and then but constantly, consistently, and in a complex and self-reinforcing interwoven pattern.

Using conflict to define and strengthen overarching values. Leaders who are engaged in constructing the organization's culture use conflict situations as opportunities for culture building. Effective managers approach conflict by seeking a creative integration through problem solving, a win-win resolution strategy. But effective leaders do this in a very special way: they look first for an overarching value that the conflicting parties agree on (or can agree on). Then, they make that value explicit and proceed to engage the parties in a constructive problem-solving approach to resolve the conflict in a manner that is consistent with and illustrates the shared value. Common values serve to anchor whatever resolution the conflicting parties come up with, thus helping to ensure that their agreement will actually work.

Conflict situations provide more of a one-short opportunity; thus the behavioral skill competency of trust or consistent action is of less importance than was the case for modeling. The other four behavioral skill competencies, however, become quite important. How can the leader get across the concept of a shared superordinate value without using clear and even vivid metaphors, thus focusing the conflicting parties on the value issue? Communication skills become critical as the leader becomes a "third party interventionist" (Walter, 1987). The leader's credence rests, in part, on the ability to show the conflicting parties that they are all equally respected, that the leader considers the issues and concerns of all of them to be legitimate and worthy of respect. Finally, a creative win-win solution will often require that the leader be willing and able to create new opportunities, to take certain risks. Recall, however, that visionary leaders do not see this sort of action as risky, due both to their high self-efficacy and to their cognitive capability, which permits them to see clearly how the proposed solution can be made to work effectively.

Strategic Reinforcement of Cultural Values

Up to now I have spoken of the strategies and tactics used by leaders to embed values within the organization's culture and to inculcate values within the organization's members. In many ways the approaches detailed so far may seem oddly mundane. What of the sort of activities so widely associated with organizational culture—ceremonies, storytelling, the use of symbols, and so on?

In this regard, I agree with Schein (1990), who calls these more popularly accepted activities "secondary articulation and reinforcement mechanisms." These sometimes appear to be the cause of culture, but that assumption is a mistake generated by the highly visible and affect-laden nature of these mechanisns. In fact, they are powerful reinforcement mechanisms, helping to make more recognized and overt the organization's important cultural values. These mechanisms have been studied in depth by Deal and Kennedy (1982) and Deal and Peterson (1990). Some of the most common are:

- telling stories about organizational heroes and heroines
- using vivid and exciting symbols
- establishing well-recognized traditions
- engaging in highly visible rituals
- conducting public ceremonies

The effective use of these secondary mechanisms for articulating and reinforcing culture is not a simple matter. Of course, effective time management (to establish traditions and engage in rituals) is required, and good planning (to conduct ceremonies) is a necessity. Certainly, good communication (to tell stories) is important. More important, the leader must design these traditions, ceremonies, and rituals, must develop clear and engaging stories, and must generally select or create meaningful symbols that connect clearly to the cultural values the leader is trying to instill within the organization and its members. All of these secondary articulation and reinforcement mechanisms must be carefully designed to have a positive emotional impact on organization members, as they make explicit and highly visible the values being expressed and reinforced.

My own research (Sashkin and Sashkin, 1990) confirms that more visionary leaders, that is, those scoring higher on my measure of visionary or transformatoinal leadership, the Leader Behavior Questionnaire (Sashkin, 1990), engage in these "symbolic leadership" activities to a much greater degree than do less visionary leaders. They do so, however, not to define and embed certain values within the culture but, rather, to make more visible, to articulate, and thus to reinforce the values that have been defined and instilled by means of the primary embedding mechanisms that I have described.

The above argument means (1) applying the leader's vision by developing a value-based organizational philosophy, (2) putting empowerment into action through value-based selection programs that empower organization members to own and construct elements of the leader's value-based vision and using reward policies that reinforce values, and (3) acting on the belief that one can have an impact on the organization by the constant, consistent, and connected modeling of value-based behaviors and by using conflict to define and strengthen overarching values.

This is not to suggest that storytelling, traditions, and so on are of little consequence; these can be powerful tools for expanding organization members' awareness and understanding of values and for reinforcing the values out of which the culture is built. But the values and beliefs that form the organization's culture are defined and embedded within the culture only through value-based actions. Those actions must involve the actual work or business of the organization. As Zaleznik (1989b) has observed, leadership involves substance, the content of organizational work, not merely process.

The Role of Behavioral Competencies

Developing a philosophy, a value-based vision, obviously requires that one believe that one's vision can make a difference. Similarly, one would not develop a vision unless one were motivated to achieve that vision (through power and influence used to empower members of an organization). Most obviously, developing a vision requires a high level of cognitive complexity; that is the basis of the ability to be visionary. But without behavioral skills, the leader's vision will remain nothing more than a concept, for it is with and through people, by empowering them to act in concert toward a common aim, that visions are made real.

The behaviors of focusing attention and effective communication are generally crucial, both for modeling and for reinforcing cultural values. Trust, developed by means of consistent actions over time, is needed for behavior modeling to be effective. Respect is important for modeling and for dealing constructively with conflict and is both used for and reflected by value-based selection, as well being necessary for reinforcing values. Risk is actually the embodiment of empowerment through leadership action, for it is by opening up new opportunities that organization members can buy into and own the leader's vision and make that vision reality.

Behavior: The Source of Charisma. By means of the behavioral skill competencies, leaders make followers see them as charismatic. That is, exceptional levels of the five behavioral skill competencies, common when the two personal practice areas are used by the leader as culture-building tactics, lead followers to feel inspired, encouraged, enthused and to conclude that the leader has charisma. Charisma is in the beholder, not the leader, and is the affective consequence, not the cause of the leader's actions.

It is important to point out this fact, because it has become common in some circles to speak of "charismatic leadership." Not only does this put the cart before the horse, confusing the cause with the effect, but it creates the expectation that effective high-level leadership is, by nature, associated with charisma. This is not necessarily the case. It is true that simply because effective visionary leaders engage in more of the charisma-producing behaviors, they are more likely to be seen as charismatic (Sashkin and Fulmer, 1985). However, this is a matter of degree, and it is quite possible for an effective visionary leader to produce a relatively low level of charismatic affect among followers.

There is a still-darker side to this issue. Howell (1988) points out that those leaders seen as extremely charismatic may well be basing their influence on followers' identification with the leader. In contrast, effective visionary or transformational leaders rely on followers' internalization of the values the leader models and inculcates as the basis for the organizational culture that can support and guide the attainment of the leader's vision. Leaders relying on the first mechanism, identification, are, in Howell's view, operating at a lower level of development of the need for power, a level that may not be prosocial but may, instead, involve the drive for power for self-aggrandizement and dominance, as part of a narcissistic personality profile. (Note that this is the type of individual identified by McClelland as very high in power need but low in impulse control.) In his latest book, Zaleznik (1989b), warns of just this sort of pseudo-leader, immersed in what he refers to as "the managerial mystique."

Such leaders are dangerous because they often have neither a vision nor the understanding needed to engage in building organizational culture. Followers identify with the leader, being deeply influenced by their charismatic feelings toward the leader, and may thus act as the leader wishes (or demands), but that action may have serious negative consequences for individuals as well as for the organization. Some might argue that Ronald Reagan was this type of leader, intensely charismatic but unable to engage in building a sound culture, as well as having a vision that was seriously flawed in that some of the basic beliefs and value assumptions it contained were proven wrong (e.g., that supply side economics would permit the nation to spend its way out of debt). Consider the consequences of having a charismatic leader whose vision is truly warped, a person such as Jim Jones who not only destroyed himself and his organization but literally led his followers to self-destruction.

Thus, the presence of exceptionally strong charismatic affect among the followers of a leader should be a cause for concern. It may mean nothing more than that the leader engages in a very high level of charisma-producing behavior as he or she goes about strategically and tactically defining and embedding the cultural values and beliefs that will facilitate attainment of the leader's organizational vision. It may mean that the leader has no vision and followers run the risk of following like lemmings into the sea. Worst of all, the presence of exceptional levels of charismatic affect may signal that the leader is out to attain a vision so destructive that only by appealing to narcissistic processes of identification among followers can the vision be enacted.

I suggest that, consistent with Howell's (1988) argument, the term *charismatic leadership* be reserved for such circumstances and that the terms *transformational leadership* (Burns, 1978) or *visionary leadership* (Sashkin, 1990) be used when referring to the sort of effective leadership at the strata that are of central concern in this chapter.

PUTTING IT ALL TOGETHER

The central notion of Stratified Systems Theory is that effective visionary leaders must have the requisite level of cognitive complexity. But this is, in fact, only a partial explication of the requisite leadership competencies. Such leaders must also have certain behavioral skill competencies and a sophisticated understanding (implicit or explicit) of organizational culture and culture building, based on their motivational competencies, that is, the other two personal capabilities—self-efficacy and need for power prosocially directed.

Behavioral competencies are important because they are the only sure means for implementing the strategies and tactics needed by visionary leaders; a purely structural approach cannot do the job of defining and guiding the attainment of an organizational vision. Neither can some sort of mysterious, magic charisma be the cause of, and force for, implementing a vision. Only concrete actions, in the real world, can have such effects, and such actions depend for their definition and execution on the behavioral skill competencies of visionary leaders.

How they implement their visions through these behavioral skill competencies truly identifies and characterizes successful visionary leaders. That is, their personal motivational capabilities (self-efficacy and socially directed power need) enable them to embed in organizational cultures and instill in organizational members the values and beliefs that make possible the realization of their visions. Here we come back to the issue of behavioral skill competencies, actions that are applied to define, embed, and reinforce values, not through what some term ''symbolic leadership'' but through use of mundane managerial activities as opportunities for culture building.

As part of one of the programs at the National Center for Research on School Leadership (at the University of Illinois) Russell Ames and Sam Krug, two senior researchers, designed what has been called ''the beeper study.'' That is, they arranged for a group of about fifty school principals in the greater Chicago area to participate in a quantitative study of time use. Each agreed to carry a paging device, the kind that makes a beep when one has an urgent telephone message or that physicians wear when on call. The beepers were programmed to go off at random, all at once, during the school day. Each time they did, every principal was to write down on a card what he or she was doing. At the end of the day this was to be entered into a logbook and elaborated as necessary.

After a few days of this procedure, the principals were near revolt—hardly a surprise. But it was then that some of the most interesting and revealing of their actions were recorded. One of the most fascinating involved two principals whose actions were compared when the beepers went off at about 3:15 p.m. What are most school principals doing then? It is a good bet they are dealing with school buses; one wrote on his card, "3:15—supervising school bus loading." But another wrote, "3:15—encouraging kids to expect more of themselves as they get on the buses."

What could be more striking! One principal was attending to a simple bureaucratic management task, dealing—effectively, one assumes—with the usual administrative problems of scheduling and loading school buses, building what Firestone and Wilson (1988) call "bureaucratic linkages." The other was doing this, too. In addition, she was at the same time (and through some of the behaviors I have been speaking of here) building what Firestone and Wilson call "cultural linkages," that is, defining, inculcating, and reinforcing the shared values and beliefs that create the organization's culture and enable attainment of the leader's vision. (Note, too, that this leader was embedding the belief of self-efficacy in "followers." Effective leaders do not simply create followers; they aim to develop followers into leaders.)

To put it simply, effective, transformational leaders implement their visions and build organizational cultures by overlaying value-laden meanings onto "normal" bureaucratic/managerial activities. This is why the tendency to separate "leadership" and "management," as though these were dichotomous categories, must be rejected. It would appear very unlikely, indeed, that one could be an effective leader unless one is able to function with a reasonable degree of effectiveness as a manager. Of course, the two are not the same; leaders build cultural linkages as a "subtext," while they engage in managerial actions, building bureaucratic linkages. Managers need perform only the latter; effective leaders must do both.

DEVELOPING COMPETENT VISIONARY LEADERS

A pure selection strategy for obtaining effective leaders based on leaders' personal capability in terms of cognitive complexity is inadequate. If there is any merit at all to the arguments I have advanced here, then it should be clear that even if individuals with the "right" level of cognitive complexity (or potential) could be identified (e.g., using the sort of assessment battery developed by Stamp, 1978, 1981) and selected, this would not guarantee the success of such individuals. If the other requisite personal capabilities I have identified are absent, if an understanding (implicit or explicit) of how one goes about building organizational culture is absent or if the requisite behavioral skill competencies are absent, the individuals selected into leadership positions will fail no matter what their level of cognitive complexity and no matter whether or not that level appropriately matches the task requirements of the stratum at which they are trying to operate.

Of course, one could simply develop a more comprehensive selection formula, by adding to cognitive complexity the behavioral skills and personal capabilities identified here, thus maintaining a pure selection strategy. This, too, is inadequate, being far too narrow an approach. I believe that any approach aimed at placing capable leaders at the appropriate levels in organizations must attend to development as well as to selection.

I raise the issue in this manner because the pure selection approach has received the most attention from Jaques (1986, 1989) and his colleagues (Jacobs and Jaques, 1987, 1990). The rationale appears to have centered on the belief that cognitive complexity is a genetically fixed variable and that an individual's cognitive development in this regard will be within a single "mode" that predicts the highest stratum a person can ever be expected to have the cognitive complexity in which to operate comfortably and effectively (Jaques, 1986). Thus, a "Mode III" person in his or her twenties may be able to perform the most complex Stratum I or the least complex Stratum II work, that is, projects with about a three-month time horizon. By about age forty, this person might develop the degree of cognitive complexity needed to deal with the one- to two-year task horizons that characterize Stratum III work.

According to Jacobs and Jaques (1987, 1990), the development of cognitive complexity is an extended process that occurs over an individual's entire life. They do admit that individuals must have experiential opportunities for effective development, and they even suggest that development, at least within a stratum, might be facilitated through a "guided discovery" learning process involving mentors who could help individuals develop fully the ability to operate in that stratum. But any planned or directed developmental process is implicitly excluded as a possibility, especially if the aim is to increase the level of cognitive complexity beyond that assessed as the individual's genetic potential and if the process involves relatively short-term training interventions.

The approach to developing leaders discussed by Jacobs and Jaques (1987, 1990, 1991) is, however, far too narrow and limited. Most obviously it ignores behavioral skill training, which Jacobs and Jaques (1987) do recognize as important, especially at certain strata. Also ignored are the personal capabilities I have identified as important for top-level leadership (in addition to cognitive complexity); there is evidence that purposeful training and development interventions can have positive impact on these factors. Thus, development calls for action on several fronts, including behavioral skill training of the sort commonly associated with leadership development (which is relatively easy), new forms of training in organizational culture and culture building (which is harder), and training centered on development of the three personal capabilities (hardest of all).

Traditional management training, which is centered on what has generally been called ''leadership'' but which is actually supervisory management at the middle and lowest organizational levels, is and will remain important. Without both knowing how to and being able to carry out basic managerial duties, individuals are not likely to be capable of using those duties as opportunities for leadership.

In addition to continued sound management training programs, future leaders would benefit from behavioral skill competency training that centers on the specific behaviors identified and discussed here. To some extent these are normally included in basic management training, but traditional management courses are less likely to include skill development segments emphasizing how to use metaphors creatively or how to build trust. These are important behavioral skills that can be taught.

Some sort of training can certainly have a positive impact on one of the three personal capabilities I have defined and discussed: self-efficacy; Bandura (1986b, 1988) has clearly demonstrated this. McClelland and Burnham (1976) have shown that a training program aimed at increasing district sales managers' prosocial power need led to improvements in organizational climate (greater sense of responsibility, organizational clarity, and team spirit), as seen by district sales personnel, and was followed by substantial improvements in sales and profits. Other power need training programs reported by McClelland and his associates have proven effective in alcoholic rehabilitation efforts (McClelland et al., 1972) and in empowering the staff of community action agencies (McClelland et al., 1975). There is no doubt that the need for power is susceptible to such developmental efforts, although in some cases the type of intervention required to modify or alter power need seems closer to therapy than to training.

Finally, I have already observed that Jacobs and Jaques (1987, 1991) appear to believe that cognitive complexity can, at best, be developed only to a minimal extent and within an individual's innately defined limits. I suggest, in contrast, that cognitive complexity is, without doubt, amenable to development in the sense that individuals can learn to use more effectively the capacity that they have. It may also be that cognitive complexity is amenable to development in the sense of extending one's span of vision and increasing one's cognitive complexity, though this is not certain.

Jacobs and Jaques appear to accept the fallacy that because a trait is innate or genetically determined, it is necessarily immutable. Angoff (1988) points out this logical fallacy and provides data-based illustrations showing that it is simply not inevitably true. Angoff admits that positive changes (such as in individuals' IQ scores) are much easier to achieve if efforts are initiated early in life as opposed to later and notes that a supportive and motivated environment may also be required. My point is not that proof exists that cognitive complexity can be developed beyond what Stamp's (1978, 1981) assessment methods would suggest; I only assert that the assumption that such development is impossible is untenable.

But let us be even less optimistic; I suggest that it is all but certain that individuals can develop increased cognitive complexity within their innate "mode." Recent research yielded some provocative findings relevant to this question. A study by psychologists at the University of Colorado of elite student violinists showed that the number of hours spent practicing was the only thing that separated potential "superstars" from others who were good but not top caliber. The researchers followed the careers of violinists studying at the Music Academy of West Berlin. By the age of eighteen, the best students had spent about 2,000 more hours in practice (on the average) than had their fellow students. If the primary differentiator of "good" from "great" violinists is hours of practice, perhaps we should take seriously the possibility that practice in the complex cognitive activity characteristic of high-level leaders may actually produce more effective leaders.

Every human ability or talent that I am aware of, whether or not it is genetically determined, can be exercised more effectively after guided practice that consists, at least in part, of structured training exercises. I could never be a great violinist, but were I willing to practice three hours a day for the rest of my life, I could guarantee that the music I produced would at least be pleasant to the untrained ear. The same must apply to cognitive complexity. We have not yet even begun to embark on the design, let alone the delivery, of the kinds of training that would be of greatest benefit for organizational leadership. My comments are chiefly a warning against closing out work toward such a goal by accepting without question the limiting assumptions offered by Jacobs and Jaques.

CONCLUSION

My aim in this chapter has been to expand Stratified Systems Theory in several respects. I have used the concept of "competencies" to identify and define a set of personal (psychological) and behavioral skill competencies that I have found to be additional requisites for effective organizational leadership (Strata IV and V). Focusing on leadership at Stratum V, I have tried to provide concrete and specific illustrations of how the various competencies are applied through leaders' actions and micro-behaviors.

Let me very briefly reframe the most essential elements of my presentation, in terms of SST. First, I believe that if SST is to gain wider attention and use as a major approach for understanding and affecting leadership in organizations, then it is crucial that we add to the single variable of cognitive complexity additional motivational competencies, namely self-efficacy and prosocial power need. Without incorporating the motivational aspect of leadership, SST is headed for a dead end.

Second, I believe that it is imperative that SST focus more on the specific actions and behaviors of leaders at all strata and particularly on interpersonal behaviors. If SST remains limited to purely structural concepts, it cannot remain a viable model of leadership in organizations.

Third and finally, SST must begin to incorporate an approach to development that goes well beyond selection and "guided discovery" (Jacobs and Jaques, 1987). Assessment of stratum requirements must become far more specific, enabling developmental actions that focus on leader behavior that is stratum-specific. Approaches must be designed to develop leaders' specific behavioral skill competencies and to help leaders develop their personal capabilities, including cognitive complexity.

Overall, SST must look to, and become open to, other approaches to leadership, especially including approaches such as those of Howell (1988), House, Spangler, and Woycke (1990), Kouzes and Posner (1987), and Sashkin (1988, 1990) that emphasize organizational leadership at Strata IV and V. Not one of these approaches (or predecessor reports) is, for example, mentioned or referenced by Jacobs and Jaques (1987, 1990). Continuing to ignore other relevant leadership theories and approaches will surely render SST sterile in the long run.

NOTE

1. Jacobs and Jaques (1987) discuss the skills needed by managers and leaders at various strata, using a model considerably different from the one to be applied here.

10

Behavioral Complexity and the Development of Effective Managers

Robert Hooijberg and Robert E. Quinn

> The authors themselves provide a very fine summary at the beginning of their
> chapter. Therefore, all we as editors do here is to emphasize the potential importance
> that we think behavioral complexity has in extending SST's cognitive complexity
> notion and enhancing readers' understandings of leadership. Particularly interesting
> and important in this regard is the authors' description of the behavioral complexity
> leader development program recently articulated by Quinn and his colleagues.

One of the essential elements of Stratified Systems Theory (SST) is cognitive complexity. While SST has focused on the relationship between cognitive complexity
and performance at the different levels of the organizational hierarchy, SST has
underemphasized the issue of skills at the behavioral level. In this chapter we introduce the concept of behavioral complexity. Behavioral complexity suggests that effective managers are not only cognitively complex but also able to perform a diverse
set of roles and skills in the explicit, behavioral realm. We first briefly review SST
and the role of the concept of cognitive complexity within SST. We then introduce
and elaborate the notion of behavioral complexity. After reviewing the empirical
support for the proposition that behaviorally complex managers are more effective,
we place behavioral complexity in an evolutionary model and ask the question of
how behavioral complexity can be increased in practicing managers. Here we review
a comprehensive educational process in which the objective is to increase the
behavioral complexity and effectiveness of middle managers in a Fortune 10 company.

SST AND THE EVOLUTION OF COGNITIVE COMPLEXITY

It is useful to start our discussion by reiterating some key SST aspects. First,
as managers move up the organizational hierarchy both the environmental complexity and the time horizon that they have to work with increase. Second, for a

manager to be effective at any given organizational level, his or her cognitive complexity has to at least match the environmental complexity. Finally, in SST, seven organizational levels are distinguished. The time horizons that managers work with range from a few weeks at level 1 to twenty years at level 7. At the first managerial level the manager deals with his or her subordinates and direct superior. At the highest level the manager oversees multiple organizations, diverse consumer markets, wide ranges of suppliers, and political issues.

The Definition of Cognitive Complexity

The concept of cognitive complexity is of central importance in SST. It sometimes is discussed as work capacity (Jaques, 1976). Work capacity refers to the extent to which a person is able to construct a project—"the subjective picture of the goal and plan for reaching it—[by] pulling together and ordering external information about the required task, and its organization into a patterned sense of the finished output accomplished in a particular block of time" (p. 123). The concept of work capacity is closely linked to the concept of time frames. That is, the longer the time span that one can oversee and plan for, the higher one's work capacity. Jaques and Clement (1991) have more recently elaborated the notion of work capacity. They now distinguish eight thinking processes that they build from two dimensions. The first dimension is the level of abstractness: (1) simple denotation, (2) symbolic labeling, (3) abstract conceptualization, and (4) universalization. The second dimension they describe concerns how information at different levels of abstraction is put together. Again they distinguish four levels in this dimension: (1) declarative, (2) systematic thinking, (3) serial processing, and (4) parallel processing. The eight thinking processes closely map onto the levels of the bureaucratic hierarchy that Jaques (1976) distinguishes. As can be seen in this volume, other authors also continue to modify the notion of cognitive complexity.

The Evolution of Cognitive Complexity

An issue of some importance is the development of cognitive complexity. How does a manager move from one level of complexity to another? While not extensively addressed by students of SST, there is some literature on the subject, and most of it takes the form of stage theory. In stage theory, it is assumed that a person moves from one predictable phase or stage to another. Here we will briefly review some key notions in this literature.

Jaques (1976) assumes that work capacity develops in stages. More precisely, he argues that the "maturational process [of work capacity] occurs in stages, with discontinuity. At stages before the full maturation of work capacity the non-matured potential in people will reveal itself in the quality of working" (p. 161). This statement indicates that Jaques believes that people have an innate upper limit of work capacity and that their environments and work experiences determine the extent to which this potential is realized: "With maturation and experience, the individual's work-capacity opens out and fills with usable information—eventually filling out to its fullest limits. The higher the capacity, the longer into adulthood this filling-out process takes" (p. 167).

Kuhnert and Lewis (1987) use Kegan's (1982) stage theory of evolving self-other relationships as a framework to understand better when managers can display transactional and transformational behaviors. Kegan (1982) proposes that the way in which we see self-other relationships changes significantly over the life course. Kuhnert and Lewis (1987) suggest that only managers who have reached Kegan's (1982) institutional stage (the fifth stage out of a possible six) can be expected to display transformational leadership behaviors. In a similar vein, Lewis and Jacobs (this volume) assert that changes in cognitive complexity follow a developmental process. More specifically, they use Kegan's (1982) theory of the evolving self to discuss how people develop increasingly broad perspectives of themselves in relation to the world.

There is some work that supports the above positions. Bartunek, Gordon, and Weathersby (1983) conclude that managers at higher stages of development can handle stress and ambiguity better than managers at earlier stages of development. Fisher and Torbert (1991), furthermore, find that managers at higher levels of development function better because they are able to examine situations from more perspectives and because they listen better to others than do those at lower levels of development.

An important aspect of Lewis and Jacobs's (this volume) model is that people do not respond directly to an objective, real world. Rather, people construct a view of the world that then becomes the world within which they live and work (Kegan, 1982). As Lewis and Jacobs point out, a "crucial point is that strategic leaders *behave* differently than lower level leaders not principally because they have better managerial skills but because they 'see' more than others see" (emphasis added). In this chapter, rather than focus on cognitive complexity, we will focus more closely on the behavior of managers.

THE EVOLUTION OF BEHAVIORAL COMPLEXITY

The above definitions of cognitive complexity and the above models of how it evolves are clearly useful. In this section, however, we propose a concept called behavioral complexity, which we place in a larger evolutionary perspective. Behavioral complexity is not meant to replace cognitive complexity. Behavioral complexity suggests that effective managers are not only cognitively complex but also able to perform a diverse set of roles and skills in the explicit, behavioral realm. Cognitive complexity is one element of behavioral complexity (R. Quinn, Spreitzer, and Hart, 1991).

Behavioral Complexity

Cognitive complexity consists of at least two key elements: the extent to which an individual can discriminate variables and the extent to which an individual can hold different variables, simultaneously, in his or her mind (Jaques, 1976). As seen above, many levels of complexity can be specified, and the more complex the individual's cognitive processes, the more effective the individual is assumed to be. This argument, however, ignores the issue of skills at the behavioral level. Effectiveness requires not only cognitive complexity inside the individual but also the ability to act out a wide array of roles in the interpersonal and organizational arena. Boal and Whitehead (this volume), in a similar vein, argue that any generalizable theory of leadership must consider both traits and behavior. The ability to behave complexly requires not only complex thinking processes but also a complex set of performance skills. Behavioral complexity is the ability to act out a cognitively complex strategy by playing multiple, even competing roles, in a highly integrated and complementary way.

The competing values model of leadership roles provides a framework for conceptualizing and measuring behavioral complexity in managers. In the framework, eight roles are modeled along two dimensions (see Figure 10.1). Each role is juxtaposed with roles on the opposite side of the model.

Figure 10.1
The Competing Values Model of Leadership Roles

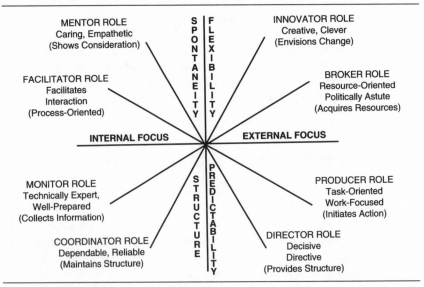

Source: R.E. Quinn (1988), *Beyond Rational Management.* Copyright 1988 by Jossey-Bass, Inc. Reprinted by permission of Jossey-Bass, Inc.

The notion of behavioral complexity suggests that more effective managers will play more roles, and play them to a greater extent, than less effective managers. More effective managers will also strike a balance among the various roles that they play. That is, they will not emphasize certain roles substantially more than other roles. The effective managers are also more likely to have the cognitive complexity to understand the four contrasting mind-sets, values, or philosophies underlying each of the quadrants and to be able to integrate behaviorally the behaviors embedded in the contrasting mind-sets (R. Quinn, 1988).

To compute a measure of behavioral complexity, we use a formula developed by Bobko and Schwartz (1984) for integrating bipolar concepts. Bobko and Schwartz were attempting to develop a continuous measure of androgyny. Instead of treating masculinity and femininity as independent concepts, as was traditionally the case, they wanted a continuous measure integrating the separate masculinity and femininity concepts. They developed an equation for constructing an index of integrative balance between the two contrasting concepts. The equation they use is as follows:

$$\text{Integration} = [(k\text{-}1) - (|X\text{-}Y|)] * [(X+Y)/2]$$

X and Y are bipolar concepts to be integrated and are measured on a common integral response scale from 1 to k. The first term is the absolute difference, or balance, between the bipolar concepts, X and Y. The second term distinguishes persons who are low on the two contrasting concepts from persons who are high on both. Thus high scores on this integration index indicate individuals who are high, yet balanced, on the two contrasting concepts (Quinn, Spreitzer, and Hart, 1991).

To demonstrate how the formula works, let us take two managers' scores on two seemingly contradictory roles, the mentor and director roles (see Quinn, 1988). The scores for the mentor role are entered for the ''X''s and the scores for the director role for the ''Y''s in the above formula. The response scale k ranges from 1 (manager almost never performs that role) to 7 (manager almost always performs that role), for both roles. Manager A scores 2 (out of a possible 7) on the mentor role and 6 on the director role. Manager B scores 4 on both the mentor and the director role. When we compute the integration scores for both managers using the above formula, we see that manager A scores 8 while manager B scores 24. While the average scores on the two leadership roles are the same for both managers, we see that manager B scores substantially higher on the integration index because he or she balances the two roles more than does manager A. To get an overall index of behavioral complexity using Quinn's (1988) competing values framework, we add up the integration scores on the four indexes of integrative balance: mentor versus director, facilitator versus producer, monitor versus broker, and coordinator versus innovator.

Evidence on Behavioral Complexity and Effectiveness

Several studies provide support for the idea that effective managers are more behaviorally complex than ineffective managers. Denison, Hooijberg, and R. Quinn (1991) studied the behavioral complexity of 176 public utility industry managers. Using the perceptions of the managers' superiors, they split the sample into effective and ineffective managers. They then used the perceptions of the managers' subordinates to assess the leadership behaviors of the managers. Denison, Hooijberg, and Quinn (1991) found that the effective managers were more behaviorally complex than the ineffective managers because their subordinates differentiated the eight leadership roles of the competing values framework more clearly and because their leadership profiles resembled more closely a circle as predicted by the competing values framework (Quinn, 1988).

Quinn, Spreitzer, and Hart (1991) used the concept of interpenetration to examine the effectiveness of managers from a Fortune 10 company. They define interpenetration as "the simultaneous operation of opposites. During interpenetration a new system emerges from the integration of the two original differentiated systems" (p. 4). These researchers treat each of the four quadrants as a differentiated system. Using the previously discussed measure for integrating bipolar concepts (Bobko and Schwartz, 1984), they then combine the opposite quadrants into one new system. Building cohesion (the human relations quadrant) and stimulating productivity (the rational goal quadrant) are combined into the "productive team-building" role. Coordinating/stabilizing behaviors (the internal process quadrant) and innovative behaviors (the open systems quadrant) are combined into the "practical revitalizing" role. Quinn, Spreitzer, and Hart found that managers who are high on productive team-building or practical revitalizing are more effective in the eyes of their subordinates, peers, and superiors than managers who do not score high on these measures. That is, managers who have the behavioral complexity to balance competing demands will do better than managers who focus on one demand over another.

Hart and Quinn (1991) studied the impact of leadership behavior on firm performance in a sample of 916 CEOs from a location in a large metropolitan area in the industrial Midwest. They defined a leadership role for each of the quadrants of the competing values framework (see Figure 10.1): vision setter (open systems quadrant), taskmaster (rational goal quadrant), analyzer (internal process quadrant), and motivator (human relations quadrant). Hart and Quinn found the CEOs who scored in the top third on all four roles (the high balanced managers) had significantly more impact on firm performance than those managers who scored in the bottom third on all four roles (the low balanced managers). The high balanced managers also tended to have more impact on firm performance than unbalanced managers (those who scored high on some roles and low on others), but not on all criteria of firm performance.

Studies that have used measures developed by Kegan and his colleagues

(Kegan, 1982; Lahey et al., 1988) to assess cognitive complexity have assessed the extent to which students can differentiate themselves from their work (Lewis and Jacobs, this volume). They have also examined the cognitive complexity of military officers. These studies of cognitive complexity assess how people think, not how they behave. Characteristic of the three studies conducted by Quinn and his colleagues is that they use assessments of the managers' behaviors, not of how managers think. Denison, Hooijberg, and Quinn (1991) and Quinn, Spreitzer, and Hart (1991) use subordinates' perceptions of their managers as independent measures and superiors' perceptions as dependent measures. Hart and Quinn use self-perceptions to assess leadership behaviors. These assessments allow us to understand the differences in behavior of effective and ineffective leaders in terms of distinct roles that they display and the balance that they strike among the different roles.

An Alternative View of Development

The literature on the development of cognitive complexity, mentioned above, takes the form of stage theory. However, there exist several problems with stage theories. The stage concept implies a hierarchical relationship among the proposed stages (i.e., later stages include, and are better than, earlier stages), invariance in the sequence of the stages, structurally universal phenomena, unconscious cognitive structures, qualitative changes, and development rather than aging (Snarey, Kohlberg, and Noam, 1983). Another assumption usually associated with the concept of stages is the epigenetic principle (Erikson, 1957). The epigenetic principle refers to the idea that there exist critical periods during which an individual is most sensitive and most likely to move on to the next stage of development. If the critical period passes without the individual's moving on to the next stage of development, development is arrested and further development becomes difficult.

Another problem with many of the developmental theories is that they have primarily focused on the individual (Fischer, 1980). It is the individual who changes from one stage to the next, with the environment's playing only a minimal role. We, however, concur with Fischer (1980) that development is the result of the joint influences of individual and environment. The environment provides the opportunities for the individual to explore new behaviors. Kuhn's (1970) theory of scientific revolutions and Hall's (1987) framework of breaking career routines are two theories that emphasize both the individual and the environment in understanding scientific/career development.

In Kuhn's developmental model of the sciences, researchers follow a certain paradigm. Researchers who work within the paradigm conduct what Kuhn calls normal science. Progress is incremental. Researchers, however, do encounter phenomena/problems that they cannot explain. These unexplainable phenomena are termed anomalies. Anomalies accumulate, and some researchers attempt to formulate theoretical frameworks that can explain the anomalies. When a new paradigm is formulated that explains all the phenomena that the old paradigm explained as well as the anomalies, Kuhn argues, a scientific revolution has taken place.

Hall (1987) provides a similar discussion. He focuses on career routines and triggers that break the routine. A person enters the career routine after he or she has gone through the entry socialization process and has acquired the knowledge, values or attitudes, and skills required of incumbents in a new role. The person then feels established in the role, experiences mastery, and enters a period in which work is more scripted, habitual, routine, and nonconscious (Louis, 1980). When the person is in the routine period, little development of skills takes place, much the same as during Kuhn's normal science period.

Kuhn and Hall have in common that they include environmental influences (anomalies, triggers) as critical factors in the developmental process. Both emphasize that periods of relative stability will be followed by periods of change, followed by stable periods again. Van Maanen (1977) described job transitions as "break points"—changes that thrust one from certainty to uncertainty or from the familiar to the unfamiliar. Similarly, the factors that may trigger changes in a person's work role routine are "break points" that provide opportunities for "unfreezing," which Lewin argued is necessary for change and development (Brett, 1984). It is what Gersick (1991) called the punctuated equilibrium paradigm: "relatively long periods of stability (equilibrium), punctuated by compact periods of qualitative, metamorphic change (revolution)" (p.12). Development, as described here, then, is a process of freezing-unfreezing-refreezing (FUR) routines. Routine role behavior "consists of bundles of routines, or strings of behavior-outcome sequences that spin out unconsciously in response to environmental stimuli. These routines unfold in a mindless fashion" (Langer, 1978, as cited in Brett, 1984, p. 157). "One does not need to think to move through a routine, though much mindful activity may be necessary to construct a routine and much may be embedded in a routine" (Brett, 1984, p. 157). We are interested in factors that break the routine, especially in such a way that the resulting routine reflects more behavioral complexity than the previous routine.

Challenges to the Work Role Routine

Hall (1987) suggests three sources of environmental influence that can trigger changes in the career routine: (1) organizational/societal (e.g., technology, labor market, and organizational culture), (2) work role sources (e.g., positive role models and opportunities for developmental relationships, either as mentor, protégé, or peer), and (3) personal sources (e.g., change in one's family, health, age, personal insight, and frustration with the status quo). Any of these three sources may provide an impetus to trigger a change in the career routine. Hall (1987) terms the events that effect changes in the career routine "triggers." The triggers in Hall's framework serve similar functions to Kuhn's anomalies. That is, both triggers and anomalies can lead individuals to make significant changes in their careers/theoretical frameworks. The triggers that Hall describes do not necessarily have to lead to career changes. The environmental influences that he describes can lead to changes in the work role routine. Getting a different mentor, for example, may led to a renewed interest in work and increased broker activities.

Most of the examples that Hall provides of factors that may trigger changes in a persons's career routine are events outside of a person's control. We propose that challenges to the work role routine can also come from the persons themselves. That is, individuals can intentionally create or alter their environment (Buss, 1987; Buss et al., 1987).

We propose, furthermore, that having to deal with challenges to the work role will elicit the enactment of new leadership roles and/or the rebalancing of leadership roles. This change, in turn, we propose, will lead to more behavioral complexity. It is the interaction between the individul and his or her environment that stimulates development. Getting a new boss, dealing with new technology in the workplace, and becoming a widow are all examples of events in a person's environment that can significantly affect how a person executes his or her job. A person can also create changes in his or her job that subsequently affect his or her behavioral complexity. A person's decision to join the union, for example, may lead the individual to very different behaviors at work from before he or she joined the union.

We also expect that those leaders who intentionally alter their work role will show the most development in behavioral complexity. People who commit themselves to new behaviors voluntarily and publicly will be more likely to stick to those behaviors than people who do not commit to new behaviors voluntarily and publicly (Staw and Ross, 1987). Leaders who persist the hardest at new behaviors, we expect, will show the most increase in behavioral complexity. Changes in the work role that are not under the control of the individual can be perceived as threatening and can lead to reactive behavior aimed at re-establishing the routine (Brett, 1984).

The environment can induce people to use new leadership roles or to balance leadership roles in new ways. The environment, however, plays an important role not only in the inducement of new behaviors but also in sustaining new behaviors (Fischer, 1980). Only if a person's work environment supports the new leadership behaviors and the new balance that people strike among the roles that they perform can changes in behavioral complexity be expected to be permanent. That is, only through practice and experience in an environment that induces and supports new behaviors do the new leadership roles and/or the new balance of leadership roles become metaprograms that guide behavior (McKnight, 1991, p. 9).

THE DEVELOPMENT OF BEHAVIORAL COMPLEXITY: LEARNING FROM PRACTICE

The question that remains to be answered is how we can provide people with environments that stimulate them to initiate changes in their work roles. More specifically, in order for changes in behavioral complexity to occur, there has to be a learning-to-learn skill, an opportunity to learn, and the capacity to learn (Jacobs and Jaques, 1987). In the following paragraphs we discuss a management training program that focuses on developing the learning-to-learn skill and provides managers with opportunities to learn. This program has served as a behavioral laboratory for applying some of the notions in this chapter. While the experience does not provide any final answers to the above question, it does provide important insights.

The Ford LEAD Program

The Ford-University of Michigan LEAD (Leadership Education and Development) program was designed to increase the behavioral complexity of all middle managers at Ford. LEAD was developed jointly by Ford Motor Company and the University of Michigan Business School faculty. The designers recognized that traditional skill training was an equilibrium-preserving activity. They felt that the middle managers of Ford needed not information, but transformation. They recognized that middle managers are really the experts and that only they can determine the right form for any given situation. The focus of the program, then, became learning, thinking, and managerial leadership. The context for the program was provided by several key issues upon which Ford focuses: corporate strategy, customer focus, quality, and continuous improvement.

LEAD provides Ford's middle managers with a theoretical framework (i.e., the competing values framework, Quinn, 1988) that helps them better understand and frame the often paradoxical nature of the problems that they encounter. The primary purpose of the LEAD program is to stimulate paradigm changes in the middle managers about their role in the organization. The organization is moving away from a sole emphasis on financial accountability and control to an emphasis on financial accountability as well as individual initiative. The program serves as a stimulus for the managers to think deeply about how they can refocus their perceptions of themselves and their work role.

The program serves as a challenge to the managers' work role routines. As one manager described it: "The program forced me to reevaluate my core values, goals, and methods of operating as a means for reinforcing them and/or changing them. I made a conscious effort to become aware of my paradigms and then expanded my own and others' mind-sets toward change." Again, the emphasis is not on teaching new skills, but rather on stimulating and providing tools for critical self-reflection and the formulation of personal action plans for individual improvement.

The above process is sometimes described as in-depth personal evaluation and cognitive reframing, which allow managers to see themselves and their environment through different lenses (Bartunek and Moch, 1987; Quinn, Sendelbach and Spreitzer, 1991). This cognitive reframing process can lead managers to enact new leadership roles and/or to rebalance their leadership roles. Expressed in behavioral terms, the LEAD program leads managers to assess their leadership behavior in terms of Quinn's competing values framework. The identification of roles that they tend to underemphasize or overemphasize may lead these managers to pay more attention to those behaviors in their work unit.

To emphasize application of what is learned at the program, the program consists of two stages: a core session and a follow-up session. During the core session the participants are encouraged to reflect on how the content and the context of the program apply to their specific job responsibilities. The content of the program consists of learning and thinking (paradigm flexibility), cross-functional teamwork, and personal fitness and managerial leadership (the competing values framework [CVF]), while key strategic issues of overall corporate strategy, customer focus, quality, and continuous improvement form the context. (For a more elaborate discussion of the Ford LEAD program, see Quinn, Sendelbach, and Spreitzer (1991).) Figure 10.2 presents the basic design of the content and context for the core session of the LEAD program.

Figure 10.2
Content of the LEAD Program Core Session

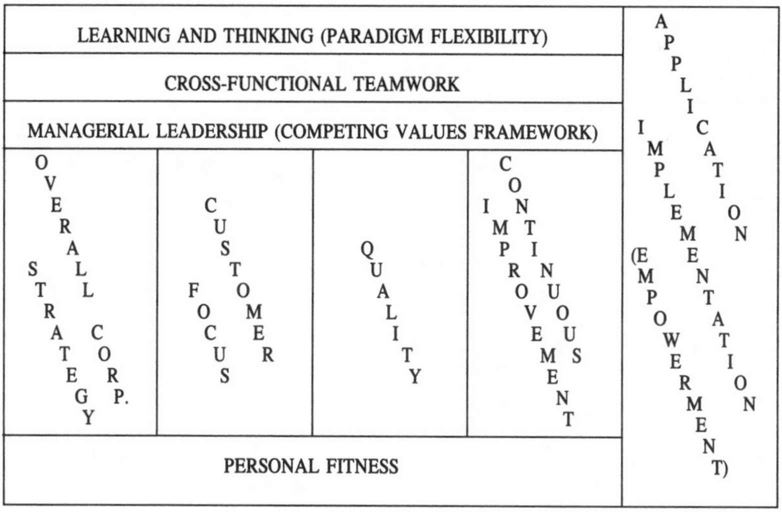

```
┌─────────────────────────────────────────────────────────────┬──────────────┐
│        LEARNING AND THINKING (PARADIGM FLEXIBILITY)          │  A           │
│                                                              │  P           │
│              CROSS-FUNCTIONAL TEAMWORK                       │  P           │
│                                                              │  L           │
│                                                              │  I           │
│  MANAGERIAL LEADERSHIP (COMPETING VALUES FRAMEWORK)          │ I      C     │
│                                                              │ M      A     │
│  O                          C                                │ P      T     │
│  V                          O                                │ L      I     │
│  E          C        I  N                                    │ E      O     │
│  R          U        M  T                                    │ M      N     │
│  A          S        P  I                                    │(E      E     │
│ S    L      T     Q  R  N                                    │ M      N     │
│ T    L   F  O     U  O  U                                    │ P      T     │
│ R        O  M  A  V  O                                       │ O      A     │
│ A  C     C  E  L  E  U                                       │ W      T     │
│ T  O     U  R  I  M  S                                       │ E      I     │
│ E  R     S     T     E                                       │ R      O     │
│ G  P.          Y     N                                       │ M      N     │
│ Y                    T                                       │ E            │
│                                                              │ N            │
│                    PERSONAL FITNESS                          │ T)           │
└─────────────────────────────────────────────────────────────┴──────────────┘
```

Source: R.E. Quinn (1991). Education and Empowerment: A Transformational Model of Managerial Skills Development. In J. Bigelow (Ed.) *Managerial Skills: Explorations in Transferring Practical Knowledge.* Copyright 1991 by Sage Publications, Inc. Reprinted by permission of Sage Publications, Inc.

At the end of the core session, each participant is asked to develop action plans for application. The follow-up session takes place six to eight months after the core session. The follow-up session extends the content and context of the core program. While the themes are the same, the purpose is now to analyze experiences that managers had in the period following the core session, to assess current conditions, and to determine required next steps. In the interval between core and follow-up session, participants are able to try out new behaviors. During the follow-up session they present and compare their failures and successes.

In sum, the process of learning and thinking and individual initiative are central aspects of the Ford LEAD program. The competing values framework and theories of learning and paradigm thinking serve as tools for self-assessment and individual growth. The purpose is to empower managers by altering their current mind-sets, implementing new behaviors, and increasing behavioral complexity.

Impact of the Program

When middle managers enter the program, they tend to be somewhat cynical. Years of experience in a large organization have taught them that the middle manager's job is not about leadership and change, but about conformity and preserving equilibrium. The system, they say, does not want change. Indeed, through interviews, surveys, and a series of factor analyses examining their change efforts in the period between the core session and the follow-up, five powerful factors seem to operate as barriers to change: lack of vision (meaning an unwillingness to commit to projects that will not pay off in the next quarter) in the levels directly above them, organizational or cross-functional conflict, bureaucratic culture, personal time constraints, and disempowered subordinates and coworkers (Quinn, Sendelbach, and Spreitzer, 1991).

The above five barriers are formidable and discouraging, yet during the period between sessions, the middle managers do, indeed, initiate new behaviors. In the same analysis five types of initiative are identified: personal attitude change, empowering subordinates, challenging the mind-sets of others, cross-functional team-building efforts, and self-empowered initiatives, including efforts that bypass many traditional control structures. Quinn, Sendelbach and Spreitzer (1991) provide examples of changes in each category.

These authors also provide an analysis of the overall impact process. This can be seen in Figure 10.3 Here we will review only the highlights.

The data suggest that the core program deeply impacts the existing mind-sets or paradigms of the middle managers and that the middle managers redefine self and role in the organization. The previously mentioned activities lead to new patterns of behavior as outlined above. The outcomes of the initiatives are valued in about 95 percent of the cases, but in 5 percent of the cases people are punished for their efforts. These people become disillusioned with the process and with the

Figure 10.3
The Cycle of Empowerment

CYCLE OF EMPOWERMENT

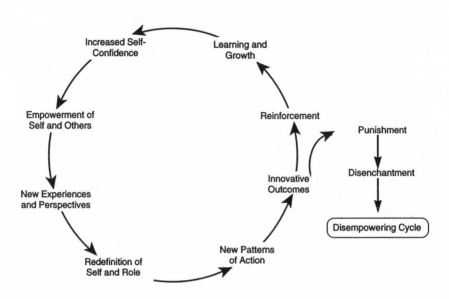

Source: R.E. Quinn (1991). Education and Empowerment: A Transformational Model of Managerial Skills Development. In J. Bigelow (Ed.) *Managerial Skills: Explorations in Transferring Practical Knowledge.* Copyright 1991 by Sage Publications, Inc. Reprinted by permission of Sage Publications, Inc.

program itself. Those who are reinforced continue to grow and increase in self-confidence. These people continue to empower self and others. Such empowerment leads to new experiences and perspectives and to further redefinition of self and role.

So extensive and explicit are the changes that take place in these managers that the company, in the face of a deep automotive downturn, has maintained, at considerable cost, a long-term commitment to the program. This pattern is a clear break with tradition in the industry. Clearly the program shows that it is possible to trigger changes in work role routines, to make deep changes in the paradigms or mind-sets of middle managers, to alter their leadership behaviors, and to increase their behavioral complexity.

CONCLUSION AND DISCUSSION

In this chapter we have introduced a new concept called behavioral complexity. Behavioral complexity focuses on the ability of managers to perform diverse roles and skills in the explicit, behavioral realm. Managers high in behavioral complexity will be able to perform many different roles and will also be able to strike a good balance among the roles. The competing values framework was introduced to provide a framework for the behavioral complexity concept.

We then placed behavioral complexity in an evolutionary context. A developmental framework was introduced that conceptualizes the development of behavioral complexity as a process of freezing-unfreezing-refreezing (FUR) patterns of leadership behavior. The FUR model of development diverges from the more traditional stage models in that it does not assume a universal progression through a set number of stages, critical periods, or unconscious structures. It also diverges from the more traditional stage models because it assigns a critical role to environmental stimuli in the development of the organism, whereas traditionally the emphasis has been solely on the individual. Four types of environmental stimuli were distinguished. Three of these are outside the control of the individual (organizational, work, personal), and one of them is under the control of the individual (self-initiated changes).

Finally, an educational program was described that combined an organizational-level intervention with self-initiated changes to affect individual development. The organizational intervention consisted of two one-week workshops that offered tools for self-reflection and stimulated the participants to formulate action plans based on the self-assessments and to implement these. The action plans formulated by the participating managers led to changes in their work role routine, and these changes are expected to lead to increased behavioral complexity.

The arguments that we have presented can be questioned on a number of issues; we discuss three that need serious attention. First, in the literature on leadership behavior, many more roles have been discussed than the eight leadership roles of the competing values framework (Quinn, 1988). Hart and Quinn (1991) discuss leadership roles that Drucker (1973), Donaldson and Lorsch (1983), Katz (1973), and Mintzberg (1973, 1975) distinguish. Hart and Quinn find that the leadership roles that these researchers distinguish map onto the competing values framework fairly well. However, there probably are leadership roles that do not easily map onto the competing values framework, for example, transformational (Tichy and DeVanna, 1986b) and charismatic leadership (Conger and Kanungo, 1987). The competing values framework, then, is not meant to be the be-all and end-all of the frameworks of behavioral complexity. Rather, the competing values framework should be viewed as a first attempt to conceptualize behavioral complexity in a way that stresses two important aspects: diversity of, and balance among leadership behaviors.

Second, is the issue of whether the environment of the manager has the resources for increased behavioral complexity. The educational program described in this chapter provides an environment that induces new behaviors in managers. What has not been discussed, however, is the actual work environment of the manager. The LEAD program may lead managers to critical self-evaluation and to the development of personal initiatives, but it does not address whether the work environment will sustain or even feed the new initiatives. Critical for the performance of one's job and for the implementation of initiatives is the support that one receives from the organization, including superiors, peers, and subordinates. Gardner and Schermerhorn (this volume) provide a more elaborate discussion of the importance of the support of the superior for managerial success.

The third issue concerns the relationship between cognitive and behavioral complexity. Jaques uses the concept of work capacity to discuss both a person's potential as well as a person's actual level. Jaques argues that a person has an innate potential work capacity and that a person's environment determines the extent to which that capacity is actualized. He believes, furthermore, that a person's potential ability shows at all stages in his or her working life. What matures over a person's life is "the ability to use his [or her] level of abstraction consistently and reliably over a full range of activities" (1976, p. 166). If we accept the notion that work capacity is determined at birth and that the environment only determines the extent to which the innate work capacity is fulfilled, then we can conceive of cognitive complexity as a person's potential work capacity and of behavioral complexity as a person's fulfilled potential. The assessments of cognitive complexity determine how well individuals can differentiate self and others (Kegan, 1982) or school from work (Lewis and Jacobs, this volume). The assessments of behavioral complexity, (Denison, Hooijberg, and Quinn, 1991; Hart and Quinn, 1991; Quinn et al., 1991) discussed in this chapter, reflect actual behavior of managers in the workplace, not only how they see themselves but also how others see them. The assessments of cognitive complexity then may reflect the potential work capacity whereas the assessments of behavioral complexity reflect actualized work capacity.

Practical Implications

The Ford Leadership Education and Development (LEAD) program was developed as a response to the question by top management: What are we doing to prepare the next generation of leaders? We have argued that the LEAD program stimulates self-reflection and personal initiative, leading to increased behavioral complexity. In that respect the program increases the behavioral complexity of the pool of middle managers, from whom the leaders of the future will rise. The program, then, not only stimulates individual growth but also contributes to the effectiveness of the organization by increasing the behavioral complexity of a whole layer of management. The middle managers can be expected to be better at their jobs as well as more responsive to environmental changes. By increasing the behavioral complexity of a whole layer of management, the chances of managers falling prey to the Peter Principle (Peter, 1969) are also reduced.

IV

Temporality and Dynamic Change Processes

11

Stratified Systems Theory and Dynamic Case Study Perspectives: A Symbiosis

James G. Hunt and Arja Ropo

The study described in this chapter, although not originally conducted with SST in mind, has been reinterpreted and extended based on selected SST concepts. This reinterpretation and extension show clearly the additional knowledge contributions that can be gained when SST concepts and those from the study's dynamic case study perspective are used to inform each other.

Specifically, the chapter shows what happens when transformational leadership is added to SST and traced across a period of frame-breaking change lasting several years. It also shows how empirical measurement of cognitive complexity, so important in SST, can be used to help explain the vastly different transformational tracks displayed by the five bank leaders included in the sample of Finnish banks.

Particularly interesting is the dynamic case study approach summarized in the chapter and used to reveal the dynamic transformational leadership tracks. The chapter then shows how the interview transcripts used as the heart of the dynamic case study approach were used to derive cognitive complexity levels for the sampled leaders.

Regardless of whatever strengths or weaknesses Stratified Systems Theory (SST) has as a leadership approach per se, we consider a major (perhaps the major) contribution of it to be a sensitization to some key issues cutting across the organizational and leadership literatures. These issues are an organizational emphasis, a temporal emphasis, and consideration of leader cognitive capabilities.

In terms of the organizational emphasis, the approach moves us from the predominant lower-level, face-to-face, direct influence thrust of current "mainstream leadership" approaches. Instead, the emphasis is on leadership of the total organization at the top, with a cascading of direct and indirect leadership effects down various hierarchical levels throughout the organization.

In terms of a temporal emphasis, SST explicitly stresses time span of feedback. That is, it focuses on differences in the length of time of such feedback at various organizational domains and levels and covers time periods as long as twenty years or more at the very top. Most mainstream leadership approaches, if they emphasize time at all, tend to look at it over relatively short periods (cf. Hunt, 1991; Williams and Podsakoff, 1989).

In terms of cognitive capabilities, the approach especially emphasizes the cognitive complexity of leaders at various organizational levels. Again, the thrust of mainstream leadership approaches has not been on cognitive capabilities (although an exception is cognitive resource theory, Fiedler and Garcia, 1987). Furthermore, we welcome the debate in the present volume, by those such as Lewis and Jacobs and Hooijberg and Quinn, concerning the relative merits of an emphasis on cognitive complexity and related notions versus other more commonly emphasized stylistic or behavioral aspects of leadership.

These organizational, temporal, and cognitive emphases serve as the backdrop for the focus of this chapter. That focus is a processual one examining organizational, temporal, and leader capability aspects within a dynamic case study framework. This examination is both a conceptual and an empirical one based on a number of higher-level leaders, involved in frame-breaking change (cf. Fry and Pasmore, 1983) over several years. The combined SST notions and dynamic case study perspective are used symbiotically to inform each other and enrich the understanding of leadership in a dynamic setting.

A DYNAMIC PERSPECTIVE

While SST sensitizes us to the importance of temporal considerations, it does not follow that SST itself is dynamic. Indeed, it is possible to consider it cross-sectionally or statically at only a single time period, both conceptually and empirically. It also can be looked at in a comparative statics mode, where relationships between or among variables are considered at more than a single point in time. However, of most interest here are the dynamic or processual aspects. Essentially, such an analysis differs from comparative statics in that it examines the path across time or between the periods examined in comparative statics (for a summary, see Hunt, 1991, chap. 12). If a static analysis is a snapshot, then a comparative statics analysis is a series of snapshots (with the periods clearly identified) and a dynamic analysis is a motion picture.

There are a number of techniques for conducting dynamic analysis (e.g., see Huber, 1992; Huber et al., 1990a; Huff, 1991; Kelley and McGrath, 1988; Ropo, 1989).[1] Most of these are what have been termed "variable-oriented" approaches (Hunt, 1991). Indeed, the currently popular structural equation approach, reflected by LISREL (Jöreskog and Sörbom, 1985), can be used in this manner if the individual variables to be modeled can be specified precisely enough (cf. Hunt, 1991). However, rather than concentrating on LISREL or one of the other variable-oriented dynamic approaches, our focus is on the holistic, dynamic case study approach.

In terms of holism, we can think of a continuum of research assumptions and strategies developed by Hunt (1991) from earlier work by Morgan and Smircich (1980). On that continuum, heavily nomothetic, objectivist approaches emphasizing cause-and-effect regularities are at one end, and subjectivist approaches culminating in extreme phenomenology, sometimes described as "solipsism" (S. D. Hunt, 1991), are at the other end. In between is the holistic cybernetic or brain orientation where, as Wilden (1980) says, "causes cause causes to cause causes" (see also Luthans and Davis, 1982, for related discussion). The hologram, where the whole is embedded in each of the parts, is a good representation, and feedback loops abound. Dynamically, we can see this kind of approach emphasized in the kind of virtuous and especially vicious circles discussed by those such as Masuch (1985) where an action taken to deal with one issue has unanticipated effects throughout the system. He shows many examples where attempts to correct dysfunctions not only do not correct them but lead to an ever-increasing spiral of vicious circles, over time. Miles (1980) uses the Watergate affair of the Nixon presidency as an example.

Miller and his colleagues (e.g., Miller and Friesen, 1980, 1984; Miller and Mintzberg, 1983) refer to this notion, in an organization theory context, as organizational configurations or archetypes. These consist of gestalts that not only can reflect relationships among many internal organizational aspects, such as structural components and behaviors, but include a fit with environmental aspects as well (some examples are provided by Mintzberg, 1979). Contingency approaches (e.g., Gupta, 1988; Osborn, Hunt, and Jauch, 1980) also involve a fit between or among various components; however, the fit is a reductionist one in contrast to the holistic emphasis here, where understanding is gained by looking at the overall design.

These configurations can be linked to each other across time by means of tracks (see Greenwood and Hinings, 1988; Hinings and Greenwood, 1988). These tracks represent the dynamic paths taken in the movement of one archetype toward another. Overall, leaders are concerned either with maintaining the current archetype or with moving toward another (as reflected in top-level strategic vision). Tracks reflect this movement, either as change or as maintenance of the status quo. Essentially, tracks are maps of the extent to which organizations move from the constraining assumptions of a given archetype and assume characteristics of an alternative archetype. The specific track, followed by an organizational archetype, is a function of the compatibility among structures and environmental/contextual contingencies, commitment to prevailing and alternative cognitive maps (including values/schemas and implicit organization theories), and the impact of various stakeholders (e.g., as emphasized by Blair and Rivera, this book).

Tracks, like organizational archetypes, can take many forms. Four of these are (1) status quo-oriented, (2) aborted excursions (a change is attempted but is unsuccessful, and there is movement back to the original archetype, (3) reorientation (the change is successful), and (4) unresolved excursions (the change is unsuccessful, and the organization remains in a kind of never-never land).

As indicated, the description above helps integrate the notions of cognitive maps, schemas/implicit theories, and so on with strategic leadership vision. There are many kinds of implicit theories (see Wegner and Vallacher, 1977), and implicit leadership theories have received special emphasis. In the present context, implicit organization theories (Downey and Brief, 1986) are seen as particularly important in influencing strategic leaders' cognitive maps of appropriate configurations and tracks at given time periods (see Hunt, 1991).

Holism Revisited

We argued above that a dynamic case study perspective emphasizes holism, rather than causality, among variables. Here we elaborate on that view within the context of the work of Tsoukas (1989). Following Bhaskar (1978) and Outhwaite (1983), Tsoukas argues that phenomena have different ontological domains: the real, the actual, and the empirical.

What follows is a brief summary of these domains based on Outhwaite (1983). The empirical domain is comprised of experiences, is obtained from direct or indirect observations, and may be distinguished from the actual domain, which includes events, whether these are observed or not. It is possible the events simply do not happen to be observed because there is no one around to see them. Or they may be too slow or too fast or too large or too small to be observed. In other words, what actually happens is not necessarily what is perceived.

Finally, the real domain differs from the actual domain (made up of events) in that it comprises the processes that generate events. The absence of an event does not necessarily mean that there are no generative tendencies or mechanisms. It may mean, instead, that these underlying tendencies are counteracted by other forces. For example, a watch has a generative mechanism that allows it to tell time. However, for that to happen, (1) the mechanism must have its causal powers intact, that is, it must not be broken; (2) the mechanism must be activated via winding or batteries, and the watch must be set to the correct time; and (3) although the watch will indicate the time twenty-four hours a day regardless of whether one observes it or not, it will tell a given person the time only if he or she observes the event of the hands pointing to a given time, an event produced by the generative mechanism.

What all this means is that in terms of theory development, the explanatory structure resides as a generative mechanism in the object of study. Be revealing a generative mechanism(s), we are in a position to redescribe our research object in a direction that is theoretically contributive. The explanatory mechanisms operate as causal powers to generate tendencies (not deterministic causal laws). The realization of these tendencies is contingent upon specific circumstances in the setting that may or may not favor the generation of certain patterns of events (the objectivist, variable-oriented literature calls this "overdetermination"; see Glick et al., 1990). In terms of empirical research efforts, one would be more interested in revealing and conceptualizing the causal capabilities of some research object, such as leaders, than in discovering recurrent regularities of actual events or empirical experiences associated stocastically with leadership.

The generalizability of the findings from such work relies on its capability to conceptualize generative mechanisms of research objects and shed light on contingent conditions under which these generative mechanisms combine and operate. The redescription of the research object can take many forms, including a type of conceptual framework, a process model, or a middle-range theory (cf. Eisenhardt, 1989a). Here, as we show below, we use the dynamic case study perspective to develop an illustrative process model.

APPLICATION OF THE DYNAMIC CASE STUDY PERSPECTIVE

Sample Overview and Theoretical Framework

With the previous discussion as background, we devote the rest of this chapter to empirical and conceptual aspects of the earlier mentioned dynamic case study of higher-level leaders. The case study was not conducted with SST as an explicit framework. However, as we have argued and will show below, the case study can be interpreted within the SST framework and thus put a dynamic "spin" on SST.

The case study involved five higher-level leaders in three different Finnish banks during a period of frame-breaking (Fry and Pasmore, 1983) change. Consistent with Yin (1989, p. 23), the study was an empirical inquiry investigating a contemporary phenomenon within its real life context; the boundaries between the phenomenon and context were not clearly evident; and multiple data sources were used.

The five banking leaders appear to have operated at SST levels IV and/or V, in the organizational domain; one was a CEO, and four were SBU heads (although one of the leaders started at a lower level and was rapidly promoted during the course of the study). All the banks came from one of the largest, nationwide banking systems in Finland. Thus, systems domain strategic leadership could be considered to provide a common strategy/policy umbrella, although, as will be evident, subsystems responses within this umbrella differed considerably.

The Finnish banking industry was chosen for its dynamic aspects as a result of three waves of industry deregulation, starting in the 1970s, with the frame-breaking change starting in the mid-1980s. The chosen banks were involved in mergers and service structure changes (from functionally oriented to profit-center-oriented) as a response to the frame-breaking environmental changes.

Indeed, these substantial structural, organizational changes served as the first criterion for selection of leaders and units for the case study. Then, following Glaser and Strauss (1967), the second selection criterion was an attempt to maximize differences among selected leaders and banks. Thus, the selected banks differed by size (monetary volume), business potential (market share, main customer group), rural versus urban environment, and performance profitability and solvency. The selected leaders within the banks varied by age (thirty-sixty years), education (less than high school-advanced university degrees), and banking experience (three-thirty years). All had a central role in the change process. The overall sampling procedure was based on Glaser and Strauss's theoretical sample—theoretical relevance, rather than statistical representativeness is emphasized. Also, data collection and data analysis were simultaneous processes.

Following the track notion discussed earlier, there was an emphasis on leadership tracks within the sampled banks. The tracks were treated over four to six years and were conceptualized in terms of their transformative nature within the turbulent environmental and structural changes brought about by the succeeding waves of deregulation.

Following both the organizational change literature (e.g., Dunphy and Stace, 1988; Tichy and DeVanna, 1986a) and recent leadership literature (e.g., Nicholls, 1987; Shamir, House, and Arthur, 1990), the study focused on leadership as a transformative force. The assumption was that for leadership, indeed, to serve as a transformative force, it would have to be change-oriented in nature. If it were, it could reinforce the frame-breaking environmental and structural forces. If it were not, it would work at cross purposes with the dynamic environmental and structural forces, and the nature of its track would differ from a transformative track.

Based on the managerial work literature (e.g., Hales, 1986, 1988; Stewart, 1989) and consistent with SST, it was further argued that the crucial linkage among environmental, organizational, and leadership aspects was managerial work or leader critical tasks (in SST terms)[2]. Consistent with Lawrence and Lorsch (1967), these changing leadership tasks were conceptualized in terms of focus, goal, and time perspective.

In summary, there were initial configurations of environmental, organizational, task, and leadership forces in complex interaction. As frame-breaking deregulation occurred, the configurations envisioned by the leaders in question were argued to change substantially to be more suitable to the deregulated environment and the systems-domain strategy/policy umbrella. Tracks showing the extent to which leadership was a transformative force were investigated over a four-to six-year time period.

Leadership was conceptualized in terms of transformational, transactional, and representational aspects. Transactional leadership activities were seen as those that stress stability, short-term perspectives, and first-order changes (cf. Levy and Merry, 1986) in the immediate workplace. This conception is consistent with that of Bass and his colleagues (e.g., Avolio and Bass, 1988; Bass, 1985).

Nicholls (1987) considers transactional leadership in terms of its emphasis on individuals as opposed to the transformative stimulus that drives organizations. He sees transformational leadership as the latter. It involves visionary and charismatic behaviors used to deal with rapid changes and to help put long-range organizational plans into place (cf. Avolio and Bass, 1988; Sashkin and Fulmer, 1988).

A third leadership aspect involved in the study was representational activities. Representational leadership is seen as facilitating aspects of individual, change-oriented linkages among the other aspects of leadership as well as task and organizational aspects. It involves the developing of new networks (e.g., Kotter, 1990) beyond conventional superior-subordinate ones (see Baliga and Hunt, 1988). These new networks are necessary in identifying new issues and linking the organization to a changing environment. As we indicated above, representational activities are argued to facilitate transformational behavior. Sayles (1964), Stewart (1976), and Osborn and Hunt (1974) are among early advocates of representational leadership.

We have provided above an overview of the nature of the sample and covered details of our theoretical framework. Now let us focus on a quick summary of the data-gathering and analyses processes.

Data Gathering and Analysis

Data consisted of interviews supplemented with archival information. The interviewing process itself lasted from three to twelve months, varying from case to case. The entire data collection process took about eighteen months, with the inclusion of the archival documents, supplementary surveys in a couple of cases, and careful verification procedures. In three cases, the interviews were conducted at the same time as the frame-breaking structural change aspects were occurring. In two of the cases, the change process started a few months earlier than the interviews and the two leaders worked in the same bank.

The sampled leaders, plus other knowledgeable informants, were asked to describe, in concrete, factual incidents or situations, the change processes the banks were undergoing. They described how the situations were handled, what had been done specifically, who else was involved, and what the response was. Retrospective information was also necessary. Essentially, it tended to cover the earlier periods of stability or relatively minor change and stable working relationships. Because of possible retrospective social constructions, there was special emphasis on checking facts, using written documents, and interviewing several informants. Also, as indicated below, coanalysts were used to cross-check the original findings.

Processual methodology (see, e.g., Miller and Friesen, 1982) was used to analyze the data. That methodology was consistent with Van De Ven's (1987) suggestions. It involved:

- Pointing out the set of concepts (organizational context, structural mode adopted, strategic behavior, economic performance); critical tasks/managerial work (focus, goal, time perspective); leadership (transactional, transformational, representational).
- Data collection in terms of interviews, archival documents, and the like.

- Tracing events and activities as a function of organizational change, critical tasks, and leadership behavior.
- Checking validity and reliability based on suggestions of Miles and Huberman (1984) and Yin (1989), among others. While details are covered in Ropo (1989) and Ropo and Hunt (1990a, b), we can note here that there was a heavy emphasis on coanalysts to cross-check findings and interpretations concerning leadership descriptions, tracks, temporal relationships, and so forth. Traditional objectivist quantitative coefficients were not appropriate for these data; however, there was a relatively high percentage of observer agreement across a number of different dimensions (see Ropo and Hunt, 1990a, for details).

Results and Discussion

Three different kinds of leadership tracks could be traced in this study: proactive (one leader), reactive (two leaders), and contractive (two leaders). While details differed for each of the leaders within each of the reactive and contractive tracks, the overall patterns for each leader were similar enough to be consistent with an overall description for their track in question.

Figure 11.1 summarizes the general nature of each of these tracks. The figure also shows the three periods of anticipating changes, strategic reorientation, and establishing a new mode, which were inferred from the case study data. While the periods are the same for each of the banks, Figure 11.1 shows that the length of time of the periods in question differs for each bank.

The three organizational change periods were seen as a function of environmental pressure (regulation of business operations, predictability of operations, nature of competition); strategic behavior (changes in major business areas and physical facilities, risk taking, and future orientation); managerial structure (higher-level management team composition and responsibilities); organization structure (functional versus customer-oriented, profit-centered structure); growth (balance sheet figures); and performance (profitability, amount of credit loss). As indicated, each bank had specific developmental features, but all were evaluated as going through the same periods.

Figure 11.1 shows that the tracks varied not only by the timing of leadership activities (in response to organizational and task needs) but also by the intensity and extent of emphasizing change-oriented leadership behaviors. The proactive track was highly progressive and proceeded without major delays. The leader acted in advance of the needs that developed later. The reactive track involved a leader's immediate behavioral response after the organizational force was actualized. The reactive track comprised large, sudden changes, in contrast to the proactive track's continuing progress. Typical of the contractive track was a reversed form of behaviors—there was an occasional peak of change-oriented behaviors but later contraction and sharp decreases in all the kinds of leadership activities.

Figure 11.1
Organizational Periods and Temporal Leadership Tracks

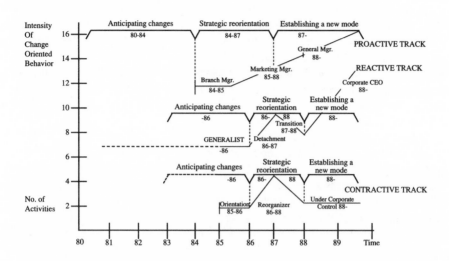

Our basic emphasis pushes us toward further consideration of how the tracks were produced, that is, toward the earlier-mentioned redescription of leadership behavior in dynamic organizational settings. Based on previous treatment and the case findings, we can conceptualize the linkages among the substantive elements of our earlier theoretical argument: organizational change, critical tasks, and leadership behavior. The argument is that the role of leadership in organizational change processes varies as a configurative function of individual and organizational capabilities that are developed over time.

Consistent with much of the literature (see, e.g., Hunt, 1991), individual capabilities here refer to a leader's personal characteristics, abilities, and skills. Organizational capabilities refer to the cumulative know-how and experience of subordinates and the know-how and experience built into the structures, strategies, policies, concrete actions, and events of the organization, and the general organizational climate or cultural change orientation.

Where both individual and organizational capabilities were judged to be high, the proactive track was able to develop. Where both were low, the contractive track developed, as it did also where individual capabilities were low and organizational capabilities were high but could not be utilized. Finally, where individual capabilities were high but organizational capabilities were evaluated as low, the reactive leadership track was identified.

We suggest, further, based on our own conclusions and those of a number of others familiar with the samples in question, that the underlying causal power providing the generative capability to produce the different tracks was a drive toward renewal. That drive was seen as being triggered by a combination of environmental forces (industry frame-breaking changes), organizational forces (strategic decisions heavily oriented toward restructuring), and individual forces (need or desire to deal with the tension between simultaneous change and continuity). The change processes took the form of both catalytic effects and regulating thermostats. These together had an impact on the formation of supportive or countervailing mechanisms as illustrated by the previously mentioned virtuous and vicious circles. Details supporting the above arguments are provided in Ropo (1989) and Ropo and Hunt (1990a, b).

At the beginning of this chapter, we argued that a major contribution of SST was its sensitization of scholars and practitioners to three key issues. The first two of these are a multiorganizational-level leadership perspective and a long- and short-term temporal emphasis.

Our dynamic case study approach and illustrative results and interpretations were an attempt to cover these two issues. In terms of the multiorganizational-level perspective, we showed the tracks of leaders in three different banks and the extent to which each track was transformational. The case description argued that the higher-level leaders whose leadership was investigated probably were operating in the SST organizational domain in response to systems domain leadership.

At the same time, it was pointed out that the proactive leader made a dynamic movement up several hierarchical levels as he was promoted as a part of the change process. Of particular interest here were the major differences in the configurations and tracks of the banks in responding to changes in the systems domain strategy/policy umbrella. The processual tracks also clearly reinforced SST's temporal emphasis, but in a way quite different from its traditional time span of feedback emphasis.

At first blush one might expect more uniformity in these responses than was found. However, we argued that though there was uniformity in terms of the underlying generative drive for renewal, the dynamic aspects of the bank as a system led to differing leadership tracks. The underlying generative forces were comprised of supporting and countervailing mechanisms. The relative impact of these across time was argued to be a function of the way that individual and organizational capabilities came together.

Cognitive Extensions

The third key SST issue mentioned at the beginning of the chapter was an emphasis on leader cognitive capabilities. We also mentioned leader capability in general as a part of our explanation for the different kinds of tracks shown in our case analysis. Here, we attempt to tie together that explanation and the SST emphasis on cognitive capability by reanalyzing some of the case data in terms of cognitive complexity.

The earlier explanation essentially argued that the proactive track developed where both organizational and individual capacity were high. The reactive track developed where there was high individual capability and low organizational capability. The contractive track developed where both were low. Thus, for the proactive track we might expect high leader cognitive complexity, other individual capability aspects being equal. For the reactive track we might also expect high leader cognitive capability. For the contractive track we would expect low cognitive capability.

The question, then, was, How might we tap cognitive complexity, given that we had not set out to measure it as a part of the original case study? What follows is a very brief description of our approach and the results obtained for one leader from each of the proactive, reactive, and contractive leadership tracks.

Cognitive Complexity Aspects of Different Leadership Tracks. Suedfeld and Tetlock (1991) have developed a cognitive complexity coding manual for analyzing speeches or writing of those from whom complexity scores are desired. The second author (Ropo) and an assistant used slight modifications of the procedures in this coding manual to analyze interviewer transcripts derived from the dynamic case study approach as described previously. The research question focused on in these transcripts was, "What is happening in your bank?"

Following key cognitive complexity dimensions set forth in the literature (cf. Hunt, 1991), two dimensions were derived using techniques in the coding manual. The first dimension was differentiation (the number of different elements described by the leaders). The second dimension was integration (the ways in which the leaders were able to put the elements together). In addition, time span (time perspectives expressed by the leaders) was obtained from the transcripts (cf. Jaques, 1986; Streufert and Nogami, 1989). Table 11.1 is a summary of the cognitive complexity dimensions for the selected leader in each track. The proactive leader received high evaluations in both differentiation and integration. His time perspective, as measured here, was from two to three years. The reactive leader was classified as moderate in differentiation and low in integration. His time span was less than a year (our original expectation was that complexity here would be high; it turned out to be moderate). The contractive leader was low in both differentiation and integration, and his time span was evaluated as less than six months.

The proactive leader was very creative in describing the bank's situation. He looked at problems from many angles (unit versus bank versus industry level, national versus international developments, and so on). He showed this perspective in the variety of jobs that he was in across time. He also demonstrated sensitivity to internal and external networking, matching functions with different objectives and the like.

The reactive leader saw industry-level developments broadly and could identify emerging pressures. However, in terms of proposed actions, his focus was at the

Table 11.1
Overview of Bank Managers' Cognitive Complexity

Dimensions	Leadership Types		
	PROACTIVE	REACTIVE	CONTRACTIVE
Differentiation[a]	high	moderate	low
Integration[b]	high	low	low
Time span	2–3 years	< 1 year	< 6 months
Overall evaluation of complexity along the scores of the manual[c]	6–7	3–4	1–2

[a]high=more than four perspectives
moderate=two or three perspectives
low=one or two perspectives

[b]high=more than four ways to link issues
low=one or two ways to link issues

[c]6–7=broad view, outcome comparison, systematic analysis, identifies contradictions
3–4=conditioned alternative views, probabilities, increased tolerance for ambiguity
1–2=dominating one view, generalizations, may identify conditioned alternative views

unit level. He had difficulties with SBU-corporate and with operative bank service-business management linkages. His movement from a specialist to a unit manager appeared to cause him difficulties.

The contractive leader suffered from a lack of accurate perception of fundamental task environment changes. He focused on a very narrow area of expertise that was becoming less and less relevant. He had difficulties dealing with several problems simultaneously.

We should note that the absolute scores and time spans in the table may not correspond exactly to those reported in the literature. The time spans appear short for people in these positions, and the proactive complexity scores are higher than those typically reported in the literature (cf. Tetlock, 1984) for high-level people. Nevertheless, their positioning relative to each other appears in line. Besides the fact that the present scores are based on single cases as contrasted to means in the literature, procedural differences might help account for the differences indicated.

- The manual assumed the text would be directly produced by the informant; here the material came from interviewer notes.
- The manual emphasized the meaning of certain English words to connote complexity; here the original text was in Finnish so these emphases could not be addressed.

- The manual stressed a mechanistic counting of elements; here content was emphasized as well, especially because there was considerable variation in the length of the interviews and notes.

Temporal and Capability Issues One More Time. The treatment above has tied together SST and dynamic case analysis in terms of temporal and capability issues. Previous discussion concerning the fit between individual leader capabilities and organizational capabilities also has a number of implications stemming from these issues.

First, we can think in terms of requisite variety (Ashby, 1952), where there needs to be a dynamic fit between individual and organizational capability. Actually, if we consider configuraitons and tracks, we can extend the notion still further by arguing along the lines of environment, organization, task, and leader behavior fits.

Second, if we return to the change periods in Figure 11.1, we can see that the tracks and the periods are closely related. For example, even though the deregulation and systems domain forces impacted the banks at the same time, the anticipating change period both started and lasted a different duration of time in each bank. There were similar differences in the other two periods. As we mentioned before, differences in these stages were interpreted as a function of a number of things. However, the major point we want to emphasize now is the importance of these periods as far as the tracks are concerned. The dynamic case study perspective has helped alert us to this, and it reinforces the importance of recognizing organizational life cycle or related kinds of stages or periods in thinking about the time spans discussed in SST.

It appears that the time span across the periods was noticeably longer in the proactive as compared with the other tracks. Part of this difference may well be due to that leader's superior cognitive complexity. At the same time, part of it also is probably a function of superior organizational capability. The point is that we would have missed some important dynamic aspects if we had not considered the periods.

Third, the configurative nature of the dynamic case study illustration is consistent with Hooijberg and Quinn's contention that while leader cognitive complexity is important, it is not sufficient. Leader behavior is also considered crucial, along with other previously mentioned aspects of the configuration. Not just any leader behavior will do—it must be change-oriented, transformational, and representational behavior. Thus, it is a part of the broad notion of leader capability, mentioned earlier, in the sense that it is considered appropriate for what needs to be done.

Of course, we do not know whether such behavior actually led to desired organizational change or not. While the literature argues for this transformationally oriented behavior, we do not have direct measures of the extent to which the behavior of the leaders actually served as the desired transformative force. Even more, we do not know the extent to which such change, if it occurred, resulted in improved bank effectiveness. While we might assume that both these things took place, they are questions left unanswered by our dynamic case study illustration.

It is important to note that this effectiveness question is also a particularly important one in SST. At present, we are unaware of any studies empirically linking SST directly with effectiveness, at whatever level is considered. Indeed, there are those who would put this question at the very top of the research agenda, for SST and its answer would determine how seriously they would consider SST.

Regardless of the answers to the above concerns, we can reiterate the point that, like some of the other authors in this book, we consider both leader cognitive complexity and leader behavior, important.

Experience, Training, and Learning How to Learn. One of the most striking aspects of the dynamic case study results was the impact of previous experience and training. The proactive track leader had relatively little traditional bank experience or specific leadership training. The other leaders, however, had considerably more of each and had a tendency to fall back on these in trying to respond to the drive for renewal. This reliance was particularly apparent in the case of the illustrative contractive track leader, who tried to follow his previous extensive experience at rejuvenating failing banks. However, that experience was no longer relevant.

Equally as striking was the tendency of these leaders to fall back on transactional leadership training stressed in previous training programs. These programs had been developed before the widespread dissemination of information about transformational leadership by those such as Bass (1985). (Ropo, 1989, provides a much more detailed description of the historical background of these leaders than we have been able to do here.)

This finding also has a fairly obvious implication in terms of SST—namely, capabilities at lower levels may not be helpful and may even be harmful at higher levels. At the very least we should heed Jacobs and Jaques's (1987) point that a developmental process needs to add to previous strengths. An even more important point, made by these authors, along with many others (e.g., Hunt and Blair, 1985), is that learning how to learn is a key object to strive for in long-term leader development programs, especially in turbulent settings. Thus, rather than specific knowledge and behaviors that may become outmoded, flexibility is the hallmark. Miller (1990) focuses on a variation of this argument in his *Icarus Paradox.* He treats current organizations as analogues to Icarus, who, with his new wings, flew too close to the sun so that his greatest asset ultimately became his greatest weakness.

SYMBIOSIS: A DEEPER LOOK

We have made the point throughout the chapter that SST and the dynamic case study approach could be used symbiotically to inform each other. While we have alluded to some aspects of this contention, here we wish to deal with it more explicitly.

In terms of a dynamic case study emphasis, SST reiterates for us the importance of cognitive complexity and, indeed, of cognition in general. Thus, we are reminded that it is useful to try to obtain congnitively oriented information, along with other kinds. This can take the form not only of cognitive schemas, maps, and the like but also of various aspects of cognitive differentiation and integration, as was done here. Stamp's CPA notions would also be appropriate (see Hunt, 1991, for a discussion).

Also, varying organizational complexity as a function of hierarchical level can be considered in some manner, and the requisite variety notion of a matching of complexity across time can be kept in mind. Finally, the varying time spans of feedback are useful to keep in mind in considering configurations and tracks. In terms of SST, the dynamic case study perspective reinforces the emphasis on temporality. As such, its tracks provide useful information that goes beyond simply arguing that time spans of feedback increase in predictable ways as a function of hierarchical location. For example, a status quo-oriented track, where the intent essentially is to try to maintain the current configuration over a number of years, would seem to be quite different from an attempted dramatic reorientation track.

The configurational aspects also reinforce SST's holistic view by calling for consideration of the overall pattern of environmental, organizational, and individual aspects. Especial emphasis was given to leader behavior in the case study illustration considered here. However, following Greenwood and Hinings (1988) and Hinings and Greenwood (1988), the tracks could emphasize structural aspects or strategic aspects. As an example, a study has recently been completed by Fox (1991) that deals with tracks in the U.S. banking industry focused on strategic issue activities as a function of the Federal government's Community Reinvestment Act (CRA). She found interesting differences between banks with a defender strategy and banks with a prospector strategy as defined by Miles and Snow (1978).

As indicated earlier, the underlying ontological and epistemological assumptions of the dynamic case study emphasis are different from those involved in more objectivist approaches. Here, the grounded theory aspects mean that theory develops simultaneously with data analysis. Also, the assumed differing ontological levels mean an emphasis on underlying generative mechanisms as opposed to causal linkages among variables. The resultant theorizing, then, is in terms of causal tendencies (e.g., an expanding proactive track versus reactive or contractive tracks).

Thus, in the illustration provided here, we talked in general terms about the tracks' being a function of individual and organizational capabilities in dealing with organizational and environmental changes. Given one set of confluences, there was one kind of track; given another set, there was another. Only in the extension involving cognitive complexity did we attempt to describe these in specific quantitative terms. Rather, less specific, generative assumptions were emphasized, and it was recognized that the final result was a function of countervailing and supportive forces.

Also, more reductionist, objectivist approaches typically involve various kinds of aggregations across differing levels of analysis. However, the configurations here, since they do not aggregate data across cases move back and forth among the levels of analysis without using such aggregation (see Dansereau, Alutto, and Yammarino, 1984; Korukonda, 1989; Rousseau, 1985, for recent treatments of unit of analysis issues). Tsoukas (1989) uses the term *embedded* to describe this phenomenon. These configurations also deal in a straightforward way with the "indirect effects" mentioned earlier in the context of SST. Aspects involved in the indirect effects are included as part of the configuration.

Of course, more objectivist-oriented individuals may be uncomfortable with various aspects of the dynamic case study perspective that we have emphasized. Particularly bothersome to some is the "grounded theory" notion where theorizing and data gathering are done simultaneously. They worry essentially that the researcher will see only what he or she expects to see. Fox's bank study, mentioned earlier, is a case in point. She knew ahead of time which banks were defenders and which were prospectors. Thus, one might argue that this knowledge biased her description of the dynamic tracks (even though she cross-checked her conclusions with others).

Following the suggestion of our colleague, Robert Phillips, double- or single-blind technique may sometimes be used in a situation like this where neither the researcher nor respondent or only one of these is aware of the underlying classification. This should not have been an issue in the Finnish study since there was no such classification. The technique would be particularly important if one were interested in effectiveness or the like. For example, do tracks differ between effective and less effective organizations? Here, not knowing about the effectiveness level ahead of time would strengthen the findings.

In summary, the above discussion, indeed, the chapter in general, has suggested a number of ways in which SST and dynamic case studies can complement each other and add to the leadership knowledge base. We have argued that the extensions in thinking involved in the two approaches are symbiotic. We invite readers to share in that symbiosis through appropriate conceptualization and empirical work.

NOTES

1. Various kinds of manned and computer-based simulations also are consistent with a dynamic perspective (for discussion, see Hunt, 1991).

2. Sometimes managerial work and leadership behavior are erroneously confused with each other in the literature (see Hales, 1986; Stewart, 1989, for discussion).

12

Effecting Strategic Change:
Biological Analogues and Emerging
Organizational Structures
Robert L. Phillips and Catherine A. Duran

There are many conceptions and classifications of change throughout a multidisciplinary literature base. This chapter presents a model of change based on biological analogues, which should be useful for strategic leaders, who are necessarily concerned with change and how to cope with and facilitate it in their organizations. Particularly interesting is the manner in which the authors characterize change in terms of adaptiveness or nonadaptiveness.

This chapter integrates a new model of strategic change with emerging organizational structures that may facilitate, and even stimulate, both graduated and punctuated types of change. Specific concepts and recommendations for actions by strategic leaders from the strategic management and practitioner literature are discussed. Phillips and Duran show parallels with some of the key concepts of SST in their discussion of change orientations in structures and top management teams.

This chapter will examine, in detail, ways of classifying and defining change by comparing and contrasting various dimensions of change from different frameworks and will present a model based upon biological analogues that, we suggest, better meets the needs of researchers and practitioners. Next, we review a significant segment of the strategic leadership, as well as the practitioner, literature in an effort to provide specific concepts and recommendations for action by strategic leaders. These concepts and recommendations also include a look at the possibility of developing modified organizational structures for the facilitation of change.

DEVELOPMENT OF A CHANGE MODEL

Theories of change have emerged in almost every discipline, including biology, chemistry, physics, mathematics, economics, and sociology, as well as management. As might be expected, some theorists have begun to employ a multidisciplinary approach (Jantsch and Waddington, 1976; Levy and Merry, 1986;

Miller and Friesen, 1984; Myer, Brooks, and Goes, 1990). However, it is both difficult and problematic to apply theories from one discipline (e.g., evolutionary theories from biology) to other types of systems (e.g., organizations). Reasons for the difficult and problematic nature of applying theories across fields include inconsistencies of level of analysis, underlying assumptions, and theoretical domains. However, cross-fertilization of ideas between disciplines can often lead to creative theory development. In fact, one prominent theorist in complex system theory suggests that the biological notion of adaptation (the view of change employed here) is one of the common threads connecting several disciplines (Gell-Mann, 1984).

Although the concept of biological adaptation is, indeed, a thread running through the field of strategic management (Foster, 1985; Henderson, 1989; Miller and Friesen, 1984; Myer, Brooks, and Goes, 1990), there appears to be a certain degree of confusion concerning its roots, as well as its application. Further, we suggest that the confusion is exacerbated due to the fact that several concepts and models of change fail to distinguish between the processes of change and the resulting change states.

Classification of Change

As indicated earlier, it seems almost every discipline presents multiple classifications of change. The management field is no exception. Such concepts as first-order change (a variation within a system that leaves the system unchanged) and second-order change (a variation that changes the system itself) (Levy and Merry, 1986) appear to dominate the literature. Several other concepts of change states, although provided different names, can be approximated by the notion of first- and second-order change. In a brief review of the literature on first- and second-order change, Levy and Merry (1986) found numerous such pairs of change concepts, for example, branch and root; executive and policy; evolutionary and revolutionary; linear and nonlinear; rational and radical; developmental and revolutionary; homeostasis and radical; transition and transformation; single-loop and double-loop learning; change and transformation; normal and paradigm; momentum and revolution; as well as others (Levy and Merry, 1986, pp. 6-8).

As an exception to the dual state change classification system, Golembiewski, Billingsley, and Yeager (1976) developed a tripartite model of change. Although two of the three change classifications (alpha and gamma) might be considered parallel to first- and second-order change, their third type of change (beta) is not. The three types of change were (1) alpha: a variation in the degree of an existential state; (2) beta: alpha change plus a change in the calibration of at least some portion of the measurement continuum; and (3) gamma: the redefinition or reconceptualization of some domain—differences in state as well as differences in degree (Golembiewski, 1986).

Snow and Hambrick (1980) go so far as to suggest that the term *strategic change* should be reserved for results that substantially alter the strategy-making process. Changes that fall short of such a criterion ought to be labeled as "adjustments."

Recently the strategic management field has introduced change classifications that generally fit the dichotomous notion of first- and second-order change, but with additional dimensions (e.g., Ginsberg, 1988; Miller and Friesen, 1984; Myer, Brooks, and Goes, 1990). Meyer, Brooks, and Goes (1990) adopted the first- and second-order change notions; however, they added a level of analysis dimension—firm and industry—that resulted in four classifications of change: (1) adaptation: firm-level, first-order change; (2) metamorphosis: firm-level, second-order change; (3) evolution: industry-level, first-order change; and (4) revolution: industry-level, second-order change.

Ginsberg (1988) proposed a framework for conceptualizing changes in strategy that involved two dimensions and four concepts. The first dimension distinguishes between viewing strategy as a position (choices of product/market domains, and so on) or as a perspective (organizational processes by which problems are discovered, decisions made, and so on). The second dimension distinguished between change as (1) changes in magnitude or (2) changes in pattern. Their model, thus, results in four categories of changes in strategy. We suggest the dimension of magnitude/pattern is similar to the notion of first- and second-order change.

Miller and Friesen (1984) begin by viewing change in the usual terms of evolutionary and revolutionary but also introduce the dimension of degree of interconnectedness, resulting in four classifications—incremental, piecemeal, dramatic, and quantum. Quantum (as opposed to piecemeal) change occurs when many things change together—change in a "multifaceted or concerted way" (pp. 208-209). Dramatic (as opposed to incremental) change occurs when "elements quickly change a great deal" (p. 209). Revolutionary change is described as change that is both dramatic and quantum. Evolutionary change is change that is both incremental and piecemeal.

Aside from the various change states, there are several frameworks of change processes based upon biological analogues. Tushman and Romanelli (1985) have developed a model of organizational evolution that includes both gradual, incremental change (i.e., a type of first-order change) and rapid, revolutionary change (i.e., a type of second-order change). Tushman and Romanelli's (1985) model of punctuated equilibrium depicts organizations as having convergent periods, characterized by long time spans of incremental change and adaptation, punctuated by strategic reorientations, or short periods of discontinuous change. In convergent periods, structures, systems, controls, and resources increasingly coalign, whereas in reorientation periods, strategies, structure, power, and systems are fundamentally transformed. Strategic orientation and reorientation reflect both corporate-level (what business the firm is in) and business-level (how a firm competes) activities (Tushman and Romanelli, 1985).

The Tushman and Romanelli (1985) punctuated equilibrium model apparently has arisen as a metaphor from a biological concept of evolution put forth by

Eldredge and Gould (1972); however, there are some fundamental differences in the Tushman and Romanelli (1985) model and the "punctuated equilibria" notion of Eldredge and Gould (1972). Eldredge and Gould (1972) and Eldredge (1985) use the term *punctuated equilibria* to describe a process of speciation (i.e., the origin of new kinds or types of organisms) characterized by rapid and episodic events that produce large-scale revolutionary patterns. The first point of difference is the level of analysis; the Tushman and Romanelli (1985) model pertains to changes within a firm (rather than the development of new types of firms), while Eldredge and Gould (1972) are referring to populations of different species of organisms. Myer, Brooks, and Goes (1990) note that in explicating strategic change processes, it is useful to distinguish between firm and industry (a population of firms) levels.

The second difference is that the convergent periods in the Tushman and Romanelli (1985) model are characterized by gradual adaptive change, whereas Eldredge and Gould (1972) and Eldredge (1985) suggest that stasis or nonchange is the dominant evolutionary theme. One interesting way to view the Tushman and Romanelli (1985) model of organizational evolutionary change is a combination of two other distinct biological notions of change (keeping in mind the shift to firm level instead of population level). One is the theory of phyletic gradualism. Phyletic gradualism is evolution that takes place by the slow, steady, gradual, progressive transformation of an entire species through time (Eldredge, 1985) and is the theory to which Eldredge and Gould (1972), proposed their alternative theory of "punctuated equilibria." The other notion is the theory of quantum evolution, which attempts to explain large evolutionary shifts within a single species, leading to major new adaptations of that particular species, rather than the origin of new types of organisms (Simpson, 1944, 1953). Phyletic gradualism could correspond to the convergent periods (at firm level), and quantum evolution might describe the strategic reorientation periods, in the Tushman and Romanelli (1985) model.

Plausible Reasons for Second-Order Strategic Change

Strategic reorientations, or second-order strategic change, whether punctuated or chaotic, may occur as a result of many events. For example, mergers and acquisitions often dramatically affect both corporate- and business-level strategies of a firm. Markets and/or products that were important before a merger or acquisition may be downplayed or eliminated, and new ones may emerge or be mandated. A firm that was following a focus differentiation strategy merged with, or acquired by, another company that follows a low-cost producer strategy may or may not be allowed to retain its original strategy, depending on the dominant merging or acquiring firm's motives. A second example would be an organization that undergoes second-order change as a result of a major technological shift in the organization's task environment.

When an organization changes members of the top management team, especially the chief executive officer (CEO), there is great potential for second-order change. The new CEO will often have a distinctive (and probably different from the past) vision of where the organization should be headed and how to get there, especially if the new CEO is coming from the outside. (However, even if coming from within, there could be radical change, e.g., Reginald Smith's replacement by Jack Welch in General Electric.)

Punctuated Equilibrium Allusions

Whatever the reason for second-order change, adaptive or nonadaptive, a punctuated equilibrium type of model may be heuristically valuable. In addition, currently in theoretical biology, punctuated equilibrium is seen as complementary, rather than exclusive of phyletic gradualism (Bodnar, Jones, and Ellis, 1989). We suggest that processes akin to phyletic gradualism and punctuated equilibrium exist simultaneously within an organization.

There have been numerous examples of "punctuated" processes of change in the organization science literature, at many different levels of analysis. For example, at the group level, Gersick (1988) proposed a model of group development with long periods of inertia, punctuated by concentrated, revolutionary periods of quantum change. Examples at the firm level include Greiner (1972), who addressed organizational development as a series of evolutionary periods of growth punctuated by times of revolutionary change. Foster (1985) described new spurts of competitive advantage obtained through radical and unpredictable changes in organizational strategies, punctuating the usual gradual and smooth adaptation to the environment. Pettigrew (1987) observed that the development of one of the United Kingdom's largest manufacturing companies showed radical periods of change interspersed with periods of incremental adjustment.

Theorists who have done studies at the industry level or above include Weiss and Birnbaum (1989) and Mokyr (1990). Weiss and Birnbaum (1989) characterized technological invention as a continuous process resulting in incremental change, punctuated by radical changes that create discontinuities that change the basic technology. Mokyr (1990) described technological systems as having long periods of stagnation and very slow change punctuated by feverishly rapid changes, through which new innovations arise.

Additionally, Tushman, Newman, and Romanelli (1986) suggest that the punctuation process is painful, dysfunctional, and a "necessary evil" and that effective firms are those that take advantage of the long convergent periods. However, other theories of change in several fields may suggest that systems and organizations retain flexibility and achieve high performance more through punctuated change, rather than graduated change. Perhaps if the change process were made routine, that is, structures modified to allow (or even force) both types of change (more on this later in the chapter), the process would be productive and adaptive, rather than painful and dysfunctional.

Toward a Modified Change Framework

In any modified framework for the classification of change, we propose that the classification framework meet at least five criteria. (Levy and Merry, 1986, and Van de Ven and Poole, 1988, have suggested criteria for theories of change. These criteria should not be confused with the criteria presented below for classifications of change states.)

First, we suggest that any new framework be commensurate with the dominant change classification models currently in the field. The reason for this suggestion is that many of the presented models have excellent theoretical value. Second, any new framework should allow for a full range of change classifications, from inertia to out-of-control change (chaos). Third, a change classification model should not confound processes of change with change outcomes. Fourth, in line with Snow and Hambrick (1980), we believe a change framework should be able to distinguish between small, and perhaps insignificant, changes (adjustments) and large, highly significant changes (strategic changes). Finally, the framework ought to be internally consistent and possess a reasonable degree of external validity.

With the above criteria in mind, we examined the underlying dimensions contained in many of the other change frameworks. From the Miller and Friesen (1984) discussion of change classifications with respect to the terms *dramatic* versus *incremenetal*, as well as from numerous other frameworks (e.g., see the discussion of first- and second-order change parallels, early in this chapter), the most common underlying dimension seems to be some concept of degree or magnitude of change over time. Thus, we selected as our basic dimension change per unit of time. When we examined the other two categories of Miller and Friesen (1984), quantum versus piecemeal, the underlying dimension appeared to be the degree of interconnectedness of a set of changes. Miller and Friesen (1984) also used the term *concerted change* to denote quantum change.

A dimension of interconnectedness would have certain advantages. For example, it would tend to separate planned from unplanned change. However, we believed such a dimension had more to do with the process of change, rather than a change outcome. Thus, we searched for another dimension that would help us meet our stated criteria.

It seemed that no model we reviewed attempted to separate functional from dysfunctional change. That is, all frameworks that used the biological notion of evolutionary change assume that the change is functional. That is, by its very definition, an evolutionary change is one that is in concert with its environment. But organizations with the cognitive ability of its strategic leaders are quite capable of fostering change that is dysfunctional, as well as functional. Perhaps organizations can change so rapidly as to induce a chaotic state. Thus, a change state framework ought to provide for such a possibility.

We selected an axis of our model labeled degree of environmental fit. There were several reasons for so doing; however, two were most important. First, the

Figure 12.1
Modified Change Framework

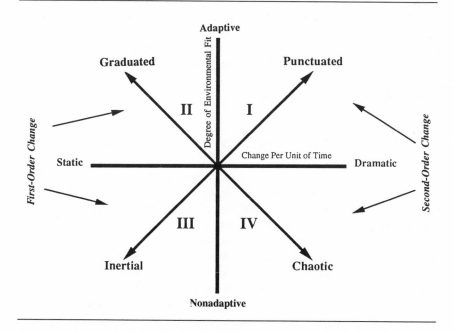

notion of environmental fit, as indicated earlier, is fundamental to any change out-come in the field of strategic management. Second, environmental fit is highly con-sistent with the biological framework on which much of the change theories are based. Figure 12.1 presents the model.

The various classifications of change can be derived from vectors in each of the four quadrants. Similar to the original Miller and Friesen (1984) notion, punc-tuated (revolutionary) change is illustrated as a combination of dramatic and adap-tive (quantum) change (see Quadrant I). There are other change possibilities rang-ing from complete inertia (Quadrant III) through graduated change (Quadrant II) to complete chaos (Quadrant IV).

We suggest the framework in Figure 12.1 meets the five criteria outlined earlier. First, it does fit with many of the existing change notions earlier discussed under the rubric of first- and second-order change. As indicated in Figure 12.1, however, first- and second-order change need not necessarily be adaptive or functional. On the other hand, one might inquire if the notion of ''changing the system itself'' is contained in the punctuated or chaotic quadrants. We would argue it is, based on the reasoning that, by its definition from both biology and organizational science, change of such magnitude affects the larger organism.

Second, it clearly does allow for a full range of change states, from inertia through chaos. Third, it distinguishes between change states (outcomes) and change processes; that is, it deals with the results of change, rather than the stimuli for change. Fourth, it does distinguish between small and large changes (adjustments/strategic changes) for the same reasons as outlined by Snow and Hambrick (1980). Finally, we believe it is internally consistent and, to the extent it is commensurate with the dominant change notions in the field, contains a degree of external validity. But, more importantly, the modified change framework, by virtue of its greater range and separation of change states from change processes, can better facilitate the formulation of change theories.

EFFECTING STRATEGIC CHANGE

It seems to us that the key lesson from the biological analogues of change and our proposed model is that strategic leaders need to ensure that the organizations for which they are responsible are structured for both graduated and punctuated types of change. Structures of organizations built for intense competition (incidentally, military organizations committed to battle face the most intense competition yet known) and intended for long-term survival must be able not only to accommodate but to facilitate both graduated and punctuated change, simultaneously. In fact, we suggest that an important criterion for the separation of the strategic level from lower organizational levels is the requirement for facilitating punctuated change, which we argue is inherent in the strategic leadership role. Our argument goes well beyond what is inherent in a single role. The impetus for change must include the organizational function in that the organizational structure needs both to stimulate innovation as well as to facilitate integration of the innovation.

Experience with punctuated change often tells us how traumatic such change is (e.g., Tushman, Newman, and Romanelli, 1986; Wittington, 1990). Wittington (1990) examined social structures of British manufacturing organizations in the 1980s and pointed out that the failure to recognize the social "embeddedness" of organizational phenomena had serious implications for the management of strategic change. Socially entrenched strategic inertia (i.e., the social and political structuring of organizations) drove two manufacturing firms into first crisis and then takeover, despite strategically well-informed attempts to change. In November 1988, the editor of the *Academy of Management Executive*, when discussing possible future themes, cited the need to know more about strategy and culture. His basic observation was that typically, organizations that implemented a change strategy frquently had implementation problems and seemed puzzled. He asserted, "Strategic implementation usually means culture change" (Burke, 1988, p. 268).

Johnson (1990) pointed out that although research on fundamental strategic change is sparse, what there is suggests that such change requires substantial cognitive shifts in which there are required interventions, often by new corporate leaders, involving political and symbolic, as well as more substantial, action. His suggestions are consistent with the "conceptual capacity" notions of Lewis and Jacobs (this book), where strategic leaders must be able "conceptually to represent highly complex, volatile, and probabilistic environments in which they operate" (Lewis and Jacobs, this book). Johnson's (1990) requirement of substantial cognitive shifts by strategic leaders may be akin to the Kegan (1982) fourth stage of development of meaning (a type of "metacognition"), where strategic leaders "think about, rather than thinking with, consensual points of view" (Lewis and Jacobs, this book).

Johnson (1990) also illustrated how changes in structure facilitated strategic change. However, he was discussing how structural change facilitated specific strategic changes; he did not discuss how structures could be formulated to facilitate generalized strategic change, which is for us a key point. The model presented by Johnson (1990)—unfreezing, some change process, refreezing—although a generalized model that has been in the literature in some form or another since the writings of Lewin (1952), may be part of the problem of social entrenchment. That is, all such models end with the word *refreezing*, with the implication that the new attitudes and behaviors are just as embedded as the old; hence, any new change would be just as traumatic as the first change.

What we are suggesting, albeit toward an ideal state, is a structure and culture (granted, there is considerable overlap between the two) that facilitate change. That is, there may be integrating mechanisms within the structure that greatly facilitate the assimilation of change, perhaps akin to the Lawrence and Lorsch (1967) notion of boundary-spanning units. It may be possible to stimulate the formation of a culture that expects and welcomes change, or, if not welcomes, at least does not put up active opposition. Hopefully, as punctuated change is seen to facilitate the accomplishment of organizational goals and as individuals in the organization have a vested interest in the accomplishment of the goals, change would be welcome.

Thus, there appears to be an organizational paradox when it comes to environmental adaptation. On one hand, members of the organization need to be highly committed to their current task—improving production, gaining proficiency with the technology in use, perhaps working on a new product. On the other hand, progress, change, and new technology are inevitable; thus, the organization requires sensors as to what is happening elsewhere and an ability to adapt to the new reality. Frequently, these two requirements are not in harmony with each other. But to be the industry leader (or to be the military force with the distinctive advantage on the next battlefield), there is a third requirement—the organization is the source of the environmental change. Successful organizations that quickly adapt to significant disturbances in their environment are frequently praised; nonetheless, such organizations are reactors to the initiatives of others. Usually, although not always, the preeminent position goes to the organization that fields (brings to market) the new idea or product (or weapons system).

In military terms, the strategic leader must encourage the effectiveness and efficiency of the military force in being while at the same time working very hard on the development of the new force (concepts for employment, synergies across services and forces of other countries, design and experimentation of new weapons). For the strategic leader of business, it means designing an organization that can "get down on the learning curve," continuously improve the product, gain market share, garner the benefits of scale, shorten cycle time, and so on, but, at the same time, plan for punctuated change in three general ways.

First, the strategic leader must design environmental scanning units that can quickly discern new developments that are relevant to the organization. Second, the strategic leader should construct integrating units within the organization that are designed to facilitate changes required to keep the organization abreast of the new developments, regardless of the source of such developments—external or internal. Finally, the strategic leader can design a structure that seeks to be the source of the punctuated change for all in the industry—again, whether the basis for such change is internally generated or acquired through acquisition.

Earlier, we spoke of the requirement for strategic leaders to be able to facilitate punctuated change. In an effort to discern current thinking on strategic change and the role of the strategic leader, we examined a segment of the literature.

In a recent study conducted jointly by Korn/Ferry International and the Columbia University Graduate School of Business (Korn/Ferry, 1989), CEOs and senior executives of twenty nations were surveyed on a host of issues, including the expected requirements of the CEO in the year 2000. Whereas there were some differences, most agreed that the CEO of the future must be able to

- convey a compelling vision of the future of the corporation,
- communicate even more frequently with customers and employees,
- link compensation to individual performance more systematically,
- promote management training and development, and
- plan for management succession with more vigor and foresight.

Jaques and Clement (1991) would agree with the above points and would probably argue that Stratified Systems Theory (SST) provides an explication of these notions. For example, they maintain that (1) CEOs must have a clearly articulated conception (vision) of where they are trying to take the company (Jaques and Clement, 1991, p. 274); (2) managers must keep their subordinates informed about company policy shifts, current market conditions, personnel changes, and many other environmental factors, as well as the subordinates keeping their managers informed of their progress in tasks and their ideas and insights (p. 161); (3) top-level corporate executives must periodically review the corporate culture and look for any inconsistencies, such as compensation policies that do not reward employees who do more complex tasks (p. 269); (4) it is necessary for companies to have a managerial leadership development program (p. 288); and (5) one of the essential components of the managerial leadership development program is a system for reviewing and evaluating existing personnel for matches with future requirements, having the top management team considering their "up-and-coming talent" (p. 288, 290).

Of the five imperatives set forth by the Korn/Ferry study (1989) and the related notions of SST, it seems to us the major challenge is the first—a compelling vision of the future of the corporation. The Korn/Ferry report points out: "The corporate leader of the 21st century must also understand and accurately interpret the rapidly changing business environment. The fate of every corporation will depend upon the CEO's ability to anticipate the competition and formulate a strategy for surmounting threats that have not yet materialized. Business leadership in the 21st century will entail fighting wars before they occur." (Korn/Ferry, 1989, p. 54).

The above quotation is not entirely foreign to the strategic leadership literature, although the part about fighting wars before they occur might have pushed the frontier somewhat. In fact, if we refer to Hooijberg and Quinn (this book) concerning a role theory framework for strategic leaders, the need for innovation is an important consideration. Although the innovation requirement is not nearly as strongly stated as in the Korn/Ferry (1989) report, there are two other aspects of strategic leadership that we believe are very important—the strategic leader's need for balance along competing roles as well as a need to perform multiple roles. That is, the role of the innovator (living with change, creative thinking, managing change) in the Quinn (1988) framework must be balanced with the role of coordinator (one who is expected to maintain the work flow and structure of the system). The more the strategic leader innovates, the greater the requirement for performance in the coordinator role. Quinn (1988) provides an example of a corporation that almost literally innovated itself out of existence. The basic structure was never allowed to assimilate change before more change was instituted. (Incidentally, we would plot such a situation in the chaos section (Quadrant IV) of the model in this chapter).

The notion of the competing values paradox (managerial behavioral balance) by Quinn (1988) is very similar to our notion of organizational paradox discussed earlier. In fact, we suggest that we have, perhaps, provided a structural analogy to Quinn's (1988) managerial behavioral model, at least on the innovation-coordination dimensions, with the possible result that the practically omniscient requirement (from the Korn/Ferry list) for the CEO of the year 2000 and beyond to "accurately interpret the rapidly changing environment" and to fight wars "before they occur" might possibly be helped by the organizational structure.

Nevertheless, in examining biological theory or organizational imperatives, one idea stands out—the need for change, whether graduated or punctuated. Although SST deals explicitly with levels across organizations, length of time of managerial decisions, and organizational outcomes, it does not explicitly recognize how to bring about change, either graduated or punctuated.

It appears to us that different types of change may be inherent at different levels of hierarchy outlined in SST. For example, in the production domain (Levels I-III), graduated change may be inherently linked to the primarily linear and sequential type of cognitive processing required at that level (see Jacobs and Lewis, this book). Although in the organizational domain (Levels IV and V), the primary cognitive processing modes are parallel and interconnected, there is still an emphasis on task trade-off and constant adjustment between organizational and environmental variables (Jacobs and Lewis, this book), thereby suggesting that graduated change would be most likely. On the other hand, in the systems domain (Levels VI and VII) there may be potential for punctuated change, as the cognitive processing required at these levels encompasses the development of networks (Jacobs and Lewis, this book). These informational and conceptual networks provide a means for the necessary anticipation of changes in the environment. The use of complex conceptual information (including culture and values) to form strategic alternatives (Jaques and Clement, 1991) may stimulate punctuated change within the organization.

As stated earlier, the need for change (graduated and punctuated) is evident. If we examine graduated change first, we discover a literature with a plethora of prescriptions. In fact, we suggest that the classical management school, as well as the ongoing management literature, contains rich prescriptions and examples of what to do to bring about graduated change in an organization. We now briefly review a few such prescriptions.

Effecting Graduated Change

We proceed from a fundamental assumption that we are discussing the variance that may be accounted for by the actions of individuals within organizations. Of course, there are theories of population ecology that may be used to explain speciation, as previously noted; however, again as noted earlier, we are talking about within-organization actions. Thus, Burgleman's (1991) concept of intraorganizational ecology of strategy making and organizational adaptation is quite appropriate. Burgleman (1991), under the intraorganizational ecology (IOE) concept, views organizations as an ecology of strategic initiatives that emerge in patterned ways and compete for limited resources. Strategy and, hence, strategic change result, in part, from selection and retention mechanisms operating on the internal variations of strategic alternatives. Variations, in turn, are induced by individuals' seeking expression of their special skills and career advancement through the pursuit of differing initiatives. Selection of alternatives (i.e., retention of initiatives) comes from retaining those initiatives that "work," which, in turn, define organizational goals, domains, and perhaps culture, at least some aspects of culture.

Burgleman (1991) proposes links between the ecological processes and different forms of adaptation—induced process (initiatives that are within the scope of the organization's current strategy) and autonomous process (initiatives that emerge outside the scope of the organization's current strategy and provide the potential for new organizational learning). Burgleman's (1991) Proposition 1 is as follows: "Firms that are relatively successful over long periods of time, say ten years or more, will be characterized by top managements that are concerned with building the quality of the organization's induced and autonomous strategic processes as well as with the content of the strategy itself,'' (Burgleman, 1991, p. 256). Burgleman's (1991) two types of adaptation (induced and autonomous) are at least suggestive of, if not similar to, our earlier presented notions of graduated and punctuated change. (Burgleman, 1991, does refer to the autonomous process as discontinuous change.)

Burgleman (1991) suggests that as an organization grows, strategy formulation becomes increasingly differentiated, involving multiple layers of the hierarchy. Organizational members in different parts of the organization perceive different strategies as having the best potential for both their own and the organization's advancement, hence, the provision of sources of variation in strategic choices. Such processes preserve the coupling of strategic initiatives to current operations, albeit with variations. In fact, such processes may have the effect of decreasing the probabilty of the organization's generating punctuated changes.

Let us pause here with IOE theory, as the second part, autonomous change, better fits with our last section (on punctuated change). However, before leaving IOE, we might draw one or two implications for strategic leaders in fostering graduated change. To accomplish graduated change, strategic leaders should foster and seriously consider change recommendations coming from all parts of the organization, regardless of hierarchical level, through a variety of mechanisms, especially through organizational experimentation (Burgleman, 1991).

The internal process portion of IOE seems to show links with the strategic management theory of logical incrementalism (J. Quinn, 1980). A description of logical incrementalism includes the flowing together of internal decisions and external events, creating a widely shared consensus for action. It is a combination of strategies from strategic subsystems that are "blended incrementally and opportunistically into a cohesive pattern" (J. Quinn, 1978). In Burgleman's (1991) IOE, induced processes result in strategic initiatives that fit with the current organizational strategy, through administrative mechanisms and/or cultural influencing.

Aside from the broad theoretical literature, as indicated earlier, there is a large amount of practitioner literature that may offer suggestions.

Tichy and Charan (1989) published the results of an interview with Jack Welch, CEO of General Electric (GE). Welch indicated that good business leaders were able to create vision, articulate the vision, passionately own the vision, and relentlessly drive the vision to completion, an idea that is somewhat removed from IOE and logical incrementalism, in that a single individual, rather than subsystems within the organization, is the primary source of change and ideas. It seems to be anchored in an imperative for the strategic leader to convince others and establish systems to assist the organization toward whatever the vision is. The GE system is built upon the answers to five questions, using five simple charts:

- What are your global market dynamics today, and where are they going over the next several years?
- What actions have your competitors taken in the last three years to upset the dynamics?

- What have you done in the last three years to affect those dynamics?
- What are the most dangerous things your competitor could do in the next three years to upset those dynamics?
- What are the most effective things you could do to bring your desired impact on those dynamics? (Tichy and Charan, 1989).

Welch sees his role as facilitating fast action to support his strategic business unit leaders to create and grow new global businesses. Further, there is a stated goal to be number one or two in virtually all business in which GE enters. However, in line with IOE, Welch views the future of GE to be a place where "people have the freedom to be creative, a place that brings out the best in everybody" (Tichy and Charan, 1989, p. 120).

Pearson (1989) presents six basics for general managers that he suggests constitute the key tasks of every general manager's job:

- Shaping the work environment, which consists of three elements—affecting the prevailing performance standards (most important of the three elements), defining what the company is like and how it operates, and shaping the people concepts and values that determine what it is like to work there.
- Setting strategy (crafting a strategic vision).
- Marshaling resources (allocate resource support to competitive strategies, not to marginal businesses, low payout projects, and so on). In short, have strategic focus.
- Developing managers—lead the annual personnel reviews, use challenging job assignments for development purposes, surround yourself with "good people."
- Building the organization—fewer layers, bigger jobs, broader responsibilities; organize the people rather than concepts or principles.
- Overseeing operations—supervise operations and implementation (Pearson, 1989).

The above recommendations fit better with the notion of a strong strategic leader focused mostly on graduated change; however, the managerial development notion might be quite consistent with creating intraorganizational variety along the lines of IOE theory. The above recommendations may also converge with SST. For example, shaping the work environment and setting strategy are part of the SST notion of aligning corporate and personal values for getting everyone in the organization moving in the direction set by the CEO (Jaques and Clement, 1991, p. 270). Marshaling resources could be achieved through project teams (Jaques and Clement, 1991, p. 234). Developing managers (especially through matching work opportunities with individual potential) is a key tenet of SST (see Jaques and Clement, 1991, pp. 88-89, 287-288). Also, SST has specific suggestions on building the organization, with a certain number of layers (no more than seven), organizing people in a particular manner according to complexity of work and human capability (Jacobs and Lewis, this book).

Finally, we will close the graduated change section by briefly discussing concepts from five prominent theorists—Zaleznik (1989a), Drucker (1988a), Kanter (1989a), Jaques (1990), and Etzioni (1989).

Zaleznik (1989a) states that psychopolitics (the balancing of expectations in the workplace) has been substituted for real work, or the actual performance of an organization, and that process has been put ahead of substance. He maintains that workers actually prefer task, rather than social, leaders and that real proficiency of work is the ultimate confidence and morale builder. These notions are consistent with Welch's five-step system for GE, where global market dynamics are the center of attention, and all GE businesses are expected (or required) to be number one or number two in their global markets. Real work and organizational performance reign supreme, yet workers have creative freedom and are continually challenged and developed.

Drucker (1988a) discusses a new type of organization where specialists will be brought together in task forces that cut across traditional departments. Information technology will be the major underlying force, and everyone will take "information responsibility" for actions (asking, Who depends on me for what information, and on whom do I depend?). Drucker's (1988a) suggestion for the creation of a vision that can unify an organization of specialists and the building of a management structure that works with task forces could facilitate a structure that Pearson (1989) might propose. That is, one of Pearson's (1989) basics for general managers—building the organization through fewer layers, bigger jobs, and broader responsibilities—might be implemented through Drucker's (1988a) unifying vision.

Kanter (1989) espouses views in line with Drucker (1988a), with even more extreme forms of collaborative work—across divisions and companies, not just across departments. She believes that there will be many horizontally functional channels through which workers collaborate and with information making managers and workers more alike (again similar to Drucker, 1988). She also asserts that managers need to master change in the two critical areas of power and motivation, consistent with Drucker's (1988) notion that the new organization will foster special managerial problems such as motivating and rewarding specialists. Kanter (1989) further states that effective managers are integrators and facilitators, rather than watchdogs. Similarly, Welch of GE sees strategic leaders as facilitators of action (Tichy and Charan, 1989).

Kanter (1989a) also maintains that hierarchy is no longer an adequate base of power and that vertical channels through the chain of command are becoming increasingly less viable. In contrast, Jaques (1990), in expanding upon SST, contends that managerial hierarchy is still the most natural and effective organizational form for a large company. He believes that hierarchy preserves accountability for getting work done (the most important aspect of a company's existence, according to Zaleznik, 1989a). Jaques (1990) discusses his view of the proper use of hierarchy as derived from the nature of work. That is, as the time span of tasks increases, so does the level of experience, knowledge, and mental stamina required to do the work. The increasing level of mental capacity puts people in the jobs they can do and allows managers to add value to the work of their subordinates. In our view, a paradigmatic shift from control to commitment (as partially advocated by Drucker, 1988a, and Kanter, 1989a) does not necessarily eliminate hierarchy, especially if one looks at hierarchy as a quite necessary vertical division of labor.

Finally, Etzioni (1989) carries the information theme of Drucker (1988a) and Kanter (1989a) into the realm of decision-making models by describing a new model that helps managers adapt to new information. Etzioni's (1989) model, which he calls "humble decision making," proposes that managers can increase the flexibility and adaptability of their decisions by using a technique of partial information use, which, in our view, has strong ties to logical incrementalism (J. Quinn, 1980). Etzioni (1989) advocates "focused trial and error" and not committing all resources to a first decision. He states that managers can put decisions off, stagger them, or break them into separate parts, as well as make decisions that are easily reversible, helping to allow them to maintain strategic reserves to take advantage of unexpected opportunities. Similarly, a key point in logical incrementalism is that early commitments are kept broad and tentative, subject to later review and change (J. Quinn, 1978). Interactive testing is another aspect of logical incrementalism in line with Etzioni's model (1989), where strategic leaders may substantially modify their original concepts, unfolding decisions with time and room for flexibility (J. Quinn, 1981).

The above discussion may suggest ways to facilitate graduated change from both a strategic leader's perspective, as well as a structural perspective.

Effecting Punctuated Change

It is important to note that we are not suggesting that functional change is only graduated or punctuated. As suggested by our change model, change can be continuous. The terms *graduated* and *punctuated* are used to represent quite different levels of change, according to the two dimensions in the model, but, by no means, are meant to suggest a dichotomous situation.

Our first look at effecting punctuated change involves a review of the military forces employed recently in the Persian Gulf. What everyone agrees is that it was not the same force that was deployed to Vietnam, nor was it expected to be. Yet, the degree of change seemed to surprise most observers.

In a recent address, General Maxwell R. Thurman (1991b), formerly the vice chief-of-staff U.S. Army, and formerly the commander-in-chief, U.S. Forces, Southern Command (where he commanded the operation in Panama), made several interesting observations. First, he suggested that the recent operation was "not a seven-month war; not a 44-day air campaign; and, not a 100-hour ground campaign." Instead, it was a result of visionary changes begun in the mid-1970s.

The innovations included five factors: the volunteer concept, the integration of the reserves and the National Guard into deployment plans, the reform of combat doctrine, the transformation in training, and the modernization of equipment. He tied the above five factors to persistent strategic leadership at the highest levels of government. Thurman (1991b) listed what he thought were the key strategic leadership competencies and provided a general strategic leadership framework. We have integrated the two as follows:

- communication (public speaking, persuasiveness, listening—broad networking, open-door policy; the use of someone else's good idea, with proper credit, of course)
- opportunity recognition (act as if you have the confidence of your boss, set timelines for action, be persistent)
- integration/synthesis (involve the knowledgeable individuals—what's right, not who's right)
- visualization
- second-order consequence management—at least a ten-year horizon
- resource trade-off analysis
- mentor the institution
- continue to learn
- institutionalization (integrate the innovations into the organization)
- set the tone—morally, enthusiastically, energetically (operate from a principle base; work hard personally; accommodate bad news)

(Many of the above factors are consistent with the expanded discussion of SST in Jaques and Clement, 1991.)

Finally, Thurman (1991b) cautioned that the tactics and the weapons systems that were seen in the Gulf must not be seen in future conflict, as "the competition" will have already developed a counterforce. There must be constant change, constant innovation if the next "competitive situation" is to have as favorable an outcome.

We are impressed with the Gulf outcome, but recall the constant reminders that business must not become bureaucratically bogged down like military organizations (e.g., Peters, 1988). Yet, we cannot help but think many researchers confuse the army in the field (the operational army engaged in battle) with the army in a garrison situation. The two "armies" do not have the same modus operandi (Etzioni, 1964; Hunt and Phillips, 1991). On one hand, there are strict procedures and what most would call highly bureaucratic behavior in the garrison army. On the other hand, there are highly adaptive behavior, leaders sharing the hardships of battle with the troops, leaders in the same uniform as the troops, all in a survival situation in the army in the field. Perhaps the future business leaders of America returned from World War II and emulated the army in garrison, whereas the future corporate leaders of Japan returned and emulated their military in the field.

Is that perhaps one reason executives in Japan are not paid with the same enormous differentials as they are in the United States, generally have not many more perks than workers, eat in the same cafeteria as the workers, and wear the same "uniform" on the factory floor?

Let us return to Burgleman's (1991) IOE theory to examine more organizationally based concepts. His Proposition 1 suggests that over a long time period, successful firms are characterized by top managers who are concerned with building the quality of both the organization's induced and autonomous strategic processes, as well as the strategic content. Further, his other two propositions contain suggestions relevant to strategic leaders concerning the structuring for punctuated change:

> Proposition 2. Firms that are relatively successful over long periods of time, say ten years or more, will be characterized by maintaining top driven strategic intent while simultaneously maintaining bottoms-up driven internal experimentation and selection processes.

> Proposition 3. The population of firms with successful strategic reorientations will contain a significantly higher proportion of firms whose strategic reorientations were preceded by internal experimentation and selection processes than the population of firms with failing strategic reorientations (Burgleman, 1991, p. 256).

We suggest the above two propositions, as well as the first proposition, are quite commensurate with our earlier expressed notion of the responsibility of the strategic leader to focus certain elements of the strategic leadership role, as well as to seek new organizational structures that facilitate both graduated and punctuated change. The Burgleman propositions further suggest an important contribution to internal experimentation.

Burgleman (1991) also suggests that logical incrementalism may need to be augmented with an autonomous strategic process. We agree, as in our earlier suggestion, that for long-term survival, an organization must be structured for simultaneous graduated and punctuated change.

More in line with our arguments and, we believe, in line with the Burgleman (1991) propositions are the recommendations made by Schoonhoven and Jelinek (1990). They suggest that the key to continued innovation success in organizations in rapidly changing environments is their careful management of structure, through the following:

- thoughtful reexamination of formal structure in light of changing technology, market needs, and, we presume, competition
- change in structure through reorganization, which provides a consistent signal to employees that change is neither undesirable nor to be resisted, exactly our point earlier
- possible structural changes, including quasi-structural elements such as cross-disciplinary, multilevel committees, task forces, and teams, which require senior management commitment

- a consistent pattern of structure (formal, quasi-formal, informal) that facilitates innovative ideas and cooperation

They conclude by observing, "Clear organizational structures, frequent reorganizations, and an extensive use of quasi-structure contribute significantly to the long-term innovative abilities of the high technology companies" (Schoonhoven and Jelinek, 1990, p. 118).

Eisenhardt and Bourgeois (1990) studied decision making by CEOs and top management teams of firms in high-velocity environments. They defined high-velocity environments as enviromments with rapid and discontinuous change in product demand, competition, technology, or regulation—continuous instability with "sharp spikes of discontinuous change" (Eisenhardt and Bourgeois, 1990, p. 74). In such environments, information is frequently not available or, if available, is inaccurate, unreliable, or obsolete. They discovered that executives in successful, as opposed to less successful, firms engaged in fundamentally different strategic decision-making processes. The differences seemed to form three distinctive paradoxes.

The first paradox was that top management teams of successful firms used highly rational processes (gathered data, used analytical techniques, examined more than one alternative, and so on) but accomplished the process in rapid fashion. In contrast, poorly performing firms reacted to outside events, conducted little analysis, and considered few alternatives, while, at the same time, taking a fairly long time to come to a conclusion—frequently, longer than a year. The second paradox was that successful firms were led by decisive and powerful CEOs, but the top management teams were equally empowered in that the functional vice-presidents were more powerful in their respective areas than the CEOs. What was also interesting was the observation that only among the low-performing firms did the CEO exercise the greatest influence in every decision area. The third paradox involved the degree of risk the top management teams were willing to assume. Top management teams of successful firms made bolder decisions and took more time, yet modulated the risk through careful implementation, usually in an incremental fashion. (This later observation seems quite consistent with Robert Quinn's, 1988, notion of balance —innovate yet coordinate, that is, let the organization assimilate the change.)

Eisenhardt and Bourgeois (1990) specified implications for strategic decision makers:

- Be alert to, and attempt to build into real-time information systems, signals that suggest the possible need for strategic change.
- Alternative options to the present strategy and strategic implementation should be continuously considered, in order to be able to react to change in the industry.
- The top management team must learn to do high-quality analysis in a short period of time.

- Do not wait for consensus. Take counsel, but act decisively.
- Plan for bold actions but guard against error by maintaining an array of options for as long as possible. This combination of planning and options will allow for modification of the decisons based upon further changes in the environment (Eisenhardt and Bourgeois, 1990).

Interestingly, Feeser and Willard (1990) examined successful (high growth) and less successful (low growth) start-up firms and found a clear focus and decisive decision making were a major difference. The experimental or "cut and try; learn as you go" approach does not pay off, at least in the early years (Feeser and Willard, 1990, p. 96). Evidently, it does not pay off in the later years as well (Eisenhardt and Bourgeois, 1990).

Pavitt (1991) examined key characteristics of large, innovating firms and observed four key properties. The first seems to place them squarely in the graduated change quadrant (Quadrant II of Figure 12.1) in that, according to Pavitt (1991), these firms developed competencies that were largely firm-specific and cumulative over time; and what they were able to do in the past strongly conditioned what they hoped to do in the future. The second characteristic also tied them to the graduated change quadrant (Quadrant II of Figure 12.1)—the firms' choices seemed to be limited to the extent that their accumulated technology was proximate to other technologies. However, the third characteristic gave hope of greater change possibility in that innovative activities involved continuous and intensive collaboration across a wide variety of professional grousp—both technical (science and engineering) and management. Finally, the fourth characteristic suggested neither quadrant. It was simply that innovative activities have remained highly uncertain.

The Pavitt (1991) observations built upon the classic Burns and Stalker (1961) notion of interfunctional integration and contained specific factors that affect successful R&D as well as implementation:

- horizontal communications across functional boundaries
- flexibility in the definition of tasks
- links with outside sources of expertise and with users
- authority and experience of responsible managers

Pavitt (1991) provides some insight in aspects of organizational structure that impede innovation, at least in multidivisional firms. Specifically, he cites three problems of M-Form (multi-divisional) organizations:

- the coordination/management of synergies across divisions
- new technology development frequently across divisional lines
- the classical centralization/decentralization tension

Pavitt (1991) provides us with two conclusions that suggest that the technical function should contribute to the definition of divisional boundaries, to the exploration of radical technologies, and to the resource allocation process.

Wagner (1991) assessed the slipping competitiveness of U.S. corporations and determined the problem to be more structural than anything else. His basic premise is that the problem of U.S. competitiveness does not derive from a lack of technological innovation; rather it occurs in moving the innovation to the marketplace. He points out three sources of innovation—research labs (e.g., AT&T's Bell Labs), the not-for-profit research labs, and the nation's research universities. (Of the three, Wagner, 1991, has found his best source of innovation to be university faculties.)

Wagner (1991) suggests that big corporations in America are structured to be good at other things than innovations transfer, even if the innovation was developed in the company's own lab. Large corporations have failed to commercialize innovative technologies as well as simply follow-on innovations due to a missing structural element—something like a catalytic agent between the company's R&D laboratory and its product divisions. Wagner (1991) introduces a model for fostering marketing innovations that he labels the "open corporation." Basically, he addresses two questions: (1) How can rapid growth be sustained? and (2) How can innovations transfer and entrepreneurship continue as the company ages?

The basic corporate philosophy that he advocates is that no matter how attractive a technology is, it has no value until it has a market. Therefore, marketing efforts should concentrate on discovering, within client companies, problems that can be solved with a given technology—an innovations-transfer process. Wagner (1991) usually begins a start-up with two entrepreneurs who, typically, are quite young, have a strong grounding in leading-edge technology, and have already shown signs of "being winners." Both are technologically based, one has an outside, sales orientation, and the other has an inside, projects orientation. The pair continue to be trained in marketing and sales, and by the time they have graduated from "school," they have grown their unit to twenty-twenty-five people and are ready to spin out to affiliate status. The new unit is highly involved in solving client needs, usually in a very small market.

The final element in the start-up methodology is the involvement of the client in the commercialization of the innovation. The process usually results in the new venture's spinning off and growing and eventually becoming a new company. (Keep in mind it may take anywhere from eight to fifteen years to spin-out.) Wagner (1991) has provided us with a specific technique to keep highly entrepreneurial elements operating within an established corporation—a feat that seems to solve our earlier organizational paradox of obtaining efficiency while simultaneously planning for punctuated change.

SUMMARY AND CONCLUSIONS

We have attempted to develop a model of organizational change, based upon biological theory, that will differentiate between adaptive and nonadaptive change, as well as the rate of change. The proposed model, we suggested, would better serve both researchers and practitioners in that it would provide a common frame of reference for the assessment of change states and would allow for dysfunctional as well as adaptive change (chaotic states, on the one hand, and inertia, on the other.) We then introduced our main thesis. When competing in volatile environments, in order for organizations to be successful, they must have strategic leaders who develop top management teams as well as organizational structures that accommodate both graduated and punctuated change. Strategic leaders need to review procedures and techniques that will result in not only graduated change but punctuated change as well, without, however, the usual cultural reactance of organizational members. We provided an integrated literature review in an attempt to present theories and recommendations concerning both graduated and punctuated change. Although we provided several recommendations from a variety of theorists, there are not many suggestions that directly address our main thesis—the need for both types of adaptive change. There are several excellent recommendations concerning the handling of change, in general, in an organization, but very few recommendations that deal directly with organizing and leading for simultaneous graduated and punctuated change. There is much more to be developed. Nevertheless, there were notions and theoretical considerations that did suggest that such dual change orientations are emerging in both structures and top management team orientations.

V

Application and Concluding Commentary

13

The Integration of Internal Operating Systems: An Application of Systems Leadership

Dandridge M. Malone

The other chapters in this book have a heavy conceptual and scholarly emphasis. In contrast, the basic thrust of this chapter is to show how some of the concepts developed in other chapters can be applied in a complex organization.

Specifically, the chapter shows how a newly appointed commander of an army combat corps went about changing the climate and structure to provide empowerment up and down the hierarchy. Given the stereotype that many have about the military, they would be surprised that the commander would want to do this. After reading the chapter, they would probably be even more surprised that the change was as successful as it appeared to be. Be that as it may, the chapter has much to say about how a number of concepts dealt with in this book were applied in an extremely complex organization.

Particularly interesting is the way in which the commander, operating at SST level VI in the systems domain, was able to focus explicitly the direct and indirect effects of his actions to provide empowerment at lower organizational levels. This empowerment perspective also reflects Malone's underlying "bottom up" philosophy and is in contrast to the "top down" philosophy reflected in SST and many of the chapters in this book.

During the first half of the 1980s, I had the opportunity to study—up close, over time, and in detail—the leadership behavior of a highly capable chief executive. This systems leader ran a large and complex organization, in a business marked by a demanding purpose, high technology, rapid change, and extremely capable competitors. His organization numbered about 50,000 people. Monthly payroll ran around $54,840,000. Annual personnel turnover was high, a little over 30 percent. Most of the organization's facilities were at a single location, which normally would have made things easier, but, due to the nature of the work, this chief executive was also responsible, around the clock, for the support and well-being of more than 50,000 wives and children of the work force—as well as for the total management, on the work site, of a complete, all-facilities, "company community" of more than 5,000 families.

The organization's primary work site was 340 square miles, with a real estate value of about $584,000,000. Scattered around the site were 4,400 buildings with 23 million square feet of floor space and $1,467,278,900 worth of major items of equipment and machinery. Included in the machinery were 6,090 wheeled vehicles and 2,250 tracked vehicles. Included in the tracked vehicles were over three acres' worth of the new M1 Abrams tanks—at about $2,500,000 a copy. The work site was located down among the mesas and mesquite bushes of central Texas; the organization was a U.S. Army combat corps; and the systems leader's "business" was planning, developing, and maintaining a continual state of high-level operational readiness for his organization's immediate war-fighting deployment overseas, including all of its tracked vehicles. You watched the workings of this kind of business on CNN some time back as the nation deployed its fighting forces to the Middle East.

You can get some idea of the scope of this particular systems leader's daily activity by looking at his daily schedule for a typical workday, about a month after he took charge of the organization:

0730: Exit Briefing by the Army IG Team	1315: Visit Armored Division Field Training Site
0815: Meet with G3 (Force Modernization)	1400: Visit Corps Artillery Training Site
0830: Army Cmdrs' Conference Update	1430: Visit Tank Maintenance Building
0840: Classified Intelligence Briefing	1500: Army Audit Agency Briefing
0900: Open Time	1600: Update on General Court Martial
0930: Update on REFORGER Exercise	1620: Open Time
1000: Quarterly Training Conference	1700: Retreat and Retirement Ceremony
1130: Battalion Commanders' Luncheon	1930: Host Dinner Honoring Allied Visiting Dignitaries
1230: Visit Tank Gunnery Range	

A quick trip through the papers lying in this systems leader's in-box on this same typical workday illustrates the sort of information he had to deal with and some of the things about which he had to make decisions:

- Last year's REFORGER After-Action Report
- Staff recommendations on American Heritage Week
- Information paper on visit of fourteen European journalists
- Letter from city manager of Killeen, Texas, concerning future city planning issues
- Information copies of staff documents:
    Installation Management System
    Installation Information System
    Corps Annual Training Program
- Information document on number and purpose of recurring meetings, conferences, and forums; and a question concerning how many of these he wants to continue
- Preconference notes for next week's Abrams Tank Conference
- Decision paper concerning NATO interoperability issues

- Itinerary of British liaison officer currently visiting Ft. Hood
- Folder of electronic message traffic from chief of staff, U.S. Army and CG, FORSCOM, concerning safety, funding cuts, force modernization, automation and information initiatives, and classified Middle East intelligence information
- Staff information paper on force modernization issues
- Letter announcing visit by team from the Soldier Support Center
- Letters for signature:
   To CG, TRADOC, concerning training inquiry
   To CG, FORSCOM, relative to annual funding concerns
   To Army Safety Office, responding to aircraft safety issues
- Information paper summarizing the gist of 1,025 inquiries from members of Congress (over a one-year period)
- Folder with names of officers rated by the corps commander
- Letter from a research psychologist friend, offering some thoughts on running a large and complex organization

This systems leader whom I was studying was an army lieutenant general, and I will just refer to him as my friend or the boss. To study his leadership requirements and his ways of meeting those requirements, I visited his corps for three or four days each quarter, over a period of three and a half years. Between visits, we also talked frequently by telephone. My friend was well-read in the leadership field—both the applied side and the scientific side. I was free to go wherever in his corps I wanted to and talk with anyone, and no subject was off-limits. Many of the subordinate leaders knew me from talks and speeches and from more than a decade's worth of journal articles I had contributed on leadership and soldiers. They trusted me. Finally, as a soldier, scientist, and leadership teacher for twenty years at every level in the army school system, I knew well how to look for, and study, army leaders and army followers doing army work in army organizations.

After the first year, my friend and I had determined that a systems leader has to work three interrelated domains. All three domains are obvious in the daily schedule and in-box inventory you read a moment ago. The first is the principal business in which the organization is engaged. In the war-fighting business, the business domain includes such things as the enemy, operation plans, intelligence, battle doctrine, tactics, military technology, support systems of all kinds, principal programs in all functional areas. The second domain is one we termed "fence riding" or "working the organizational interfaces"—the interfaces being those instances, processes, and arrangements whereby the organization interacts with external organizations, agencies, and groups. In my friend's case, some of these external interfaces were with other major commands, higher headquarters, local communities, state government, the news media, the army research community, defense contractors, test agencies, NATO agencies, members of Congress, various governmental agencies and departments, and commanders and officials in likely areas of overseas deployment.

Finally, the third, and most apparent, systems leadership domain was what we termed, "the integration of internal operating systems." Simply put, these are the main things that actually make the organization "run." Draw a circle around the entire corps organizational chart and then identify all of the processes involved in directing and supporting the mission accomplishment of all those line components and staff functions, and you will have a good handle on "internal operating systems," at least the obvious ones. You might also get at this doman by viewing the traditional management functions—planning, organizing, coordinating, directing, and controlling—as internal operating systems. Or you might be able to describe internal operating systems in terms of organizational functions—personnel, logistics, intelligence, communications, operations, and the like. But naming and defining are not the real challenge.

The challenge in this third systems leadership domain seemed to be one of integrating effort among organizational components, that is, establishing common understanding, achieving mutual support, and eliminating internal friction and nonproductive competition—"orchestrating." This particular domain—the integration of internal operating systems—corresponds most closely to the leadership required of the systems leader, and the remainder of this chapter will be directed to this particular area. Further, I will describe and discuss not what the systems leader should do, but what this particular systems leader actually did. (A couple of years after my friend completed his three and a half years of commanding the corps, in an effort to pass on some "lessons learned" to others, we put together an operational definition of this particular kind of systems leadership and then formulated a set of principles for its application. The numbers that follow selected paragraphs herein indicate one or more applications of these principles and are keyed to our set of principles, listed separately at the end of this chapter.)

Starting out, this new corps commander had no written plan for how he was going to run a corps. He know the job was about ten orders of magnitude larger, in all respects, than his previous job as commander of a 17,000-person armored division in Europe. He knew he would have to do many things differently, do some things he had never done before, and eliminate some things altogether. All the time that he had been an immediate subordinate to his own corps commander, he had also been an immediate student of that corps commander, and he studied actively. Finally, he also had working for him about ten straight years of command experience prior to taking charge of his corps.

His first major undertaking as new boss (and systems leader) of this large and complex organization was to think through, then lay out, his own personal leadership philosophy for his senior commanders and staff. In the years I had been watching him lead line organizations of ever-increasing size, he had never used this particular philosophy. But there were clear similarities and a basic continuity over time. This philosophy was an "upgrade," a vision, and a challenge. It was a one-sentence statement that went like this: "If we can create a climate, wherein leaders at all levels can lead, the organization will grow in productivity." (2, 5) It was simple. It was also systemic, in that he did not focus on productivity directly.

He went at it indirectly. He wanted to make productivity grow, but he wanted the leadership, at all levels, to know that the challenge always to be better—to grow in productivity—was theirs and that they had his trust and confidence. Further, it was systemic in that, rather than a special program, with a special task force, a special director, and a blizzard of workshops, slogans, speeches, bells, whistles, and bumper stickers about more and better leadership, he made a supporting organizational climate the principal gateway to improved leadership. This systemic emphasis clearly brought together the organization's primary climate-shapers: the boss himself, his deputy, his chief of staff, and the senior line and staff members. He put his scientific knowledge of leadership to work in his leadership philosophy by using the concept of organizational climate, which is itself a systemic concept.

What the new boss did next was call in his corps G1 (personnel director) and give him a mission to be completed by about four or five months after the philosophy was introduced. This mission was a large-scale three-day leadership conference. Participants would be a corps "organizational slice" of about 120 leaders from all over the corps—commanders, staff officers, army civilian employees, soldiers, dependents. They would confer in four small mixed groups (and smaller subgroups) to identify issues that seemed to have a major impact on "the ways things are in this outfit" and to develop solution concepts for dealing with the issues. The teams would be required to brief each other to achieve a common understanding across the whole large group and, at the end, to brief the senior leaders of the corps on the issues and what things needed to be started, left alone, or stopped. The mission was fully achieved, but what might help you most in getting their insights about "climate" are the lists the work groups came up with for identifying "the way things are in this outfit." Following are the four main issues and some of the related subjects listed under each:

JOB SATISFACTION
Meaningful and satisfying duty
Adequate working conditions
Mismatch of man-hour requirements
Use of soldier's day productivity
Supply of tools, equipment, supplies
Match of garrison to field duty
Soldiers' expectations, and trust
Inexperience or incompetence
Sound mind; sound body
Leadership and supervision

ORGANIZATIONAL CONSISTENCY
AND REINFORCEMENT
Pay, incentives, rewards, punishment
Goals, priorities, actions, incongruities
Professional development for
advancement
Inspections, reports, statistics, taskings
Power-down taught/practiced at top first
Micromanagement and commander's
CYA("cover your _____") statistics
Abuse of commander's signature
requirement
Excessive administrative trivia
Tolerance of honest mistakes

OFF-THE-JOB INFLUENCES	JOB STRESS
Personal problem referral	Job stress reduction
Family life issues	Commander's tour length versus staff
Single soldier issues	tour length
Family versus career	Combat stress reaction
Adequate living conditions	Delayed stress syndrome
Coordinating social services	Communicative skills training
Concerned commanders	Identifying symptoms of excessive stress
	Transience of soldiers and their families

If you could have listened to the talk of the groups during those three days, you would have had a good approximation of the "climate" in that 50,000-person organization. If you had watched them briefing the boss that last evening, you would have seen the beginnings of a leadership philosophy starting to work and the initial outlines of a shared plan for "creating a climate wherein leaders can lead." (1, 3)

In plain terms and from your perspective as an experienced leader, the climate of an organization is the overall "feel" or sensing of the organization that you get when you visit it for the first time and walk around for an hour or so, looking at bulletin boards, talking to people, and watching people and teams at their work. The notion of climate evolved from what the early industrial psychologists used to call "job satisfaction." The concept of "culture" can be thought of as climate, over time. Likert, in *The Human Organization* (1967), described climate as a systemic phenomenon resulting from the interactive effects of all the major components of the human side of organizational life: leadership, motivation, communications, decision making, goals, and control. Each of these components can be operationally defined by the questions Likert used to measure the climate of an organization. Let me illustrate the concept of climate. First, think of a past assignment to a large and complex headquarters, like the Pentagon, and then think of "what it was like to work in that organization." Read through the questions of Likert's climate measure, which follows, and, without getting overly serious, score each question, roughly, on an imaginary scale ranging from 1 (Not So Good) to 10 (Good).

- Leadership:
  How much confidence is shown in subordinates?
  How free do they feel to talk to superiors about their job?
  Are subordinates' ideas sought and used, if worthy?
- Motivation:
  Is predominant use made of fear or fear of involvement?
  Where is responsibility felt for achieving the organization's goals?
  How much cooperative teamwork exists?
- Communications:
  What is the direction of information flow?
  How is downward communication accepted?

How accurate is upward communication?

How well do superiors know problems faced by subordinates?

- Decision making:

    At what level are most decisions made?

    Are subordinates involved in decisions related to their work?

    How much does the decision-making process contribute to motivation?

- Goals:

    How are organizational goals established?

    How much covert resistance to goals is present?

- Control:

    How concentrated are control and review functions?

    Is there an informal organization resisting the formal one?

    What are cost, productivity, and other control data used for?

(Likert, 1967, pp. 197-211).

Now, let me summarize all we have said about climate. An organization's climate is all of the answers to all of these questions by all of its people, over a period of time—a vast array of perspectives, all mixed and blended together into how an organization "feels" when you are inside it. So a senior leader can often get the "feel" of an organization in no more than twenty minutes of just walking around because time and experience have taught him or her what to look for and who and what to listen to. It is not just that the people of an organization are shaped by its climate, even more so, climate also shapes the organization's leadership. People will follow their leaders, but their leaders will thrive in some climates, die in others, lie dormant in others, and, in some, just dry up and blow away, as climate, evolving slowly over time, becomes culture.

Let us go next to the part of the command philosophy that says "wherein leaders at all levels can lead." The words *all levels* have some special significance. My friend, in each of his previous commands, had always stressed heavily the need continually to push trust, authority, power, and responsibility downward through the levels of leadership. In his view, decisions should be made at the lowest level capable of making the decision, with true delegation occurring only when the leader had delegated to his own immediate subordinate until he, the leader, actually felt vulnerable to his own immediate superior.

Coincidentally, at about the time my friend took over the corps, the army was just beginning to field its brand new battle doctrine called "The AirLand Battle" (cf. Hunt and Blair, 1985). Because of electronic technology that could quickly detect, and bring heavy fire on, any efforts to mass combat forces, this battle doctrine envisioned a "distributed battlefield" of highly dispersed and relatively small units. The doctrine identified leadership as the primary determinant of who would win the AirLand Battle and decentralized leadership as the specific kind of leadership required on the distributed battlefield. One of the word pictures used, as the AirLand Battle doctrine was being introduced, described the decentralized leadership needed for the distributed battlefield in these terms: "A thousand young leaders, alone with their units, out there on a thousand hills." (1, 4, 8)

The new battle doctrine also laid out some criterion statements to set the standards for the degree of decentralization that the AirLand Battle would require. Here are some relevant terms and phrases abstracted from FM 100-5, *Operations,* the army field manual that laid out the bedrock of battle doctrine: "Subordinate leaders are to be given freedom and responsibility. . . .Refuse to permit the battle to be decided by automatic and compartmented processes that inevitably work their way to a pre-determined conclusion. . . .Mission-type orders will be required at every level of command. . . .As battles bcome more complex and unpredictable, decision-making must be more and more decentralized. . . .Commanders must trust their subordinates' ability to make on-the-spot decisions. . . .Risk-taking and an atmosphere that supports it." (2, 3, 4, 8, 11)

In our discussions, both of us—the leader and the watcher—agreed that the philosophy would be "in place and working" only when we could see inspired, quick, take-charge, innovative leaders as the norm, down there on the true "bottom line," running the tank crews and rifle squads and gun crews and maintenance teams. This bottom line would have been my friend's primary criterion measure anyway, even without the battle doctrine. After all, if we are talking about the leadership of an organization, it is worthwhile to keep in mind that, in large and complex organizations, about 75 percent of the organization's leaders are found down there at the organization's bottom two-three levels. (8)

Most new bosses today know that, at the outset, they have to spell out, clearly, their own philosophy of leadership. My friend did more than this. He purposefully set out actually to teach his philosophy to his senior subordinates. He taught it in many different ways, until he could be sure that they understood its complexity, as well as its implications for virtually all that this large and complex organization would do. This philosophy, what it meant, and the shared in-depth understanding of what it meant, across the senior levels of the organization, were the anchor point for his entire effort to integrate internal operating systems.

His teaching of the corps's senior line and staff leaders began soon after the words of the philosophy were put on paper. He put someone else to work with the staff, but he himself worked primarily with the top two or three levels of line commanders. He used hard sell, no implied threats, no direct mention of the philosophy per se, but he did use much personal discussion, some small meetings, one informal off-site weekend, some written things that went down through command channels, some speeches, breakfasts, luncheons, talks, and 100 funny stories that people could laugh at and later remember and repeat for others and only then, after remembering and repeating, realize that this funny story had, buried somewhere within it, a theme or point that clearly and purposefully gave more meaning to the boss's philosophy. Thus they began looking for the boss's philosophy in almost everything he said and did, and sure enough, it was always there. (2)

He taught the senior staff in a different way. He had relaxed, informal, individual talks with them and some workshops and social affairs, but he did most of his teaching of the staff another way—indirectly, systemically, through his chief of staff. At the outset, he probably gave teaching the chief higher priority than teaching the senior line commanders. The chief told me about all this teaching later. (6, 7, 8, 14)

The chief was exceptionally intelligent, with a long record as a good leader. He did not play favorites among the staff members; he never abused his relationship with the boss; and he was not hesitant to give the boss bad news. The chief told me it took him about two months before he really understood the boss's philosophy. He would get a paper for the boss's signature from one of the staff members, check it out, not just for appearance, but also, carefully, for content and implications, and as it would look great, he would send it in. All too often, at least from the chief's point of view, the boss would say, "Chief, let's talk about this paper a little." They would then have a short discussion about the paper, not about format, but about content, mainly about implications, that is, systemic effects. The chief called these sessions "discussions," but they really were classes, with the boss teaching the chief his leadership philosophy and, as he did with the senior line commanders, without every once referring to the written-down statement of his own leadership philosophy. (2, 3, 6)

Finally, one day, after about two months, the chief sat down, penciled five simple questions on a 3x5 card, propped the card against his desk lamp, and then started checking every paper that came in from the staff against his "filter"—the five handwritten questions. After that, the boss and the chief still had plenty of discussions, but no more classes. The chief then began doing some teaching of his own with the senior staff leaders. In time, the meaning of the boss's leadership philosophy was understood and at work in all the various staff channels as well as the command channel.

Here are the five key questions the chief had written down on his 3x5 card:

- Is it consistent with our basic mission priorities?
- Is it consistent with "authority to the lowest level"?
- Does it reflect reciprocal trust—no implied threats or assumptions of value differences?
- Does it support the authority of the command?
- Is it reasonable and rational? (7, 8, 12)

At this point, my friend had reached a major leadership milestone with his teaching. His philosophy was not just distributed and known. It was, instead, installed, understood, and at work at the upper echelons, in both line and staff channels. The senior subordinates—both line and staff—now knew the essence of the boss's intent, his frame of reference, and what he expected. These senior subordinates, directly and indirectly, aided by some good stories, were themselves beginning to teach what they had learned to their own subordinate leaders. The chief, with his 3x5 pony, was now teaching the corps's principal staff members. A neat, articulate, well-written, properly formatted staff paper would come across the chief's desk. He would read it, study it a bit, then pick up the phone: "John, let's talk about this paper a little." (6, 7)

He had also reached another major and too often never-achieved systemic milestone. Central to any systems thinking are the information channels, information flows, and the total "information metabolism" within the system of interest. This is what actually runs the system. The corps now had an understanding of the boss's expectations, working its way down through the command channels. The same understanding was working its way down through all the many staff channels. The philosophy was thus becoming a part of the organization's information metabolism. That is a systemic phenomenon. It is also probably the "golden screw" for the integration of internal operating systems, that is, consistency, congruence, and coherence within and among the principal information flows that run the total system—and, incidentally, it is also one of the primary means whereby leaders at each level can meet their fundamental responsibility to their subordinates, that is, the reduction of uncertainty. (3, 7)

Getting his leadership philosophy clearly articulated and commonly understood across the upper echelons was the tough part of integrating internal operating systems. It took about six months to do this. Next came the time-consuming part, and it was still going on when my friend left his corps three and a half years later. Two major "integration offensives" are involved, and we will deal with each separately, even though they were interwoven across time and function.

All the staff recommendations, decisions, and actions that the chief was checking with his 3x5 card represented most of the corps's policy-making system and process. Additional policy came down from the two higher headquarters above the boss's, and hs line commanders were adding policy of their own. Policy reaches across all functions, so does something else: climate. There is no way to build climate without doing something with policy, and my friend did, big time. He looked at policy, overall, as the central downward-flowing stream of information that determined what the corps did and, more importantly, set the broad parameters for how the corps did it. Policy, therefore, was one of the pricipal determinants of climate, which was the key to increased productivity. (He was approaching productivity indirectly, systemically, through climate.) If the chief's 3x5 worked right, the policy coming out of the chief's staff would be consistent with the boss's philosophy.

Sometimes it was not; some of the staff's policy that made it through the chief's filter was just plain dumb, and so was some from the boss, some from the higher headquarters above the corps, and some from the old policy left behind by previous leaders (although it might be noted here that he took over a basically solid, well-led outfit). Recognizing this clearly, my friend's next move in the integration of internal operating systems was a studied effort to identify, throughout the corps, any downward-flowing, policy-related information in the line and staff channels that was inconsistent, incongruent, or incoherent with the mission of the corps, the leadership philosophy, or good common sense. With the boss doing the initial teaching, the line commanders and the staff had learned the meaning and implications of the boss's philosophy. Now, the boss set out to teach the organization about dumb policy. (2, 3, 5, 7)

What he did was to declare an open hunting season on dumb policy—his own, his staff's, his boss's, and his subordinate commanders'. But he did it easily, with understanding, careful explanation, and humor, an as an upgrade to the normal sort of policy questioning that a good leader expects from his younger line commanders, and he did this with no special program. It started one day at a routine "leadership meeting," which he had started holding about every quarter with the corps's upper 150 line and staff officers and noncommissioned officers (NCOs). During the fifteen minutes just before the session began, while small groups of people were standing around socializing, the boss and his sergeant major were moving here and there, talking, laughing, and handing out copies of an unusual poop sheet that no one had ever seen before in any unit. It was a one-page "policy quiz." On it, there were twenty true-false questions about corps policies. Were they in fact corps policies? Should they be? Why? (2, 4, 6, 7, 9)

Some people filled out the policy quiz. Others figured they were not really supposed to. All of them read it. Was it a trick or a joke? As the meeting began, after a couple of good stories, my friend simply mentioned the quiz, gave the correct answers, explained some in more detail, changed a couple, and then continued the meeting. From that time on, the one-page policy quiz, complete with fun and stories, was a probable part of most of the relaxed and informal group meetings that he had with commanders and senior staff. What he was doing, indirectly, systemically, was teaching, showing his key people that he expected them to study and question all policy, including his own and their own, in terms of command philosophy, consistency, congruence, coherence, and common sense—and then pass on and support these policies with vigor and with confidence. (2, 5, 7)

The policy quiz was only one of a whole purposeful system of "sensors," openly put in place here and there among the internal operating systems of the organization, to identify policies that just did not seem to make good sense. Most obvious and readily available to anyone was a "DUMB-Line" telephone system, open twenty four hours a day to receive complaints, problems, and suggestions from soldiers and family members who were having difficulties with, or wanted to question, any policy. Calls could be anonymous, or the caller's name could be left so that a reply could be given. Each call with a name received a written response within a reasonable period of time. Some triggered a response in the corps newspaper. Some got a personal note from the boss. He read all of the comments and some of the responses. But the DUMB-Line was only a small part of the total sensing system. (1, 7)

You know from the daily schedule we saw earlier that my friend held monthly meetings with battalion commanders. He also had meetings, in his office, with company commanders, about twelve at a time. He used both of these occasions to help the lower-level line commanders identify dumb policies and to clarify others. Even here, he was teaching, and these were never "bitch sessions." They knew this was an excellent opportunity to lay out, directly to the boss, policies and procedures that did not make good sense. But, at the very first one of these meetings, after each commander had been given the opportunity to point out policies that were not working right, the boss went back to the first commander and asked each commander to identify and share, with his peers, policies and procedures that, from his perspective, were exceptionally good. He was teaching them a valuable lesson about balance. The word got around, and the opportunity to sit down with the corps commander and help identify dumb policies never became just another "bitch session." (1, 7)

Because training for war was the overriding concern within the corps, my friend devised a special survey to isolate distractors to training. A series of discussions with staff and commanders led to developing a list of a couple dozen items, such as "short-fuse requirements." This list was next pared down to the top ten items through discussions with the most affected group, battalion and company commanders. This final list of distractors was then the basis of a quarterly survey of approximately half of the 120 company commanders of the corps. They would rate each item as "Getting Better," "Getting Worse," "About the Same," or "No Problem for Me." Summaries of their input were provided to major unit commanders and the corps staff and used as the basis for further analysis and action. The process of identifying the distractors was itself a stress ameliorator, and discussions of progress overall, and then within particular units, provided another vehicle for reinforcing success and for fixing the persistent items that continued to be irritants.

The boss had learned about, and used, survey technology many years earlier in graduate school. Now he put his smarts to work and, working closely with the scientists of the Army Research Institute, developed a 100-item unit climate survey instrument. It measured items in categories similar to those you have just seen, but in military context. The survey could be administered by a leader at any level, and the information used in any way the leader desired. Safeguards for protecting chain of command integrity were built into the administration procedures. This survey was used widely, not just within the corps but, later, armywide. There were a number of other, more pointed questionnaires that helped identify policy problems. For example,

There was an "Inspect the Inspector" report that lower echelon line commanders filled out after any inspection by an IG (Inspector General) or staff representative. This one-page, check-the-block and fill-in-the-space survey was used, by the unit commander, to provide feedback to inspection teams on the comprehensiveness, fairness, and helpfulness of their inspections. In addition to identifying policy disconnects of various kinds, it also served to build cooperation and remove hostilities between the inspectors and those being inspected, and helped maintain the right balance of power. Once in a while—very rarely in fact—it also resulted in a replaced inspector. (8, 10, 11)

The boss spent a considerable part of each day visiting various units and headquarters. He did much more than visit. He used these visits also to gather more input on the climate and the policies that helped shape it. He and the corps command sergeant major, in conjunction with these visits, frequently handed out and explained simple, one to two page survey instruments, designed to identify the impacts of policy. The "One Question Open Response Survey" is a good example. There was only one question on this kind of survey, and it varied over time according to climate conditions, or policies and policy issues that the boss wanted to know more about. The question might read like this: "Of all the many training, supply, personnel, maintenance and leadership programs and policies that affect your ability to train your unit well these days, list three—of any kind—that significantly help you do your job." This kind of question was usually used with battalion and company commanders, and worked unobtrusively into a luncheon or meeting of some kind. This technique complemented the quarterly input from company commanders to collect data on progress toward solving their top ten problems. (1, 2, 4, 8, 11)

Quite often, on some of the more complex or restrictive policies that came in for approval and signature, the boss would personally explain the policy or procedure to the whole organization. He would first sign the paper, then, in his own handwriting, he'd write some of his own comments in the margins, carefully explaining the policy, and the all-critical "why" for its implementation. He did this frequently with policies coming down from his own two higher headquarters. That is the way these policies were published and distributed—boss's handwriting and all. They, too, like any of the others, were challenged, but, basic standards for combat readiness and integrity were not challengeable! (2, 12)

These are only a few of the "user-end" policy-checking sensors or filters openly put in place to help ensure consistency, congruence, and coherence in the directive information flowing downward through the corps. Now what I have called the "policy offensive" represents achieving consistency, congruence, and coherence by filtering the downward-flowing information through the leadership philosophy. The boss also figured out another way to enhance consistency, congruence, and coherence in "the way we do things around here" by running the upward-flowing information through essentially the same filter as the policies. This had a major positive impact, not just on the corps's climate, but on its mission achievement as well. While you have heard of this subject before, there is about an 80 percent chance that you have never thought of it as a leadership technique. However, it is particularly applicable in this case, since we are discussing systems leadership and since "feedback" is central to systems thinking. (3)

In 1970, when my friend and I were both teachers at the Army War College, we had worked on a study of the army's moral and ethical climate, designed to assess and repair major damage caused in part by Robert McNamara's body count-based measurement system in Vietnam. After that in-depth look at the long-term, second-and third-order systemic effects of the measurement system, my friend from then on always took a close interest in this particular "internal operating system" in any organization he commanded. We had talked about measurement from time to time. One day we started wondering about the total measurement system in an organization and what the magnitude of such a system might be. I had an answer:

> Magnitude of the measurement system . . . . well, I'll tell you. A general named Meloy, charged with keeping the Eighty-second Airborne Division constantly ready for instant deployment, but continually harried by numbers and required reports, once ordered an audit of, as he put it, "every damn routine, upward-flowing, required letter, report, form, statistical account, data extract, or what-the-hell-ever that exists today, here, in the Eighty-second Airborne Division!" He was mad, and he was hot, so there wasn't much room to sidestep. The audit showed that right there, in the division that was supposed to be the army's most streamlined, instantly ready "fire brigade," the total number of upward-flowing reports came to 521! General Meloy, at that point, implemented on the spot, a "zero-based" measurement system in the Eighty-second and gave the people who were requiring the reports two weeks to justify, to him, any report they wanted to keep receiving. After the justification session, the total was reduced to half.

But all that is another story. Over the years of teaching how to run an organization, I had always seen measurement treated as a management tool—related to the control function and full of squirrelly formulas and long arguments about efficiency and effectiveness, reliability and validity, and the "Heisenberg effect." I had never found anything in the literature that explained the right way to set up and run a measurement system from the leadership perspective until I visited my friend in his office one morning, about six months after he had assumed command. As we sat down, he skittered a single page across the table and said, "What do you think of this?" He had written it himself. On that single page (both sides), he had laid out the essence of the most important things he had learned about measurement in all his years of commanding army units. That page was the underpinnings of a "leadership-based measurement system." It was also the principal document that would be used later that very day in another one of those big, quarterly, 150-person corps leadership meetings." (6, 13)

When the meeting got under way, the boss taught the content of the single page to the top three levels of line and staff leaders. They next broke down into smaller groups (mixed line and staff) and then, together, proceeded to run the whole corps measurement system through what they had just learned, discussing corps measurements from the perspectives of both the staff leaders who required the reports and the line leaders who had to submit them. The whole group came together again for a plenary session and discussed with the boss their findings about the corps's measurement system in general and about certain required reports in particular. He then gave them a measurement system "homework" requirement, and the leadership meeting ended. (4)

Two months later, the homework was due. At that time, the boss, accompanied by the senior members of his principal staff, visited each of the major component headquarters, this time for a formal briefing covering two things: (1) the changes they were going to make in their own measurement systems, and why; and (2) the changes they recommended the boss make in his, and why. With that, the entire measurement system within the corps began to change, and the total leadership of the corps learned a valuable lesson in leadership-based measurement. It will be worth your time to study one of the things that were printed on that single page—one of the things that the corps line and staff used to rebuild and upgrade the whole array of upward-flowing required reports in their large and complex organization. Here, abstracted from the one-pager my friend skittered across the table that morning, are nine general principles of leadership-based measurement that he himself first developed, then taught to his corps:

- Measuring things accurately and reliably is both an art and a science.
- Measurement techniques themselves have a powerful influence on operations and are de facto promulgators of priority.
- Measurement techniques and the production of associated statistics can generate both useful insights and dysfunctional side effects.
- Measurement techniques have enormous impact on climate and are closely related to concepts of mutual trust and to expectations regarding competence.
- The leader's skill in measuring things is a major component of both his effectiveness as a manager and his reputation as a credible leader.
- Measurement techniques and systems are closely related to communications within the organization, particularly with respect to feedback concepts.
- Inappropriate or poorly designed measurement systems are major sources of junior leader frustration and ethical dilemmas.
- Measurement techniques can be used to educate, motivate, sensitize, or act as a deterrent.
- The subjective costs associated with measurement may be higher than the objective ones: confusion regarding organizational priorities, misperceptions regarding trust and decentralization, fears regarding use of collected data. (1, 2, 3, 5, 7, 8, 9, 10, 11, 13, 14)

What gets measured, who measures it, how it is measured, how often it is measured, and what is done with the measurements have major impacts on both the climate and the leadership of a large organization. Less obvious is that these aspects also characterize the nature of most of the upward-flowing information in any large organization. If you compare these measurement principles for upward-flowing information with the chief's 3x5 filter for downward-flowing information, you will see that they both have much the same meaning and that both are clearly related to my friend's "anchor point" leadership philosophy. What he was doing with the measurement system was using it for additional integration of internal operating systems—building additional consistency, congruence, and coherence in information flow, not just laterally, between line and staff channels, but also vertically, between what was coming down and what was going up.

In summary, then, here is an interrelated, bare-bones, already test-fired set of four practical lessons for the systems leader tackling the challenges inherent in the integration of internal operating systems:

- Do not start out with a leadership philosophy that merely sounds impressive. Start with one that you believe in, and thus will be obvious to other people, in much of what you say, write, and do.
- Purposefully teach—do not just talk—this philosophy to your senior-level line and staff, in a number of different ways and contexts, until they demonstrate the real value of your stated and taught philosophy, that is, their ability accurately to predict your actions and responses to situations, events, developments, both good and not so good.
- Using both line and staff, filter two critical information flows through your philosophy: downward-flowing policy and upward-flowing measurement.
- Assess the end-state effectiveness of your efforts to integrate internal operating systems by the degree to which your front-line leaders—down there in the trenches four or five levels below you—can see and can describe positive examples of the one thing that they are always looking for and that will always reduce their uncertainty—consistency, congruence, and coherence in both the talk and the walk of "all them no-good bastards up there at platoon headquarters!" (1, 2, 3, 4, 5, 7, 9, 10)

How successful was my friend's approach? There were real achievements, all directly related to productivity, that could "prove" that it worked very well. But, that would take a bunch of those numbers. I would rather answer the question subjectively.

The ultimate criterion for a combat organization is how well it can fight. Much of that is determined by army battle doctrine. Recall that the army's battle doctrine at the time stressed leadership as its most important factor and that the demands of this new doctrine's "distributed battlefield" made it clear that success on this battlefield would rest squarely on the initiative and leadership capabilities of all those small unit leaders "alone with their units, out there on a thousand hills." Recall also that as our systems leader put together his philosophy, he realized that he could never consider it fully implemented and at work until he could clearly see its widespread inpact down at the levels of the small unit leaders. So I would like to answer the question of how well the approach worked with two stories about the small unit leaders of this large and complex organization.

The first story happened in the last half of the second year. The leadership philosophy and the policy and measurement initiatives were taking hold well at the upper levels, but there seemed to be some sort of hang-up for a while at the middle levels. Then, one day, it happened, down there in the trenches, with all of the NCOs in one battalion. They told me they started off at first just talking among themselves at morning coffee breaks in the mess hall, after work, and at all those other times and places in between, where front-line leaders, in any kind of organization, do their really heavy "coordinating." They plotted, schemed, and most certainly conspired, and soon, they came up with a plan to test "the system." Three or four days later, three of the NCO ringleaders went to see the battalion commander.

"Sir, the NCOs have gotten together and, well, we'd like to do some training."

"Say, that's fine! What kind of training?"

"Sir, we'd like to run a full-scale tactical exercise in the field."

"That's the best kind of training there is. Tell me some more."

"Well, we want to run a big one, sir. Three days. Out in the field. Whole battalion. Run by the NCOs. Test all our people and equipment and all the things the battalion is supposed to be able to do on the battlefield."

The NCOs did run the whole three-day battle exercise—not the best that the battalion had ever done, but better than what was often done. Soon the word got around, and staff officers from the corps headquarters, from different units, and from various levels went to talk to the NCOs in the battalion about what happened. Some were surprised, some were not. Some were thinking: As battles become more complex and unpredictable, decision making must become more and more decentralized. . . .Initiative. . . .Risk taking and an atmosphere that supports it. . . .Commanders must trust their subordinates' ability to make on-the-spot decisions.

That is one "measure" of how well things went when the systems leader of a large and complex organization led the leadership of that organization in a concerted effort to create a climate wherein leaders at all levels could lead.

The last story (perhaps an anecdotal measure?) is, at least for me, both good news and not so good news. It is also, perhaps, a lesson for those who speak of changing something as complex as the climate of an organization (or even its culture) as if it were nothing more than a pair of drawers or a coat of paint. This last story, very short, is my own. One of my friend's midlevel leaders, nearly a year or so after my visits to the corps had ended and after my friend was gone, told me that, about two months after the boss left the corps, his successor, a leader who habitually "liked to stay on top of things" (many things), remarked one day, somewhat irritably, to a member of his staff, "You know, the sergeants around this place act like they're running the damn army!" (14)

A SET OF PRINCIPLES FOR THE APPLICATION OF SYSTEMS LEADERSHIP

("Systems leadership" is the executive process of creating a productive organization through the planned integration of internal operating systems.)

1. First, get in touch, and then stay in touch, with what is really going on and what people are thinking about.
2. Spend time (continuously) articulating the vision and clarifying the goals and priorities; make it easy for individuals and teams to question whether or not a particular policy is out of line with organizational values.
3. Develop a clear plan for creating and sustaining a climate that is routinely supportive, trusting, and in every respect integrated. (Drafting this plan must be a team effort.)
4. Always explain the intent of directives and rules so that subordinates can use initiative and independent action to achieve the desired objectives.
5. Focus organizational energy on priority matters; identify and attack nonproductive policies and meaningless routines; and keep some energy free for adaptation and innovation.
6. Insist that key leaders set the example in representing the organization's values and priorities. (Take prompt action when key leaders do not reinforce the values and support the vision.)
7. Ensure that the staff acts to reinforce the leader's intent and the organization's vision and priorities, through coordination and integration of programs and policies, and establish and maintain communication channels for uncovering disconnects and dysfunctions.
8. Ensure that leaders at a given level do not routinely handle actions that could be done as well by subordinate leaders and that latitude to act is described for each level. Explain and draw attention to the model of an empowered leader—the authority, the boundaries, and the patterns of mutual trust.
9. Assume good intent and, when something goes wrong, check first for flaws in the system. (Trust people, but be suspicious of systems.)
10. Test, measure, and transmit evaluation data carefully and openly, with clear intent and flexible format, so that the vision, goals, and priorities are clarified and supported by the overall measurement scheme.
11. Reinforce outstanding individual and team accomplishments with an appraisal and reward system whose rules are straightforward and open to discussion and that is consistent with organizational goals, values, priorities, and quality standards. (Encourage risk taking and trust building while simultaneously focusing on quality output.)
12. Ensure that policy changes are always explained first to leaders, so that they may, in turn, explain to their subordinates the rationale for those changes before the changes are announced and implemented.
13. Eliminate any competition that hampers idea sharing across the organization.
14. Attend to personnel selection and assignment so that the organization identifies and educates potential leaders who want responsibility consistent with the values of the organization. Plan carefully for succession and transition of key leaders.

14

A Critique and Extension
of the Stratified Systems
Theory Perspective

Kimberly B. Boal and Carlton J. Whitehead

If researchers are to be of much help to leaders at the strategic apex of organizations, they must develop models of leadership that specifically address issues of
selection, development, and effectiveness of strategic leaders.

SST offers a useful beginning. However, Boal and Whitehead argue that it and
other approaches to leadership that focus on either leadership traits or behaviors
have not adequately integrated them. To that end, these authors suggest the need
to examine the leader's behavioral flexibility and cognitive complexity. Furthermore, the degree to which leaders seek, as well, to use information is seen as
crucial. Finally, the importance of the environment, time, and other individual
differences is examined in terms of implications for strategic leadership in general
and for SST in particular.

BEHAVIORAL FLEXIBILITY

Stewart (1982a) notes that top management leadership consists of three components:
demands (what must be done), constraints (that limit what can be done), and choices
(discretion in choosing what to do or how to do it). As Mischel (1977) points out,
some situations are so demanding (powerful) with respect to situational cues and
incentives to behave that virtually everyone would view the situation similarly and
have uniform beliefs regarding appropriate behaviors. However, Hambrick and
Finkelstein (1987) argue that organizations differ significantly in terms of the latitude
of action they afford their leaders.

Thus, while individual characteristics, such as cognitive complexity, may serve
to enhance the leader's discretion, other variables in either the task environment
(e.g., powerful outside forces) or internal organization (e.g., forces for inertia)
may serve to limit the latitude of managerial action. Limits on discretion reduce
the potential importance of cognitive complexity as a necessary individual difference.

Consistent with the above point, we argue that SST's cognitive complexity and time span are useful but fundamentally inadequate to develop a generalized strategic leadership theory and prescriptions (cf. Bass, 1990; Hambrick, 1989). Although most current models of leadership emphasize style or behavior, SST returns to earlier trait approaches that emphasize leader characteristics. While it is clear that any understanding of leadership must afford traits a central role (House, Howard, and Walker, 1991), it is not clear that cognitive complexity, among various traits, should take center stage.

House and Baetz (1979), among many others, have reviewed the research on leader traits and concluded there is a wide constellation of traits, cognitive complexity being only one of many, commonly associated with leadership. Indeed, as Bass (1990) warns, "A person does not become a leader by virtue of the possession of some combination of traits, but the pattern of personal characteristics of the leader must bear some relevant relationship to the characteristics, activities, and goals of the followers" (p. 76).

While SST focuses on the repertoire of mental maps that leaders bring to the situation, it ignores the repertoire of behaviors that leaders can and/or will use in a given situation. Some people are behaviorally more flexible than others. Gangestad and Snyder (1985) show that some individuals, labeled "high self-monitors," will adapt their behavior to fit the situation, but others, "low self-monitors," will not. Dobbins, et al. (1990) found that high self-monitors emerged more frequently as leaders, and Zacarro, Foti, and Kenny (1991) found that high self-monitors were rated more favorably by their subordinates and engaged in more task-related behaviors. Thus, any generalizable theory must consider both traits and behaviors. Contrasting cognitive complexity with behavioral flexibility suggests four possibilities (Figure 14.1).

Figure 14.1
Behavioral Flexibility and Cognitive Complexity Typology

| | | Behavioral Flexibility (Self Monitoring) | |
		High	Low
Cognitive Complexity	High	Informed Flexibles Many Schemas Many Behavioral Responses	Programmed Many Schemas But Limited Behavioral Responses
	Low	Scatter Shooters Few Schemas But Many Behavioral Responses	Plodders Few Few

Cell 1 represents the situation where the leader has both a wide array of cognitive maps with which to interpret the situation and a wide array of behavioral responses. We label these leaders "informed flexibles." Cell 2 represents the situation where cognitive complexity is high, but the leader's repertoire of behavioral responses is low. We label these leaders "programmed." Note that SST as currently formulated would not distinguish between these two types. We believe such a distinction would be particularly important in situations characterized as hyper-turbulence or punctuated equilibrium. Cells 3 and 4 represent situations where the leader has few cognitive maps with which to understand the situation but may either be flexible behaviorally (Cell 3—"scatter shooters) or rigid (Cell 4—"plodders"). Scatter shooters could be successful, even in turbulent environments, if they engage in trial-and-error learning. The problem lies in the inherent inefficiency of this approach compared with one where a person already possesses appropriate cognitive maps. Plodders, who are low in both cognitive complexity and their behavioral repertoire are unlikely to be successful except in highly stable environments.

Finally, while both trait and behavioral approaches to leadership add to our understanding, both approaches underemphasize the importance of the leader's specific task-relevant knowledge. Bass (1990) concluded, in his review of the literature, that task-relevant specialized knowledge was an important contributor to leadership. We argue that what people think is a function of what they know, and what they know determines how they think. In addition, people know what they do and do what they know. Thus, knowledge links thinking and action. Change knowledge and you change both thinking (i.e., cognitive complexity) and behavior, at least potentially.

ENVIRONMENTAL LINKAGES

SST as developed by Jaques (1976, 1989) and summarized by Jacobs and Lewis in this book, presents what Jaques considers to be a universal model of bureaucratic organization design. Bureaucracies are viewed as managerial employment hierarchies, which include most formal organizations (exceptions include political organizations, entrepreneurs, university academic departments, and so on). Although SST is a unique model, it is consistent with the rational system models developed in organizational theory (Scott, 1987). It adopts and extends the three managerial levels developed by Parsons (1960) and proposes that organizations should have a maximum of seven strata within the three levels (Strata VI and VII—systems level, Strata IV and V—organizational level, and Strata I-III—the production or operational level). The SST model is characterized as a one best way to view organization design and increasing managerial omniscience from level I through VII.

Jacobs and Jaques (1987) and Jacobs and Lewis (this book), in extending the SST model to leadership, considerably refine SST by infusing the analysis with concepts from open systems, contingency, information, and exchange theory. In our opinion, these pieces represent a major refinement of SST but still do not overcome its deterministic and manager-centered perspective and assumptions. Since our primary concern is strategic leadership, it will be the key focus of our discussion of the implications of SST for organization-environmental linkages. A brief overview of the leadership perspective, focused at the strategic (VI and VII) level, will be presented, and then the environmental linkage will be discussed.

Jacobs and Jaques's theory (1987, p. 50) views the core of strategic leadership as uncertainty reduction (mapping external environment and envisioning desirable and attainable futures) through acquiring and interpreting information to determine appropriate courses of action for the organization. SST leadership theory is built around three basic concepts:

1. Adaptation requirements—the need for organizations to adapt to the environment, characterized by varying degrees of dynamism and complexity, in order to acquire scarce resources and use them efficiently.
2. Requisite frame of reference (cognitive map/complexity) for appropriate exercise of discretion. Leadership is discretionary behavior beyond those behaviors specified by task structure. The level of complexity for frame of references needs to increase with strata since the levels of interdependencies and environmental complexity and uncertainty increase.
3. Information acquisition and use. Since uncertainty reduction is the core of the leadership role at the systems-level, requisite complexity for acquiring and interpreting information to cope with uncertainty due to the lack of information, equivocality, and/or ambiguity is a key factor to successful strategic leadership.

Organizational-Environmental Linkage

The SST position is that systems-level managers are the mechanism for keeping the organization coaligned with its environment, and successful linkage is a function of the cognitive complexity and time perspective of the executive. Jacobs and Jaques (1987) emphasize organization adaptation to the environment. However, as Meyer, Brooks, and Goes (1990) observe, adaptation represents first-order change in response to environmental evolution (relatively slow incremental change). Second-order change involves frame-breaking change at the firm level in response to revolutionary (punctuated, quantum) change in the environment (Meyer, Brooks, and Goes, 1990).

For numerous reasons, environmental turbulence created by revolutionary change poses a major challenge to the generalizability of SST (for a discussion of organization change models, see Duran, Phillips, and Whitehead, 1991; Gersick, 1991; Phillips and Duran, this book). First, bureaucratic organizations can adapt effectively to environments experiencing slow evolution but have problems in responding appropriately to revolutionary changes (Burns and Stalker, 1961; Kanter, 1990; Lawrence and Lorsch, 1967; Miller and Friesen, 1984).

Second, the complexity of a turbulent environment will exceed the requisite cognitive complexity of any CEO or executive group (Terreberry, 1968), especially if this is a relatively homogeneous group, which might be predictable from an SST perspective. Thus, organizations relying on level VII leaders or the combined capacities of VI and VII are likely to experience severe organization-environmental interface problems. Murray (1989) suggests that when competition is intense, homogeneity in top management team compositions is to be preferred, but under turbulent conditions, a heterogeneous team is preferable. As Hurst, Rush, and White (1989) point out, because a variety of behaviors is needed at the strategic apex (Stratum VII in Jaques's terms), each of which is associated with a different cognitive style, the top management team should be heterogeneous with respect to the cognitive styles of its members. Research by Norbum and Birley (1988) suggests that successful top management teams are heterogeneous with respect to the functional backgrounds of team members. These results suggest the importance of task-relevant knowledge combined with multiple frames of reference.

Third, and closely related to the previous point, second-order organization changes are frame breaking. SST leadership theory emphasizes the progressive development of the appropriate systems domain leaders' frames of reference for mapping and interpreting the environment (Jacobs and Jaques, 1987) and emphasizes the significance of the embeddedness of leadership in the organization structures and processes. To the extent that these frameworks are rooted in adaptive change perspectives and action programs, it is questionable whether the leaders can be expected to generate the appropriate frame-breaking organization changes. Perhaps this is one reason that bureaucracies are consistently better prepared to fight the last, as opposed to the current, war.

Fourth, SST emphasizes hierarchical differences in power and capacity. This orientation is not likely to develop the organization culture conducive to capturing and using the expertise located below the strategic levels in the system. In frame-breaking change situations, the expertise, perspective, and proclivity for developing the appropriate organization response might be more prevalent in the strata below the systems domain.

Fifth, consistent with Daft and Lengel (1986), SST strategic leadership recognizes the increasing levels of uncertainty, lack of information, equivocality (conflicting interpretations), and ambiguity (inadequate quality). Revolutionary environmental change creates all of these informational uncertainties and the need for frame-breaking individual change. "Wicked" as opposed to "tame" problems are associated with revolutionary environmental change (Rittel and Webber, 1973). Tame problems can be defined, structured, and solved through obtaining and/or developing additional information and applying the appropriate analytic techniques. However, wicked problems are indeterminate and cannot be definitively formulated, and hence no agreed-upon criteria can be developed to ascertain if or when a solution has been found.

We believe SST is more oriented toward solving tame problems. Time span of feedback and the individual's cognitive complexity are important variables in categorizing the environment and selecting leaders who can solve tame problems. However, cognitive complexity may be less essential for dealing with wicked problems. Because of their indeterminate nature, wicked problems may lead the cognitively complex leader to be overcome with analysis paralysis. In addition to or perhaps rather than cognitive complexity, we will suggest that the construct of "street smarts" (Wagner and Sternberg, 1990) may be more useful for selecting leaders who must deal with wicked problems. This is because of its explicit focus on types of knowledge and its implicit recognition of the need for behavioral flexibility.

TIME

Time is a critical variable in SST leadership theory; however, the theory fails to deal explicitly with time as a nonlinear, multidimensional, and cultural phenomenon. Given the uncertainty absorption and environmental interpretation role (most likely involving both multinational and multicultural dimensions) ascribed to executive leaders, understanding the cultural nature of time is critical to the theory. We will use the complementary frameworks proposed by Hall and Hall (1987) (monochronic, polychronic, and rhythmic time) and Kelly and McGrath (1988) (Newtonian, Einsteinian, and transactional perspectives of time) in developing our conclusions about the significance of the cultural nature of time and our argument that the SST perspective is overly simplistic.

The culturally dominant view of time in the United States (and the one we think is implicit in SST as currently formulated) is Newtonian (Kelly and McGrath, 1988) or monochronic time (Hall and Hall, 1987). Here time is viewed as atomistic but homogeneous, abstract and absolute, linear, segmented, and tangible. In monochronic-time cultures, time is a fundamental structuring variable, characterized by a clock and calendar orientation and driven by schedules and agendas. For example, things like being on time, time management, and saving, wasting, or losing time are perspectives characteristic of this orientation.

Time also can be viewed from an Einsteinian or polychronic perspective, the antithesis of the monochronic time orientation. Here, time is viewed as indivisible but differentiated, abstract but relational with the simultaneous occurrence of many things, and multidimensional. Within this framework time might be identified in terms of movement, and, to some degree, the radar scope captures this notion. The event time between plans is a function of their current location and relative movement. As they change location, so does the event time between them. Organizations and people do not operate in a vacuum.

Hall and Hall (1987, p. 18) propose that the orientation of polychronic people differs substantially from that of monochronic people. For example, polychronic people tend to be less focused, more distractible and flexible, less time-and schedule-conscious, and more oriented to relationship, family, and people (e.g., people are more important than schedules), and they have a longer time frame than monochronic people. These differences have substantial implications for leadership in a multicultural environment.

A third view of time is transactional. Here time is cyclical, not linear. One interesting aspect of the cyclical concept—circadian rhythm—leads to "entrainment" of various physiological and behavioral responses. Entrainment is the phenomenon in which one cyclic process becomes captured by, and set to oscillate in rhythm with, another process (Kelly and McGrath, 1988). The four elements of entrainment are rhythm, mesh (synchronization), tempo, and pace. Entrainment thus becomes a process that integrates temporally differentiated activities and behaviors. Organizational strategies such as planning, scheduling, and group-task forces may be viewed as attempts to induce temporal complementarity among temporally asymmetric worlds (Bluedorn and Denhardt, 1988).

The cross-cultural nature of most large bureaucratic organizations, viewing time as a cultural and variable phenomenon, and the role of time span of feedback in SST emphasize some implications of time perspective for the theory. First, the time span of feedback is not constant but is a function of changes in other variables inherent in the environment in which an action is taken as well as the response of others to the action taken. One of the things being observed in large business organizations is that the time span between idea to marketplace is being greatly compressed, as is the time span between an organization's actions and a competitor's reaction. In fact, Peters (1990) suggests that the next great arena of competition will be time. Those who can compress it will win. This suggests that rather than time span of feedback, the relative time span of learning and response is most important.

The transnational nature of organizations creates multicultural environments as the domains in which the leader must cope with several different perspectives of time and spans of feedback. In addition, because of the networked nature of many of these systems, multiple time perspectives could be encompassed within the systems domain in which executive leadership operates. Examples of situations with high potential for time diversity at the strategic leadership level include alliances among countries (such as NATO) and joint business ventures between a monochronic and polychronic time culture. Problems between Japanese and Americans are, at least partially, attributable to differences in time orientations, such as relationship versus "let's do it now" perspectives, or the concept of appropriate age versus merit for executive leaders (that is, the relationship between time and competence), and so forth (Hall and Hall, 1987).

Finally, by focusing on only the calendar time span of feedback, SST has not addressed other equally important aspects of time: synchronization, sequence, rate, and allocation. As Bluedorn and Denhardt (1988) point out, one of the most important aspects of time concerns bringing the right objects to the right place at the right time and in the right order. In addition, if time is viewed as a commodity (McGrath and Rotchford, 1983), then it must be rationed and allocated among competing demands.

PERSON

Person/trait variables play a central role in SST in two ways. First, similar to Ashby's (1956) theory of requisite task variety, Jacobs and Jaques (1990) hypothesize that for successful performance to occur, there must be a match between the complexity of the environment (as assessed by the time span of feedback of critical tasks) and the cognitive complexity of the individual (as currently assessed by the Career Path Appreciation technique, Stamp, 1988). The second person trait variable is referred to as "temperament." A reflection of the person's temperament is his or her "proclivity" to develop complex mental models (cognitive maps). In support, Levi and Tetlock (1980) found that the cognitive complexity of an individual was significantly correlated with the complexity of the cognitive maps developed to portray the same event.

This proclivity, or cognitive style (cf. Streufert and Nogami, 1989) ultimately prepares the person with sufficient cognitive complexity to cope with the task demands at the highest level. Jacobs and Jaques (1990) speculate that the Myers-Briggs Type Indicator may be a measure of this "proclivity." Before reviewing the role of temperament and proclivity, we turn to the literature on information processing to place these two constructs in perspective. Much of the research on human information processing has recently been reviewed by Lord and Maher (1990), and we use their review as a jumping-off point.

Information Processing

Lord and Maher (1990) suggest there are four basic models that can be used to describe human information processing. They are the rational, limited capacity, expert, and cybernetic. Rational models, though more prescriptive than descriptive, are widely used in economic theory (Becker, 1976), motivation theory (Vroom, 1964), and subjective utility models of decision making (Edwards and Tversky, 1967). These models assert that individuals do, or should, assign probability and utility values to hypothetical events and choose among available alternatives to maximize expected utility. While rational models are not highly descriptively accurate, because of limited, short-term memory capacity, it is also true that, with the help of decision aids, rational models are widely used to solve tame problems. Examples of decision aids would be linear programming models, stochastic inventory models, and capital asset pricing models.

Limited capacity models, recognizing the limitations of cognitive processing, focus on how people simplify information processing through the use of heuristics (Hogarth, 1981; Tversky and Kahneman, 1974) and implicit theories and schema (Gioia, 1986; Nisbett and Ross, 1980); or how they limit the decision-making tasks by using suboptimal decision rules (e.g., Simon's 1955 satisficing model). Two points are of interest to us. First, while the use of certain heuristics may result in predictable biases, they do not always lead to errors in judgment. Secondly, although it is thought that there are general heuristics common across people, Sherman and Corty (1984) point out that experts use different heuristic principles than do novices. Thus, the role of task-specific expertise must be considered. Both Goodwin, Wofford, and Harrison (1990) and Scott (1969), among others, argue and provide support for the contention that cognitive complexity is task-specific and nontransferable.

Expert models of information processing assume that individuals rely on already developed knowledge structures to supplement simplified means of processing data. Experts differ from novices both in the use of more elaborate schema (Chi, Glaser, and Reese, 1982) derived from their knowledge of the subject matter (Glaser, 1984) and in how they process information (Glaser, 1982). However, as Lord and Maher (1990) point out, experts are not superior in a general sense but only within their limited domain of expertise. Knowledge structures are task-specific. Chi, Glaser, and Farr (1988) suggest that the superior performance of experts is a function of the interaction between knowledge structures and the processes of reasoning and problem solving. This line of research needs to emphasize the acquisition of knowledge structures. As Glaser (1984) notes, quoting Siegler and Richards (1982), "Knowledge of specific content domains is a crucial dimension of development in its own right and changes in such knowledge may underlie other changes previously attributed to the growth of capabilities and strategies" (p. 98).

Unlike the previously discussed models, cybernetic models are dynamic, rather than static, and temporal, rather than atemporal. Feedback plays a key role in altering behavior, learning, and cognitive processes. Rather than using sophisticated processes to achieve optimization, as the rational model suggests, optimization occurs through learning and adaptation. Hogarth (1981) argued that heuristics that apply suboptimal decision rules in discrete decision situations may yield optimal decisions in continuous environments when decisions are recurring. However, the usefulness of cybernetic models diminishes when the time span of feedback is lengthy or courses of action are costly to reverse.

The importance of environmental dynamism is of particular importance when viewing information-processing models. Drawing on the review of forecasting research methods by Pant and Starbuck (1990), we conclude that complex models work better in stable environments but the opposite also is true, that is, simple models predict better in turbulent environments where complex models mistake noise for information. Models that predict trends well in stable environments do not preduct turning points in turbulent environments. Unfortunately, turning points can be discovered only retrospectively. The best predictor of the future in the short run is the immediate past, but in the long run no single model works well, and complex models do worse (Pant and Starbuck, 1990). As Pant and Starbuck (1990) point out, quoting Niels Bohr, "Prediction is very difficult, especially about the future."

This line of research raises questions about the general usefulness of equating time span of feedback with cognitive complexity, with focusing on cognitive complexity as a generic trait, devoid of context, and, most importantly, assuming that complexity is always to be preferred. Under crisis or turbulence less cognitively complex persons may be more successful. Schroder, Driver, and Streufert (1967) suggest, for example, that the relationship between cognitive complexity and environmental complexity could be visualized as a set of inverted U curves, with optimal functioning occurring at some intermediate level of environmental complexity.

In addition, under crisis, time spans become compressed, especially the response time span. Under crisis, decision makers consider less information, focus on shorter-term consequences, and stereotype more. These effects are likely to hold true irrespective of the level of cognitive complexity (Weick and Bougon, 1986). Complex models may lead to analysis paralysis unless coupled with a bias for action (Peters and Waterman, 1982). Under turbulence, especially involving changes of direction, models that worked well in the past become dysfunctional, a la the "failure of success" syndrome (O'Toole, 1985). Miller (1990) points out that organizations sow the seeds of their own destruction by focusing on, and overemphasizing, their core competences to the neglect of other organizational needs.

Cognitive Complexity

Cognitive complexity contains two basic dimensions: differentiation, which refers to the number of characteristics or dimensions of a problem that are included, and integration, which refers to the number of connections, and the rules governing those connections, among differentiated concepts. Both dimensions are thought to vary widely across individuals, and it is assumed by SST that both dimensions, within limits, are fixed in the person. However, within organizations it is likely that for any particular problem, one or both of these dimensions will be constrained. Shull, Delbecq, and Cummings (1970) coined the term *bounded discretion* to point out that technically sound solutions are often constrained by laws, customs, and ethical considerations and therefore are not acceptable, even for discussion.

Thus, it is possible for the individual's cognitive complexity to exceed the complexity of the allowable solution space. SST, it seems to us, assumes that higher leader complexity will always be functional, an assumption that we believe is an empirical question and may be problematical. In SST, cognitive complexity is thought to be necessary to deal with the many variations in the environment facing the leader. However, one of the functions of leadership is the creation of meaning (Boal and Bryson, 1988; Smircich and Stubbart, 1985).

Hence, we agree that strategic leadership requires, among other things, the ability to simplify the many into the few—in the vernacular, "to separate the wheat from the chaff." It is not clear that this is necessarily related to cognitive complexity (e.g., President Ronald Reagan). Noel (1989), for example, points out that the CEOs he studied had narrow obsessions that drove their behavior. Furthermore, of various salient capacities required of different types of strategic leaders, it is unclear if cognitive complexity is related to them (cf. Shrivastava and Nachman, 1989; Westley and Mintzberg, 1989). In contrast to Hunt and Ropo (this book), Bass's (1990) review of current theories of charismatic and transformational leadership does not suggest that cognitive complexity plays much, if any, role. In fact, as currently formulated, SST views charismatic leadership as a breakdown in the system and therefore a sign of ineffectiveness. Our position is that this is increasingly likely at the strategic level under conditions of equivocality and turbulence.

Boal and Bryson (1988) argue that there are two types of charismatic leaders. The first type arises under conditions of crises. They suggest that crises sever the linkage between action and outcomes. According to Boal and Bryson, leaders who reestablish this linkage, restoring systems' effectiveness, are seen as charismatic. We believe that leaders who are cognitively complex and behaviorally flexible are more likely to respond effectively to crisis situations. Thus, unlike current formulations of SST, we think it could be extended to encompass this form of charismatic leadership. They imply that Admiral W. F. "Bull" Halsey may have been such a leader.

The second type of charismatic leader, according to Boal and Bryson, arises in situations where the linkage between values and action has been severed. Leaders whose visions reconnect this linkage are also seen as charismatic. We argue that at the strategic level, conflicts over goals and a lack of consensus are likely to prevail (Cameron, 1986). Quinn (1988) argues that the master manager is able to achieve a balance in these competing values. We see this as problematic. Rather, we argue that one or more stakeholders (Freeman, 1984) are likely to be ignored by the leader, the result of which is a severing of the linkage between their values and their actions.

It is unclear whether SST is applicable to leaders who have charismatic effects because of their visions. However, analysis of the speeches and writings of such leaders, e.g., Martin Luther King, could suggest whether the core construct of SST, cognitive complexity, was related to the emergence of this type of charismatic leadership. A key issue separating this form of charisma versus crisis produced is that visions, unlike crises, have no necessary time limit for resolution. Thus, the idea of linking cognitive complexity to the time span of feedback, as SST currently does, limits the extendability of SST for understanding this form of strategic leadership. In any case, among various trait approaches to leadership, only SST affords cognitive complexity such a central role.

Proclivity

Jacobs and Jaques (1990) suggested that the Myers-Briggs Type Indicator (MBTI) might reflect a person's proclivity to build mental models. In addition, they suggest that as people move progressively higher in their organizations, SST would predict that the proportion of intuitive-thinking types would increase. While not directly addressing this issue, McCaulley (1990) reviewed all the data collected by the Center for Applications of Psychological Type. She concluded that while managers, in general, were more heavily weighted toward sensing types, as opposed to intuitive types, top managers were more evenly divided between sensing and intuitive types. She did not address the proportion of thinking versus feeling types in her review, but the data she presents show that thinking types are in the majority in fifty-one of fifty-nine samples studied. It is not clear whether this dimension discriminated across leadership levels. McCaulley (1990) suggests that, overall, top executives are somewhat more likely to be extrovert-intuitive-thinking-judgmental (ENTJ) types.

Extroverts favor quick action as opposed to introverts, who emphasize conceptualizing the problem clearly and engaging in thoughtful deliberation before making decisions. Intuitive types are more concerned with the "big picture" and visions as opposed to sensing types, who favor practical experience. Thinking types favor logical analysis of causes and effects as opposed to feeling types, who decide by weighting the relative importance or value of competing alternatives. Finally, judging types enjoy organizing, planning, and moving quickly to a decision as opposed to perception types, who are curious and open to change and prefer to keep their options open.

With respect to time, extroverts see time as more episodic, and introverts view it more continuously. Intuitives are more future-oriented, and sensing types are more oriented to the present. Thinking types view time as a past-present-future continuum and do not emphasize any special stage. Judging types are less oriented to the past than are feeling types. Finally, meeting objectives by target dates comes more easily to sensing-thinking-judgmental (STJ) types. It must be noted, however, that all types are found among top managers. While the evidence supports the contention that some types are proportionately more represented, it does not show that leaders of one type are more successful than leaders of another type.

In fact, Barr and Barr (1989) argue that leaders need to develop all the processes of type—both those that come naturally to a person and those that do not. We speculate that equivocality and turbulence require one type of leader but that clarity and stability require another. The good staff general is not necessarily a good field general, especially in times of battle. The opposite is also true. A good field general may be ill-suited to lead a peacetime army (cf. Hunt and Phillips, 1991).

Jacobs and Jaques (1987) suggest that intuitives, as measured by the MBTI, have a greater proclivity to develop mental models and would be expected, ceteris paribus, to be more cognitively complex. However, Bensimon (1987) did not find that the use of multiple frames of reference by college presidents was related to whether or not they identified themselves as intuitive. A follow-up study by Birnbaum (1990) reported that those presidents who were identified as both being intuitive and having complex multiframe perspectives were more problem-oriented and likely to engage in active information search processes.

However, Ruble and Cosier (1990) did not find that cognitive style, as measured by the Myers-Briggs Type Indicator, was related to prediction accuracy on a multiple-cue probability learning task. Furthermore, it is well known that confidence in one's decisions increases proportionately to increases in information; however, the correctness of the decision does not. In fact, there is often a negative correlation between the accuracy of a decison and the confidence in the decision. Usually those who have data in statistical form make better decisions than those who have raw data (Hogarth, 1981).

Information Seeking and Using

The discussion up to this point has focused on how individuals process information, but we have not addressed, nor does SST, the degree to which individuals actively seek and use information. Individuals differ in both the degree to which they actively seek new information for problem solving as well as the kinds of information they seek (Einhorn and Hogarth, 1985; Hershey, et al. 1990). In addition, they differ in the degree to which they use the information (Ashton and Ashton, 1990; Ross and Lepper, 1980). By contrasting seeking with using behavior, we develop the typology in Figure 14.2.

Figure 14.2
Information Seeking and Using Typology

		Degree to Which New Information Is Actively Sought	
		Low	High
Degree to Which the Leader Incorporates Information and Revises Beliefs/Mental Models	Low	Information Avoiders	Information Discarders
	High	Information Sensitives	Information Junkies

Cell 1 represents the situation where the leader neither actively seeks nor uses information. We label these leaders information avoiders. Novices often evidence information searches that lack both coherence and efficiency (Chi, Feltovich, and Glaser, 1981; Larkin et al., 1980), and when coupled with a relative insensitivity to new evidence (Edwards, 1968; Einhorn and Hogarth, 1978), we have a case approximating cell 1. It is doubtful, but not impossible, that many top executives would be like this—for instance, a situation when nontask-related criteria are used as the primary basis for selection, for example, family firms. The cell 2 leader, whom we label the information discarder, evidences a strong decision confirmation bias. Evidence consistent with prior beliefs is used more often to make decisions than evidence that is inconsistent with prior beliefs (Ross and Lepper, 1980). Mitroff's (1974) study of highly regarded NASA scientists found that if data were inconsistent with their "pet" theories, they ignored the data.

Information sensitives (cell 3) do not actively scan the environment for data but will incorporate data presented to them in revising their decisions. There is some evidence that sensitivity toward the use of data is the result of professional training (Ashton and Ashton, 1990). Those who actively seek and use information (cell 4) we label information junkies (a label Ted Turner is said to have used to describe his motivation to start CNN). SST, like most other models of leadership, does not sufficiently consider the importance of information seeking and usage. However, studies by Daft, Sormunen, and Parks (1988) and Eisenhardt (1989b) find that organizational success is influenced by the degree to which top management seeks and uses information.

A partial reconciliation of SST and the above findings is the realization that search processes are not usually distributed across problem identification, alternative generation, and choice. As Simon (1987) points out, expert chess players will choose an alternative fairly quickly but may spend considerable time checking to see that a plausible move does not have a hidden weakness. Perceived weaknesses are a function of the degree to which current data deviate from schemas, scripts, or knowledge structures.

Early theories of leadership emphasized the traits of leaders, much as SST does by focusing on cognitive complexity and temperament examples. More recent models of leadership emphasize leader behaviors and style. We argue that each approach adds understanding but is not sufficient (see House and Baetz, 1979). If it was, we would expect leaders to be transferable across organizational contexts. But Shetty and Perry (1976) found that outsiders who became CEOs, were effective only if they possessed relevant industry knowledge.

Thus, we believe, more emphasis needs to be placed on understanding the schemas and scripts that executives possess. Or, to paraphrase Sam Ervin, "What did the President know, and when did he know it?" A major difference between schemas and scripts (whether personal or organization) and cognitive complexity is that the former can be codified and shared while the latter can be developed only within the person's genetic endowment. That is, Jaques (1978, 1989) argues that some/most people are genetically not equipped to develop the levels of cognitive power required to function successfully at higher levels in the organization.

To close this section and to introduce the next, we quote Bruner (1957, pp. 132-133). "Presented with a complex stimulus, the subject perceives in it what it is ready to perceive; the more complex or ambiguous the stimulus, the more perception will be determined by what is already 'in' the subject and the less by what is in the stimulus" (Cited in Huber, 1991, pp. 104).

Schemas

Four types of schemas are discussed in the literature—self, person, event, and person-in-situation (Lord and Foti, 1986). Self schemas contain information about one's own personality and behavior. Person schemas focus on trait and behavior information common to certain groups or types of people, for example, leaders (cf. Hunt, Boal, and Sorenson, 1990). Event schemas (scripts) entail knowledge about the typical sequence of events in a given situation. Event schemas are especially important but may be dysfunctional for wicked problems or under environmental turbulence because they might lead to applying old solutions to new problems. Person-in-situation schemas contain information about people and behavior typically found in particular situations. Understanding schemas is particularly important because they affect the perception and retrieval of information and the normative appraisal of events, people, and objects, influence what is learned, and serve as a guide for action (Feldman, 1986; Isenberg, 1986; Lord and Foti, 1986).

Isenberg (1986) has argued that managers engage in plausible reasoning, as opposed to logical reasoning and probabilistic thinking. Both allow managers to cope with uncertainty and ambiguity, and both are embedded in the schemas and the structure of knowledge one possesses. Little is known about how or why individuals change their schemas. Clearly, the more the situation is routine, the more the decision maker will automatically involve schemas rather than thinking. Nystrom and Starbuck (1984) argue that if organizations are to avoid crises, they must unlearn, that is, discard, old schemas (that are assumed no longer to be functional) and learn new schemas (that are assumed to be functional). Continued failure, as well as novelty, promotes unlearning (cf. Langer, 1978), but this is hardly a recipe for success unless experimentation allows the leader to pilot-test different possible strategies while limiting potential losses. Feldman (1986) suggests that the less knowledge possessed by the individual, the more likely inappropriate generalizations will be made and that learning is determined by the interaction of knowledge and experience. He suggests experiences that contradict existing schemas promote the most learning.

Bedeian (1986) suggests four potential sources of experiences that contradict existing schemas. They include:

1. Borrowing from other organizations. Institutional theory suggests that under conditions of uncertainty, coerciveness, and professional training leaders are likely to mimic the behaviors of others (DiMaggio and Powell, 1983; Levittt and Nass, 1989).
2. Introducing changes in current procedures based on feedback from the environment. This approach is often utilized in action research. Argyris and Schön (1978) point out that individuals possess a cognitive theory, referred to as the espoused theory, which represents a normative ideal regarding how they should behave, and a theory-in-use, which actually guides their behavior. They argue that learning involves a change in the theory-in-use. However, Fiol and Lyles (1985) contend that learning requires understanding and cognition of the reasons beyond an event. Thus, we argue that feedback that results in either a change in the espoused theory, a change in the theory-in-use, or recognition of the discrepancy between them should be termed learning.
3. Original innovations. Einstein is often quoted as saying, "Imagination is more important than knowledge." How to increase the likelihood of creativity and innovation at both the individual and organizational level has been a recurring theme in management (cf. Cosier and Schwenk, 1990; Morgan, 1986; Taggart and Robey, 1981; Zaltman, Duncan, and Holbeck, 1973). Usually suggestions focus on either identifying and overcoming individual, group, and organizational barriers to innovation or advocating the use of certain techniques such as devil's advocate and dialectical inquiry (Mason and Mitroff, 1981; Schwenk, 1989).
4. Blind variations. Population ecology (Aldrich, McKelvey, and Ulrich, 1984) suggests that organizations continually experience random variations. Variations that enhance effectiveness are retained, and those that do not are selected out. Unlike previous approaches, population ecology does not suggest that these variations be conscious and purposeful.

Street Smarts

Recently, Wagner and Sternberg (1990) have suggested three kinds of tacit knowledge collectively referred to as "street smarts," which differentiate successful managers and executives from less successful ones. The three kinds of tacit knowledge are knowledge about managing oneself, managing others, and managing tasks. Managing oneself refers to knowledge regarding self-motivation and self-organization, such as overcoming procrastination. Managing others refers to knowledge concerning subordinates, peers, and superiors. An example would be how to negotiate with important organizational stakeholders (see Savage, Blair, and Sorenson, 1989).

Managing tasks refers to knowledge about how to do specific managerial tasks well, such as conducting a performance appraisal review. As such, each type of the above forms of tacit knowledge represents different schema possessed by successful managers. Recent theoretical and empirical work has emphasized the importance of learning to manage oneself under the rubric of self-leadership (Manz, 1986; Manz and Sims, 1980), while traditional transactional theories of leadership (e.g., path-goal) emphasize managing others. The third component, task knowledge, is usually not emphasized in discussions of leadership (see Hunt, Boal, and Sorenson, 1990, for an exception). Based upon our earlier discussion, we believe this is a serious omission.

Wagner and Sternberg (1990) note that what one learns from experience, not experience per se, is sufficient for the acquisition of street smarts. How best to structure the environment to promote learning thus becomes a key task for the leader and by the leader. Feldman (1986) offers four suggestions for improving the likelihood that individuals will learn from experience. They are:

1. Increase the amount and immediacy of useful feedback. This can be enhanced by requiring that specific predictions as to results be made and by setting up data collection and interpretation systems to make feedback inevitable.
2. Create an environment that promotes learning. One way to do this would be to institutionalize the role of devil's advocate.
3. Hire or train employees to be experts in both substance and process.
4. Do not expect infallibility. Allow for failure. As Feldman (1986) says, "Everyone wants to learn, but nobody wants to be wrong" (p. 283). Besides experience, leaders can learn vicariously or through imitation, though these approaches appear to be more useful in stable, rather than turbulent, environments (cf. Huber, 1991).

CONCLUSION

In this chapter we argue that as presently conceptualized, SST leadership theory is both incomplete and situation-bound. It appears to be most relevant for leaders in bureaucratic organizations operating in a relatively stable environment. In this situation, strategic leaders are more likely to possess the requisite cognitive complexity and time perspective to perform the key uncertainty absorption role, through environmental interpretation and mapping role, as envisioned by SST theory. We have suggested that SST needs to (1) consider the behavioral flexibility, as well as cognitive complexity, of the leader; (2) focus on the degree to which the leader seeks and uses information as well as his or her capacity to process information; and (3) take into account the leader's knowledge and schemas. In addition, we have argued that a broader conception of time needs to be incorporated in SST. We believe the insights developed in this chapter can be used to strengthen SST theory.

15

Some Concluding Thoughts
James G. Hunt and Robert L. Phillips

This book has attempted to broaden the conception of leadership by emphasizing its strategic aspects as opposed to its common but highly restrictive treatment as lower-level, face-to-face influence. This thrust has meant a focus on the total organization and consideration of organizational theory, organization design, and strategic management considerations, in addition to those considerations covered in traditional leadership theory. The focus has been oriented around a hierarchical approach (Stratified Systems Theory), which, as we pointed out in Chapter 1, those such as Lessem (1991) have argued is representative of a European "third force" counterbalance to Anglo-American individualistic approaches and sharply contrasts with Japanese management perspectives and their current spin-offs (e.g., Ouchi's, 1981, Theory Z).

A number of authors, with a range of different backgrounds, have contributed to our multiple-organizational-level perspective by discussing their work from the standpoint of its potential interplay with stratified systems—that is, how their work can extend stratified systems and how stratified systems notions can extend their work. In addition to the major focus of each of these chapters, we indicated that there were also a number of "crosscutting themes," common to more than one chapter. These crosscutting themes were summarized briefly in Table 1.1.

We consider these themes as a useful underlying framework for this chapter on concluding thoughts, and they are discussed in the sequence shown in the table. In these concluding thoughts we do not systematically discuss each of the book's chapters per se, but rather refer to them as they relate to the theme in question. We are especially interested in bringing in a wide range of additional literature so that it, along with the book's earlier content, will encourage future directions for leadership research and application.

CROSS-CUTTING THEMES

Organizations as Hierarchies

The book's title, reinforced by arguments from the literature, has emphasized a hierarchical focus. However, not surprisingly, given the mix of the contributors selected and their charge, that view has not gone unchallenged. Contributions focusing most strongly on this issue are Gardner and Schermerhorn's and Boal and Whitehead's. Indeed, some alternative organizational designs are discussed by Phillips and Duran in the context of different kinds of change.

These challenges raise the question of the generality of SST, which serves as the point of departure for this book's multiple-level approach. In other words, to what extent is the book's point of departure based on a general versus a midrange theory? Boal and Whitehead contend that SST purports to be a general theory. However, Jacobs and Jaques (1987) make the point that SST, as currently formulated, is limited to industrial and commercial organizations, to federal and local civil service, health, education, and social service organizations, and to the armed forces. They argue that it does not apply to entrepreneurships or partnerships or to church or political organizations and the like. Jaques and Clement (1991) make a similar argument in their later work. Clearly, these authors see SST as a midrange, rather than a general, theory, even though its boundaries are wide.

Gardner and Schermerhorn's chapter briefly discusses Mintzberg's (1979) five types of organizations: simple structure, machine bureaucracy, professional bureaucracy, divisionalized bureaucracy, and adhocracy. The chapter argues essentially that SST ignores these. Our interpretation is that it does not claim to apply to the first and that it is not inconsistent with the second, third, and fourth types.

The fifth type, the adhocracy, as a broad category, encompasses the vast range of "antihierarchy" organization types mentioned in Chapter 1 (Kanter's, 1989b, "network organizations"; Peters, 1988, "focused anarchies," Drucker's, 1988, technology-based "synchronies"; Lawler's, 1988, "high-intensity organizations"; and various kinds of self-managed team organizations, consistent with Lessem's European "third-force" organizations; and the like). Jaques and Clement (1991) argue that these participative and team-type setups are better handled within hierarchies, and Robbins's (1990) careful review of the literature leads him to argue that an adhocracy's success and progression in its life cycle will drive the organization toward stabilization, standardization, differentiation and formalization, or death.

While we believe this is an empirical question, Robbins's argument basically reinforces the dynamic thrust of Part IV, where configurations, tracks, and types of change are emphasized. Also, while Blair and Rivera do not address the hierarchy-adhocracy notion explicitly, their emphasis on the strategic management of various kinds of stakeholders provides additional insight on the question.

Finally, a very different perspective related to this general issue is presented by Tosi (1991). He spins out a very complex theory that considers different organizational typologies and incorporates leadership concepts from selected mainstream leadership approaches.

Critical Tasks, Managerial Work

All of the chapter authors have addressed, in one way or another, some of the critical tasks of strategic leaders. A number of these authors (e.g., Blair and Rivera; Gardner and Schermerhorn) examine these in greater or lesser depth by hierarchical level. Jacobs and Lewis point out the requisite variety notion (Ashby, 1952) in Stratified Systems Theory, where leader complexity must match complexity of the organization. In other words, individual complexity must be appropriate to match that required by leader critical tasks or managerial work. There has been discussion throughout the book of the nature of critical tasks and managerial work, starting with the general notions of mission, strategy goal settting, and organizational design functions at the top, to tasks cascading with increasing concreteness down the organization (Figure 2.1 provides a summary consistent with this description). Key notions articulated there and, indeed, throughout the book are the increasing time span of decision-making feedback as one moves up the organization.

Recall that SST argues that these time spans have been derived empirically by Jaques and associates and are based on the time required to receive feedback concerning performance of the longest task for which a worker or leader at a given level is accountable. As pointed out earlier, this can run to twenty years or even longer at the very top (e.g., long-range weapons systems, time required to find out success of high capital investments made by a large corporation). Jacobs and Jaques (1990) provide some evidence bearing on this for army general officers at different ranks.

Boal and Whitehead question the linear thinking implied in using time span of feedback as the measure of task complexity. This view is also consistent with change-oriented chapters such as Phillips and Duran's, and Hunt and Ropo's, as well as the immense environmental changes discussed by Segal and Hitt and Keats.

All of this suggests additional ways of getting at task complexity, in addition to, or in place of, time span of feedback. Hunt (1991), building on the work of Bentz (1987) and Stewart (1982b, 1989), suggests a couple of possibilities. Indeed, Jaques himself, in his most recent work with Clement (Jaques and Clement, 1991), has developed a complexity approach that, while consistent with time span of feedback is independent of it. Essentially, that approach conceives of the following four types of task complexity:

- Direct action and immediate situational response. Problems can be dealt with as they are encountered.
- Diagnostic accumulation. Problems must be anticipated and resolved by determining and acquiring important information and assembling it to anticipate problems and overcome difficulties.

- Alternative serial plans: devising possible ways of carrying out and evaluating a task and choosing and planning one of the alternatives. The plan is then followed, with the possibility of changing to an alternative plan, if necessary.
- Mutually interactive programs. Here, a number of interactive, serially planned projects are required, and there must be mutual adjustment with regard to resources and timing as the work proceeds in order to keep everything on target.

Jaques and Clement combine the four types of task complexity above with four orders of information complexity (A,B,C, and D). As an example, A represents first-order complexity of information in a concrete world while C represents the second order of abstraction of the conceptual order of ideas and language. Thus, there are information complexity orders from A-1 to A-4, B-1 to B-4, C-1 to C-4, and D-1 to D-4. Jaques and Clement argue that only the categories from B-1 to B-4 and C-1 to C-3 apply to managers in SST's seven hierarchical levels. They then describe the combination of task complexity and information complexity for each level in the organization and show the correspondence with the time span of feedback for each level.

This approach, as well as those mentioned earlier, has the potential of going beyond time span of feedback, which has received increasing amounts of criticism. It appears as if the Jaques-Clement approach might provide one way of dealing with the notion of "compressed time," encountered in crisis or very fast-moving situations where it has been argued that the linear time span of feedback notion is not appropriate (see Jacobs, 1991; Boal and Whitehead). In this sense the Jacobs-Clement thrust may deal with the equifinality question raised by Hunt (1991) when comparing complexity of time span of feedback with what might be involved in such fast-moving, dynamic situations. It also appears to deal with a point raised by Jacobs (personal communication, 1991) that Jaques's time spans for each of the SST levels were heavily driven by investment decisions and hence might be particularly biased toward the specific kinds of organizations encountered in Jaques's earlier work.

Capacity, Skills, Competencies, Behaviors

The concepts considered here both constitute a major thrust (capabilities) in Part II and cut across virtually very other chapter in the book. Also, in our opinion, the current treatment of many of them by Jaques and Clement (1991) reflects what appears to be at least a major shift in emphasis, if not a substantial position shift. The shift is away from an almost exclusive emphasis on cognitive complexity (or its equivalent) to a combined emphasis on some other capability aspects in addition to complexity.

Such additional aspects were given much less emphasis in previous works (e.g., Jacobs and Jaques, 1987; Jaques, 1989). Indeed, this relative lack of emphasis can be seen as contributing to the arguments in several of the chapters (particularly Sashkin's and Boal and Whitehead's) that SST is too narrowly conceived. The later, more comprehensive Jaques and Clement treatment was not available to many of these authors at the time they wrote their chapters.

Let us briefly consider this revisionist SST position and its implications in terms of the present volume. As before, Jaques and Clement argue first and foremost for cognitive complexity. However, to this they add four additional factors. The first is values, divided into those reflecting underlying philosophies or ethical positions and specific ones (more like traditional attitudes), such as things one currently gives priority to or seeks to satisfy. Jaques and Clement argue for the importance of "overarching corporate values nested within basic societal values" that are consistent with people's generic values. Their values appear as somewhat akin to self-efficacy (used by Sashkin; Cowan, Fiol, and Walsh; and Gardner and Schermerhorn) and to Sashkin's socially oriented power.

The second factor is knowledge and skills, and these terms are basically consistent with their usage by others in the literature (cf. Hunt, 1991). The third factor is what they term "wisdom" or the soundness of an individual's judgment about the ways of the world, about what individuals are like and how they are likely to respond. This factor, in many ways, appears similar to Wagner and Sternberg's (1990) "street smarts" variable, discussed in Boal and Whitehead's chapter.

The final factor differs from the others in that it is expressed in terms of T and minus T. T is argued to consist of an extremely wide set of temperament or personality variables that can have a positive impact up to some limit, beyond which the variable in question is harmful (e.g., tenacity becoming stubbornness). Minus T consists of a wide range of variables, any one of which could disqualify a leader otherwise qualified (e.g., obsessive, heartless, untrustworthy). This way of dealing with "personality" traits is, indeed, quite different from their usual treatment in the leadership literature (cf. Bass, 1990; Yukl, 1989a).

Having said all this, we still see important differences between SST and the leadership literature in general; between SST and the contents of this book; as well as among some of the chapters in the book. As pointed out earlier, in contrast to SST, most leadership approaches have tended to emphasize behaviors at the expense of underlying capacities. Conversely, a number of chapters in this book take a different stance. Lewis and Jacobs, for example, tend virtually exclusively to emphasize what they call "cognitive capacity." However, other chapters (e.g., Sashkin; Cowan, Fiol, and Walsh; Hunt and Ropo) call for some combination of that concept with a range of other variables.

Particularly important for present purposes is the combination of cognitive capacity (complexity) and behavioral flexibility or behavioral complexity. Boal and Whitehead develop a four-celled, cognitive/behavioral flexibility matrix. Hooijberg and Quinn, speaking in terms of complexity, rather than flexibility, develop the concept of behavioral complexity and see cognitive complexity as a part of behavioral complexity. For them, then, it is a necessary, but not sufficient, part of behavioral complexity.

In contrast, Boal and Whitehead's four-celled matrix suggests (if we speak of complexity, rather than flexibility) that the two concepts may be independent. If Hooijberg and Quinn are correct, we should be interested in cognitive complexity primarily for what it can tell us about behavioral complexity and its development rather than its importance per se (a view in stark contrast to that espoused by Lewis and Jacobs and even the Jacobs-Clement description of SST).

If Boal and Whitehead are correct, then we should be interested in the combinations of the concepts. An important implicit question in the latter hypotheses is the extent to which there may be null sets of cells encountered in organizations. Perhaps only the high/high or low/low combinations would be found, in which case we would have essentially the Hooijberg-Quinn formulation. We should note that either of these treatments would provide a much-needed marriage of cognitive and behavioral approaches that have typically been separate in the leadership literature. Hooijberg and Quinn provide some preliminary evidence on how to measure behavioral complexity using Quinn's competing values instrument. Additional work with that, as well as other measures (cf. Bass, 1990; Hunt, 1991; Yukl, 1989a), is needed and a start has been made by Bullis (1992).

A related focus emphasizing cognitive aspects is the association of the cognitive notions of SST with the cognitive thrust of Streufert and associates (cf. Streufert and Nogami, 1989; Streufert and Swezey, 1986) based on aspects of cognitive differentiation and integration. Particularly important, given the dynamism and change notions stressed so heavily in this book, is an emphasis on the impact of cognitive complexity in fast-changing situations.

An article by Streufert, Pogash, and Piasecki (1988) examines this issue, using a specially designed quasi-experimental simulation technique. Here, such measures as diversity of action (number of decision categories), use of strategy (forward integrations), and the like are measured within the context of managerial decisions in the simulation. Inclusion of Streufert and associates' work would move it into a more central role than it has previously occupied in the study of leadership.

Finally, increasingly popular cognitive mapping notions, as mentioned by Boal and Whitehead and Hunt and Ropo, also are important in the consideration of cognitive complexity. Huff (1990) and Walsh (1990) discuss these in some detail in a strategic management context. Forsythe and Barber (1991) show how such maps are related to differentiation, integration, and some of the recent complexity notions, indicated in the Lewis and Jacobs chapter and elaborated on by Jaques and Clement (1991).

Transformational, Visionary, Charismatic Leadership

Many now argue that with works by those such as Bass (1985), Burns (1978), Conger (1989), Conger and Kanungo (1988), House (1977), and Sashkin (1988), charisma, transformational, and visionary emphases provide a new genre or new generation of leadership studies in organizations. Chapters by Sashkin and by Hunt and Ropo are consistent with that theme, as are references to these concepts in many other chapters (see Table 1.1). In stark contrast, Jaques and Clement (1991) argue:

> Our research over many years reveals that there are no special traits or personality qualities which are associated specifically with something called leadership. Charisma is the negation of effective role leadership, since it leads to blind followership and diminishes competent working together. And qualities such as courage, initiative, proactivity, energy, flexibility, open-mindedness, imaginativeness, and all other factors that appear on lists of 'leadership qualities' are nothing more than the everyday qualities that are needed for ordinary working in a wide range of roles (p. 307).

Clearly, in this extended quote and in other places in their book (e.g., where they argue that charisma is suitable only in a cult), these authors take as extreme a stand as possible against this type of leadership. Interestingly, while vision and visionary leadership are frequently tied into charisma (cf. treatments in Conger and Kanungo, 1988), Jaques and Clement, not surprisingly, deal with vision in a very nonmystical manner. Vision is treated as the long-term, overarching strategic goal. In this sense it is consistent with Conger's (1989) work which contrasts visions of charismatic and noncharismatic leaders, and with Kotter's (1990) work, which speaks in terms of the different kinds of "agendas" set by "leaders versus managers."

Be that as it may, much of the work in the present book argues that this genre of leadership has the potential of adding considerably to the contributions of SST. Of this charismatic work, one of the most interesting is the discussion by Boal and Whitehead, based on the approach originally proposed by Boal and Bryson (1988), a part of which was tested in a laboratory study by Pillai and Meindl (1991).

Recall that the first of Boal and Bryson's charismatic leaders is the crisis-induced one. For Boal and Whitehead, it is the earlier-mentioned cognitively and behaviorally flexible leader who is able to restore the broken link between action and outcomes that occurs during times of crisis. In reestablishing this linkage and thus restoring important aspects of effectiveness, charisma is attributed to this crisis-induced leader.

If Boal and Bryson's (1988) first kind of charisma is a function of the reestablishment of a linkage between action and outcomes, their second kind of charismatic leader establishes the linkage between values and action. The leader does this by means of visionary leadership. Thus, whereas charisma is attributed to the first kind of charismatic (crisis-induced charismatic) as a function of the leader's response to crisis, the second kind of charismatic (visionary charismatic) obtains charisma from the nature of the vision.

Along with the Boal and Whitehead treatment, Sashkin's arguments concerning the importance of visionary leadership and Hunt and Ropo's emphasis on the link between cognitive complexity and transformational leadership argue strongly for the latter's addition in the present context, as does the literature reviewed by Hunt (1991).

Organizational Culture, Climate

Jacobs (1991a) mentions the important role of organizational culture and organizational climate in SST, and the Jaques and Clement (1991) book emphasizes organizational culture. Sashkin links organizational culture to visionary leadership, Hitt and Keats discuss it in the content of downsizing, and Malone emphasizes the importance of organizational climate and ways to influence it. Other chapters also stress culture/climate in one way or another. This thrust is entirely consistent with the overall organization culture emphasis in the literature since the early 1980s and the more recent resurgence of organizational climate as an important concept (for a discussion see Hunt, 1991).

Sometimes the two notions are used interchangeably, sometimes one but not the other is used, and sometimes both are used in combination to reflect related aspects of an underlying construct. For example, Schneider and Rentsch (1988) consider climate to be the message conveyed by organizational routines (policies, practices, procedures, and so on) and the reward system (supports, expectations, and various kinds of rewards). They define culture as the values and norms underlying such organizational routines and rewards, in addition to the shared assumptions about organizational life reflected in these norms and values. They see culture as communicated through interpretations of routines and rewards. For them, the organizational routines measured in climate research are the ''what,'' interpreted and given meaning (the ''why'') by organization members, as assessed in culture research.

Jaques and Clement (1991) do not consider climate but describe culture as the established ways of thinking and doing things in the institution. They include policies, rules, procedures, customs, practices, shared values and belief systems, traditions and assumptions, and the nature of the language used to communicate throughout the organization. Malone considers climate to be the overall ''feel'' that one gets from visiting an organization for the first time and culture to be climate over time.

Clearly, these concepts, whether separated or not, capture much the same thing for the authors above as they also do for the other contributors. They also serve in one way or another for Jaques and Clement and the chapter contributors as linkages between mission, strategic vision, values, policies, procedures, and the like and organizational outcomes.

Organizational culture, more than most leadership and organizational concepts, has been caught up in the debate between objectivist and subjectivist philosophy of science assumptions. This debate is reflected in how one conceives of organizational culture and how it is measured. A shorthand way of thinking about this is,

Is it something an organization is (a root metaphor) or something an organization has (a variable)? If it is seen as the former, then subjectivist approaches must be used. If it is seen as the latter, it can be measured with questionnaires. Questionnaires traditionally have been used for tapping climate.

Finally, a particularly useful way of dealing with this issue is to see culture as made up of deeper and more shallow layers, with different assumptions and approaches used to tap given layers of culture (e.g., questionnaires for surface layers and clinical, ethnographic approaches for deeper layers; cf. Ott, 1989; Rousseau, 1990).

While the major emphasis in this volume has been on conceptual and empirical work, Malone's chapter is particularly insightful in showing how a new leader went about changing the culture in an army corps (level VI in SST terms). Malone's case description suggests that the leader appeared to be at least reasonably successful. A culture that one might assume was not very participative apparently became far more participative over a three-and-a-half-year period. The techniques used are particularly interesting. A book by Frost, et al. (1985) and a later version by Frost et al. (1991) provide a number of additional organizational culture insights relating to conceptual, empirical, and applications aspects relevant to leadership.

Leader Succession: Selection, Development, Training

Unlike population ecologists who take the stance that leaders are unimportant, the obvious position in this book is that leaders and leadership do make a difference in organizational functioning. Hence, succession and its selection, development, and training implications are very important. Our discussion below concentrates on development and training aspects since these help explain how one acquires the qualities needed for selection.

Several of the currrent chapters discuss various aspects of leader succession within the book's multiple-level perspective. Segal provides particular food for thought when he discusses internal versus external labor markets. The military is an example of an internal market, where all new positions are entry-level. This is in contrast to organizations utilizing external labor markets, where individuals can be hired from the outside. The succession implications are quite different between the two.

Segal's work is joined by detailed treatments of various aspects of succession in chapters by Jacobs and Lewis, Lewis and Jacobs, Sashkin, and Hooijberg and Quinn. The heart of these treatments is concerned with the difference between increasing what Lewis and Jacobs term "conceptual capacity" and enhancing skills or competencies.

The most extreme view concerning conceptual capacity is held by Jaques and does not seem to have been altered appreciably in his latest work with Clement

(Jaques and Clement, 1991). As shown earlier in this book, that view essentially argues that capacity (individual complexity) matures across an individual's life and can be assessed quite early using the Career Path Appreciation approach developed by Stamp (1988). The key underlying point here is Jaques's argument that while capacity increases across time (as an individual ages), it will not increase beyond the growth track or mode in which the individual has been classified by the CPA approach.

For us, unlike Jaques, this is still an open question, as it also appears to be for Jacobs and Jaques (1987). We agree with Sashkin that even if the restriction to growth track does turn out to be true, there are still developmental implications within the tracks. Indeed, this is where the developmental work of Lewis and Jacobs has strong implications. They make the point that increases in conceptual capacity call for the provision of challenging job assignments that require upward revision of the thinking and envisioning processes. For them, mentoring and role modeling as a part of job assignments are extremely important ways of reinforcing this developmental process.

While not denying the importance of such development, Sashkin emphasizes the importance of skill training for a much wider range of capabilities than do Lewis and Jacobs. Interestingly, so do Jacobs and Clement, in spite of their stand on cognitive capacity. For their other characteristics (e.g., values, knowledge, skills), they advocate traditional training.

Quinn and associates' work, as discussed in Hooijberg and Quinn's chapter, is oriented primarily toward development as the term is used above. However, Quinn also takes a competency-oriented approach in a recent text-oriented book (Quinn et al. 1990). There a program is emphasized that is designed systematically to develop twenty-four "competencies" underlying the eight roles dealt with in Hooijberg and Quinn's chapter.

Whereas that program emphasizes competency skill training in a manner consistent with Sashkin's discussion, the development (Leadership Education and Development, LEAD) approach emphasizes behavioral complexity notions discussed by Hooijberg and Quinn and is much different. Recall that the emphasis in the LEAD program was to stimulate paradigm changes in middle managers about their role in the organization. A key part of that was described in terms not of teaching new skills but rather of "stimulating and providing tools for critical self-reflection and the formulation of personal action plans for individual improvement . . . the purpose is to empower managers by altering their current mind-sets, implementing new behaviors, and increasing behavioral complexity." (pp. 170, 172)

It is important to note that the emphasis on experience as a key aspect of the developmental thrust emphasized here is in line with in-depth discussions in Kotter's recent books (1985), 1988), 1990) and by others such as McCall, Lombardo, and Morrison (1988) and Ruderman, Ohlott, and McCauley (1990). Hunt (1991) deals with these discussions within a much broader education, training, and experience context, based on a framework by Heisler and Benham (in press).

Environmental Changes

External environment is a very important aspect of SST. It impacts virtually all components of the approach, particularly leader critical tasks. The societal culture component of the external environment also has an obvious relationship to organizational culture/climate. However, important as environment is, SST provides no explicit conceptualization of it, and SST's time span of feedback, so important in picking up organizational complexity, does not adequately reflect environmental dynamism. The strategic management and organization theory literatures are rich with the kinds of environmental conceptualizations alluded to above (cf. Draft, 1989; Osborn, Hunt, and Jauch, 1980; Robbins, 1990; Scott, 1987).

Insights into long-term environmental change and implications for various aspects of SST are most heavily emphasized by Segal, Hitt and Keats, Hunt and Ropo, Phillips and Duran, and Boal and Whitehead. All of these, in various ways, reinforce the importance of moving away from short-term, static treatments of leadership and organizations. Phillips and Duran's discussion of different kinds of change and their implications is particularly relevant here. So also are Hinings and Greenwood's (1988) configuration and track notions as dealt with in the Hunt and Ropo chapter.

Temporal Aspects

Aspects of temporality have been reflected throughout the book's contributions and especially in the previous discussion of environmental change. Of most interest in the present discussion, however, is the treatment of time by Boal and Whitehead. Their discussion of culturally dominant perspectives of time in terms of monochronic versus polychronic orientations and consideration of cyclical, as opposed to linear, concepts of time are especially important. So, too is their brief treatment of time span of feedback in terms of considering additional aspects such as synchronization, sequence, rate, and allocation. As they make abundantly clear, awareness of the different temporal orientations is at least partly a reflection of culture and thus is becoming more and more important with the increasing internationalization of organizations. Neither SST nor any other current leadership approach deals adequately, if at all, with this issue.

Indeed, even though there have been periodic admonitions to take time more seriously in various organization and leadership approaches, it is only recently that time has begun to be recognized as a crucial variable in its own right (cf. McGrath and Kelly, 1986). Recent works by Bluedorn and Denhardt (1988), Clark (1984), Heller (1984), Kelly and McGrath (1988), and McGrath and Kelly (1986), as well as those cited in Boal and Whitehead's chapter, are helping to deal with the underemphasis on time. The treatments by Phillips and Duran and Hunt and Ropo, as well as by Hunt (1991), also reinforce a temporal perspective and provide references to a range of methodologies needed for the serious study of time in organizational and leadership approaches.

CONCLUSION

This volume has focused on strategic leadership and looked at it from a multiple-organizational-level perspective. That perspective recognizes the organizational implications of strategic-level leaders and leadership. These implications consider not ony external environment and societal culture but direct and indirect effects of top-level strategy, mission/goals, policies, and organizational design, as these cascade down the organization in ever more concrete forms.

This multiple-level approach to strategic leadership uses Stratified Systems Theory (SST) as the point of departure for a collection of cutting-edge chapters from authors with leadership, organization theory, and strategic management backgrounds. These authors contribute to the multiple-organizational-level perspective by discussing the interplay of their work with SST. That is, they use their work to critique and extend SST, and vice versa. In so doing, they move SST out of its extremely narrow literature base, where it spins in its own orbit, and provide many ideas for future research.

One of the more important of these directions involves newer conceptualizations and measures of leader and individual complexity, beyond those in earlier SST formulations. Another involves the expansion of the underlying hierarchy concept in SST and European "third force" organizations, within a dynamnic context. Especially relevant here are the leadership and organizational implications of dynamism and different kinds of change. Other directions are discussed throughout the book, and many of these were summarized in earlier parts of this concluding chapter.

In summary, the book has attempted to provide a multiple-organizational-level perspective concerning strategic leadership. That perspective brings together cutting-edge work from a wide range of literature in order to encourage future research and applications.

16

Afterword: Stratified Systems Theory and Leadership: Where We Go From Here

Robert J. House

House raises a number of important points in this short Afterword. First, he classifies SST as a "compensatory" approach and this classification leads to a comparison of it with a number of other leadership approaches with which it is not usually grouped. Second, he proposes a way to conceptualize and measure leader position incumbency from an organization-wide perspective. Third, extending some of the earlier work in this volume, he emphasizes the importance of systematically relating affect, motivation, and cognition in determining leader behavior. Accompanying this emphasis, he reinforces earlier arguments in this book that there must be a concern with both cognitive capacity and behavioral flexibility. In many cases, the cognitive and dispositional aspects of this emphasis may mean an insufficient ability to deal with major organizational change. Such inability may call for the necessity of replacing CEO's or entire top management teams. House adds to this contention by pointing out the difficulty of actually obtaining these replacements because of the institutionalization of power. He uses the lack of real responsiveness of General Motors as an example. Since he wrote these words, it appears that General Motors may finally be beginning to address the kinds of issues he raises. However, it required pressure from outside board members to move the corporation in this direction.

House argues that SST raises many questions and that these are both new and conceptually and practically important. Furthermore, much of the evidence presented on SST has not undergone the normal editorial review process in social scientific journals. For House, this more rigorous kind of review is necessary to really move SST forward.

The framework for this book is the Stratified Systems Theory (SST) advanced by Jacobs and Jaques (1987) and extended by Jaques and Clement (1991). It is an expansion of Jaques's (1964, 1976) earlier theorizing on managerial time span of discretion. Essentially, this book represents attempts to integrate the work of several leadership and strategic management scholars within the SST framework. SST is used throughout this book to conceptualize several normative, midrange theories of strategic leadership. For the most part, these midrange theories are complementary and conceptually overlapping and consistent. There are very few positions taken in the chapters presented in this book that contradict or are inconsistent with the fundamental assumptions or propositions of SST. The two exceptions to this statement are the chapters by Sashkin and Boal and Whitehead. In both of these chapters the authors question whether the cognitive capacity construct of SST theory is sufficient to differentiate effective from ineffective leaders and suggest additional leader cognitive or personality characteristics that need to be considered as well.

While not all of the contributors initially based their conceptualizations and investigations on SST, most of them articulated logical linkages between their work and SST. In this chapter I will discuss how SST fits within current organization and leadership theory. I will discuss some of the underlying assumptions and implicit assertions of SST and attempt to specify some criteria that need to be met if the multi-organizational-level perspective of strategic leadership advanced in this book is to attain credibility as a social scientific theory of leadership.

RELATIONSHIP TO CURRENT THEORY

SST is a theory of leadership of hierarchical organizations. As Jacobs and Lewis state, the theory is intended to apply to accountability hierarchies—organizations chartered and governed by higher bodies such as boards of directors, external constituencies, and shareholders, not to "associations," such as universities, churches, or collegial organizations. It is not clear whether or not SST can be applied to quasi-hierarchical organizations, of the kind mentioned by Hunt and Phillips, that are referred to in the literature as organic organizations, adhocracies, or professional bureaucracies. The essential criterion to be applied in determining the kind of organization to which SST applies is whether the organization is structured in hierarchical form. Since almost all organizations consisting of moderate to large numbers of members (100 or more) are necessarily structured somewhat hierarchically, SST may apply to a broader class of organizations than those mentioned above. However, such application may require modest modifications of SST if it is to have meaningful and valued application.

The editors note earlier that this book is designed to be context-free, that is, intended to apply to military and nonmilitary organizations alike. It appears that the theory applies to almost all large organizations since hierarchical stratification of authority and responsibility is necessarily a characteristic of such organizations (Simon, 1977).

SST is similar to current theories of leadership in that leaders are described as "adding value" over and above the value contributed to performance by the formal organization. The contribution of leaders is described as discretionary; that is, the leader exercises discretion to fill gaps in the formal organizational system

(Hunt and Osborn, 1982). The specific gaps, or deficiencies, of the formal system that the leader fills concern the coordinative, motivational, or supportive functions of leaders. Jacobs and Lewis also note that the vision and direction provided by leaders give meaning to the work of organizational members and that meaningfulness is a motivational property of work.

Because the theory asserts that leaders "add value," it can be considered a compensatory theory of leadership (cf. Evans, 1973). Following Katz and Kahn (1978), leaders are assumed to complement hierarchical, formal organization by providing strategic direction for the organization and by systematically and rationally integrating the multiple levels of organization. Other compensatory leadership approaches are Graen and Cashman's (1975) Vertical Dyadic Linkage Theory (VDL), Hunt and Osborn's (1982) Multiple-Influence Model of Leadership (MIML), and House's (1970) Path-Goal Theory (PGT) of leadership. In contrast to the above approaches, SST stresses the need for a match between the cognitive demands of managerial positions and the cognitive capacities of position incumbents. Also in contrast to other thrusts, SST stresses the role of leadership in strategy formulation and implementation and focuses primarily, but not exclusively, on top management.

Until recently there has been a controversy concerning whether leaders make a difference in organizational performance. Put succinctly, the debate concerns whether leaders make the times (or the organization) or whether the times (the organization and its environment) make individuals appear to be great leaders (Meindl, Ehrlich, and Dukerich, 1985; Pfeffer, 1977; Salancik and Pfeffer, 1977b; Tolstoy, 1904, epilogue). Recent evidence (House, Spangler, and Woycke, 1990b; Thomas, 1988) shows that leaders do, indeed, significantly affect the overall performance of complex organizations, after controlling for the effect of organizationally exogenous forces.

THE SCIENTIFIC STATUS OF THE COGNITIVE CAPACITY CONSTRUCT

SST asserts that effective organizational performance results from a high level of congruence between the intellectual work demands of positions within an organization and the cognitive capacities of the incumbents of these positions. This assertion is based on Jaques's (1964, 1976) earlier theoretical work concerning the time span of descretion associated with organization-hierarchical levels, and is consistent with current theory of effective cognitive processing (Streufert and Nogami, 1989; Streufert and Streufert, 1978; Suedfeld and Tetlock, 1990).

More specifically, the theory asserts that as one proceeds up the organizational hierarchy, the work of managing becomes increasingly complex and, consequently, position incumbents need to have higher levels of cognitive ability. The theory can be criticized on the basis of two arguments. First, as will be discussed below,

the theory focuses predominantly on leader cognitive capacity, with minor attention devoted to task knowledge, personality, and motivational characteristics of
leaders (cf. Jaques and Clement, 1991). Second, the cognitive capacity construct
is still at the conceptual stage and requires substantial developmental work to be
adequately operationalized. The evidence in this book reviewed by Jacobs and Lewis
and Hooijberg and Quinn, and that reported by Hunt and Ropo provides tentative
support for the major assertions of the theory. However, it should be noted that
with the exception of a limited amount of work by Stamp (1978, 1988) the measures
are approximate measures of the cognitive capacity construct of the theory and
require further development and validation. Cognitive capacity is conceptualized
in SST as two-dimensional: cognitive information processing and conceptual abstraction. The empirical evidence reported in this book concerning cognitive capacity
appears to relate to integrative complexity (Suedfeld and Tetlock, 1990).

No evidence is presented concerning position incumbents' capacity for abstract
reasoning. Additional work remains to be conducted to measure the two dimensions of the cognitive capacity construct. Further, since the evidence cited in this
book is, for the most part, not available in the public domain for independent evaluation and since the manuscripts reporting this evidence have not undergone the normal editorial review process in social scientific journals or book reviews, the quality
and strength of evidence remain unassessed by independent scholars of leadership
or cognitive psychology.

THE LEVEL OF ANALYSIS ISSUE

Since organizational effectiveness is the primary dependent variable addressed
by SST, an aggregate construct reflecting overall position-incumbent congruence
(PIC) is needed to derive predictions of aggregate organizational effectiveness. SST
does not offer specific guidance with respect to the conceptualization of an organiza-
tionwide PIC construct. However, SST is sufficiently articulated to permit scholars
to conceptualize and operationalize such a construct. Here I will suggest how an
aggregate PIC might be conceptualized.

It is most likely a reasonable assumption that not all of the positions at any given
level will be staffed by individuals who have congruent cognitive capacities. At
each level there will presumably be only some proportion of positions for which
incumbents have adequate cognitive capacities. Therefore, one component of the
aggregate PIC will be the proportion of positions whose incumbents have cognitive
capacities that are congruent. This component may be expressed as

Aggregate PIC $=$ (P/Total Pi) n

Where

P equals the number of individual-position congruencies

Total Pi equals the total number of positions at level i

n equals the number of levels in the organization

The theory does not specify the relative importance of PIC with respect to function or level. In times of stability, in mechanistic organizations, organizational efficiency and productivity are primarily determined by lower-level organizational members who produce the products or services of the organization. Under such conditions, the top management of organizations often plays primarily a custodial and symbolic role and may have little influence on the performance effectiveness of organizations. In times of instability, organizational effectiveness is primarily determined by the adaptability and implementation of organizational strategy (Tushman and Romanelli, 1985). Thus, it may well be that PIC is more important at lower levels in highly mechanistic bureaucracies during times of environmental stability and more important at higher levels during times of environmental instability. It is also possible that PIC is more important at lower levels in highly organic organizations as compared with highly mechanistic organizations because organic organizational effectiveness is a function of the ability of lower level-members to generate strategic innovations.

Thus the relative importance of PIC may be a function of both organizational form and environmental stability. If this is, indeed, the case empirically, the (1) the relative weight given to PICs at different levels, performing different functions, will be specific to the organization under study and the characteristics of its environment and (2) auxiliary propositions need to be developed to link cognitive capacity to both organizational form and environmental characteristics.

Alternative assumptions also might be suggested with respect to PIC depending on the size of the organization under consideration, the relative ease of replacing position incumbents at each level, the training and socialization time and costs associated with positions at each level, and the relative strategic and tactical influence of positions at each level. The conclusion to be drawn from the above discussion is that for adequate empirical testing of SST predictions of organizational effectiveness, it will be necessary to more precisely specify the conceptual components of aggregate PIC and the relative weight to be allocated to each position within the organization.

At the position level of analysis, SST predicts that PIC is predictive of individual performance effectiveness. This assertion requires that a metric be established that can be used to determine position cognitive demands for individual performance and that a metric be established that can be used to determine individual cognitive capacity. Finally, these two measures must have equivalent metrics such that individual cognitive capacity can be subtracted from position demands for cognitive capacity in order to determine the degree of congruence between the two measures. Jaques and Clement (1991) provide careful conceptual definitions of these constructs. However, until these constructs are operationalized, the predictions of SST concerning individual performance effectiveness cannot be tested empirically.

NONCOGNITIVE DETERMINANTS OF LEADER EFFECTIVENESS

SST asserts that the primary determinant of leader effectiveness is the congruence between position cognitive demands and the cognitive capacity of leaders. Setting measurement issues aside, this assertion gives primacy to cognitive processes over affective or motivational processes. As Sashkin (in this book) has argued, leader motivation has been shown to be a significant determinant of leader effectiveness. Sashkin also has forcefully argued that leader self-efficacy is implicated in leader effectiveness. Sashkin's argument is consistent with a substantial amount of empirical evidence that individual self-confidence, or level of efficacy expectations, is predictive of motivated behavior (Bandura, 1986b). Without sufficient self-confidence, individuals in management positions are not likely to attempt to influence others, including those whom they manage, and are not likely to obtain the satisfaction from leading that is necessary to sustain their leadership efforts.

There is substantial evidence that affective and motivational variables are implicated in the prediction of behavior and the manner in which individuals employ and enact their cognitive capacities (Abramson and Martin, 1981; Fazio, 1986; Higgins, Klein, and Strauman, 1985; Hoffman, 1984; Isen et al., 1982; Norem and Cantor, 1984; Trope, 1980). The conclusion to be drawn from studies concerning relationships among affect, motivation, and cognition is that affect and motivation interact with cognitive processes to produce behavior. Affect and motives determine, significantly, the way individuals focus attention, process information, and make cognitive representations of reality, which, in turn, determine the direction and nature of their behavior. While SST recognizes leader motivation and personality characteristics other than leader cognitive capacity, it has little to say about the ways such variables operate. Future developments of SST will need to include assertions about the moderating effect of affect and motives on leaders' abilities to enact their cognitive capabilities.

SST AND ORGANIZATIONAL CHANGE

As noted by Boal and Whitehead, the cognitive capacity construct of SST implies both individual ability to engage in higher-order complex information processing and individual behavioral flexibility. To date, no measure of such cognitive capacity has been developed. The measure of cognitive integrative complexity used by Hunt and Ropo closely approximates the information-processing component of the cognitive capacity construct of SST. The findings reported by Hunt and Ropo suggest that higher levels of integrative complexity are associated with effective adaptation of managers and their organizations to changing and to increasingly complex organizational environments. Since the findings reported by Hunt and Ropo are based on only five managers, their results can be considered only suggestive. However, both SST and the Hunt and Ropo findings suggest that managerial cognitive integrative complexity facilitates adaptation to changing demands imposed on organizations by their environments.

It is not clear, however, whether integrative complexity is associated with higher-order information processing only or whether it is also associated with flexibility of behavioral responses to changing organizational conditions. Boal and Whitehead suggest that higher-level cognitive capacity may be associated with so much information gathering and processing that individuals who have such capacity may be victims of analysis paralysis. Further, they suggest that cognitive complexity may inhibit leaders' decisiveness and immediacy of action in response to crises.

It is likely that cognitive capacity, as articulated in SST, is a stable person characteristic consisting of dispositional, as well as cognitive, components. If this is the case, then managerial responses to changing and increasingly complex work demands are likely to be inadequate for those whose dispositions are incongruent with such demands. Thus major organizational change, such as organizational turnarounds, may well require replacement of CEOs or entire top management teams.

There is a practical problem associated with the need to replace top managers to bring about major organizational change. Individuals in positions of significant formal authority—institutionalized power—are likely to have gained their positions as a result of possessing strong dispositions to acquire power and high levels of skills required for the acquisition and exercise of power (House, 1991). Such individuals are very likely to be motivated to protect and retain their positions. Consequently, it may be that major organizational change can occur only after involuntary removal of top managers from their position. However, such removal may be either very difficult or impossible to accomplish. As Salancik and Pfeffer (1977b) have stated, "While in power, a dominant coalition has the ability to institute constitution, rules, procedures, and information systems that limit the potential power of others while continuing their own" (p. 391).

The institutionalization of power in the form of legitimate authority, together with the motives and skills possessed by those in power, provides for them significant resources to maintain the status quo and thus to maintain their own power. Consider, for example, the responses of General Motors to changes in fuel emission regulations, oil prices, and international competition in the 1970s. In response to these environmental threats, GM's board chairman, Roger Smith, ordered a reorganization of the operating divisions of GM. However, he stipulated that the reorganization be concerned with the regrouping of GM plants and that neither the top management levels nor the GM corporate headquarters be affected by the reorganization (Keller, 1990). The result of the reorganization was the maintenance of the prevailing distribution of power and protection of those already in power. To date, GM has not solved the continued decline in market share and profits that began in the early 1970s. Plant closings and massive employee layoffs have continued through 1991. Clearly, SST predicts that unless the cognitive capacities of the top management team become congruent with the increasingly complex and unstable environment, GM is doomed to continued decline. Since the top management team is likely neither to replace itself nor to increase its cognitive capacity, continued decline is predicted. As Salancik and Pfeffer (1977b) noted prophetically: "The structures created by dominant powers sooner or later become fixed and unquestioned features of the organization. Eventually this can be devastating" (p. 392).

CONCLUSION

SST is an ambitious theory of leadership. It addresses two major issues in the leadership literature. The first issue concerns the appropriate distribution of cognitive capacities throughout complex hierarchical organizations and the matching of position-incumbent cognitive capacities to position requirements. The second issue concerns the role of leaders in the formulation and implementation of strategy and the vertical integration of multilevel hierarchical organizations. Both of these issues are of major importance to the functioning of complex organizations. As with most theories in early developmental stages, SST raises more questions than it answers. The questions are both new and theoretically and practically important. Hopefully, this book will stimulate further theoretical development and empirical research concerning these issues.

References

Abramson, L., and D. Martin (1981). Depression and the causal inference process. In J. Harvey, W. Ickes, and R. Kidd (Eds.), *New Directions in Attribution Research*, Vol. 3, pp. 117-168, Hillsdale, NJ: Erlbaum.

Ackoff, R. L. (1970). *A Concept of Corporate Planning*. New York: Wiley.

Ahbrandt, R. S., Jr., and A. R. Blair (1986). What it takes for large organizations to be inventive. *Research Management* 29 (March-April): 34-37.

Aldrich, H., W. McKelvey and D. Ulrich (1984). Design strategy from the population perspective. *Journal of Management* 10(1):67-86.

Allard, C. K. (1990). *Command, Control, and the Common Defense*. New Haven: Yale University Press.

Amburgey, T. L., D. Kelly and W. P. Barnett (1990). *Resetting the clock: The dynamics of organizational change and failure*. Unpublished manuscript, University of Wisconsin.

Andrews, K. R. (1980). *The Concept of Corporate Strategy*. Homewood, IL: Irwin.

Angoff, W. H. (1988). The nature-nurture debate, aptitudes, and group differences. *American Psychologist*. 43:713-720.

Argyris, C. (1985). *Strategy, Change and Defensive Routines*. Boston, MA: Pitman.

Argyris, C., and D. Schön (1978). *Organizational Learning*. Reading, MA: Addison-Wesley.

Ashby, W. (1952). *Design for a Brain*. New York: Wiley.

_____. (1956). *An Introduction to Cybernetics*. New York: Wiley.

Ashton, R. H. and A. H. Ashton (1990). Evidence-responsiveness in professional judgment: Effects of positive versus negative evidence and presentation mode. *Organizational Behavior and Human Decision Processes* 46(1):1-19.

Astley, W. G., and A. H. Van de Ven (1983). Central perspectives and debates in organization theory. *Administrative Science Quarterly* 28:245-273.

Avolio, B. J., and B. M. Bass (1988). Transformational leadership, charisma and beyond. In J. G. Hunt, B. R. Baliga, H. P.Dachler, and C. A. Schrieshiem (Eds.), *Emerging Leadership Vistas,* pp. 29-50. Lexington, MA: Lexington Books.

Baliga, B. R., and J. G. Hunt (1988). An organizational life cycle approach to leadership. In J.G. Hunt, B.R. Baliga, H.P. Dachler, and C.A. Schriesheim (Eds.), *Emerging Leadership Vistas,* pp. 129-149. Lexington, MA: Lexington Books.

Bandura, A. (1977a). Self-efficacy: Toward a unifying theory of behavioral change. *Psychological Review* 84:191-215.

———. (1977b). *Social Learning Theory.* Englewood Cliffs, NJ: Prentice-Hall.

———. (1978). Reflections on self-efficacy. *Advances in Behavioral Research and Therapy* 1:237-269.

———. (1982). Self-efficacy mechanism in human agency. *American Psychologist* 37:122-147.

———. (1986a). The explanatory and predictive scopy of self-efficacy theory. *Journal of Social and Clinical Psychology* 4:359-373.

———. (1986b). *Social Foundations of Thought and Action: A Social Cognitive Theory.* Englewood Cliffs, NJ: Prentice-Hall.

———. (1988). Self-regulation of motivation and action through goal systems. In V. Hamilton, G. Bower, and N. Frijda (Eds.), *Cognitive Perspectives on Motivation and Emotion.* Dordrecht, The Netherlands: Kluwer Academic.

———. (1989). Human agency in social cognitive theory. *American Psychologist* 44:1175-1184.

Barnard, C. I. (1938). *Functions of the Executive.* Cambridge: Harvard University Press.

Barney, J. B. (1986). Strategic factor markets: Exceptions, luck and business strategy. *Management Science* 32:1231-1241.

———. (1988). Returns to bidding firms in mergers and acquisitions: Reconsidering the relatedness hypothesis. *Strategic Management Journal* 9 (Special Issue):71-78.

Barr, L. and N. Barr (1989). *The Leadership Equation: Leadership, Management, and the Myers-Briggs.* Austin, TX: Eakin Press.

Barr, P. S., and J. L. Stimpert (1990). A cognitive explanation of organizational decline. Paper presented at Academy of Management meetings, San Francisco.

Bartunek, J. M., J. R. Gordon, and R. P. Weathersby (1983). Developing a "complicated" understanding of administrators. *Academy of Management Review* 8(2):273-284.

Bartunek, J. M., and M. K. Moch (1987). First-order, second-order, and third-order change and organization development interventions: A cognitive approach. *Journal of Applied Behavioral Science* 23(4):483-500.

Bass, B. M. (1985). *Leadership and Performance Beyond Expectations.* New York: Free Press.

———. (1990). *Bass & Stodgill's Handbook of Leadership: Theory, Research, & Managerial Implications,* 3d ed. New York: Free Press.

Becker, G. S. (1976). *The Economic Approach to Human Behavior.* Chicago: University of Chicago Press.

Bedeian, A. G. (1986). Contemporary challenges in the study of organizations. *Journal of Management* 12:185-201.

Beehr, T. A. (1985). The role of social support in coping with organizational stress. In T.A. Beehr and R.S. Bhagat (Eds.), *Human Stress and Cognition in Organizations,* pp. 375-398. New York: Wiley.

Behn, R. D. (1988). The fundamentals of cutback management. In K. S. Cameron, R. I. Sutton, and D. A. Whetten (Eds.), *Readings in Organizational Decline,* pp. 347-351. Cambridge: Ballinger.

Bennis, W. (1966). The coming death of bureaucracy. *Think* 32 (November-December): 30-35.

——. (1984). The four competencies of leadership. *Training and Development Journal* 38(8):15-18.

Bennis, W., and B. Nanus (1985). *Leaders: Strategies for Taking Charge.* New York: Harper and Row.

Bensimon, E. M. (1978). The meaning of "good presidential leadership": A frame analysis. Paper presented at National Meeting of the Association for the Study of Higher Education, Baltimore, MD.

Bentz, V. J. (1987). *Explorations of Scope and Scale: The Critical Determinant of High-Level Effectiveness* (Technical Report 31). Greensboro, NC: Center for Creative Leadership.

——. (1990). Contextual issues in predicting high-level leadership performance: Contextual richness as a criterion consideration in personality research with executives. In K. E. Clark and M. E. Clark (Eds.), *Measures of Leadership.* West Orange, NJ: Leadership Library of America.

Bhaskar, R. (1978). *A Realist Theory of Science.* Hassocks, U. K.: Harvester.

Birnbaum, R. (1990). "How'm I doing?": How college presidents assess their effectiveness. *Leadership Quarterly* 1(1):25-40.

Blair, J. D., and M. D. Fottler (1990). *Challenges in Health Care Management: Strategic Perspectives for Managing Key Stakeholders.* San Francisco: Jossey-Bass.

Blair, J. D., and J. G. Hunt (1986). Getting inside the head of the management researcher one more time: Context free and context specific orientations in research. *1986 Yearly Review of Management of the Journal of Management,* 14:299-320.

Blair, J. D., T. W. Nix, G. T. Savage, C. J. Whitehead, and M. F. Fottler (1990, November). Managing organizations strategically: Using stakeholder management concepts to integrate strategic approaches at macro and micro levels of analysis. Paper presented at the annual meeting of the Southern Management Association, Orlando, FL.

Blair, J. D., G. T. Savage, and C. Whitehead (1989). A strategic approach for negotiating with hospital stakeholders. *Health Care Management Review* 14:13-23.

Blair, J. D., and C. Whitehead (1988). Too many on the seesaw: Stakeholder diagnosis and management for hospitals. *Hospital & Health Services Administration* 33:156-166.

Blau, G. (1981). An empirical investigation of job stress, social support, service length, and job strain. *Organizational Behavior and Human Performance* 27:279-302.

Bluedorn, A. C., and R. B. Denhardt (1988). Time and organizations. *Yearly Review of Management of the Journal of Management* 14:299-320.

Boal, K. B., and J. M. Bryson (1988). Charismatic leadership: A phenomenological and structural approach. In J. G. Hunt, B. R. Baliga, H. P. Dachler, and C. A. Schriesheim (Eds.), *Emerging Leadership Vistas,* pp. 111-28. Lexington, MA: Lexington Books.

Bobko, P., and J. P. Schwartz (1984). A metric for integrating theoretically related but statistically unrelated constructs. *Journal of Personality Assessment* 48(1):11-16.

Bodnar, J. W., G. S. Jones, and C. H. Ellis, Jr. (1989). The domain model for eukaryotic DNA organization 2: A molecular basis for constraints on development and evolution. *Journal of Theoretical Biology* 137:281-320.

Bouchard, D. T., Jr., D. T. Lykken, M. McGue, N. L. Segal, and A. Tellegen (1990). Sources of human psychological differences: The Minnesota study of twins reared apart. *Science* 250:230-250.

Bradley, G. W. (1978). Self-serving biases in the attribution process: A reexamination of the fact or fiction question. *Journal of Personality and Social Psychology* 36:56-71.

Brett, J. M. (1984). Job transitions and personal and role development. *Research in Personnel and Human Resource Management* 2:155-185.

Brockner, J., J. Davy, and C. Carter (1988). Layoffs, self-esteem, and survivor guilt: Motivational, affective, and atittudinal consequences. In K. S. Cameron, R. I. Sutton, and D. A. Whetten (Eds.), *Readings in Organizational Decline*, pp. 279-290. Cambridge: Ballinger.

Bruner, J. A. (1957). On perceptual readiness. *Psychological Review* 64:132-133.

Bullis, R. C. (1992). The impact of leader behavioral complexity on organizational performance. Working paper, College of Business Administration, Texas Tech University, Lubbock.

Bureau of National Affairs. (1990). *Employee Relations Weekly* 8(39):1121-1222.

Burgleman, R. A. (1991). Intraorganizational ecology of strategy making and organizational adaptation: Theory and field research. *Organization Science* 2(3):239-262.

Burke, W. W. (1988). From the editor. *Academy of Management Executive* 2(4):268.

Burns, J. M. (1978). *Leadership.* New York: Harper and Row.

Burns, T., and G. M. Stalker (1961). *The Management of Innovation.* London: Tavistock.

Buss, D. M. (1987). Selection, evocation, and manipulation. *Journal of Personality and Social Psychology* 53(6):1214-1221.

Buss, D. M., M. Gomes, D. S. Higgins, and K. Lauterbach (1987). Tactics of manipulation. *Journal of Personality and Social Psychology* 52(6):1219-1229.

Byrd, R. E. (1987). Corporate leadership skills: A new synthesis. *Organizational Dynamics* 16(1):34-43.

Byrne, J. A. (1988). Caught in the middle: Six managers speak out on corporate life. *Business Week* (Industrial/Technology Edition), Issue 3069:80-88.

Cameron K. S. (1986). Effectiveness as paradox: Consensus and conflict in conceptions of organizational effectiveness. *Management Science* 32:539-553.

Cameron, K. S., S. R. Freeman, and A. Mishra (1990). Effective organizational downsizing: Paradoxical processes and best practices. Paper presented at Academy of Management meetings, San Francisco.

Cameron, K. S., M. U. Kim, and D. A. Whetten (1988). Organizational effects of decline and turbulence. In K. S. Cameron, R. I. Sutton, and D. A. Whetten (Eds.), *Readings in Organizational Decline,* pp. 207-224. Cambridge: Ballinger.

Cameron, K. S., R. I. Sutton, and D. A. Whetten (1988). Issues in organization decline. In K. S. Cameron, R. I. Sutton, and D. A. Whetten (Eds.), *Readings in Organizational Decline,* pp. 3-19. Cambridge: Ballinger.

Campbell, J. P. (1977). The cutting edge of leadership: An overview. In J. G. Hunt and L. L. Larson (Eds.), *Leadership: The Cutting Edge,* pp. 221-235. Carbondale: Southern Illinois University Press.

Campbell, J. P., and R. J. Campbell (1988). Industrial-organizational psychology and productivity: The goodness of fit. In J. P. Campbell, R. J. Campbell, and Associates, *Productivity in Organizations: New Perspectives from Industrial and Organizational Psychology,* pp. 82-93. San Francisco: Jossey-Bass.

Carroll, A. B. (1989). *Business and Society: Ethics and Stakeholder Management.* Cincinnati, OH: South-Western.

Carroll, G. R. (1984). Dynamics of publisher succession in newspaper organizations. *Administrative Science Quarterly* 29:93-113.

Cattell, R. B. (1948). Concepts and methods in the measurement of group syntality. *Psychological Review* 55:48-63.

———. (1951). New concepts for measuring leadership, in terms of group syntality. *Human Relations* 4:161-184.

Chandler, A. D., Jr. (1962). *Strategy and Structure: Chapters in the History of American Industrial Enterprise.* Cambridge: MIT Press.

Chi, M. T. A., P. J. Feltovich, and R. Glaser (1981). Categorization and representation of physics problems by experts and novices. *Cognitive Science* 5:121-152.

Chi, M. T. A., R. Glaser, and M. J. Farr (1988). *The Nature of Expertise.* Hillsdale, NJ: Erlbaum.

Chi, M. T. A., R. Glaser, and E. Rees (1982). Expertise in problem solving. In R. J. Sternberg (Ed.), *Advances in the Psychology of Human Intelligence,* pp. 7-75. Hillsdale, NJ: Erlbaum.

Child, J. (1972). Organizational structure, environment, and performance: The role of strategic choice. *Sociology* 6:1-22.

Christensen, C. R., K. R. Andrews, J. L. Bower, and R. G. Hamermesh (1982). *Business Policy: Text and Cases.* Homewood, IL: Irwin.

Churchman, C. W. (1971). *The Design of Inquiring Systems.* New York: Basic Books.

Clark, K. (1987): Investment in new technology and competitive advantage. In D. J. Teece (Ed.), *The Competitive Challenge: Strategies for Industrial Innovation and Renewal,* pp. 59-81. Cambridge: Ballinger.

Clark, P. A. (1984). Part 5 integrative comments: Leadership theory—the search for a reformulation. In J. G. Hunt, D-M. Hosking, C. A. Schriesheim, and R. Stewart (Eds.), *Leaders and Managers,* pp. 375-381. Elmsford, NY: Pergamon.

Conger, J. A. (1989). *The Charismatic Leader: Behind the Mystique of Exceptional Leadership.* San Francisco: Jossey-Bass.

Conger, J. A., and R. N. Kanungo (1987). Toward a behavioral theory of charismatic leadership in organizational settings. *Academy of Management Review* 12:637-647.

Conger, J. A., and R. N. Kanungo (1988). *Charismatic Leadership.* San Francisco: Jossey-Bass.

Cosier, R. A., and C. R. Schwenk (1990). Agreement and thinking alike: Ingredients for poor decisions. *Academy of Management Executive* 4:69-74.

Covey, Stephen R. (1989). *The 7 Habits of Highly Effective People.* New York: Simon and Schuster.

Curphy, G. J. (1990). An empirical evaluation of Bass' (1985) theory of transformational and transactional leadership. Ph.D. diss., Department of Psychology, University of Minnesota.

Daft, R. L. (1989). *Organization Theory and Design.* St. Paul, MN: West.

Daft, R., and R. H. Lengel (1986). Organization information requirements, media richness and structural design. *Management Science* 32(5):554-571.

Daft, R. L., J. Sormunen, and D. Parks (1988). Chief executive scanning, environmental characteristics, and company performance: An empirical study. *Strategic Management Journal* 9(2):123-139.

Daft, R. L., and K. E. Weick (1984). Toward a model of organizations as interpretation systems. *Academy of Management Review* 9:284-296.

Dansereau, F., J. A. Allutto, and F. J. Yammarino (1984). *Theory Testing in Organizational Behavior: The Varient Approach.* Englewood Cliffs, NJ: Prentice-Hall.

Deal, T. A., and A. A. Kennedy (1982). *Corporate Cultures.* Reading, MA: Addison-Wesley.

Deal, T. A., and K. D. Peterson (1990). *The Principal's Role in Shaping School Culture.* Washington, DC: Government Printing Office.

Denison, D. R., R. Hooijberg, and R. E. Quinn (1991). Paradox and performance: A theory of the behavioral complexity of effective leaders. Working paper.

Dess, G. G., and D. W. Beard (1984). Dimensions of organizational task environments. *Administrative Science Quarterly,* 19:45-59.

Digman, J. M. (1990). Personality structure: Emergence of the five-factor model. In M. R. Rosenzweig and L. W. Porter (Eds.), *Annual Review of Psychology,* pp. 417-440. Palo Alto, CA: Annual Reviews.

DiMaggio, P., and W. Powell (1983). The iron cage revisited: Institutional isomorphism and collective rationality in organizational fields. *American Sociological Review* 48:147-160.

Dobbins, G. H., W. S. Long, E. J. Dedrick, and T. C. Clemons (1990). The role of self-monitoring and gender on leader emergence: A laboratory and field study. *Journal of Management* 16(3):609-618.

Donaldson, G., and J. Lorsch (1983). *Decision Making at the Top.* New York: Basic Books.

Donnellon, A. (1986). Language and communication in organizations: Bridging cognition and behavior. In H. P. Sims, Jr., and D. A. Gioia (Eds.), *The Thinking Organization,* pp. 136-164. San Francisco: Jossey-Bass.

Downey, H. K., and A. P. Brief (1986). How cognitive structures affect organizational design. In H. P. Sims, Jr. and D. A. Gioia (Eds.), *The Thinking Organization,* pp. 165-190. San Francisco: Jossey-Bass.

Doz, J. L., and C. K. Prahalad (1981). Headquarters' influence and strategic control in MNCs. *Sloan Management Review* 23 (Fall):15-29.

Dreyfus, H. I., and S. E. Dreyfus (1986). *Mind over Machine: The Power of Human Intuition and Expertise in the Era of the Computer.* New York: Free Press.

Dreyfus, S. E. (1982). Formal models vs. human situational understanding: Inherent limitations on the modeling of business expertise. *Office Technology and People* 1:133-165.

Driver, M. J., K. R. Brousseau, and P. L. Hunsaker (1990). *The Dynamic Decisionmaker: Five Decision Styles for Executive and Business Success.* New York: Ballinger Division of Harper and Row.

Drucker, P. (1973). *Management: Tasks, Responsibilities, Practices.* New York: Harper and Row.

Drucker, P. F. (1988a). The coming of the new organization. *Harvard Business Review* 66 (January-February):45-53.

_____. (1988b). Leadership: More doing than dash. *Wall Street Journal,* (January 6) p. 16.

Duffey, J. (1988). Competitiveness and human resources. *California Management Review* 30:92-100.

Dumaine, B. (1990). The new turnaround champs. *Fortune* 122 (July 16):36.

Dunbar, R. L. M., and S. A. Nachman (1989). Pattern in adaptive strategy: A review of empirical studies of the Miles and Snow typology. Working paper, New York University.

Dunphy, D. C., and D. A. Stace (1988). Transformational and coercive strategies for planned organizational change: Beyond the O. D. model. *Organizational Studies* 9:317-334.

Duran, C. A., R. L. Phillips, and C. J. Whitehead (1991). An integrated outcome model of strategic change. In D. F. Ray (Ed.), *Southern Management Association Proceedings*, pp. 23-25. Starkville, MS: Mississippi State University.

Durkheim, E. (1964). *Moral Education*. Glencoe, IL: Free Press.

Dutton, J. E., and R. B. Duncan (1987). The influence of the strategic planning process on strategic change. *Strategic Management Journal*. 8:103-116.

Dutton, J. E., L. Fahey, and V. K. Narayanan (1983). Toward understanding strategic issue diagnosis. *Strategic Management Journal* 4:307-323.

Dutton, J. E., and S. E. Jackson (1987). Categorizing strategic issues: Links to organizational action. *Academy of Management Review* 12:76-90.

Eden, D. (1990). *Pygmalion in Management: Productivity as a Self-Fulfilling Prophecy*. Lexington, MA: Lexington Books.

Eden, D., and U. Leviatan (1975). Implicit leadership theory as a determinant of the factor structure underlying supervisory behavior scales. *Journal of Applied Psychology* 60:736-741.

Edwards, W. (1968). Conservatism in human information processing. In B. Kleinmuntz (Ed.), *Formal Representation of Human Judgment*. New York: Wiley.

Edwards, W., and A. Tversky (1967). *Decision-making*. Baltimore: Penguin Books.

Einhorn, H. J., and R. M. Hogarth (1978). Confidence in judgment: Persistence of the illusion of validity. *Psychological Review* 85:395-416.

_____. (1985). A contrast/surprise model of updating beliefs. Unpublished manuscript, Graduate School of Business, University of Chicago.

Eisenhardt, K. M. (1989a). Building theories from case study research. *Academy of Management Review* 14:532-550.

_____. (1989b). Making fast strategic decisions in high-velocity environments. *Academy of Management Journal* 32(3):543-576.

Eisenhardt, K. M., and L. J. Bourgeois III (1990). Charting strategic decisions in the microcomputer industry: Profile of an industry star. In M. A. von Glinow and S. A. Mohrman (Eds.), *Managing Complexity in High-Technology Organizations*, pp. 74-89. New York: Oxford University Press.

Eldredge, N. (1985). *Time Frames: The Rethinking of Darwinian Evolution and the Theory of Punctuated Equilibria*. New York: Simon and Schuster.

Eldredge, N., and S. J. Gould (1972). Punctuated equilibria: An alternative to phyletic gradualism. In T. J. Schopf (Ed.), *Models in Paleobiology*, pp. 82-115. San Francisco: Freeman, Cooper.

Erikson, E. H. (1957). *Childhood and Society*, 2d ed. New York: W. W. Norton.

Etzioni, A. (1964). *Modern Organizations*. Englewood Cliffs: Prentice-Hall.

_____. (1989). Humble decision making. *Harvard Business Review* 67(4):122-126.

Evans, M. G. (1973). Discussant's comments. In E. A. Fleishman and J. G. Hunt (Eds.), *Current Developments in the Study of Leadership*. Carbondale, IL: Southern Illinois University Press.

Executive Leadership (1988). U.S. Army War College, Carlisle Barracks, PA.

Fahey, L., and K. H. Christensen (1986). Evaluating the research on strategy content. *Yearly Review of Management of the Journal of Management* 12(2):167-184.

Fazio, R. (1986). How do attitudes guide behavior? In R. Sorrentino and E. Higgins (Eds.). *Handbook of Motivation and Cognition*. New York: Guilford Press.

Feeser, H. R., and G. E. Willard (1990). Founding strategy and performance: A comparison of high and low growth high-tech firms. *Strategic Management Journal* 11(2):87-98.

Feldman, J. (1986). On the difficulty of learning from experience. In H. P. Sims, Jr., D.A. Gioia, and Associates (Eds.), *Dynamics of Organizational Social Cognition*, pp. 263-292. San Francisco: Jossey-Bass.

Festinger, L., S. Schachter, and K. W. Back (1950). *Social Pressure in Informal Groups*. New York: Harper.

Fiedler, F. E., and J. E. Garcia (1987). *New Approaches to Effective Leadership*. New York: Wiley.

Finkelstein, S. (1988). Managerial orientations and organizational outcomes: The moderating roles of managerial discretion and power. Ph.D. diss. Columbia University.

Fiol, C. M., and M. A. Lyles (1985). Organizational learning. *Academy of Management Review* 10:803-813.

Firestone, W. A., and B. L. Wilson (1988). Using bureaucratic and cultural linkages to improve instruction: The principal's contribution. *Educational Administration Quarterly* 21(2):7-30.

Fischer, K. (1980). A theory of cognitive development: The control and construction of hierarchies of skills. *Psychological Review* 87(6):477-531.

Fisher, A. B. (1988). The downside of downsizing. *Fortune* 117(11):42-52.

Fisher, D., K. Merron, and W. R. Torbert (1987). Human development and managerial effectiveness. *Group and Organizaton Studies* 12(3):257-273.

Fisher, D., and W. R. Torbet (1991). Transforming managerial practice: Beyond the achiever stage. In R. Woodman and W. Pasmore (Eds.), *Research in Organizational Change and Development*. Greenwich, CT: JAI Press.

Fleishman, E. A. (1973). Current developments in leadership: An overview. In E. A. Fleishman and J. G. Hunt (Eds.), *Current Developments in the Study of Leadership*. Carbondale: Southern Illinois University Press.

Forsythe, G. A., and H. F. Barber (1991). *Cognitive representations in strategic thinking*. Unpublished manuscript, Department of Behavioral Sciences and Leadership, U.S. Military Academy, West Point, NY.

Foster, L. W. (1985). From Darwin to now: The evolution of organizational strategies. *Journal of Business Strategy* 5(4, Spring): 94-98.

Fottler, M. D., J. D. Blair, C. Whitehead, M. D. Laus, and G. T. Savage (1989). Assessing key stakeholders: Who matters to hospitals and why? *Hospital & Health Services Administration* 34:525-546.

Fox, S. J. (1991). *The influence of institutional context, organizational context, and issue context on strategic issue processing: An explanatory study*. Ph.D. diss. College of Business Administration, Texas Tech University, Lubbock.

Freeman, R. E. (1984). *Strategic Management: A Stakeholder Approach*. Marchfield, MA: Pitman.

Friedman, S. D., and H. Singh (1989). CEO succession and stockholder reaction: The influence on organizational context and event content. *Academy of Management Journal* 32:718-744.

Frohman, M. A., and M. Sashkin (1985, August). Achieving organizational excellence: Development and implementation of a top-management mind set. Paper presented at the annual meeting of the Academy of Management, Organization Development Division, San Diego.

Frost, P. J., L. F. Moore, M. R. Louis, C. C. Lundberg, and J. Martin (Eds.) (1985). *Organizational Culture*. Newbury Park, CA: Sage.

———. (1991). *Reframing Organizational Culture*. Newbury Park, CA: Sage.

Fry, R. E., and W. A. Pasmore (1983). Strengthening management education. In S. Srivastva (Ed.), *The Executive Mind,* pp. 269-296. San Francisco: Jossey-Bass.

Gamson, W. A., and N.A. Scotch (1964). Scapegoating in baseball. *American Journal of Sociology* 70:69-72.

Gangestad, S., and M. Snyder (1985). To carve nature at its joints: On the existence of discrete classes in personality. *Psychological Review* 92:317-349.

Gell-Mann, M. (1984). *The concept of the institute*. In D. Pines (Ed.), *Emerging Synthesis in Science,* Vol. 1, pp. 1-15. Redwood City, CA: Addison-Wesley.

Gersick, C. J. (1988). Time and transition in work teams: Toward a new model of group development. *Academy of Management Journal* 31(1, March): 9-41.

Gersick, C. J. G. (1991). Revolutionary change theories: A multilevel exploration of the punctuated equilibrium paradigm. *Academy of Management Review* 16(1):10-36.

Ghemawat, P. (1986). Sustainable advantage. *Harvard Business Review* 86(5):53-58.

Ginovsky, J. (1990). Major commands to cut 4,600 slots by '93. *Air Force Times,* September 24, p. 3.

Ginsberg, A. (1988). Measuring and modelling changes in strategy: Theoretical foundations and empirical directions. *Strategic Management Journal* 9(6):559-575.

Gioia, D. (1986). Symbols, scripts, and sense-making: Creating meaning in the organization experience. In H. P. Sims, Jr., D. A. Gioia and Associates (Eds.), *Dynamics of Organizational Social Cognition,* pp. 49-74. San Francisco: Jossey-Bass.

Gist, M. E. (1987). Self-efficacy: Implications for organizational behavior and human resource management. *Academy of Management Review* 12:472-485.

Glaser, B. G., and A. L. Strauss (1967). *The Discovery of Grounded Theory: Strategies for Qualitative Research*. New York: Aldine.

Glaser, R. (1982). Instructional psychology: Past, present, and future. *American Psychologist* 37:292-305.

———. (1984). Education and thinking. *American Psychologist* 39:93-104.

Glick, W. H., G. P. Huber, C. C. Miller, D. H. Doty, and K. M. Sutcliffe (1990). Studying changes in organizational design and effectiveness: Retrospective event histories and periodic assessments. *Organization Science* 1:293-312.

Golembiewski, R. T. (1986). Contours in social change: Elemental graphics and a surrogate variable for gamma change. *Academy of Management Review* 11(3):550-566.

Golembiewski, R. T., K. Billingsley, and S. Yeager (1976). Measuring change and persistence in human affairs: Types of change generated by OD designs. *Journal of Applied Behavioral Science* 12:134-140.

Goodwin, V. L., J. C. Wofford, and D. Harrison (1990). Measuring cognitive complexity in the organizational domain. Paper presented at the Academy of Management meetings, San Francisco.

Graen, G., and J. F. Cashman (1975). A role-making model of leadership in formal organizations: A developmental approach. In J. G. Hunt and L. L. Larson (Eds.), *Leadership Frontiers*. Kent, OH: Comparative Administrative Research Institute, Graduate School of Business Administration, Kent State University.

Grant, J. H., and W. R. King (1982). *The Logic of Strategic Planning*. Boston: Little, Brown.

Greenberg, E. R. (1989). The latest AMA survey on downsizing. *Personnel* 66(10):38-44.

Greenwood, R., and C. R. Hinings (1988). Organizational design types, tracks and the dynamics of strategic change. *Organization Studies* 9:293-316.

Greiner, L. E. (1972). Evolution and revolution as organizations grow. *Harvard Business Review* 50(July-August):37-46.

Gupta, A. K. (1988). Contingency perspectives on strategic leadership: Current knowledge and future research directions. In D. C. Hambrick (Ed.), *The Executive Effect: Concepts and Methods for Studying Top Managers*, pp. 141-178.

Gupta, A. K., and V. Govindarajan (1984). Business unit strategy, managerial characteristics and business unit effectiveness at strategy implementation. *Academy of Management Journal* 27:25-41.

———. (1986). Resource sharing among SBUs: Strategic antecedents and administrative implications. *Academy of Management Journal* 20:695-714.

Hackman, J. R. (1976). Group influences on individuals. In M. D. Dunnette (Ed.), *Handbook of Industrial and Organizational Psychology*, pp. 1455-1526. Chicago: Rand McNally.

———. (1987). The design of work teams. In J. W. Lorsch (Ed.), *Handbook of Organizational Behavior*, pp. 315-342. Englewood Cliffs, NJ: Prentice-Hall.

Hage, J. (1980). *Theories of Organizations: Form, Process, & Transformation.* New York: Wiley Interscience.

Hales, C. (1986). What do managers do? A critical review of the evidence. *Journal of Management Studies* 23(1):88-115.

———. (1988). *Management processes, management divisions of labour, and managerial work: Towards a synthesis.* Paper presented at the Workshop on the Study of Managerial Labour Processes, Brussels: European Institute for Advanced Studies in Management.

Hall, D. T. (1987). Breaking career routines: Midcareer choice and identity development. In D. T. Hall and Associates (Eds.), *Career Development in Organizations.* San Francisco: Jossey-Bass.

Hall, E. T. and M. R. Hall (1987). *Hidden Differences: Doing Business with the Japanese.* New York: Anchor Books.

Hambrick, D. C. (1983). Some tests of the effectiveness and functional attributes of Miles and Snow's strategic types. *Academy of Management Journal* 26:5-26.

———. (1989). Guest editor's introduction: Putting top managers back in the strategy picture. *Strategic Management Journal* 10:5-16.

Hambrick, D. C., and G. Brandon (1988). Executive values. In D. C. Hambrick (Ed.), *The Executive Effect: Concepts and Methods for Studying Top Managers.* Greenwich, CT: JAI Press.

Hambrick, D. C., and S. Finkelstein (1987). Managerial discretion: A bridge between polar views of organizational outcomes. In L. L. Cummings and B. M. Staw (Eds.), *Research in Organizational Behavior*, Vol. 9, pp. 369-406. Greenwich, CT: JAI Press.

Hambrick, D. C., and P. A. Mason (1984). Upper echelons: The organization as a reflection of its top managers. *Academy of Management Review* 9:193-206.

Hamel, G., and C. K. Prahalad (1989). Strategic intent. *Harvard Business Review* 67(3):63-69.

Harris, P., and K. Lucas (1991). *Executive Leadership: Requisite Skills and Developmental Processes for Three- and Four-Star Assignments* (Draft Technical Report). Alexandria, VA: U.S. Army Research Institute.

Hart, S. L., and R. E. Quinn (1991). Executive leadership and firm performance: An integrative model and some preliminary evidence. Working paper. Graduate School of Business Administration, University of Michigan.

Heisler, W. J., and P. O. Benham. (In press). The challenge of management development in North America in the 1990s. *Journal of Management Development*.

Heller, F. A. (1984). The role of longitudinal method in management decision-making studies. In J. G. Hunt, D. M. Hosking, C. A. Schriesheim, and R. Stewart (Eds.), *Leaders and Managers*, pp. 283-302. Elmsford, NY: Pergamon.

Henderson, B. D. (1989). The origin of strategy. *Harvard Business Review* 67(6):139-143.

Hershey, D. A., D. A. Walsh, S. J. Read, and A. S. Chulef (1990). The effects of expertise on financial problem solving: Evidence of goal-directed, problem-solving scripts. *Organizational Behavior and Human Decision Processes* 46(1):77-101.

Higgins, E., R. Klein, and T. Strauman (1985). Self-concept discrepancy theory: A psychological model for distinguishing among different aspects of depression and anxiety. *Social Cognition* 3:51-76.

Hinings, C. R., and R. Greenwood (1988). *The Dynamics of Strategic Change*. Oxford, U.K.: Blackwell.

Hitt, M. A., and R. E. Hoskisson (1991). Strategic competitiveness. In L. Foster (Ed.), *Applied Business Strategy*, pp. 1-36. Greenwich, CT: JAI Press.

Hitt, M. A., R. E. Hoskisson, and R. D. Ireland (1990). Mergers and acquisitions and managerial commitment to innovation in M-Form firms. *Strategic Management Journal* 11(Special Issue):29-47.

Hitt, M. A., and R. D. Ireland (1985). Corporate distinctive competence, strategy, industry and performance. *Strategic Management Journal* 6:273-293.

————. (1986). Relationships among corporate-level distinctive competencies, diversification strategy, corporate structure and performance. *Journal of Management Studies* 23:401-416.

Hoerr, J. P. (1988). *And the Wolf Finally Came*. Pittsburgh: University of Pittsburgh Press.

Hoffman, M. (1984). Interaction of affect and cognition in empathy. In C. Izard, J. Kagan, and R. Zajonc (Eds.), *Emotions, Cognition and Behavior*, pp. 103-131. New York: Cambridge University Press.

Hogan, R. T., and N. P. Emler (In press). Personal and moral development. In W. Kurtines and J. L. Gerwitz (Eds.), *Moral Development*. New York: McGraw-Hill.

Hogan, R. T., R. Rashkin, and D. Fazzini (1990). The dark side of leadership. In *Measures of Leadership*. West Orange, NJ: Leadership Library of America.

Hogarth, R. M. (1981). Beyond discrete biases: Functional and dysfunctional aspects of judgmental heuristics. *Psychological Bulletin* 90:197-217.

Holden, P., L. Fish, and H. Smith (1941). *Top Management Organization and Control*. Palo Alto, CA: Stanford University Press.

Hollander, E. P., and J. W. Julian (1969). Contemporary trends in the analysis of leadership process. *Psychological Bulletin* 71:387-397.

Hoskisson, R. E., and M. A. Hitt (1988). Strategic control and relative R&D investment in large multiproduct firms. *Strategic Management Journal* 9:605-621.

Hoskisson, R. E., M.A. Hitt, and C.W.L. Hill (1991). Managerial incentives and investment in R&D in large multiproduct firms. *Organization Science*, 2(3):296-314.

Hoskisson, R. E., M. A. Hitt, T. Turk, and B. Tyler (1989). Balancing corporate strategy and executive compensation: Agency theory and corporate governance. In G. R. Ferris and K. M. Rowland (Eds.), *Research in Personnel and Human Resources Management,* Vol. 7, pp. 25-57. Greenwich, CT: JAI Press.

Hosmer, L. T. (1982). The importance of strategic leadership. *Journal of Business Strategy* 3:47-57.

House, J. S. (1981). *Work Stress and Social Support.* Reading, MA: Addison-Wesley.

House, R. J. (1971). A path goal theory of leader effectiveness. *Administrative Science Quarterly* 16(3):321-338.

_____. (1977). A 1976 theory of charismatic leadership. In J. G. Hunt and L. L. Larson (Eds.), *Leadership: The Cutting Edge,* pp. 189-207. Carbondale: Southern Illinois University Press.

_____. (1988). Leadership research: Some forgotten, ignored, or overlooked findings. In J. G. Hunt, B. R. Baliga, H. P. Dachler, and C. A. Schriesheim (Eds.), *Emerging Leadership Vistas.* Lexington, MA: Lexington Books.

_____. (1991). The distribution and exercise of power in complex organizations: A meso theory. *Leadership Quarterly* 2(1):23-58.

House, R. J., and M. L. Baetz (1979). Leadership: Some empirical generalizations and new research directions. In B. M. Staw (Ed.), *Research in Organizational Behavior,* pp. 341-423. Greenwich, CT: JAI Press.

House, R. J., A. Howard, and G. Walker (1991). The prediction of managerial success: A competitive test of the person-situation debate. In J. L. Wall and L. R. Jauch (Eds.), *Academy of Management Best Paper Proceedings, 1991* pp. 215-219. Monroe, LA: Northeast Louisiana University.

House, R. J., and T. R. Mitchell (1974). Path-goal theory of leadership. *Journal of Contemporary Business* 3:81-97.

House, R. J., W. D. Spangler, and J. Woycke (1990a). Personality and charisma in the U.S. presidency. Paper presented at the annual meetings of the Academy of Management, San Francisco.

_____. (1991). Personality and charisma in the U.S. presidency: A psychological theory of leadership effectiveness. *Administrative Science Quarterly* 36:364-396.

Howell, J.M. (1988). Two faces of charisma. In J. A. Conger and R. N. Kanugo (Eds.), *Charismatic Leadership: The Elusive Factor in Organizational Effectiveness,* pp. 213-236. San Francisco: Jossey-Bass.

Howell, J. P., D. E. Bowen, P. W. Dorfman, S. Kerr, and P. M. Podsakoff (1990). Substitutes for leadership: Effective alternatives to ineffective leadership. *Organizational Dynamics* 19:21-37.

Huber, G. P. (1991). Organizational learning: The contributing processes and the literatures. *Organization Science* 2(1):88-115.

Huber, G. P. (1992). *Organizational Change and Redesign.* New York: Oxford University Press.

Huber, G. P., A. H. Van de Ven, W. H. Glick, and M. S. Poole (1990a). *Organization Science* (Special Issue, Part One) 1:213-335.

_____. (1990b). *Organization Science* (Special Issue, Part Two) 1:375-430.

Huff, A. S. (1991). *The dynamics of organization and industry change.* Academy of management symposium proposal, Department of Business Administration, University of Illinois at Urbana-Champaign.

Huff, A. S. (Ed.) (1990). *Mapping Strategic Thought.* Chichester, U.K.: Wiley.

Huff, A. S., and R. K. Reger (1987). A review of strategic process research. *Yearly Review of Management of the Journal of Management* 13(2, Summer):211-236.

Hunt, J. G. (1991). *Leadership: A New Synthesis.* Newbury Park, CA: Sage.

Hunt, J. G., and J. D. Blair (Eds.) (1985). *Leadership on the Future Battlefield.* Washington D.C.: Pergamon-Brassey's.

Hunt, J. G., K. B. Boal, and R. L. Sorenson (1990). Top management leadership: Inside the black box. *Leadership Quarterly* 1(10):41-66.

Hunt, J. G., and R. N. Osborn (1982). Toward a macro-oriented model of leadership. An odyssey. In J. G. Hunt, U. Sekaran, and C. A. Schriesheim (Eds.), *Leadership: Beyond Establishment Views,* pp. 96-221. Carbondale: Southern Illinois University Press.

Hunt, J. G., R. N. Osborn, and H. J. Martin (1981). *A Multiple Influence Model of Leadership* (Techincal Report 520). Alexandria, VA: U. S. Army Research Institute for the Behavioral and Social Sciences.

Hunt, J. G., U. Sekaran, and C. A. Schriesheim (Eds.) (1982). *Leadership: Beyond Establishment Views.* Carbondale: Southern Illinois University Press.

Hunt, S. D. (1991). *Modern Marketing Theory: Critical Issues in the Philosophy of Marketing Science.* Cincinnati: South-Western.

Hurst, D. K., J. C. Rush, and R. E. White (1989). Top management teams and organizational renewal. *Strategic Management Journal* 10(2): 87-105.

Ilgen, D. R., and H. J. Klein (1988). Individual motivation and performance: Cognitive influences on effort and choice. In J. P. Campbell, R. J. Campbell, and Associates, *Productivity in Organizations: New Perspectives from Industrial and Organizational Psychology,* pp. 143-176. San Francisco: Jossey-Bass.

Isen, A., B. Means, R. Patrick, and G. Nowicki (1982). Some factors influencing decision-making strategy and risk taking. In M. Clark and S. Fiske (Eds.), *Affect and Cognition: The 17th Annual Carnegie Symposium on Cognition,* pp. 243-262. Hillsdale, NJ: Earlbaum.

Isenberg, D. J. (1985). Some hows and whats of managerial thinking: Implications for future army leaders. In J. G. Hunt and J. D. Blair (Eds.), *Leadership on the Future Battlefield.* Washington, D.C.: Pergamon-Brassey's.

_____. (1986). The structure and process of understanding: Implications for managerial action. In H. P. Sims, Jr., D. A. Gioia, and Associates (Eds.), *Dynamics of Organizational Social Cognition,* pp. 238-262. San Francisco: Jossey-Bass.

Jackofsky, E. E., and J. E. Slocum, Jr. (1988). CEO roles across cultures. In D. C. Hambrick (Ed.), *The Executive Effect,* pp. 67-100. Greenwich, CT: JAI Press.

Jackson, S. E., and J. E. Dutton (1988). Discerning threats and opportunities. *Administrative Science Quarterly* 33:370-387.

Jacobs, T. O. (1991a). Military applications of Stratified Systems Theory. Unpublished working paper. U. S. Army Research Institute, Alexandria, VA.

_____. (1991b, February). *Strategic leadership competencies.* Paper presented before U.S. Army War College, Carlisle, PA.

Jacobs, T. O., and E. Jaques (1987). Leadership in complex systems. In J. Zeidner (Ed.), *Human Productivity Enhancement,* Vol. 2. New York: Praeger.

_____. (1989). *Executive Leadership.* Alexandria, VA: U.S. Army Research Institute, Alexandria, VA.

_____. (1990). Military executive leadership. In K. E. Clark and M. B. Clark (Eds.), *Measures of Leadership,* pp. 281-295. West Orange, NJ: Leadership Library of America.

_____. (1991). Executive leadership. In R. Gal and A. D. Manglesdorff (Eds.), *Handbook of Military Psychology.* Chichester, U.K.: Wiley.

Jacobson, G., and J. Hillkirk (1987). *Xerox: American Samurai.* New York: Collier.

Jantsch, E., and C. H. Waddington (Eds.) (1976). *Evolution and Consciousness: Human Systems in Transition.* Reading, MA: Addison-Wesley.

Jaques, E. (1964). *Time-Span Handbook.* Arlington, VA: Cason Hall.

_____. (1968). *Progression Handbook.* Carbondale: Southern Illinois University Press.

_____. (1974). *Time-Span Handbook.* London: Heinemann.

_____. (1976). *A General Theory of Bureaucracy,* Exeter, NH: Heinemann.

_____. (1979). Taking time seriously in evaluating jobs. *Harvard Business Review* 57(5):124-132.

_____. (1986). The development of intellectual capacity. *Journal of Applied Behavioral Science* 22:361-383.

_____. (1989). *Requisite Organization.* Arlington, VA: Cason Hall.

_____. (1990). In praise of hierarchy. *Harvard Business Review* 68(1):127-133.

Jaques, E., and S. D. Clement (1991). *Executive Leadership: A Practical Guide to Managing Complexity.* Arlington, VA: Cason Hall.

Jaques, E., S. Clement, C. Rigby, and T.O. Jacobs (1986). *Senior Leadership Performance Requirements at the Executive Level* (RR 1420). Alexandria, VA: U.S. Army Research Institute.

Jaques, E., R. O. Gibson, and D. J. Isaac (1978). *Levels of Abstraction in Logic and Human Action.* London: Heinemann.

Jensen, M. C., and K. J. Murphy (1990). Performance pay and top management incentives. *Journal of Political Economy* 98:225-264.

Johnson, G. (1990). Managing strategic change: The role of symbolic action. *British Journal of Management* 1(4):183-200.

Jöreskog, K. G. and D. Sörbom. (1985). *LISREL VI: Analysis of Linear Structural Relationships by the Method of Maximum Likelihood.* Chicago: National Educational Resources.

Kalish, D. E. (1990). Big companies slashing work forces. *Arizona Republic,* October 15, p. B4.

Kanter, R. M. (1989a) The new managerial work. *Harvard Business Review* 67(6):85-92.

_____. (1989b). *When Giants Learn to Dance.* New York: Simon and Schuster.

_____. (1990). When a thousand flowers bloom: Structural, collective, and social conditions for innovation in organization. In B. M. Staw and L. L. Cummings (Eds.), *Research in Organizatoinal Behavior,* Vol. 10, pp. 169-211. Greenwich, CT: JAI Press.

Kantrowitz, B., A. Miller, K. Springen, and R. Pyrillis (1990). How safe is your job? *Newsweek,* November 5, pp. 44-55.

Katz, R. (1970). *Cases and Concepts in Corporate Policy.* Englewood Cliffs, NJ: Prentice-Hall.

_____. (1973). Skills of an effective administrator. *Harvard Business Review* 52 (November-December):156-167.

Katz, D., and R. L. Kahn (1966). *The Social Psychology of Organizations,* 1st ed. New York: Wiley.

_____. (1978). *The Social Psychology of Organizations,* 2d ed. New York: Wiley.

Kegan, R. (1982). *The Evolving Self: Problem and Process in Human Development.* Cambridge: Harvard University Press.

Kegan, R., and L. L. Lahey (1984). Adult leadership and adult development. In B. Kellerman (Ed.), *Leadership: Multi-Disciplinary Perspectives.* Englewood Cliffs, NJ: Prentice-Hall.

Keller, M. (1990). *Rude Awakening: The Rise, Fall, and Struggle for Recovery of General Motors.* New York: Harper Collins.

Kelly, J. R., and J. E. McGrath (1988). *On Time and Method.* Newbury Park, CA: Sage.

Kelman, H. C. (1958). Compliance, identification, and internalization: Three processes of attitude change. *Journal of Conflict Resolution* 2:51-60.

Kerr, J., and E. Jackofsky (1989). Aligning managers with strategies: Management development versus selection. *Strategic Management Journal* 10:157-170.

Kerr, J., and J. W. Slocum, Jr. (1987). Managing corporate culture through reward systems. *Academy of Management Executive* 1:99-107.

Kerr, S., and J. Jermier (1978). Substitutes for leadership: Their meaning and measurement. *Organizational Behavior and Human Performance* 22:375-403.

Kirton, M. J. (1976). Adaptors and innovators: A description and measure. *Journal of Applied Psychology* 61:622-629.

Klauss, R., D. Fisher, L. R. Flanders, L. Carlson, M. Griffith and M. Hoyer (1981). *Senior Executive Service Competencies: A Superior Manager's Model.* Washington, DC: U.S. Office of Personnel Management.

Korn/Ferry International and Columbia University Graduate School of Business. (1989). *A Journal on Critical Issues Affecting Senior Executives and the Board of Directors: Reinventing the CEO.* New York: Korn/Ferry International.

Korukonda, A. R. (1989). Mixing levels of analysis in organizational research. *Canadian Journal of Administrative Sciences,* 6(2) June:12-19.

Kotter, J. P. (1982). *The General Managers.* New York: Free Press.

_____. (1985). *Power and Influence: Beyond Final Authority.* New York: Free Press.

_____. (1988). *The Leadership Factor.* New York: Free Press.

_____. (1990). *A Force for Change: How Leadership Differs from Management.* New York: Free Press.

Kouzes, J., and B. Z. Posner (1987). *The Leadership Challenge.* San Francisco: Jossey-Bass.

Kuhn, T. S. (1970). *The Structure of Scientific Revolutions,* 2d ed. Chicago: University of Chicago Press.

Kuhnert, K. W., and P. Lewis (1987). Transactional and transformational leadership: A constructive/developmental analysis. *Academy of Management Review* 12(4):648-657.

Lahey, L., E. Souvaine, R. Kegan, R. Goodman, and S. Felix (1988). The subject/object interview: A guide to its administration and analysis. Unpublished manuscript, Harvard Graduate School of Education, Cambridge, MA.

Lange, C. J., and T. O. Jacobs (1960). *Leadership in Army Infantry Platoons: Study II* (Research Report 5). Alexandria, VA: Human Resources Research Organization.

Langer, E. J. (1978). Rethinking the role of thought in social action. In J. H. Haney, W. J. Ickes, and R. F. Kidd (Eds.), *New Directions in Attribution Research,* Vol. 2. Hillsdale, NJ: Erlbaum.

Larkin, J. H., J. McDermott, D. P. Simon, and H. A. Simon (1980). Expert and novice performance in solving physics problems. *Science* 208:1335-1342.

Lawler, E. E. III (1988). Choosing an involvement strategy. *Academy of Management Executive* 2:197-204.

Lawrence, P., and J. Lorsch (1967). *Organization and Environment*. Cambridge: Harvard Business School.

Lax, D. A., and J. K. Sebenius (1986). *The Manager as Negotiator: Bargaining for Cooperation and Competitive Gain*. New York: Free Press.

Lei, D., M. A. Hitt, and R. A. Bettis (1990). Core competencies and the global firm. Unpublished working paper, Southern Methodist University.

Lessem, R. (1991). Foreword: Requisite leadership—Managing complexity. In E. Jaques and S. D. Clement, *Executive Leadership: A Practical Guide to Managing Complexity,* pp. xiii-xxi. Arlington, VA: Cason Hall.

Levi, A., and P. E. Tetlock (1980). A cognitive analysis of Japan's 1941 decision for war. *Journal of Conflict Resolution* 24:195-211.

Levitt, B., and C. Nass (1989). The lid on the garbage can: Institutional constraints on decision making in the technical core of college-text publishers. *Administrative Science Quarterly* 34:190-207.

Levy, A., and V. Merry (1986). *Organizational Transformation*. New York: Praeger.

Lewin, K. (1952). Group decision and social change. In G. E. Swanson, T. M. Newcomb, and E. L. Hartley (Eds.), *Readings in Social Psychology,* pp. 459-473. New York: Holt, Rinehart.

Lieberson, S., and J. F. O'Connor (1972). Leadership and organizational performance: A study of large corporations. *American Sociological Review* 37:117-130.

Likert, R. (1967). *The Human Organization*. New York: McGraw-Hill.

Lindblom, C. E. (1959). The science of muddling through. *Public Administration Review*. 19(2, Spring):79-88.

Locke, E. A., G. Latham, L. M. Saari, and K. N. Shaw (1981). Goal setting and task performance: 1969-1980. *Psychological Bulletin* 90:125-152.

————. (1990). *A Theory of Goal Setting & Task Performance*. Englewood Cliffs, NJ: Prentice-Hall.

Loevinger, J. (1976). *Ego Development*. San Francisco: Jossey-Bass.

Lord, R. G., and R. J. Foti (1986). Schema theories, information processing, and organizational behavior. In H. P. Sims, Jr., D. A. Gioia and Associates (Eds.), *Dynamics of Organizational Social Cognition,* pp. 20-48. San Francisco: Jossey-Bass.

Lord, R. G., and K. J. Maher (1990). Alternative information-processing models and their implications for theory, research, and practice. *Academy of Management Review* 15(1):9-28.

Louis, M. R. (1980). Surprise and sense making: What newcomers experience in entering unfamiliar organizational settings. *Administrative Science Quarterly* 25:226-251.

Luthans, F., and T. R. V. Davis (1982). An idiographic approach to organizational behavior research: The use of single case experimental designs and direct measures. *Academy of Management Review* 7:380-391.

Lyles, M. A., and I. I. Mitroff (1980). Organizational problem formulation: An empirical study. *Administrative Science Quarterly* 25:61-75.

Mackinlay, J. (1989). *The Peacekeepers*. London: Unwin Hyman.

Mann, R. D. (1959). A review of the relationship between personality and performance in small gruops. *Psychological Bulletin* 56:241-270.

Manz, C. C. (1986). Self-leadership: Toward an expanded theory of self-influence processes in organizations. *Academy of Management Review* 11:585-600.

Manz, C. C., and H. P. Sims (1980). Self-management as a substitute for leadership: A social learning theory perspective. *Academy of Management Review* 5:361-367.

March, J. G., and J. P. Olsen (1979). Attention and the ambiguity of self-interest. In J. G. March and J. P. Olsen (Eds.), *Ambiguity and Choice in Organizations,* 2d ed., pp. 38-53. Bergen, Norway: Universitetsforlaget.

March, J. G., and H. A. Simon (1958). *Organizations.* New York: Wiley.

Markessini, J. (1991). *Executive Leadership in a Changing World Order: Requisite Cognitive Skills* (Draft Technical Report). Alexandria, VA: U.S. Army Research Institute.

Martin, J., M. S. Feldman, M. J. Hatch, and S. Sitkin (1983). The uniqueness paradox in organizational stories. *Administrative Science Quarterly* 28:449.

Martin, T. N., J. R. Schermerhorn, Jr., and L. L. Larson (1989). Motivational consequences of a supportive work environment. In M. L. Maehr, and C. Ames (Eds.), *Advances in Motivation and Achievement: Motivation Enhancing Environments,* Vol. 6, pp. 179-214. Greenwich, CT: JAI Press.

Mason, R. O., and I. I. Mitroff (1981). *Challenging Strategic Planning Assumptions.* New York: Wiley.

Masuch, M. (1985). Vicious circles in organizations. *Administrative Science Quarterly* 30:14-33.

McCall, M. W., and M. M. Lombardo (1983). *Off the Track: Why and How Successful Executives Get Derailed* (Technical Report 21). Greensboro, NC: Center for Creative Leadership.

McCall, M. W., Jr., M. M. Lombardo, and A. M. Morrison (1988). *The Lessons of Experience.* Lexington, MA: Lexington Books.

McCauley, C. D., and M. M. Lombardo (1990). Benchmarks: An instrument for diagnosing managerial strengths and weaknesses. In K. E. Clark and M. B. Clark (Eds.), *Measures of Leadership.* West Orange, NJ: Leadership Library of America.

McCaulley, M. H. (1990). The Myers-Briggs Type Indicator and leadership. In K. E. Clark and M. B. Clark (Eds.), *Measures of Leadership,* pp. 381-481. West Orange, NJ: Leadership Library of America.

McCaulley, M. H. (1981). Jung's theory of psychological types and the Myers-Briggs Type Indicator. In P. McReynolds (Ed.), *Advances in Psychological Assessment,* Vol. 5. San Francisco: Jossey-Bass.

McClelland, D. C. (1961). *The Achieving Society.* New York: Van Nostrand.

———. (1975). *Power: The Inner Experience.* New York: Irvington.

McClelland, D. C., and R. E. Boyatzis (1982). Leadership motive pattern and long-term success in management. *Journal of Applied Psychology* 67:737-743.

McClelland, D. C., and D. Burnham (1976). Power is the great motivator. *Harvard Business Review* 54(2):100-111.

McClelland, D. C., W. B. Davis, R. Kalin, and E. Wanner (1972). *The Drinking Man: Alcohol and Human Motivation.* New York: Free Press.

McClelland, D. C., S. Rhinesmith, and R. Kristensen (1975). The effects of power training on community action agencies. *Journal of Applied Behavioral Science* 11:92-115.

McGrath, J. E., and J. R. Kelly (1986). *Time & Human Interaction: Toward a Social Psychology of Time.* New York: Guilford.

McGrath, J. E., and N. L. Rotchford (1983). Time and behavior in organizations. In L. L. Cummings and B. M. Staw (Eds.), *Research in Organizational Behavior,* pp. 57-101. Greenwich, CT: JAI Press.

McKnight, M. R. (1991). Management skill development: What it is. What it is not. In J. Bigelow (Ed.), *Managerial Skills: Explorations in Transferring Practical Knowledge*. Newbury Park, CA: Sage.

Meindl, J. R., S. B. Ehrlich, and J. M. Dukerich (1985). The romance of leadership. *Administrative Science Quarterly* 30:78-102.

Merron, K., D. Fisher, and W. R. Torbet (1987). Meaning making and management action. *Group and Organization Studies* 12(3):274-286.

Merton, R. K. (1948). The self-fulfilling prophecy. *Antioch Review* 8:193-210.

――――. (1957). *Social Theory and Social Structure*, rev. ed. New York: Free Press.

Meyer, A. (1982). Adapting to environmental jolts. *Administrative Science Quarterly* 27:515-538.

Meyer, A. D., G. R. Brooks, and J. B. Goes (1990). Environmental jolts and industry revolutions: Organizational responses to discontinuous change. *Strategic Management Journal*, 11(Special Issue):93-110.

Miewald, R. D. (1970). The greatly exaggerated death of bureaucracy. *California Management Review*, 13(Winter):65-69.

Miles, M. B., and A. M. Huberman (1984). *Qualitative Data Analysis: A Sourcebook of New Methods*. Newbury, CA: Sage.

Miles, R. E. (1989). A new industrial relations system for the 21st century. *California Management Review* 31:9-28.

Miles, R. E., and C. C. Snow (1978). *Organization Strategy, Structure, and Process*. New York: McGraw-Hill.

Miles, R. H. (1980). *Macro Organizational Behavior*. Santa Monica, CA: Goodyear.

Miller, D. (1980). *The Icarus Paradox*. New York: Harper Business.

――――. (1990). *The Icarus Paradox: How Exceptional Companies Bring About Their Own Downfall*. New York: Harper Business.

Miller, D., and C. Droge (1986). Psychological and traditional determinants of structure. *Administrative Science Quarterly* 31:539-560.

Miller, D., and P. H. Friesen (1980). Archetypes of organizational transition. *Administrative Science Quarterly* 25:268-299.

――――. (1982). The longitudinal analysis of organizations: A methodological perspective. *Management Science* 28:1013-1034.

――――. (1984). *Organizations: A Quantum View*. Englewood Cliffs, NJ: Prentice-Hall.

Miller, D., M. F. R. Kets de Vries, and J. M. Toulouse (1984). Top executive locus of control and its relationship to strategy-making, structure, and environment. *Academy of Management Journal* 27:25-41.

Miller, D., and H. Mintzberg (1983). The case for configuration. In G. Morgan (Ed.), *Beyond Method: Strategies for Social Research*, pp. 57-73. Newbury Park, CA: Sage.

Miller, D. T., and M. Ross (1975). Self-serving biases in the attribution of causality: Fact or fiction? *Psychological Bulletin* 82:213-225.

Miller, J. G. (1978). *Living Systems*. New York: McGraw-Hill.

Miner, J. B. (1978). Twenty years of research on the role-motivation theory of managerial effectiveness. *Personnel Psychology* 31:739-760.

Mintzberg, H. (1973). *The Nature of Managerial Work*. New York: Harper and Row.

――――. (1975). The manager's job: Folklore and fact. *Harvard Business Review* 53(July-August):49-61.

――――. (1978). Patterns of strategy formation. *Management Science* 24:934-948.

_____. (1979). *The Structuring of Organizations*. Englewood Cliffs, NJ: Prentice-Hall.

_____. (1983). *Structure in Fives: Designing Effective Organizations*. Englewood Cliffs, NJ: Prentice-Hall.

_____. (1989). *Mintzberg on Management: Inside Our Strange World of Organizations*. New York: Free Press.

Mintzberg, H., and A. McHugh (1985). Strategy formation in an adhocracy. *Administrative Science Quarterly* 30:160-197.

Mintzberg, H., D. Raisinghani, and A. Theoret (1976). The structure of unstructured decision processes. *Administrative Science Quarterly* 21:246-275.

Mintzberg, H., and J. A. Waters (1983). The mind of the strategist. In S. Srivastva (Ed.), *The Executive Mind*. San Francisco: Jossey-Bass.

_____. (1984). Of strategies, deliberate and emergent. *Strategic Management Journal* 6:257-272.

Mischel, W. (1977). The interaction of person and situation. In D. Magnusson and H. S. Endler (Eds.), *Personality at the Crossroads: Current Issues in Interactional Psychology*. Hillsdale, NJ: Erlbaum.

Mitchell, T. R. (1984). *Motivation and Performance*. Chicago: Science Research Associates.

Mitchell, T. R., S. G. Green, and R. E. Wood (1981). An attributional model of leadership and the poor performing subordinate: Development and validation. In B. M. Staw and L. L. Cummings (Eds.), *Research in Organizational Behavior*, Vol. 3, pp. 197-234. Greenwich, CT: JAI Press.

Mitroff, I. I. (1974). Norms and counter-norms in a select group of the Apollo moon scientists: A case study of the ambivalence of scientists. *American Sociological Review* 39:579-595.

_____. (1983). *Stakeholders of the Organizational Mind*. San Francisco: Jossey-Bass.

Mokyr, J. (1990). Punctuated equilibria and technological progress. *American Economic Review* 80(2):350-354.

Morgan, G. (1986). *Images of Organization*. Newbury Park, CA: Sage.

Morgan, G., and L. Smircich (1980). The case for qualitative research. *Academy of Management Review* 5:491-500.

Murray, A. I. (1989). Top management group heterogeneity and firm performance. *Strategic Management Journal* 10:125-141.

Murray, E. A. (1978). Strategic choice as a negotiated outcome. *Management Science* 24(9, May):960-972.

Myer, A. D., G. R. Brooks, and J. B. Goes (1990). Environmental jolts and industry revolutions: Organizational responses to discontinuous change. *Strategic Management Journal* 11(Special Issue):93-110.

Myers, I. B., with P. B. Myers (1980). *Gifts Differing*. Palo Alto, CA: Consulting Psychologists Press.

Nadler, D. A., and M. L. Tushman (1990). Beyond the charismatic leader: Leadership and organizational change. *California Management Review* 32(Winter):77-97.

Neal, S. M., and F. Fiedler (1968). Leadership functions of middle managers. *Psychological Bulletin* 70:313-329.

Nicholls, J. (1987). Leadership in organizations: Meta, micro, and macro. *European Management Journal* 6:16-25.

Nisbett, R., and L. Ross (1980). *Human Inference: Strategies and Shortcomings of Social Judgment*. Englewood Cliffs, NJ: Prentice-Hall.

Noel, A. (1989). Strategic cores and magnificent obsessions: Discovering strategy formation through the daily activities of CEOs. *Strategic Management Journal* 10 (Special
Issue):33-50.

Norbum, D., and S. Birley (1988). The top management team and corporate performance.
Strategic Management Journal 9(3):225-237.

Norem, J., and N. Cantor (1984). Pessimism as a cognitive cushion. Paper presented at
the Midwestern Psychological Association, Chicago.

Nussbaum, B. (1988). Needed: Human capital. *Business Week,* September 19, pp. 100-102.

Nutt, P. C. (1984). Types of organizational decision processes. *Administrative Science
Quarterly* 29:414-450.

Nystrom, P. C., and W. H. Starbuck (1984). To avoid organizational crises, unlearn.
Organizational Dynamics 12(Spring):53-65.

Odiorne, G. S. (1987). *The Human Side of Management.* Lexington, MA: Lexington Books.

O'Reilly, C. A., III (1983). The use of information in organizational decision making:
A model and some propositions. In L. L. Cummings and B. M. Staw (Eds.), *Research
in Organizational Behavior,* Vol. 5, pp. 103-139. Greenwich, CT: JAI Press.

Osborn, R. N., and J. G. Hunt (1974). An empirical investigation of lateral and vertical
leadership at two organization levels. *Journal of Business Research* 2:209-221.

Osborn, R. N., J. G. Hunt, and L. R. Jauch (1980). *Organization Theory: An Integrated
Approach.* New York: Wiley.

O'Toole, J. (1985). *Vanguard Management.* Garden City, NY: Doubleday.

Ott, J. S. (1989). *The Organizational Culture Perspective.* Monterey, CA: Brooks/Cole.

Ouchi, W. G. (1981). *Theory Z: How American Business Can Meet the Japanese Challenge.*
Boston: Addison-Wesley.

Outhwaite, W. (1983). Toward a realist perspective. In G. Morgan (Ed.), *Beyond Method:
Strategies for Social Research,* pp. 321-330. Newbury Park, CA: Sage.

Oviatt, B. M. and W. D. Miller (1989). Irrelevance, intransigence, and business professors.
Academy of Management Executive 3:304-312.

Oxford English Dictionary, The Compact Edition, Vol. 1. (1971). Oxford: Oxford University Press.

Oxford English Dictionary, The Compact Edition, Vol. 2. (1971). Oxford: Oxford University Press.

Pant, P. N., and W. H. Starbuck (1990). Innocents in the forest: Forecasting and research
methods. *Journal of Management* 16(2):433-460.

Parsons, T. (1960). *Structure and Process in Modern Societies.* Glencoe, IL: Free Press.

Pasztor, A. (1990). Colleges feel impact of post-cold-war cutbacks as once-reviled ROTC
slows output of officers. *Wall Street Journal,* July 17, p. A14.

Pavitt, K. (1991). Key characteristics of the large innovating firm. *British Journal of
Management* 2:41-50.

Pearson, A. E. (1989). Six basics for general managers. *Harvard Business Review*
67(4):94-101.

Peter, L. J. (1969). *The Peter Principle.* New York: W. Morrow.

Peters, L. H., and E. J. O'Connor (1980). Situational constraints and work outcomes:
The influences of a frequently overlooked construct: *Academy of Management Review*
5:391-397.

Peters, T. J. (1988). Restoring American competitiveness: Looking for new models of
organizations. *Academy of Management Executive,* 1(May):103-109.

_____. (1990). Time-obsessed competition. *Management Review* 2(September):16-20.

Peters, T. J., and R. H. Waterman, Jr. (1982). *In Search of Excellence.* New York: Harper and Row.

Pettigrew, A. M. (1987). Context and action in the transformation of the firm. *Journal of Management Studies* (UK) 24(6):649-670.

Pfeffer, J. (1977). The ambiguity of leadership. *Academy of Management Journal* 2:104-112.

Pillai, R., and J. R. Meindl (1991). The effect of a crisis on the emergence of charismatic leadership: A laboratory study. In J. L. Wall and L. R. Jauch (Eds.), *Academy of Management Best Papers Proceedings 1991*, pp. 235-239. Monroe, LA: Northeast Louisiana University.

Poole, M. S., and A. H. Van de Ven (1989). Using paradox to build management and organization theories. *Academy of Management Review* 14(4):562-578.

Porter, M. E. (1980). *Competitive Strategy.* New York: Macmillan.

_____. (1985). *Competitive Advantage.* New York: Free Press.

_____. (1990). The competitive advantage of nations. *Harvard Business Review* 68(March-April):73-93.

Prahalad, C. K., and R. A. Bettis (1986). The dominant logic: A new linkage between diversity and performance. *Strategic Management Journal* 7:485-501.

Prahalad, C. K., and G. Hamel (1990). The core competence of the corporation. *Harvard Business Review* 68(May-June):79-93.

Provan, K. G. (1989). Environment, departmental power and strategic decision making in organizations: A proposed integration. *Journal of Management* 15:21-34.

Quinn, J. B. (1978). Strategic change: Logical incrementalism. *Sloan Management Review* 20(1):7-21.

_____. (1980). *Strategies for Change: Logical Incrementalism.* Homewood, IL: Irwin.

_____. (1981). Formulating strategy one step at a time. *Journal of Business Strategy* 1(3):42-63.

_____. (1985). Managing innovation: Controlled chaos. *Harvard Business Review* 63(May-June):73-78.

_____. (1988). *Beyond Rational Management: Mastering the Paradoxes and Competing Demands of High Performance.* San Francisco: Jossey-Bass.

Quinn, R. E., S. R. Faerman, M. P. Thompson, and M. R. McGrath (1990). *Becoming a Master Manager.* New York: Wiley.

Quinn R. E., N. B. Sendelbach, and G. M. Spreitzer (1991). Education and empowerment: A transformational model of managerial skills development. In J. Bigelow (Ed.), *Managerial Skills: Explorations in Transferring Practical Knowledge.* Newbury Park, CA: Sage.

Quinn, R. E., G. M. Spreitzer, and S. Hart (1991). Challenging the assumptions of bipolarity: Interpenetration and managerial effectiveness. In S. Srivastva and R. Fry (Eds.), *Executive Continuity.* San Francisco: Jossey-Bass.

Raser, J. R. (1966). Personal characteristics of political decision makers. Peach Research Society. *International Papers* 5:161-181.

Reid, D. M. (1989). Operationalizing strategic planning. *Strategic Management Journal* 10:553-567.

Rittel, H. (1972). On the planning crisis: Systems analysis of the "first and second generations." *Bedriftsokonomen.* NRB:390-396.

Rittel, H.W.J., and M. Webber (1973). Dilemmas in a general theory of planning. *Policy Sciences* 4(2):155-169.

Robbins, S. P. (1990) *Organization Theory: Structure, Design and Applications* 3d ed. Englewood Cliffs, NJ: Prentice-Hall.

Romanelli, E., and M. L. Tushman (1988). Executive leadership and organizational outcomes: An evolutionary perspective. In D. C. Hambrick (Ed.), *The Executive Effect: Concepts and Methods for Studying Top Managers,* pp. 129-146. Greenwich, CT: JAI Press.

Ropo, A. (1989). *Leadership and Organizational Change.* Tampere, Finland: University of Tampere.

Ropo, A., and J. G. Hunt (1990a). Dynamic case studies in organizational and management research. Unpublished manuscript, College of Business Administration, Texas Tech University, Lubbock.

_____. (1990b). Leadership and organizational change: A dynamic analysis. Unpublished manuscript, College of Business Administration, Texas Tech University, Lubbock.

Rosenthal, R. (1976). *Experimenter Effects in Behavioral Research,* enlarged ed. New York: Irvington.

Ross, L., and M. R. Lepper (1980). The perseverance of beliefs: Empirical and normative considerations. In R. A. Shueder (Ed.), *Fallible Judgment in Behavioral Research.* San Francisco: Jossey-Bass.

Rothbaum, F., J. R. Weisz, and S. S. Snyder (1982). Changing the world and changing the self: A two-process model of perceived control. *Journal of Personality and Social Psychology* 42(1):5-37.

Rotter, J. B. (1966). Generalized expectancies for internal versus external control of reinforcement. *Psychological Monographs* 80 (1, Whole No. 609).

Rousseau, D. M. (1985). Issues of level in organizational research: Multi-level and cross-level perspectives. In L. L. Cummings and B. M. Staw (Eds.), *Research in Organizational Behavior,* Vol. 7, pp. 1-37. Greenwich, CT: JAI Press.

_____. (1990). Quantitative assessment of organizational culture: The case for multiple measures. In B. Schneider (Ed.), *Frontiers in Industrial and Organizational Psychology,* Vol. 3. Lexington, MA: Lexington Books.

Rowe, A. J., R. O. Mason, K. E. Dickel, and N. H. Snyder (1989). *Strategic Management: A Methodological Approach.* Reading, MA: Addison-Wesley.

Ruble, T. L., and R. A. Cosier (1990). Effects of cognitive styles and decision setting on performance. *Organizational Behavior and Human Decision Processes* 46(2):283-295.

Ruderman, M. N., P. J. Ohlott, and C. D. McCauley (1990). Assessing opportunities for leadership development. In K. E. Clark, and M. B. Clark (Eds.), *Measures of Leadership,* pp. 547-562. West Orange, NJ: Leadership Library of America.

Salancik, G. R., and J. Pfeffer (1977a). Constraints on administrator discretion: The limited influence of mayors on city budgets. *Urban Affairs Quarterly* 12:475-498.

_____. (1977b). Who gets power and how they hold on to it: A strategic contingency model of power. *Organization Dynamics* 5, 3:3-21.

Sashkin, M. (1984). *The Organizational Beliefs Questionnaire.* King of Prussia, PA: Organization Design and Development.

_____. (1987). A new vision of leadership. *Journal of Management Development* 6(4):19-28.

_____. (1988). The visionary leader. In J. A. Conger and R. N. Kanungo (Eds.), *Charismatic Leadership: The Elusive Factor in Organizational Effectiveness*, pp. 120-160. San Francisco: Jossey-Bass.

_____. (1989a). *Managing Conflict Constructively*. King of Prussia, PA: Organization Design and Development.

_____. (1989b). The visionary leader. In R. L. Taylor and W. E. Rosenbach (Eds.), *Leadership: Challenges for Today's Manager*, pp. 45-52. New York: Nichols.

_____. (1990). *The Leader Behavior Questionnaire*, 3d ed., rev. King of Prussia, PA: Organzation Design and Development.

Sashkin, M., and W. W. Burke (1990). Understanding and assessing organizational leadership. In K. E. Clark and M. B. Clark (Eds.), *Measures of Leadership*, pp. 297-325. West Orange, NJ: Leadership Library of America.

Sashkin, M., and R. M. Fulmer (1985, July). A new framework for leadership: Vision, charisma, and culture creation. Paper presented at the Biennial International Leadership Symposium, Texas Tech University, Lubbock.

_____. (1988). Toward an organizational leadership theory. In J. G. Hunt, B. R. Baliga, H. P. Dachler, and C. A. Schriesheim (Eds.), *Emerging Leadership Vistas*. Lexington, MA: Lexington Books.

Sashkin, M., and M. G. Sashkin (1990, April 20). Leadership and culture building in schools: Quantitative and qualitative understandings. Paper presented at the annual meeting of the American Educational Research Association as part of the Division A refereed symposium, "Leadership and culture: Qualitative and quantitative research approaches and results," Boston.

Savage, G. T., J. D. Blair, and R. L. Sorenson (1989). Consider both relationship and substance when negotiating strategically. *Academy of Management Executive* 3:37-48.

Savage, G. T., T.W. Nix, C. J. Whitehad, and J. D. Blair (1991). Strategies for assessing and managing stakeholders, *Academy of Management Executive* 2:61-75.

Sayles, L. (1964). *Managerial Behavior: Administration in Complex Organizations.* New York: McGraw-Hill.

Schein, E. H. (1985). *Organizational Culture and Leadership.* San Francisco: Jossey-Bass.

_____. (1990). Organizational culture. *American Psychologist* 45(2):109-119.

Schendel, D. E., and C. W. Hofer (1978). *Strategic Management: A New View of Business Policy and Planning.* Boston: Little, Brown.

Schermerhorn, J. R. (1986). Team development for high performance management. *Training & Development Journal* 40(November):38-41.

Schermerhorn, J. R., Jr., W. L. Gardner, and T. N. Martin (1990). Management dialogues: Turning on the marginal performer. *Organizational Dynamics* 18(Summer):47-59.

Schneider, B., and J. Rentsch (1988). Managing climates and cultures: A futures perspective. In J. Hoge (Ed.), *Futures of Organizations*. Lexington, MA: Lexington Books.

Schoonhoven, C. B., and M. Jelinek (1990). Dynamic tension in innovative, high-technology firms: Managing rapid technological change through organizational structure. In M. A. von Glinow and S. A. Mohrman (Eds.), *Managing Complexity in High-Technology Organizations*, pp. 90-118. New York: Oxford University Press.

Schroder, H. M., M. J. Driver, and S. Streufert (1967). *Human Information Processing.* New York: Holt, Rinehart, and Winston.

Schwenk, C. (1989). A meta-analysis on the comparative effectiveness of devil's advocacy and dialectical inquiry. *Strategic Management Journal* 10:303-306.

Scott, W. A. (1969). Structure of natural cognitions. *Journal of Personality and Social Psychology* 12:261-278.

Scott, W. R. (1987). *Organizations: Rational, Natural and Open Systems.* Englewood Cliffs, NJ: Prentice-Hall.

Segal, D. R. (1981). Leadership and management: Organization theory. In J. H. Buck and L.J. Korb (Eds.), *Military Leadership,* pp. 41-69. Beverly Hills, CA: Sage.

_____. (1989). *Recruiting for Uncle Sam.* Lawrence: University Press of Kansas.

Segal, D. R., and J. D. Blair (1976). Public confidence in the U.S. military. *Armed Forces & Society* 3:3-11.

Segal, D. R., and M. W. Segal (1991). Demographics of the Total Force: Quantity, quality, and training. In R. L. Pfaltzgraff, Jr., and R. Shulz (Eds.), *The United States Army: Challenges and Missions in the 1990s.* Lexington, MA: Heath.

Segal, M. W. (1989). The nature of work and family linkages. In G. L. Bowen and D. K. Orthner (Eds.), *The Organization Family: Work and Family Linkages in the U.S. Military,* pp. 3-36. New York: Praeger.

_____. (1990). Personnel. In J. Kruzel (Ed.), *American Defense Annual 1990-1991,* pp. 153-169. Lexington, MA: Heath.

Seltzer, J., and B. M. Bass (1990). Transformational leadership: Beyond initiation and consideration. *Journal of Management* 16:693-703.

Selye, H. (1976). *The Stress of Life,* rev. ed. New York: McGraw-Hill.

Selznick, P. (1957). *Leadership in Administration.* New York: Harper and Row.

Shamir, B., R. J. House, and M. Arthur (1990). The transformational effects of charismatic leadership: A motivational theory. Unpublished manuscript, Department of Sociology/Anthropology, the Hebrew University, Israel.

_____. (in press). The motivational effects of charismatic leadership. *Organization Science.*

Sherman, S. J., and E. Corty (1984). Cognitive heuristics. In R. S. Wyer, Jr., and T. K. Srull (Eds.), *Handbook of Social Cognition,* Vol. 1, pp. 189-286. Hillsdale, NJ: Erlbaum.

Shetty, Y. K., and N. S. Perry (1976). Are top executives transferable across companies? *Business Horizons* 19:23-28.

Shrivastava, P., and S. A. Nachman (1989). Strategic leadership patterns. *Strategic Management Journal* 10:51-66.

Shull, F. A., Jr., A. Delbecq, and L. L. Cummings (1970). *Organizational Decision Making.* New York: McGraw-Hill.

Siegler, R. S., and D. D. Richards (1982). The development of intelligence. In R. J. Sternberg (Ed.), *Handbook of Human Intelligence,* pp. 897-971. Cambridge: Cambridge University Press.

Simon, H. A. (1955). A behavioral model of rational choice. *Quarterly Journal of Economics* 69:99-118.

_____. (1987). Making management decisions: The role of intuition and emotion. *Academy of Management Executive* 1:57-64.

Simon, H. (1977). *The New Science of Management Decision,* 3d ed. Englewood Cliffs, NJ: Prentice-Hall.

Simpson, G. G. (1944). *Tempo and Mode in Evolution.* New York: Columbia University Press. Reprinted, 1984.

_____. (1953). *The Major Features of Evolution.* New York: Columbia University Press.

Smircich, L. (1983). Concepts of culture and organizational analysis. *Administrative Science Quarterly* 28:339-358.

Smircich, L., and C. Stubbart (1985). Strategic management in an enacted world. *Academy of Management Review* 10:724-736.

Smith, E. E., and D. L. Medin (1981). *Categories and Concepts.* Cambridge: Harvard University Press.

Smith, K. G., J. P. Guthrie, and M. J. Chen (1989). Strategy, size, and performance. *Organization Studies* 10:63-81.

Smith, K. K. (1984). Rabbits, lynxes, and organizational transitions. In J. R. Kimberly and R. E. Quinn (Eds.), *Managing Organizational Transitions.* Englewood Cliffs, NJ: Prentice-Hall.

Smith, P. B., and M. F. Peterson (1988). *Leadership, Organizations and Culture.* London: Sage.

Snarey, J., L. Kohlberg, and G. Noam (1983). Ego development in perspective: Structural stage, functional phase, and cultural age-period models. *Developmental Review* 3(3):303-338.

Snow, C. C., and D. C. Hambrick (1980). Measuring organizational strategies: Some theoretical and methodological problems. *Academy of Management Review* 5(4):527-538.

Snow, C. C., and L. G. Hrebiniak (1980). Strategy, distinctive competence and organizational performance. *Administrative Science Quarterly* 25:317-336.

Spangler, W. D. (In Press May 1992). The validity of questionnaire and TAT measures of need for achievement: Two meta analyses. *Psychological Bulletin.*

Spreitzer, G. M. (1991). When organizations dare: The dynamics of empowerment in the workplace. Ph.D. diss. proposal, University of Michigan.

Stamp, G. (1978). Assessment of individual capacity. In E. Jaques, R. O. Gibson, and D. J. Isaac (Eds.), *Levels of Abstraction in Logic and Human Action.* London: Heinemann.

———. (1981). Levels and types of managerial capability. *Journal of Management Studies* 18:111-124.

———. (1986). Listening to my story has been really interesting: A guide to career path appreciation., Unpublished manuscript, Brunel Institute of Organization and Social Studies, Brunel Unviersity, Uxbridge, Middlesex.

———. (1988). *Longitudinal Research into Methods of Assessing Managerial Potential.* (Technical Report DAJA45-86-C-0009). Alexandria, VA: U.S. Army Research Institute for the Behavioral and Social Sciences.

Starbuck, W. H. (1983). Organizations as action generators. *American Sociological Review* 48:91-102.

Starbuck, W., and B. Hedberg (1977). Saving an organization from a stagnating environment. In H. Thorelli (Ed.), *Strategy + Structure = Performance,* pp. 249-258. Bloomington: Indiana University Press.

Staw, B. M., and J. Ross (1987). Behavior in escalation situations: Antecedents, prototypes, and solutions. *Research in Organizational Behavior* 9:39-78.

Stewart, R. (1976). *Contrasts in Management: A Study of the Different Types of Managers' Jobs, Their Demands and Choices.* New York: McGraw-Hill.

———. (1982a). *Choices for the Manager.* Englewood Cliffs, NJ: Prentice-Hall.

_____. (1982b). The relevance of some studies of managerial work and behavior to leadership research. In J. G. Hunt, V. Sekaran, and C. A. Schriesheim (Eds.), *Leadership: Beyond Establishment Views,* pp. 11-30. Carbondale: Southern Illinois University Press.

_____. (1989). Studies of managerial jobs and behavior: The ways forward. *Journal of Management Studies* 26:1-10.

Stewart, S. R., and D. C. Angle (April 1992). *Correlates of Creative Problem-Solving* (Technical Report). Alexandria, VA: U.S. Army Research Institute for the Behavioral and Social Sciences.

Stogdill, R. M. (1948). Personal factors associated with leadership: A survey of the literature. *Journal of Psychology* 25:35-71.

_____. (1974). *Handbook of Leadership: A Survey of the Literature.* New York: Free Press.

Streufert, S. (1986). How top managers think and decide. *Executive Excellence* 3:7-9.

Streufert, S., and G. Nogami (1989). Cognitive style and complexity: Implications for I/O psychology. In C. L. Cooper and I. Robertson (Eds.), *International Review of Industrial and Organizational Psychology,* pp. 93-143. Chichester, U.K.: Wiley.

Streufert, S., G. Y. Nogami, R. W. Swezey, R. M. Pogash, and M. T. Piasecki (1988). Computer-assisted training of complex managerial performance. *Computers in Human Behavior* 4:77-88.

Streufert, S., R. M. Pogash, and M. T. Piasecki (1988). Simulation-based assessment of managerial competence: Reliability and validity. *Personnel Psychology* 41:537-555.

Streufert, S., and S. C. Streufert (1978). *Behavior in the Complex Environment.* New York: Wiley.

Streufert, S., and R. W. Swezey (1986). *Complexity, Managers and Organizations.* Orlando, FL: Academic Press.

Stubbart, C. I. (1989). Managerial cognition: A missing link in strategic management research. *Journal of Management Studies* 26:325-347.

Suedfeld, P., and P. E. Tetlock (1990). Integrative complexity: Theory and research. Unpublished manuscript, University of British Columbia and University of California, Berkeley.

Suedfeld, P., and P. E. Tetlock (1991). *Integrative Complexity Scoring Manual.* Berkeley: Department of Psychology, University of California.

Tabory, M. (1986). *The Multinational Force and Observers in the Sinai.* Boulder, CO: Westview.

Taggart, W., and D. Robey (1981). Minds and managers: On the dual nature of human information processing and management. *Academy of Management* 6(2):187-196.

Taylor, C. W. (1990). *Creating Strategic Visions.* Carlisle Barracks, PA: Strategic Studies Institute, U.S. Army War College.

Taylor, S., and J. Crocker (1981). Schematic bases of social information processing. In E. Higgins, P. Herman, and M. Zanna (Eds.), *Social Cognition: The Ontario Symposium,* Vol. 1, pp. 89-134. Hillsdale, NJ: Erlbaum.

Terreberry, S. (1968). The evolution of organizational environments. *Administrative Science Quarterly* 12(4):590-613.

Tetlock, P. E. (1984). Cognitive style and political belief systems in the British House of Commons. *Journal of Personality and Social Psychology* 46:365-375.

Thomas, A. B. (1988). Does leadership make a difference to organizational performance? *Administrative Science Quarterly* 33:388-400.

Thompson, J. D. (1967). *Organizations in Action*. New York: McGraw-Hill.

Thompson, J. D., and A. Tuden (1959). *Comparative Studies in Administration*. Pittsburgh: University of Pittsburgh Press.

Thurman, M. (1991a, February). Paper presented at Strategic Leadership Conference, U.S. Army War College, Carlisle Barracks, PA.

_____. (1991b, September 5). Paper presented to faculty and students, College of Business Administration, Texas Tech University, Lubbock.

Tichy, N.M. (1987). Training as a lever for change. *New Management* 4(3):39-41.

Tichy, N., and R. Charan (1989). Speed, simplicity, self-confidence: An interview with Jack Welch. *Harvard Business Review* 67(5):112-120.

Tichy, N. M., and M. A. DeVanna (1986a). The transformational leader. *Traning and Development Journal* 40(7):27-32.

_____. (1986b). *Transformational Leadership*. New York: Wiley.

Tichy, N. M., and D. O. Ulrich (1984). SMR Forum: The leadership challenge—a call for the transformational leader. *Sloan Management Review* 26(Fall):59-68.

Tolstoy, L. (1904). *War and Peace*. Translated by C. Garnett. New York: Random House.

Tosi, H. J., Jr. (1982). Toward a paradigm shift in the study of leadership. In J. G. Hunt, U. Sekaran, and C. A. Schriesheim (Eds.), *Leadership: Beyond Establishment Views*, pp. 222-234. Carbondale: Southern Illinois University Press.

_____. (1985). Why leadership isn't enough. In J. G. Hunt and J. D. Blair (Eds.), *Leadership on the Future battlefield*, pp. 119-132. Washington, DC: Pergamon-Brassey's.

_____. (1991). The organization as a context for leadership theory: A multilevel approach. *Leadership Quarterly* 2(3):205-228.

Tregoe, B. B., J. W. Zimmerman, R. A. Smith, and P. M. Tobia (1989). *Vision in Action: Putting a Winning Strategy to Work*. New York: Simon and Schuster.

Trice, H. M., and J. M. Beyer (1984). Studying organizational cultures through rites and ceremonies. *Academy of Management Review* 9:653-669.

Trope, Y. (1980). Self-assessment, self-enhancement and task performance. *Journal of Experimental Social Psychology* 16:116-129.

Tsoukas, H. (1989). The validity of idiographic research explanations. *Academy of Management Review* 14:551-561.

Tushman, M., W. H. Newman, and E. Romanelli (1986). Convergence and upheaval: Managing the unsteady pace of organizational evolution. *California Management Review* 29(1, Fall):29-44.

Tushman, M., and E. Romanelli (1985). Organizational evolution: A metamorphosis model of convergence and reorientation. In L. L. Cummings and B. M. Staw (Eds.), *Research in Organizational Behavior*, Vol. 7, pp. 171-222. Greenwich, CT: JAI Press.

Tversky, A., and D. Kahneman (1974). Judgments under uncertainty: Heuristics and biases. *Science* 185:1124-1136.

Van de Ven, A. H. (1987). Review essay: Four requirements for processual analysis. In A. Pettigrew (Ed.), *The Management of Strategic Choice*. Oxford, U.K.: Blackwell.

Van de Ven, A. H., and M. S. Poole (1988). Paradoxical requirements for a theory of organizational change. In R. E. Quinn and K. S. Cameron (Eds.), *Paradox and Transformation: Toward a Theory of Change in Organization and Management*. Cambridge: Ballinger.

Van Maanen, J. (1977). Experiencing organizations: Notes on the meaning of careers and socialization. In John Van Maanen (Ed.), *Organizational Careers: Some New Perspectives.* London: Wiley.

Van Maanen, J., and S. R. Barley (1984). Occupational communities: Cultures and control in organizations. In B. M. Staw and L. L. Cummings (Eds.), *Research in Organizational Behavior,* Vol. 6, pp. 287-366. Greenwich, CT: JAI Press.

Vroom, V. H. (1964). *Work and Motivation.* New York: Wiley.

Wagner, G. W., J. Pfeffer, and C. A. O'Reilly (1984). Organizational demography and turnover in top management groups. *Administrative Science Quarterly* 29:74-92.

Wagner, H. E. (1991). The open corporation. *California Management Review* 33(4):46-60.

Wagner, R. K., and R. J. Sternberg (1990). Street smarts. In K. E. Clark and M. B. Clark (Eds.), *Measures of Leadership,* pp. 493-504. West Orange, NJ: Leadership Library of America.

Walsh, J. P. (1990). Knowledge structures and the management of organizations: A research review and agenda. Unpublished manuscript, University of Michigan, Ann Arbor.

Walsh, J. P., and G. R. Ungson (1991). Organizational memory. *Academy of Management Review* 16:57-91.

Walton, R. E. (1987). *Managing Conflict: Interpersonal Dialogue and Third-Party Roles,* 2d ed. Reading, MA: Addison-Wesley.

Wegner, D. M., and R. R. Vallacher (1977). *Implicit Psychology.* New York: Oxford University Press.

Weick, K. E. (1979). *The Social Psychology of Organizations,* 2d ed. Reading, MA: Addision-Wesley.

———. (1983). Managerial thought in the context of action. In S. Srivastva and Associates (Eds.), *The Executive Mind,* pp. 221-242. San Francisco: Jossey-Bass.

Weick, K. E., and M. G. Bougon (1986). Organizations as cognitive maps: Charting ways to success and failure. In H. P. Sims, Jr., D. A. Gioia, and Associates (Eds.), *Dynamics of Organizational Social Cognition,* pp. 102-135. San Francisco: Jossey-Bass.

Weiss, A. R., and P. H. Birnbaum (1989). Technological infrastructure and the implementation of technological strategies. *Management Science,* 35(8):1014-1026.

Westley, F., and H. Mintzberg (1989). Visionary leadership and strategic management. *Strategic Management Journal* 10:17-32.

Wheeler, K. G., D. A. Gray, J. Giacobbe, and J. C. Quick (1990). Organizational and human resource results of corporate restructuring problems, pitfalls, and benefits. Paper presented at Academy of Management meetings, San Francisco.

Whetten, D. A. (1988). Sources, responses, and effects of organizational decline. In K. S. Cameron, R. I. Sutton, and D. A. Whetten (Eds.), *Readings in Organizational Decline,* pp. 151-174. Cambridge: Ballinger.

White, R. W. (1959). Motivation reconsidered: The concept of competence. *Psychological Review* 66:297-333.

Whitehead, C. J., J. D. Blair, R. R. Smith, T. W. Nix, and G. T. Savage (1989). Stakeholder supportiveness and strategic vulnerability. *Health Care Management Review* 14:65-76.

Wilden, A. (1980). *System and Structure.* London: Tavistock.

Williams, L. J., and P. M. Podsakoff (1989). Longitudinal field methods for studying reciprocal relationships in organizational behavior research: Toward improved causal analysis. In L. L. Cummings and B. M. Staw (Eds.), *Research in Organizational Behavior,* Vol. 2, pp. 247-292. Greenwich, CT: JAI Press.

Winter, D. (1973). *The Power Motive.* New York: Free Press.

———. (1987). Leader appeal, leader performance, and the motives profile of leaders and followers: A study of American presidents and elections. *Journal of Personality and Social Psychology* 52:96-202.

Wittington, R. (1990). Social structures and resistance to change: British manufacturers in the 1980s. *British Journal of Management* 1(4):201-213.

Wood, R., and A. Bandura (1989). Social cognitive theory of organizational management. *Academy of Management Review* 14:361-384.

Wood, R., A. Bandura, and T. Bailey (1990). Mechanisms governing organizational performance in complex decision-making environments. *Organizational Performance and Human Decision Processes* 46:181-201.

Woodward, J. (1985). *Industrial Organization: Theory and Practice.* London: Oxford University Press.

Yin, R. K. (1989). *Case Study Research: Design and Methods,* 2d ed. Newbury Park, CA: Sage.

Young, J. A. (1988). Technology and competitiveness: A key to the economic future of the United States. *Science* 241:313-316.

Yukl, G. A. (1989a). *Leadership in Organizations,* 2d ed. Englewood Cliffs, NJ: Prentice-Hall.

———. (1989b). Managerial leadership: A review of theory and research. *Journal of Management* 15:251-289.

Zacarro, S. J., R. J. Foti, and D. A. Kenny (1991). Self-monitoring and trait-based variance in leadership: An investigation of leader flexibility across multiple group situations. *Journal of Applied Psychology* 76(2):308-315.

Zajac, E. J., and S. M. Shortell (1989). Changing generic strategies: Likelihood, direction, and performance implications. *Strategic Management Journal* 10:413-430.

Zakheim, D. S. (1990). The defense budget. In Kruzel, J. (Ed.), *American Defense Annual 1990-1991,* pp. 53-72. Lexington, MA: Heath.

Zaleznik, A. E. (1977). Managers and leaders: Are they different? *Harvard Business Review* 55(5, May-June):67-80.

Zaleznik, A. (1989a). Executives and organizations: Real work. *Harvard Business Review* 67(1):57-64.

———. (1989b). *The Managerial Mystique: Restoring Leadership in Business.* New York: Harper and Row.

———. (1990). The leadership gap. *Academy of Management Executive* 4(1):7-22.

Zaltman, G., R. Duncan, and J. Holbeck (1973). *Innovations and Organizations.* New York: Wiley-Interscience.

Zuckerman, M. (1979). Attributions of success and failure, revisited, or: The motivational bias is alive and well in attribution theory. *Journal of Personality* 47:245-287.

Name Index

Subject Index

About the Contributors

JOHN D. BLAIR is Professor of Management and Program Director, for the Institute for Management and Leadership Research, College of Business Administration, at Texas Tech University.

KIMBERLY B. BOAL is Associate Professor of Management, at Texas Tech University.

DAVID A. COWAN is Assistant Professor of Management, at Miami University, Ohio.

CATHERINE A. DURAN is a Ph.D. candidate, strategic management, and Director of Administration for the Institute for Management and Leadership Research, at Texas Tech University.

C. MARLENE FIOL is Associate Professor of Strategic Management, at the University of Colorado at Denver.

WILLIAM L. GARDNER III is the Hearin-Hess Assistant Professor of Management, at the University of Mississippi.

MICHAEL A. HITT is the T.J. Barlow Professor of Business Administration, at Texas A & M University.

ROBERT HOOIJBERG is a Ph.D. candidate, industrial/organizational psychology, at the University of Michigan.

ROBERT J. HOUSE is the Joseph Frank Berstein Professor of Organization Studies, Wharton School, at the University of Pennsylvania.

JAMES G. (JERRY) HUNT is the Paul Whitfield Horn Professor of Management; Professor of Health Organization Management; and Director of the Program in Leadership for the Institute for Management and Leadership Research, at Texas Tech University.

T. OWEN JACOBS is Technical Chief for Leadership and Management for the Army Research Institute.

BARBARA W. KEATS is Associate Professor of Strategic Management, at Arizona State University.

PHILIP LEWIS is Professor of Psychology, at Auburn University.

DANDRIDGE M. MALONE is a former military officer and current consultant on organizational dynamics and leadership.

ROBERT L. PHILLIPS is Director for the Institute for Management and Leadership Research and Associate Dean for Research and External Affairs, College of Business Administration, at Texas Tech University.

ROBERT E. QUINN is Professor of Organizational Behavior, at the University of Michigan.

JOAN B. RIVERA is a Ph.D. candidate, organization studies, at Texas Tech University.

ARJA ROPO is Assistant Professor of Business Administration, at the University of Tampere, Finland.

MARSHALL SASHKIN is OERI Senior Associate, at the U.S. Department of Education.

JOHN R. SCHERMERHORN, JR., is Charles G. O'Bleness Professor of Management, at Ohio University.

DAVID R. SEGAL is Professor of Sociology, at the University of Maryland.

JAMES P. WALSH is Associate Professor of Organization and Management, at the University of Michigan.

CARLTON J. WHITEHEAD is Professor and Department Chair of Management, at Texas Tech University.